What's Wrong with Antitheory?

What's Wrong with Antitheory?

Edited and with an introduction by
Jeffrey R. Di Leo

BLOOMSBURY ACADEMIC
LONDON • NEW YORK • OXFORD • NEW DELHI • SYDNEY

BLOOMSBURY ACADEMIC
Bloomsbury Publishing Plc
50 Bedford Square, London, WC1B 3DP, UK
1385 Broadway, New York, NY 10018, USA
29 Earlsfort Terrace, Dublin 2, Ireland

BLOOMSBURY, BLOOMSBURY ACADEMIC and the Diana logo
are trademarks of Bloomsbury Publishing Plc

First published in Great Britain 2020
Paperback edition first published 2021

Copyright © Jeffrey R. Di Leo and contributors, 2020

Jeffrey R. Di Leo and contributors have asserted her right under the Copyright,
Designs and Patents Act, 1988, to be identified as Authors of this work.

For legal purposes the Acknowledgements on p. xiii constitute
an extension of this copyright page.

Cover design: Eleanor Rose

All rights reserved. No part of this publication may be reproduced or
transmitted in any form or by any means, electronic or mechanical,
including photocopying, recording, or any information storage or retrieval
system, without prior permission in writing from the publishers.

Bloomsbury Publishing Plc does not have any control over, or responsibility for,
any third-party websites referred to or in this book. All internet addresses given
in this book were correct at the time of going to press. The author and publisher
regret any inconvenience caused if addresses have changed or sites have
ceased to exist, but can accept no responsibility for any such changes.

A catalogue record for this book is available from the British Library.

A catalog record for this book is available from the Library of Congress.

ISBN: HB: 978-1-3500-9611-0
PB: 978-1-3502-3447-5
ePDF: 978-1-3500-9612-7
eBook: 978-1-3500-9613-4

Typeset by Integra Software Services Pvt. Ltd.

To find out more about our authors and books visit
www.bloomsbury.com and sign up for our newsletters.

… every generation… produces some individuals exceptionally preoccupied with theory.

—William James (1911)

The antitheory message to Theory is clear: get back where you belong, the appreciation of literature. Put first things first. Reverse the tragic decline. Restore the canon. Fall in line. Declare your love for literature. I love literature. Say it loud, I LOVE LITERATURE.

—Vincent B. Leitch (2019)

Contents

Notes on Contributors	ix
Acknowledgments	xiii
Introduction: Antitheory and Its Discontents *Jeffrey R. Di Leo*	1

Part 1 Antitheory as Theory

1	Antitheory 2.0: The Case of Derrida and the Question of Literature *Jeffrey T. Nealon*	25
2	Crisis Theory after Crisis *Peter Hitchcock*	40
3	Epic Fail: Prolegomenon to Failing Again, Finally *Irving Goh*	60
4	Antitheory, Positivism, and Critical Pedagogy *Kenneth J. Saltman*	73
5	Down with Theory!: Reflections on the Ends of Antitheory *Jeffrey R. Di Leo*	92

Part 2 Reading as Antitheory

6	Critique Unlimited *Robert T. Tally Jr.*	115
7	How Not to Be Governed Like That: Theory Steams On *Robin Truth Goodman*	134
8	Antitheory in Postcolonial Perspective *Nicole Simek*	149
9	Eaten Alive, or, Why the Death of Theory Is Not Antitheory *Christian Haines*	165
10	Theory as Meat Grinder *Harold Aram Veeser*	187

Part 3 Philosophy, Theory, and Antitheory

11	Theory Does Not Exist *Paul Allen Miller*	199
12	(Anti)Theory's Resistances *Tom Eyers*	220
13	Forget Latour *Zahi Zalloua*	236
14	After Anti-Foundationalism: Ten Theses on the Limits of Antitheory *Christopher Breu*	250

Index	272

Notes on Contributors

Christopher Breu is Professor of English at Illinois State University, where he teaches classes in critical theory and contemporary literature and culture. He is the author of *Insistence of the Material: Literature in the Age of Biopolitics* (2014) and *Hard-Boiled Masculinities* (2005). He is the coeditor of *Noir Affect* (forthcoming) and the recent "Materialisms" special issue of *symplokē*. His work has also appeared in *Cultural Critique, The Comparatist, Textual Practice, ELN, Callaloo, Twentieth-Century Literature, Humanities, Modern Fiction Studies, Men and Masculinities*, and *English Journal*, among other places. He is currently at work on two monographs, one tentatively entitled, *In Defense of Sex* and the other, *Infrastructure and Biopolitics*.

Jeffrey R. Di Leo is Professor of English and Philosophy and Dean of the School of Arts and Sciences at the University of Houston-Victoria, USA. He is Editor of the *American Book Review*, Founding Editor of the journal *symplokē*, and Executive Director of the Society for Critical Exchange and its Winter Theory Institute. His recent books include *Corporate Humanities in Higher Education: Moving beyond the Neoliberal Academy* (2013), *Criticism after Critique: Aesthetics, Literature, and the Political* (2014), *Dead Theory: Death, Derrida, and the Afterlife of Theory* (2016), *Higher Education under Late Capitalism: Identity, Conduct and the Neoliberal Condition* (2017), *American Literature as World Literature* (2017), *Bloomsbury Handbook of Literary and Cultural Theory* (2019), and *The End of American Literature: Essays from the Late Age of Print* (2019).

Tom Eyers is Associate Professor of Philosophy and English at Duquesne University. He is the author of three books: *Lacan and the Concept of the Real* (2012); *Post-Rationalism: Psychoanalysis, Epistemology and Marxism in Postwar France* (2013); and *Speculative Formalism: Literature, Theory, and the Critical Present* (2017). Recent writing has appeared in *Critical Inquiry, boundary 2, Mediations*, and *Revue Internationale de la Philosophie*. His next book has the title *Romantic Abstraction*.

Irving Goh is President's Assistant Professor of Literature at the National University of Singapore. He was recently Franke Visiting Faculty Fellow at the Whitney Humanities Center at Yale in the fall of 2018. His first book, *The Reject: Community, Politics, and Religion after the Subject* (2014), won the MLA Aldo and Jeanne Scaglione Prize for Best Book in French and Francophone Studies. His second monograph, *L'existence prépositionnelle*, appeared in 2019. He is now completing his next monograph, *Touching Literature, or the Experience of the Limit* and working with Jean-Luc Nancy on a conversation book, *The Deconstruction of Sex*. His new project is on failure across French thought, affect theory, and contemporary literature.

Robin Truth Goodman is Professor of English at Florida State University. Her published works include: *The Bloomsbury Handbook of 21st-Century Feminist Theory* (edited collection, 2019); *Promissory Notes: On the Literary Conditions of Debt* (2018); *Gender for the Warfare State: Literature of Women in Combat* (2016); *Literature and the Development of Feminist Theory* (edited collection, 2015); *Gender Work: Feminism After Neoliberalism* (2013); *Feminist Theory in Pursuit of the Public: Women and the "Re-Privatization" of Labor* (2010); *Policing Narratives and the State of Terror* (2009); *World, Class, Women: Global Literature, Education, and Feminism* (2004); *Strange Love, or How We Learn to Stop Worrying and Love the Market* (cowritten with Kenneth J. Saltman, 2002); and *Infertilities: Exploring Fictions of Barren Bodies* (2001). She is currently editing another volume for Bloomsbury called *Understanding Adorno, Understanding Modernism*.

Christian P. Haines is Assistant Professor of English at Pennsylvania State University. He is the author of *A Desire Called America: Biopolitics, Utopia, and the Literary Commons* (2019) and the coeditor of a special issue of *Cultural Critique*, "What Comes after the Subject?" (2017). He is also a contributing editor for *Angelaki: Journal of the Theoretical Humanities*. He's currently writing a book on finance and culture titled, *The Scored Life*.

Peter Hitchcock is Professor of English at the CUNY Graduate Center and Baruch College of the City University of New York. He is also on the faculty of Women's Studies and Film Studies at the Graduate Center. He is Associate Director of the Center for Place, Culture, and Politics at the Graduate Center. His books include *Dialogics of the Oppressed* (1992); *Oscillate Wildly: Space, Body, and Spirit of Millennial Materialism* (1999); *Imaginary States: Studies in Cultural Transnationalism* (2003); *The Long Space: Transnationalism and Postcolonial Form*

(2010); *The New Public Intellectual: Politics, Theory, and the Public Sphere* (2016; coedited with Jeffrey R. Di Leo); *Labor in Culture, or, Worker of the World(s)* (2017); and, most recently, *The Debt Age* (2018; coedited with Jeffrey R. Di Leo and Sophia McClennen). His next project is called "The World, The State, and Postcoloniality."

Paul Allen Miller is Vice Provost and Carolina Distinguished Professor at the University of South Carolina. He has held visiting appointments at the University of the Ruhr, the University of Paris 13, and Beijing Language and Culture University. He is the former editor of *Transactions of the American Philological Association*. He is the author of *Lyric Texts and Lyric Consciousness* (1994), *Latin Erotic Elegy* (2002), *Subjecting Verses* (2004), *Latin Verse Satire* (2005), *Postmodern Spiritual Practices* (2007), *Plato's Apology of Socrates* (2010) with Charles Platter, *A Tibullus Reader* (2013), *Diotima at the Barricades: French Feminists Read Plato* (2015), and *Understanding Horace* (2019). He has edited fourteen volumes of essays and published more than seventy articles on Latin, Greek, French, and English literature, theory, and philosophy.

Jeffrey T. Nealon is Edwin Erle Sparks Professor of English and Philosophy at Penn State University, where he has been toiling in the vineyards of antitheory for more than twenty-five years. His most recent efforts are *Post-Postmodernism; or, The Cultural Logic of Just-in-Time Capitalism* (2012); *Plant Theory: Biopower and Vegetable Life* (2016); and *I'm Not Like Everybody Else: Biopolitics, Neoliberalism, and American Popular Music* (2018).

Kenneth J. Saltman is Professor at the University of Massachusetts Dartmouth. His books include *Capitalizing on Disaster: Taking and Breaking Public Schools* (2007); *The Gift of Education: Public Education and Venture Philanthropy* (2010); *The Failure of Corporate School Reform* (2012); *Neoliberalism, Education and Terrorism* (with Jeffrey R. Di Leo, Henry A. Giroux, and Sophia A. McClennen, 2013); *Toward a New Common School Movement* (with Noah De Lissovoy and Alexander Means, 2014); *Scripted Bodies: Corporate Power, Smart Technologies and the Undoing of Public Education* (2016); *The Swindle of Innovative Educational Finance* (2018); *The Wiley Handbook of Global Education Reform* (2018); and *The Politics of Education: A Critical Introduction, 2nd Edition* (2018).

Nicole Simek is Professor of French and Interdisciplinary Studies at Whitman College. She specializes in French Caribbean literature, with research interests in the intersection of literature and politics, trauma theory, and postcolonial critique. Her publications include *Hunger and Irony in the French Caribbean: Literature, Theory, and Public Life* (2016) and *Eating Well, Reading Well: Maryse Condé and the Ethics of Interpretation* (2008), as well as the coedited volumes *Feasting on Words: Maryse Condé, Cannibalism, and the Caribbean Text* (2006) and an issue of Dalhousie French Studies on Representations of Trauma in French and Francophone literature (2007).

Robert T. Tally Jr. is NEH Distinguished Teaching Professor in the Humanities and Professor of English at Texas State University. His books include *Spatiality* (2013); *Utopia in the Age of Globalization* (2013); *Fredric Jameson: The Project of Dialectic Criticism* (2014); *Poe and the Subversion of American Literature* (2014); *Topophrenia: Place, Narrative, and the Spatial Imagination* (2019); and, as editor, *Geocritical Explorations* (2011); *Literary Cartographies* (2014); *Legacies of Edward W. Said* (2015); *Ecocriticism and Geocriticism* (2016); *The Routledge Handbook of Literature and Space* (2017); and *Teaching Space, Place, and Literature* (2018). The translator of Bertrand Westphal's *Geocriticism: Real and Fictional Spaces* (2011), Tally is also the general editor of "Geocriticism and Spatial Literary Studies," a Palgrave Macmillan book series.

H. Aram Veeser is Professor at the City College of New York (English Department) and the CUNY Graduate Center (Middle East and Middle-Eastern American Center). His publications include four volumes he has edited on literary theory and theorists, as well as his own book, *Edward Said: The Charisma of Criticism* (2010). In addition, he has worked as a journalist and addressed, in print, a nonacademic readership. He has conducted interviews that were published in books and magazines. Currently, he is completing *The Greatest Generation*, a book based on original interviews with fifteen contemporary literary theorists.

Zahi Zalloua is the Cushing Eells Professor of Philosophy and Literature and a professor of French and Interdisciplinary Studies at Whitman College and Editor of *The Comparatist*. He is the author of *Žižek on Race: Toward an Anti-Racist Future* (forthcoming), *Theory's Autoimmunity: Skepticism, Literature, and Philosophy* (2018), *Continental Philosophy and the Palestinian Question: Beyond the Jew and the Greek* (2017), *Reading Unruly: Interpretation and Its Ethical Demands* (2014), and *Montaigne and the Ethics of Skepticism* (2005). He has edited volumes and special journal issues on globalization, literary theory, ethical criticism, and trauma studies.

Acknowledgments

My primary debt of gratitude goes to the contributors to this book for sharing their thoughts on antitheory. I have come to know and admire each of them through my work as editor of *symplokē* and executive director of the Society for Critical Exchange and its Winter Theory Institute. This is a group of individuals committed to the future of theory, and I appreciate their willingness to address with good will work that directly challenges theory. Not only have I benefited greatly from my conversations with them about this topic and others but also I have come to be even more convinced that in spite of the relentless—and dare I also say "fashionable"—challenges of antitheorists that theory is stronger now than ever. I greatly value the collegiality and joy they bring to the pursuit and defense of theory in dark and troubling times for both the academy and our society.

At Bloomsbury, I would like to thank David Avital for encouraging the publication of this volume and for helping to steer it through the peer review and publication process. I have worked with him now on a number of projects, including the massive *Bloomsbury Handbook of Literary and Cultural Theory*, and am always energized by his unbridled passion for theory and impressed with his professional commitment to its publication.

I am also grateful to Vikki Fitzpatrick for her unfailing administrative assistance and to Keri Farnsworth for the help she has given me in preparing this manuscript for publication.

Finally, I would like to thank my wife, Nina, for her unfailing encouragement, support, and patience.

Introduction: Antitheory and Its Discontents

Jeffrey R. Di Leo

Antitheory is nothing new. As long as there has been theory, there has also been antitheory. The two fit together in a codependent relationship that has served not to enervate the other, but rather to energize it. The rise, then, of antitheory coincides with the rise of literary and cultural theory in the 1970s. Moreover, just as theory in the new millennium is stronger and more robust than it has ever been in its roughly fifty-year history, so too is antitheory. New directions in antitheory arise on a regular basis albeit with more or less the same mandate: to express discontentment with theory.

At its most rudimentary level, antitheory takes the form of opposition to some of the major mandates of theory. For example, there is a faction of antitheory that opposes the use of race, class, gender, and sexuality in the analysis of literature and culture. There is another that rejects critique and calls for forms of criticism that do not involve ideological analysis. There is still another form of antitheory that rejects the epistemological and metaphysical project of structuralism and poststructuralism and its so-called social construction of knowledge. In short, antitheory has a long and varied list of complaints about theory that can include but are not limited to the commitments of structuralism; poststructuralism; multiculturalism; and race, class, gender, and sexuality studies.

But there are other complaints by antitheorists that really have nothing to do with specific theories. Rather, these complaints are directed at the general tenor of theory, which is viewed as replete with "inflated claims," "facile slogans," and "political pretensions." There are also complaints from these antitheorists about the lack of "reason and science" in theory, its "paucity of evidence," "the incoherence of certain theorists," its "flagrant identity politics," its neglect of aesthetics, its lack of logic, and, its "fashionableness." Of the last complaint, one wonders though if the zeal of antitheorists would wane, if it were not that theory has a knack for eliciting critical interest and generating scholarly excitement in the humanities. Shiny objects are well known to attract attention.

Still perhaps the ultimate complaint of antitheorists is the alleged way in which theory impairs our appreciation of literature. "All [antitheorists] share an affection for literature," write a couple of prominent antitheorists—share "a delight in the pleasure it brings, a respect for its ability to give memorable expression to the vast variety of human experience, and a keen sense that we must not fail in our duty to convey it unimpaired to future generations."[1] In short, theory destroys our appreciation of literature, and it will continue to do so until it is cast out of the house of literary criticism. By eliminating theory from the academy, the valiant warriors of antitheory will have thereby rescued it from appreciative peril. Antitheory, writes the novelist Mario Vargas Llosa, "returns sanity and rationality to literary criticism," rescuing it from the esotericism, jargon, and delusions under which it [has] been buried by the 'theorizers'"—something he feels that "lovers of genuine literature and criticism" desperately desire.[2]

Nevertheless, to say there are central tenets to antitheory would be misguided. Though its discontentment is generally localized to what it regards as "theory," just as there are many different types of theory, so too are there many different types of antitheory. Moreover, unlike other terms with the same prefix such as *anti*foundationalism, which refers to a rejection of foundational beliefs or principles in philosophical inquiry, and *anti*-essentialism, which refers to the nonbelief that things or ideas have essences, antitheory *does not necessarily imply the rejection of theory* or a nonbelief in theory. In fact, in many cases, *antitheory* simply means another type of theory. This is one of the things that make antitheory a fascinating topic for consideration.

One of our contributors, Jeffrey T. Nealon, who self-professedly "has been toiling in the vineyards of antitheory for more than twenty-five years,"[3] recognizes well the theoretical nature of antitheory. "Antitheory" writes Nealon, "has long been a venerable brand of theory." His comment might seem odd to those who view antitheory like antifoundationalism, that is, as a rejection of theory. But he is correct in his branding assessment. The only question is what "brand of theory" is antitheory? In Nealon's case, antitheory was initially movements that offered theoretical alternatives to structuralism and poststructuralism such as cultural studies, globalization studies, feminism, race and gender studies, queer theory, postcolonialism, Marxism, and new historicism, but has now in its later stages of development moved on to some new brands of theory.

Nealon's assumption in his contribution is that the "theory" in "antitheory" refers to "structuralism and post-structuralism," which he describes as "a loose grab-bag of movements also dubbed 'the linguistic-turn.'"[4] Antitheory, then, is not work that directly follows from the linguistic turn like the

> far-reaching revolutions in thinking about everything from the nature of kinship systems (Claude Lévi-Strauss) and historical events (Hayden White) to the workings of political power (Louis Althusser) or sex and gender (Judith Butler), all the way to the workings of African-American cultural production (Henry Louis Gates's "signifyin'") and even the unconscious itself (Jacques Lacan's famous dictum that the unconscious is structured like a language is specifically scaffolded on Saussure's relation between the signifier and the signified).

Rather, antitheory is work that takes *another* "turn," specifically, one that is not linguistically based. So, for Nealon (and others) antitheory is theory that does not directly follow from the linguistic turn. Or, otherwise stated, antitheory is work that is more closely associated with the theoretical movements that are *not* considered part of the linguistic turn, which is, of course, not a small body of theory.

What is interesting about this position is that antitheory is *not* the rejection of theory. Rather, on this view, antitheory is the *multiplication* of theories—a way to build out the house of theory beyond the constraints of the linguistic turn, or, if you will, beyond the parameters of structuralism and poststructuralism. In effect, then, antitheory from this perspective involves discontentment with only one form of theory and offers, in its stead, other forms of theory. This version of antitheory opens the path to regarding, for example, not only the very long list of "studies" today as antitheory (e.g., debt studies, sound studies and surveillance studies) but also new materialism, object-oriented ontology, and surface reading. On this view, the house of theory is large and regularly expanding through the multiplication of antitheories.

Nevertheless, for some, the rejection of theory does not entail the adoption of another version of it. Rather, it is the simple and categorical rejection of theory—*all* theory, no exceptions. This rejection holds equally for structuralism, poststructuralism, cultural studies, globalization studies, feminism, race and gender studies, queer theory, postcolonialism, Marxism, new historicism, and so on. Vincent Leitch, who, like Nealon, may also be described as having "toiled in the vineyards of antitheory for a very long time," has said that this group of antitheorists includes "traditional literary critics; aesthetes; critical formalists; political conservatives; ethnic separatists; some literary stylisticians, philologists, and hermeneuticists; certain neopragmatists; champions of low and middlebrow literature; creative writers; defenders of common sense and plain style; plus some committed leftists."[5] I too have toiled in the vineyards of antitheory probably just as long as Nealon and can say too from my professional experience in comparative literature and philosophy departments that some first-generation champions of "comparative literature" as well as most analytic philosophers need to be added to Leich's list. I know all too well their scorn for theory.

But even so, this level of antitheory is perhaps easier claimed than accomplished. It assumes that these so-called antitheorists have no theoretical position of their own or that it is possible to regard them as theory "neutral." Otherwise, they would be in the same boat that Nealon puts his antitheorists, though with one major difference: their "theory" would not be the "linguistic turn." Rather, it would be one of a host of "earlier" alternatives such as philology, stylistics, formalism, aestheticism, hermeneutics, or, even, dare I say, some other version of "philosophy" other than that found in the works of Ferdinand de Saussure, Jacques Derrida, Richard Rorty, and others. So, for example, the proponents of "stylistics" as their preferred theory might argue that everything that comes *after it* is "antitheory."

Still, what if we posited that "theory" is not just the linguistic turn or the structuralism-poststructuralism dyad? And that one of the lessons of theory is that *it is no longer possible to be theory neutral*? Moreover, isn't this just the assumption of folks who call themselves "antitheorists" only to brand their own work as another version of theory? The difference between those who formulate their theoretical positions in comparison to the work of structuralists and poststructuralists and those who do not is merely, then, a historical contingency. Just because the antitheoretical "new historicists" happened to formulate their positions *after* the theoretical work of the structuralists and poststructuralists, it does not make their work any less theoretical than the philologists whose positions were established *before* the theoretical work of the structuralists and poststructuralists.

There are parallels here too with the case of philosophy. Just as we do not believe that pre-Socratic thinkers such as Pythagoras, Heraclitus, and Parmenides were not *philosophers* because they "preceded" Socrates, the "father" of philosophy, by the same token we should also not contend that pre-Saussurean or pre-Derridean thinkers were not also theorists. Perhaps, as a concession to the formative powers of Socrates, Saussure, and Derrida, we might respectively then dub these thinkers "early philosophers" and "early theorists," but we surely would not dismiss any of them from philosophical or theoretical consideration.[6]

But the point regarding the history of philosophy goes forward too. For example, consider the case of Friedrich Nietzsche, who was widely rejected as a "legitimate" philosopher by many twentieth-century American analytic philosophers because of his aphoristic style. Just as philosophy is not just Socratic philosophy or analytic philosophy, so too is theory not just Derridean theory and its variants. In addition, just because one does not self-identify as a philosopher or theorist, it does not mean that one should not be considered one. Same too with antitheorists.

The discontents then of antitheory are many. First and foremost among them is an inability to escape or make a clean break from theory. This is especially true in the new millennium, where the reach of theory is greater now than at any time in history. Today there is arguably no nontheoretical position from which one can claim to read literature or study culture. Theory now consumes all possible approaches to literature and culture—or at least this is the belief of those who choose to observe the theoretical field as a whole, rather than merely view it from only their own position within it, which can lead to the mistaken view that one's own approach is somehow "outside" of or "beyond" the purview of theory.

Stepping back from our critical practices and reading positions to situate them within the theoretical field is one of the central tasks of those who are committed to a progressive future for the humanities. There are many things wrong with antitheory, but perhaps the biggest one is that it promotes the illusion that it is possible for the humanities to consider literature and culture without theory. Fifty years ago it was still possible for the humanities to consider literature without theory. Twenty-five years ago it was still *debatable* whether this was possible. Today, however, it is not possible to be a legitimate humanities scholar *and* at the same time an antitheorist who categorically rejects theory. To attempt the impossible, that is, to claim to be a humanities scholar *and* categorically reject theory, is at this moment in history to place not only theory in jeopardy but also the future of the humanities. In short, antitheory of this ilk is wrong because it plays dice with both the future of theory and the humanities.

Antitheory as Theory

The chapters in this volume are all written by committed theorists who care deeply about the future of the humanities. Antitheory is viewed by them—albeit in differing ways—as wrongheaded. Hence, the title of this volume is "What's Wrong with Antitheory?" as opposed to "What's Right about Antitheory?" To a large extent then the question posed by this title is the common theme of the chapters in this volume. However, this question is pursued from a number of different directions, and the chapters, in the process, also pursue a number of related issues.

The chapters in the first part, "Antitheory as Theory," take up the notion that antitheory is really just disagreement with a particular version of theory. The first chapter, Jeffrey Nealon's "Antitheory 2.0: The Case of Derrida and the Question of Literature," discusses how today's antitheory movements are like and unlike prior ones—which is to ask, are today's antitheory theories similar to the antitheory challenges of cultural studies, or Marxism, or Deleuze and Guattari, or new historicism? Or is there something decisively different going on today? For Nealon, the 1980s and 1990s antitheory wars were largely wars concerning interpretive paradigms, and attempts to open up the question of where something like "meaning" comes from, outside the strict poststructuralist conception of the text. In other words, the first rounds of antitheory theory wars were largely a series of attempts to open up the question of hermeneutics beyond a myopic Saussurean focus on the signifier.

Nealon identifies the second round of antitheory as the new materialist deconstruction of the nature/culture opposition and examines its impact on the future of literature as compared to that of the first round of antitheory. He reminds us that because the first round of antitheory was centered on the linguistic turn, it never strayed far from questions regarding the various ways to interpret literature. This was even the case when Steven Knapp and Walter Benn Michaels infamously presented their arguments "Against Theory" in *Critical Inquiry* back in 1982.[7]

Even though their version on antitheory, as John McGowan has observed, "pushed back against the metaphysical and transcendental proclivities of French theory by insisting that 'theory' in no way influences [reading] practice,"[8] it is a version of antitheory that always already keeps the reading of literature in the forefront of its concerns. But, as the second round of antitheory via new materialism has as its "project ... to abandon language, and abandon the question of hermeneutics," will it lead as well to the abandonment of literature? While both the first and second rounds of "antitheory [have] been good for theory," Nealon is not sure if the same holds for literature with the second round of antitheory.

The next chapter, "Crisis Theory after Crisis" by Peter Hitchcock, continues the discussion of antitheory as theory albeit from a different angle. Whereas

Nealon is concerned with the relationship between first- and second-generation antitheory, and its impact on the future of literature, Hitchcock wants to look at the political and institutional implications of antitheory and their impact on the "crisis" in the humanities. He is concerned with the notion put forward by some antitheorists that they are "defending the humanities." Hitchcock finds this position wrongheaded.

According to Hitchcock, the financial crisis of 2007–2008 "teaches us that the role of theory in the crisis has shifted in favor of the logic of financialization, rather than pivoting on either the *ratio* of the state or the humanities' dependence on the public university as the crisis mode of thinking humanism." For him, "it is not the extravagance of theory that proves the irrelevance of the Humanities but its relative paucity in measuring crisis as a specific socio-economic form." Consequently, against the claims of the antitheorists who argue that the crisis in the humanities can be resolved by avoiding theory, Hitchcock argues "crisis after crisis tells us that returning better theory to the public university to temper the Humanities is salutary." Our challenge though "is to see crisis in the Humanities as crisis theory itself," which is something that antitheorists are reluctant to do. In short, for Hitchcock, antitheory is a problem for the humanities—not one of its solutions.

The next chapter in this volume, "Epic Fail: Prolegomenon to Failing Again, Finally" by Irving Goh, asks a question implied by the rise of antitheory, namely, in what way is antitheory the result of the failure of theory? Goh then calls for a reconsideration of the role of "failure" in theory. For him, antitheory that targets structuralism and deconstruction represents a "certain failure of theory." Structuralism and deconstruction, claims Goh, is a

> brand of theory [that] has always been calling for the freedom of all existences, the affirmation and respect of others and differences, the revolutionizing of politics to accommodate the idea of "unconditional hospitality" where none would exclude another, and the complete overhaul, if not sidestepping, of capitalist principles and practices in order to end exploitation or to even entertain the possibility of the "an-economic."

However, "we are witnessing not only some form of regression from decades of such theoretical work, but also, admittedly, the failure of theory to effectuate a real paradigm shift in thinking and acting in the world." Thus, for Goh, to abandon ourselves to this failure is "perhaps … what it means to be 'antitheory' today." Ultimately, for him, perhaps there is nothing more that can or should be done or said regarding antitheory as theory "except, maybe: fail."

In "Antitheory, Positivism, and Critical Pedagogy," Kenneth J. Saltman extends the reach of antitheory by discussing its role in education and journalism. For Saltman, this is accomplished by examining the dominance of positivism in education and journalism, and the contradiction between the simultaneous fetishization of fact and disregard for fact, evidence, argument, and truth. The first section of his chapter takes this contradiction up in education, the second part addresses journalism, and the third discusses how both can be understood as the alienation of fact and the replacement of fact with faith.

Against the "bad alienation of fact" that decontextualizes and dehistoricizes truth claims, that is, education and journalism's version of antitheory, Saltman argues that critical pedagogy puts forward what we could call a "good alienation of fact" that seeks to contextualize and comprehend not only the theoretical assumptions and ideological underpinnings but also the broader material interests, social forces, and symbolic contests that are imbricated with claims to truth. Critical pedagogy estranges experience, denaturalizing it and holding it out as an object of analysis. It reinvests claims to truth with the conditions of their production—that is, the history, context, and social contests that give truth claims meaning. It provides an approach to knowledge that emphasizes how acts of interpretation of fact can form the basis for social intervention. As such critical pedagogy asserts the potential for fact, when theorized and interpreted, to be a source of agency rather than an oppressive alienated force. As both liberals and conservatives continue to embrace positivist forms of education and journalism, they contribute to the alienation of fact and the crisis of truth it makes. Perhaps at the present historical moment, they must confront the possibility that the only antidote to the epidemic of lies is critical pedagogy.

If Nealon's chapter is ultimately concerned with fate of literature in the academy and Hitchcock's deals with the crises facing the humanities, then the final chapter in this volume might be seen as bringing these two concerns together to ask what it means to be an antitheorist at a time when the study of literature seems to be on the decline and the humanities are continuously in crisis. In "Down with Theory!: Reflections on the Ends of Antitheory," Jeffrey R. Di Leo argues that antitheory that works against the interests of literature, the humanities, and the academy may be theory, but it is "bad" theory.

He begins by revisiting William James's take on the "down with philosophy" moment at the turn of the twentieth century and uses it to provide some insight on our current "down with theory" moment. Di Leo finds it ironic that philosophy not so long ago found itself in a situation similar to the one that theory finds itself today though with a fatal twist: whereas the anti-philosophy of the early twentieth century did not destroy academic philosophy, twentieth-century antitheory has the potential not only to bring down its home departments, but also to destroy the humanities, if not bring down the academy itself.

Di Leo argues that "theory is not nor should it be simply the product of an individual rejecting or opposing the views of others just because they can." "Rather," he maintains, "theory involves the *shared pursuit* of values that ultimately have the potential to make the academy a better site of education—and give it the best chances to have a positive and transformative impact in the world." Consequently, "when we consider the role of theory versus antitheory in overcoming some of the problems facing the humanities and the academy, the progressive potential of theory trumps the innovative potential of antitheory." He concludes, "the best way to destroy the humanities and the academy is to become an antitheorist who categorically rejects theory." For him this "is a counter-narrative to the antitheorists who claim that they are *saving* the humanities and the academy by rejecting the mandates of theory." Nonetheless, Di Leo believes "theorists know better."

Reading as Antitheory

Vincent Leitch has humorously said that "theorists refer to antitheorists as the 'I love literature crowd.'" And while some antitheorists tolerate theory, he continues, it is only as "a handmaiden to appreciation of literary texts."[9] While the others argue that literary criticism and scholarship does not need a handmaiden—and that the study of literature is better off without theory. Again, antitheory arguments like this go back to the institutional rise of theory in the 1970s. And while this line of thinking preceded Steven Knapp and Walter Benn Michaels's 1982 provocation "Against Theory," antitheorists found in this chapter an antitheory "argument" to rally around.

Still, there has perhaps been no higher profile *and* higher *funded* antitheory movement not just of late but ever than the one initiated by Rita Felski just a few years ago. The funding came in the form of a $4.2-million grant in 2016 from the Danish National Research Foundation. A press release from her university announcing the grant says that it stems from work done in her 2015 book, *The Limits of Critique*, which "encouraged her fellow scholars to explore alternatives to increasingly predictable and formulaic styles of 'suspicious reading.'"[10] Felski, continues the release, says,

> literary scholars should spend less time looking behind a text for hidden causes and suspicious motives and more time placing themselves in front of it to reflect on what it suggests, unfolds or makes possible. What literary studies needs, she said, is less emphasis on "de" words—demystifying, debunking, deconstructing—and more emphasis on "re" words—literature's potential to remake, reshape and recharge perception.[11]

Felski claims that she will use the grant to "develop new frameworks and methods for exploring the many social uses of literature," something she has already begun in her course, "Theories of Reading," where "students first learn to become skeptical readers, drawing on ideas from Freud, Foucault or feminism to criticize the works of the canon or to challenge their assumptions of their favorite TV shows" and then learn "to reflect on why they love certain novels or movies and to develop more sophisticated vocabularies for describing and justifying these feelings."[12]

Felski's comments here are important to note because they betray the basic parameters of her antitheory. For her, theory has become "predicable and formulaic," and she aims to provide it with "new frameworks and methods." These new "frameworks and methods," that is to say, "antitheories," will establish "more sophisticated vocabularies for describing and justifying" why we "love certain novels and movies"—and, of course, television shows. Given this, perhaps we need to alter Leitch's pronouncement to the "I love Netflix crowd."

Each of the chapters in Part Two, titled "Reading as Antitheory," in part responds to this latest attack by the "I love literature—but especially Netflix—crowd" on theory, while offering its own positive assessment of the state of theory. Part Two takes its title from the ways in which this version of antitheory builds off of discontentment with the type of reading championed by "theory"—and aims to provide a "new" theory in its stead. As such, the chapters in Part Two also recall the general lesson of Part One, namely, that much extant antitheory is just another version of theory—something that Felski, for example, is more than happy to report openly as the use for her multi million-dollar grant. The massive funding of efforts like this one to develop "better theory" is perhaps a cause for celebration for it marks not the end of theory, but the hope for new directions in it. Still, not everyone sees this type of antitheory in such a positive light.

In "Critique Unlimited," Robert T. Tally Jr. is highly critical of Felski's "postcritical" approach to antitheory. For Tally, Felski's approach is "symptomatic of a greater capitulation to what has been thought of as neoliberalism in higher education, which has involved a consumerist ethos and a degradation of thinking in all corners of its fields of influence." Her efforts "to appeal to a public discourse fundamentally at odds with criticism and theory" is a "discourse wholly committed to perpetuating a certain status quo and to limiting both the critique thereof and speculation over alternatives."

Contra Felski, who believes that "the era of Theory with a capital *T* is now more or less over,"[13] and contra Nealon, who situates it with structuralism and poststructuralism, Tally argues that "there really was no heyday of theory." Part of his argument here is that it is only through a "parochial focus on English, as opposed to other languages and literature," that we come to view theory as having a "heyday" or involving a "capital *T*." Not only was there "plenty of 'theory' before the New Criticism and its detractors," but Felski's arguments against critique "are far closer to the antitheory discourse of the 1980s than is perhaps recognized."

Her argument against critique and its hermeneutics of suspicion "reads like a rambling polemic against largely unnamed straw men, 'critics' whose rhetoric and tone," writes Tally, "much more than their actual arguments and conclusions, are considered objectionable to her and to the field she claims to be protecting and defending." Ultimately, Tally has a difficult time locating Felski's actual argument against critique and offers his own "anti-antitheory" in the wake of her argumentative failures. Tally's anti-antitheory is a "ruthless critique of all that exists," something more valuable "in an epoch like ours, in which fake news, truthiness, and new normal reigns"—a position which in the end complements the earlier arguments of Saltman.

In "How Not to Be Governed Like That: Theory Steams On," Robin Truth Goodman continues the critique of Felski's postcritique through an examination of the legacy of a mid-Victorian crisis in credit and value. She argues that Anthony Trollope's 1873 novel *The Eustace Diamonds* treats as narrative a transition in the concept of property the necklace represents: a type of property that depends on a distance or noncomplicity between the object and its representation, like credit, currency, and debt, all of which are based on fictions of value rather than referentiality. "Just as Lizzie Eustace," the protagonist of Trollope's novel, "could not afford to accept conferrals of meaning on objects by social elites and financial enforcers, defenders, exploiters, administrators, and professionals," argues Goodman, "we must engage with facts to limit today's social and political rationalizations—the coercion of knowledge—in the face of which we should be skeptical, and we must keep asking how not to be governed *like that*."

For Goodman, as critique, Lizzie's story illustrates the major problem with Felski's position. That is, whereas "Felski believes that the Humanities needs to accommodate itself to the 'what is' even if the 'what is' is destructive to the Humanities," Goodman believes that "close reading, pure description, and unmediated experience of texts are not going to fend off a 'legitimation crisis' in literary studies in the face of market culture." Moreover, argues Goodman, "literary studies is not really even facing a legitimation crisis at all but a defunding of educational institutions and a demonizing of educators, caused by market culture, that is part of an attack on critique involving Felski herself." Thus like Tally, Goodman concludes that the current political climate is the wrong time for the humanities to turn away from critique. In spite of her claims to the contrary, Felski's work is doing more harm to the humanities than aiding them in their hour of need.

Nicole Simek's "Antitheory in Postcolonial Perspective" continues the examination of surface reading, description, and antihermeneutics as species of antitheory. However, because she does so from the point of view of the consequences of this current antitheory on postcolonial studies, she is arguably—particularly if you follow Nealon's Antitheory 1.0 and 2.0 model—looking at the consequences of an earlier form of antitheory (postcolonial studies) on later forms of antitheory (surface reading, description, and antihermeneutics).

For Simek, these current forms of antitheory seem

> to strike at the very foundation of postcolonial studies, which is built on a commitment to critique, to a hermeneutics of suspicion, in the service of political progress and social justice, and on an understanding of scholarship as an activity necessarily implicated in politics, economics, and culture, rather than a neutral or objective practice that can be separated from these other spheres of human activity.

Postcolonial studies has been traversing its own crisis of conscience and methodology over the past decades, pondering questions about its own efficacy and future that in some ways intersect with broader debates over the use or uselessness of "theory" in literary criticism. She finds that even though postcolonial studies has been reevaluating its models of critique, its "investment in critique and a hermeneutics of suspicion" leads it to be skeptical about the value placed on "neutrality, interpretive-free or interpretive-light description, or the benevolence of algorithms and machine-assisted research invoked by [antitheorists] thinkers like Moretti or Best and Marcus." She finds a puzzling convergence and divergence between the aims of these antitheorists and the hermeneutic traditions they seek to overturn. "In privileging neutral description over prescriptive critique, surface readers, for example, argue that we need to correct for what some scholars view as the critical overreach, hubris, and overinvestment in a hermeneutics of suspicion marking twentieth-century theory," writes Simek. "In so doing," however, she comments, "they aim to cultivate a respectful humility that is not so far removed from critical theory's desire to root out instrumental rationality, or postcolonial studies' goal of elucidating and reforming relations of domination and exploitation." Her chapter then goes on to examine the dynamics between this convergence and divergence with the aim of providing insight into one of the major problem spaces of contemporary literary criticism and theory.

But in addition to debating the strength or limits of antitheory and postcritique arguments like Felski's, one might also approach them from the level of affect as Christian Haines does in "Eaten Alive, or, Why the Death of Theory Is Not Antitheory." Haines begins with the observation that some antitheorists claim that because theory can "throw students into a state of confusion, inhibition and loss," it brings about a form of death to students and the humanities. "Too busy attempting to achieve a posture of 'academic cool,' theory-driven (anti-) humanists," reports Haines, have been said to "sacrifice the liveliness of students to the altar of professional achievement." A view of theory that in part leads folks like Felski to approaches like understanding better why students love Netflix—more than theory.

While Haines agrees that theory must be associated with death, it is not the kind of death where theory is "eating students alive." For him, "theory is a place which life and death mix together." He goes on to provide a biopolitics of theory that undermines efforts by antitheorists to disempower theory by associating it with death, and bolsters arguments for the biopower of theory. For Haines, theory is a scene that plays out "as a drama of life and death, gift and sacrifice, subjectivization and desubjectivization." For him, the rise of surface reading, the "descriptive turn," and postcritique as modes of antitheory "preempts speculation and allows lines of theoretical inquiry to go into attrition." These versions of antitheory also "involve a fantasy of self-presence—specifically, a fantasy of the object's presence to itself without mediation—that is more about security (institutional security but also self-security) than fidelity to the text or to the matters of life."

As an alternative to these modes of antitheory, Haines proposes another way of considering the relations among death, textuality, interpretation, and speculation. For him, "it is only by reckoning with the death at the heart of theory that thought exceeds the order of things, that it introduces the possibility of another world." In other words, Haines fully embraces the role of death in theory as "a thinking of life by way of death." Antitheory is not the death of theory but is rather its foreclosure. In the end, "one is only a teacher of theory to the extent that one is a student of theory, and to be a student of theory is not only to sacrifice one's sense of security; it is also to discover the pleasure of being eaten alive."[14]

In "Theory as Meat Grinder," Harold Aram Veeser draws on his extensive interviews with some of our most well-known literary theorists to promote a very life-affirming view of theory *and* antitheory. While continuing the line of discussion that theory is a place where life and death mix together, Veeser comes to the conclusion that "theory can improve your life." By this, of course, he means something very different than "discovering the pleasure of being eaten alive" by theory. For him, "theory has become part of the background, the common sense and the premise of daily life." Though there are many metaphors for theory, for example, theory is the fluoride in the water, or an illuminating flash of lightning, by far though the most prominent metaphor he finds among contemporary theorists is "theory as meat grinder." But what is ground up are not students or scholars. Rather, it is a description of the process of making theory today, which he views as a "machinery" that "has entered the human psyche and made us, in a happy way, post-human."

For Veeser, the meat grinder metaphor of theory allows us to read theorists and antitheorists in nonoppositional terms. For him, Felski and Benn Michaels, as meat grinders, are doing the normal work of theory, even if it is work that may have a "shocking effect" on some theorists and theory. In the case of Felski, she describes to him in an interview her "antitheory" as simply "a shift way from the rhetoric of unmaking and undermining and disrupting towards how do we theorize our passion about things, how do we theorize our attachment?" For her, antitheory as postcritique is a kind of "moral" project to move beyond the "counterpolicing and hyperpolicing" tendencies of theory. In other words, her problem with critique is not that it grinds meat, but rather that it makes moral judgments about how others grind meat.

Whether Veeser's meat-grinding metaphor gets Felski and Benn Michaels off of the "meat hook" of antitheory though is debatable. William Germano, who was also interviewed by Veeser, and was one of the most influential theory publishers of his generation when he worked at Routledge, says that while theory swings in and out of fashion, he "doesn't really like the pendulum theory because part of it would be to imply that we are ready to go back to drawing the blinds and just reading Tennyson." Perhaps though instead of Tennyson he should have said watching television and movies with our students because this is the fault line for reading today: Do we read what our students want us to read or do we read what we want them to read? And it is antitheory as agent of the neoliberal condition in higher education that is pushing us toward doing what our students tell us to do in the classroom—rather than the opposite.

Philosophy, Theory, and Antitheory

If some antitheorists can be described by theorists as the "I love literature crowd," then it is only fitting that some theorists can be described by antitheorists as the "I hate literature crowd." This, of course, has been a very common version antitheory, but as we saw earlier, it may be the case that it only holds for certain types of antitheory (i.e., "Antitheory 2.0"). Commonly called "new materialism," this form of antitheory, whether it is the speculative realism of Quentin Meillassoux, the object-oriented ontology of Timothy Morton, or the actor-network theory of Bruno Latour, has deep roots in the Western philosophical tradition. Thus leading to the question of whether *philosophy* is in some way responsible for this version of antitheory.

In the long view, then, the "I hate literature crowd" might be simply translated as yet another chapter stemming from the ancient quarrel between philosophy and poetry. While Plato did attack poetry in the *Republic*, he also recognized that though there is a "quarrel" between philosophy and poetry, there is still an important relationship between them. Philosophy does not entail the "death of poetry," and vice versa for poetry. In this long view then of philosophy, poetry is not antiphilosophy, but rather something else. It is this something else that Paul Allen Miller reminds us of in his provocatively entitled chapter, "Theory Does Not Exist," the first chapter of several in Part Three that consider antitheory in view of the relationship between philosophy and theory.

Part Three, titled "Philosophy, Theory, and Antitheory," thus begins with Miller reminding us that philosophy is never "pure"; rather, it is "always derivative from rhetoric and poetry, from various practices of embodiment." "Philosophy," argues Miller, "is a response to a pre-existing set of conversations, acts of imagination, acts of truth, and acts of persuasion." His chapter, drawing extensively on Plato, Foucault, and Derrida, argues that theory with a capital *T* does not exist. He motivates this by challenging the reader to "think seriously about what do we mean when we say we teach *theory*, we use *theory*, we apply *theory*, or we have moved beyond/after *theory*?" It is the potential of postulating theory as a thing that leads him to the counterintuitive conclusion that "Theory, as such, does not exist." "Theory," argues Miller, "is the precondition, supplement, and transcendence of philosophy." "Theory is antitheory, and as theory qua theory, as a *thing*, it does not exist." What does exist though is the practice of philosophy, a "conversation, across the centuries, across genres, ultimately across entire civilizations, that reflects, produces, and criticizes acts of truth."

Miller's point here is not to create trouble for those who believe in theory with a capital *T*, for he ultimately as a theorist is one of those people—and so too are many of his friends. Rather, he wants us as theorists to recognize that a mistake is made when one argues "for or against theory, as if theory were a thing that can be simply refused or accepted, any more than philosophy or rhetoric, at least within a world in which people still seek to discuss, persuade, or imagine." As academics, if we wish to save the humanities from demise within the university, then we must "expose the myriad ways in which the very possibility of the existence of our civilization is dependent on this work, on the continuity of this work, even when it might appear to those outside that we are doing nothing." This "work," of course, is the work of "philosophy constituted as itself and its other, as both theory and antitheory."

Like Miller, Tom Eyers too is concerned with the interrelations between philosophy and theory as well as the very identity of the latter. Nevertheless, instead of following the long road from Plato to Foucault and Derrida to establish their relationship, Eyers opts instead to approach his topic in "(Anti)Theory's Resistances" from the shorter path of the resistances of Lacan, Freud, and de Man. "Theory, as a retrospectively constructed and romanticized 'outsider' discourse, one temporarily, institutionally grounded at the very moment of its upmost claim to outsiderness, was, among other things," claims Eyers, "displaced philosophy." "Antitheory, then," for him, "is inexplicable without some understanding of its relation to philosophy, philosophy being the shadow that ghosts the former's often passive aggressive addresses to literary and cultural theory *tout court*." "Philosophy," writes Eyers, "haunts theory, in turn, even as theory is, perhaps, also self-haunted, constitutively afraid of its own shadow."

Eyers claims "antitheory, understood as a heterogeneous constellation of interventions and critical moods that advance a more or less self-cancelling critique of critique, emerges in part out of defensive moments of resistance to the very auto-resistance or constitutive self-dislocation *in theory itself*." His notion of "auto-resistance" is based on the "now unfashionable" work of Paul de

Man in "The Resistance to Theory," where he says "the resistance to theory is a resistance to the use of language about language."

Eyers argues that while antitheory "is more than happy to recognize difference per se (it, too, adores lists)," it has a more difficult time with "*self*-difference, the material-linguistic, peskily internal gap that both makes critique a possibility and that prevents its collation into an empirically satisfying whole, entirely eludes its shiny apertures." In short, because "auto-resistance is by definition absent in antitheory," it is wrongheaded to regard antitheory as a species of theory—as was done, for example, in Part One of this collection. "Without the redoubling awareness of auto-resistance that, I have argued, characterizes theory 'proper,'" concludes Eyers, "antitheory seems driven to cast undue suspicion on its ostensible opponents, while corseting itself in its own ghostly imagining of that with which it does phantom battle."

Zahi Zalloua, who Miller reminds us in his contribution, sees theory as defined by its opposition to philosophy, namely, by arguing that "if philosophy seeks a world of pure thought, then theory is messy, impure, interdisciplinary," looks more closely in his piece, "Forget Latour," at speculative realism and object-oriented ontology. Much like Knapp and Benn Michael's "Against Theory" two decades earlier, Latour's 2004 article "Why Has Critique Run Out of Steam?" has become a touchstone for many current antitheorists. According to Zalloua, the piece could have just as well been entitled "Why Has Theory Run Out of Steam?" Moreover, similar to Tally's complaints about the weakness of Felski's arguments for postcritique, Zalloua finds very little evidence for the major charges made against theory by Latour concerning "theory's overreach, unproductive habits, and waning relevance."

Zalloua pushes back on Latour's antitheory arguing that actor-network theory aligns closely with the work of speculative realism, which he views "as a strictly philosophical response to the idealism of the linguistic turn, to the strand of continental philosophy that gave us theory—at the moment that philosophy, in the eyes of theory's detractors, took a decisively wrong *linguistic turn*." Zalloua demonstrates the limits of Latour's approach to literary studies through an analysis of Ari Folman's 2008 Israeli animated docu-film *Waltz with Bashir*, a film "that deals with the trauma of the 1982 Sabra and Shatila massacre." Zalloua says that his "imperative to 'forget Latour' is meant as a call to reinvest in theory's critique, an invitation to exit our current inhospitable climate to theory." Ultimately, he finds Latour's "crucial distinction" between constructivism and deconstruction "a dubious one" and says that we need to respond to the question "constructivism or deconstruction?" with the witty, inclusive response, "Yes, Please!"

The final chapter in this book, Christopher Breu's "After Antifoundationalism: Ten Theses on the Limits of Antitheory," is a manifesto. He argues that theory, far from being unnecessary or outmoded in our twenty-first-century moment, has merely changed shape. According to Breu, the forms of antifoundational critique, so central to the work of theory in the late-twentieth-century moment of high poststructuralism have merely and only partially given way to forms of theory that are willing to venture foundationalist claims. Thus, in twenty-first-century theory, contends Breu, categories avoided by antifoundationalism, such as ontology, realism, materialism, biology, nature, ecology, and infrastructure, have all made returns.

For Breu, at its best, this return of the foundational does not abjure critique—and is not antitheory as some of our other contributors have argued. Instead, it works to situate the critical and the constructive, the foundational and antifoundational in productive tension and relationship with each other. According to Breu, we both need the forms of denaturalization that are central to poststructuralist critique and we need to take the risk of tentatively (re-)naturalizing or rendering foundational certain concepts.

Like some of our other contributors, Breu regards theory and antitheory "as different theoretical accounts of the existence of theory as such." "To argue that even antitheory is a theory," comments Breu, "seems to preclude the need for argument about the advantages and limitations of theory, antitheory, and posttheory as positions." "If everything is a theory," he asks, "then why argue for or against theory as such?"

But Breu, like the other contributors to Part Three, is also concerned with the relationship between philosophy and theory though he wants to move "past the hard and fast opposition between theory and philosophy." Unlike, say, Fredric Jameson, who makes a distinction between theory and philosophy, Breu want the two "to be understood as necessarily entangled." If we take Breu's "capacious definition" of theory as "speculative thought," "then philosophy and its history can be folded into the category of theory and the opposition vanishes." In short, he contends that theory today needs to partially "turn back to philosophy."

His chapter, though, contains many other ideas as to how theory in the new millennium needs to be different from its predecessors. Chief among them is a turn to work in speculative realism and new materialism as the answer to the woes of theory. While he has some issues with work "published under the name speculative realism, the name itself," writes Breu, "I think may be the best descriptor there is for what theory is at its best."

Conclusion

Antitheory encompasses a wide range of discontentment with theory. Like theory, it exhibits both periods in the spotlight as well as those of relative quietude. Today it is in the spotlight, whereas tomorrow it may not be. Felski and Latour have done a lot to put the spotlight on antitheory of late with their critique of critique just as Knapp and Benn Michaels lit it up decades ago with their clever theory against theory. While it is painful for some theorists to respond to the antitheories of Felski and Latour, oppositional work such as theirs in the end only serves to rally theorists to redouble their efforts to make theory stronger.

Moreover, as an inhabitant of the neoliberal university, which now only attaches value to work in the humanities when it raises the bottom line of the university, I would wager that by drawing millions of grant dollars to their work, Felski may have unintentionally also raised the bar for the next wave of antitheory. The antitheory of Knapp and Michaels only sparked debate, which might have been sufficient in the early years of the neoliberal university, but now that we are well within its heyday, opposition without outside financial support for it will not be good enough when antitheory makes its next move against theory.

What is odd though about antitheory is not the oppositional work it does with respect to theory, but rather that discontentment with theory is viewed the opposite or other of theory—as some way or other against or *anti*theory. To get a sense of this oddity, again, look at how oppositional ideas are dealt with in philosophy.

In the philosophical world, dualists have long lived next to monists, but no dualist has ever called a monist an "anti-philosopher." Nor have the many rationalists who reside in the big house of philosophy denied empiricists access to it. Sure they fight like cats and dogs over which is the preferable position, but the rejection of proponents of oppositional positions *as philosophers* is not something that has not traditionally been done. Moreover, not only has materialism long coexisted with its other, idealism, it has also dueled with naturalism and realism for philosophical superiority. So, why should the current internal squabbles within theory be any different? Why are we so quick today as theorists to look at alternate positions as a *threat* to theory?

But maybe, like philosophy, discontentment in theory will one day just become part of the very fabric of theory. It might even be argued that those who see a family resemblance within the world of theoretical difference fashion it more like the philosophical world than the world of antitheory.

In conclusion, the major questions of antitheory today are not whether theory is "dead" or what comes "after" theory. Those have been *de facto* sorted out by the emergence of robust new forms of antifoundationalist theory that offer novel opportunities and challenges for academe. Theory can no more die than philosophy or literature or rhetoric. Ultimately, the discontentment of antitheorists is not so much from outside of theory but from within. While some might be inclined to view postcritique or speculative realism as battles "against theory," as we have seen, others view them as local struggles within theory for institutional dominance. Whether we regard theory as the legacies of antifoundationalism or the rise of alternatives to it, the dialectics of theory must be regarded as an essential aspect of its rise and dominance in the academy over the past fifty years. So, what's wrong with antitheory? If we just focus on its role in fortifying theory over the past fifty years, then perhaps nothing. But if we focus instead on its efforts to destroy theory, then *everything*.

Notes

1. Daphne Patai and Will H. Corral, "Introduction," in *Theory's Empire: An Anthology of Dissent*, ed. Daphne Patai and Will H. Corral (New York: Columbia University Press, 2005), 14. All of the quoted descriptions in this paragraph come either from their introduction or from their description of the book on the back cover. Moreover, the work of the forty-seven contributors to the Patai and Corral volume is as fine a place as any to survey this particular type of antitheory, which they ironically view as "unorthodox" compared to the "ubiquitous orthodoxy" of theory.
2. Blurb in support of Daphne Patai and Will H. Corral's collection, *Theory's Empire*.
3. See his Contributor's Note in this volume.
4. There were two "linguistic turns," each very different: one in literary and cultural theory, and one in analytic philosophy. Chapter 1, by Nealson, deals with the former, whereas the latter is discussed in Chapter 5, my contribution to this volume.
5. Vincent Leitch, "Antitheory," in *Bloomsbury Handbook of Literary and Cultural Theory*, ed. Jeffrey R. Di Leo (London and New York: Bloomsbury Academic, 2019), 373.
6. For a wonderful introduction to the idea of "early theory," see Paul Allen Miller's article of the same title in *The Bloomsbury Handbook of Literary and Cultural*

7   See Steven Knapp and Walter Benn Michaels, "Against Theory," *Critical Inquiry* 8.4 (1982): 723–742. In "Revisionary Madness: The Prospects of American Literary Theory at the Present Time," *Critical Inquiry* 9.4 (1983): 726–742, Daniel T. O'Hara argues that the emerging "against theory" movement, beginning with Michaels and Knapp's chapter, appears to be an institutional form of *psychosis*. O'Hara claims it is a blind revisionism, in the service of a new professional hierarchy of one-time theorists and/or their students who, under the guise of the latest interpretive community at the time, would put a limit to theory and its certified pragmatic users. This self-serving and (self-)deceptive syndrome only ends, O'Hara claims, in the self-destructive repetition of the vicious cycle without end. Michaels and Knapp's chapter and O'Hara's critical response, along with many others, including one from Stanley Fish, Michaels and Knapp's teacher and at the time a famous theorist, are collected in *Against Theory: Literary Studies and the New Pragmatism*, ed. W. J. T. Mitchell (Chicago: University of Chicago Press, 1985).

Theory, ed. Jeffrey R. Di Leo (London and New York: Bloomsbury Academic, 2019), 17–26.

8   John McGowan, "Neopragmatism," in *The Bloomsbury Handbook of Literary and Cultural Theory*, ed. Jeffrey R. Di Leo (London and New York: Bloomsbury Academic, 2019), 590. McGowan here too concurs with Nealon's observation that antitheory is just another brand of theory, writing that Knapp and Michael's "description of reading" in "Against Theory" is "itself, [just another] a general theoretical account."

9   Vincent Leitch, "Antitheory," 373.

10 Lorena Perez, "UVA English Professor Lands Large Danish Grant to Explore Literature's Social Use," *UVAToday*. May 25, 2016. https://news.virginia.edu/content/uva-english-professor-lands-large-danish-grant-explore-literatures-social-use.

11 Ibid.

12 Ibid.

13 Rita Felski, *The Limits of Critique* (Chicago: University of Chicago Press, 2015), 25.

14 See Jeffrey R. Di Leo, ed., *Dead Theory: Derrida, Death, and the Afterlife of Theory* (London and New York: Bloomsbury, 2016), for a number of other "anti-antitheory" accounts of the role of "death" in theory.

Works Cited

Di Leo, Jeffrey R., ed. *Dead Theory: Derrida, Death, and the Afterlife of Theory*. London and New York: Bloomsbury, 2016.

Felski, Rita. *The Limits of Critique*. Chicago: University of Chicago Press, 2015.

Knapp, Steven and Walter Benn Michaels. "Against Theory." *Critical Inquiry* 8.4 (1982): 723–742.

Leitch, Vincent. "Antitheory." In *The Bloomsbury Handbook of Literary and Cultural Theory*. Ed. Jeffrey R. Di Leo. London and New York: Bloomsbury Academic, 2019. 343–354; 373.

McGowan, John. "Neopragmatism." In *The Bloomsbury Handbook of Literary and Cultural Theory*. Ed. Jeffrey R. Di Leo. London and New York: Bloomsbury Academic, 2019. 589–590.

Miller, Paul Allen. "Early Theory." In *The Bloomsbury Handbook of Literary and Cultural Theory*. Ed. Jeffrey R. Di Leo. London and New York: Bloomsbury Academic, 2019. 17–26.

Mitchell, W. J. T., ed. *Against Theory: Literary Studies and the New Pragmatism*. Chicago: University of Chicago Press, 1985.

O'Hara, Daniel T. "Revisionary Madness: The Prospects of American Literary Theory at the Present Time." *Critical Inquiry* 9.4 (1983): 726–742.

Patai, Daphne and Will H. Corral. "Introduction." In *Theory's Empire: An Anthology of Dissent*. Ed. Daphne Patai and Will H. Corral. New York: Columbia University Press, 2005.

Perez, Lorena. "UVA English Professor Lands Large Danish Grant to Explore Literature's Social Use." *UVAToday*. May 25, 2016. https://news.virginia.edu/content/uva-english-professor-lands-large-danish-grant-explore-literatures-social-use.

Part One

Antitheory as Theory

1

Antitheory 2.0: The Case of Derrida and the Question of Literature

Jeffrey T. Nealon

Antitheory has long been a venerable brand of theory. I recall for example being on a "theory versus cultural studies" panel at the Modern Language Association (MLA) convention in 1994, with Vincent Leitch and Emily Apter—back in the days when theory people used to growl derisively about an antitheory brand of "Madonna studies." However, I think we came to the conclusion that theory was cultural studies, and vice versa. In any case, literary theory was in those days taking a historicist and social turn (away from the hermeneutic formalism of the text), while cultural studies was from the beginning dedicated to what Stuart Hall called "the detour through theory," so it may have been not Madonna studies but literary studies that was trending "antitheory" in those days. In any case, the problem was solved that afternoon in San Diego by deploying the old Hegelian trick of finding an opposition to be in fact a form of agreement, if you look at it from a higher level of abstraction. Though of course over the years before and after 1994, there were myriad other conference sessions dedicated to the "antitheory" challenges-from-within posed by Walter Benn Michaels, Eve Sedgwick, Deleuze and Guattari, Badiou, or [fill in the blank]. The session I was in, and many others like it, was a symptom of this venerable antitheory genre of theory itself.

In this chapter, I want to think about how today's "2.0" antitheory movements are like and unlike prior ones. Which is to ask, are today's antitheory theories similar to the antitheory challenges posed by—among many other movements—cultural studies, globalization studies, feminism, race and gender studies, queer theory, postcolonialism, Marxism, or new historicism? Or is there something decisively different going on today? To put it bluntly, I argue that the 1980s and 1990s antitheory wars were largely internecine wars concerning interpretive paradigms, and attempts to open up the question of where something like "meaning" comes from when we read a literary work, beyond the strict formalist conception of the text. In other words, the first rounds of "1.0" antitheory wars were largely a series of attempts to open up the question of interpretation beyond a myopic Saussurean focus on the text itself as the only legitimate linchpin for literary hermeneutics.

To recall just the most obvious and banal point concerning Saussure's thinking, he demonstrates that the signifier-signified relation is a conventional one. In short, Saussure shows us that language is a constructed network of systematic effects, not a list of Adamic names whose meaning is guaranteed by an essential link between the word and the existence its referent in the world. Famously, for Saussure that relation between the signifier and the signified is arbitrary and social, not necessary and essential: as Saussure memorably puts it, "In language, there are only differences, *without positive terms*."[1] This insight about the workings of language became the linchpin of almost all structuralism and poststructuralism, a loose grab bag of movements also dubbed "the linguistic turn," which entailed far-reaching revolutions in thinking about everything from the nature of kinship systems (Claude Lévi-Strauss) and historical events (Hayden White) to the workings of political power (Louis Althusser) or sex and gender (Judith Butler), all the way to the workings of African American cultural production (Henry Louis Gates's "signifyin"), and even the unconscious itself (Jacques Lacan's famous dictum that the unconscious is structured like a language is specifically scaffolded on Saussure's relation between the signifier and the signified). The truism that "there are no positive terms, only differences" got translated far beyond Saussure's insight into the workings of human language, and in the end this linguistic insight found itself exploded into the near-universal claim that there is no meaning in itself (against the "essentialist" position that takes meaning to inhere in an essence within persons and things); rather, on the Saussurean reasoning of the linguistic turn, there is only a series of differential, social (re)productions of meaning—a social (re)production machine that pretends to be based on natural or self-evident truths, but is in reality laden with ideological power plays and hidden political interests that require constant critical demystification. In short, Saussure's insights into the social nature of meaning in language became the subtending structure or logic animating a series of critical insights into the socially constructed nature of everything.

In doing so, however, the Antitheory 1.0 critique of the signifier largely *extended* (rather than *rejected*) that very logic of the signifier—which entailed less a complete rethinking of Saussure's account of signification than it comprised a shift in emphasis from one Saussurean pole to another, stressing the social construction of signified meaning *in the social world* rather than a strict attention to the undecidable signifier *in the text*.

However, precisely because of this linguistic social construction paradigm and its saturation within structuralism and poststructuralism, Saussure's work has not been well placed to survive the backlash against the linguistic turn that has emerged in the twenty-first century—the various critiques of the linguistic turn's primary anti-essentialist modus operandi, whereby any given *realist* or *essentialist* claim is shown to be *constructed* in and through the conventions and language of social power. The era of the linguistic turn was simultaneously the era of social constructionism, and its axiomatic sense that any claim to transhistorical truth (any claim to a final signified of guaranteed meaning) was in fact a contextual linguistic power play (a series of socially constructed signifiers) dressing itself up in the language of unassailable objectivism. This wide-ranging unmasking of essentialism was, it seems to me, the primary warrant for critical work in the age of Antitheory 1.0: the hermeneutics of suspicion was exported from the literary text and set loose on the social world of politics, identity formation, race, class, gender, ethnicity, disability, and so on.

Fast-forward to the adolescence of the twenty-first century, though, and the major buzzword in antitheory theory circles these days is "realism"—a rallying cry for myriad movements that only half a generation ago would have been branded naïve or, worse yet, essentialist. (And take it from me, students, there was no label more damning, in the late 1980s or early 1990s, than being called an essentialist.) These new realisms all share a kind of flight from the signifier, from the pivot of language, and from the question of reading or social critique as grounded in a hermeneutics of suspicion. Most obvious here would be the antilinguistic turn in object-oriented philosophy and speculative realism, as well as various forms of vibrant or agential matter (in the work of Jane Bennett and Karen Barad, for example), but one could also look to gender studies, which was ruled a generation ago by the sign- and language-based theories of performativity (say, Judith Butler). However, it's recently gone in a series of other "new materialist" directions (see, for example, the essays in Stacy Alaimo and Susan Hekman's *Material Feminisms*); in literature departments, think of the critique of commentary in Gregg Lambert's work on Deleuze, or the recent antihermeneutic methodological rise of data analysis, most convincingly thematized as distant reading (Franco Moretti), not to mention emergent methods like surface reading (Stephen Best and Sharon Marcus), descriptive reading (Heather Love), a resurgence of Eve Sedgwick's reparative reading, or postcritical reading (Rita Felski); likewise, consider various kinds of scientific, neuroscientific, and new media approaches to literature—examining everything from the nonhuman networks in which we act (Bruno Latour) to the brain chemistry of reading or the evolutionary functions of storytelling (Lisa Zunshine). All the way to animal studies and posthumanism, with their stinging critiques of linguistic anthropomorphism (say, Cary Wolfe's work). In short, if we look closely at the signposts concerning the present, it begins to look like we are postsigns, on the other side of the postmodern linguistic turn.

Language 2.0? Rethinking Derrida on Language

In fact, the driving apparatus of the linguistic turn—the hermeneutics of suspicion and its axiom that any claim can be endlessly recontextualized—becomes the linchpin of Bruno Latour's critique of deconstruction, taken up by Rita Felski in *The Limits of Critique*: they share the sense that "context stinks" as a way to think about social determinations of meaning, because sooner or later, you simply have to give up on that endless contextualization, precisely because it's otherwise an interminable process (akin to the Hegelian "bad infinite").[2] If, as Derrida concisely puts it, "no can be determined out[side] of context, but no context permits saturation,"[3] then maybe the larger grid of intelligibility offered by linguistic context has to go, at least in part because that skeptical procedure of endless recontextualization has in the twenty-first century mutated from a tool used primarily by leftist hermeneuts of suspicion, to become the preferred tactic of right-wing climate change deniers and political purveyors of "alternative facts." In any case, the Antitheory 2.0 critique of contextual meaning is that formerly prized moment of factual conclusion or consensus—scientific, literary, or otherwise—is downgraded to the moment of the process's arbitrary exhaustion (you have to stop somewhere), arrived at not by satisfactorily completing the contextual deliberative process, but by simply running out of time, throwing up your hands or shrugging your shoulders.

From Derrida's point of view, however, giving up on endless contextualization is thematized not as a moment of frustrated surrender, but the generative moment of decision—the event where one engages an outcome that's never guaranteed by the process (in the moment of deliberation, you can't know if it's the "right" decision), and (luckily) always open to recontextualization. As Derrida writes in the Afterword to *Limited Inc.*,

A decision can only come into being in a space that exceeds the calculable program that would destroy all responsibility by transforming it into a programmable effect of determinate causes. There can be no moral or political responsibility without this trial and this passage by way of the undecidable. Even if a decision seems to take only a second and not to be preceded by any deliberation, it is structured by this *experience and experiment of the undecidable*.[4]

While there is no theoretical limit to the performative events of iterability and recontextualization (such an iterability of the mark, a gesture's repetition that nevertheless introduces difference, is the compulsory "real" in Derrida), there certainly is a practical limit to endless recontextualization—the necessity of action and decision without which there would be no ethics or politics. But that ethical decision or political action is based not on the sureties of intentional states and guaranteed outcomes, but on the undecidable calculations of contextual possibilities. Derrida will elsewhere call this iterable contextuality "justice" (the necessity that everything is so calculated that calculation does not have the last word over everything)—so named because any given ethico-political decision is inexorably open to revision in the future (for better or worse): to speak phenomenologically, the "event" that is today is part of a mesh with the retention of yesterday, and the protention of tomorrow. This explains why for Derrida justice is "undeconstructable": because justice is deconstruction itself.

And thereby any narrow linguistically based example of this deconstructive larger process, like the contextual emergence of meaning or the process of subjective decision making, is necessarily carried along by a structurally more powerful set of disseminating forces that go by many iterable and recontexualized names in Derrida's work—the aforementioned justice, for example, or iteration, the structure of the remnant, pharmakon, supplement, shibboleth, trace, différance, the performative, hospitality, chora, and so on. The most famous general moniker he gives to those disseminating forces is "writing," but of course that immediately leads us back to the (still-dominant) thematization of Derrida as a hopelessly "linguistic turn" figure, who suggests that human language—in the form of textuality—is finally what makes the world go round: there is nothing outside the text. On this line of reasoning, deconstruction shows us the embarrassing fact that we used to think the really real was to be found in the intentional metaphysics of presence that animates human speech, but Derrida may seem to teach us the opposite—that the real is (un)grounded in a metaphysics of difference and deferral modeled on human writing practices.

Such a narrowly linguistic understanding of Derrida, however, seriously underestimates the stakes of his notion of writing, which he insists should be taken not as synonymous with human inscription, but in a more general (let's call it universal, just to be provocative) sense as "the iterability of the *mark beyond all human speech acts*. Barring any inconsistency, ineptness, or insufficiently rigorous formulation on my part, *my statements on this subject should be valid beyond the marks and society called 'human.'*"[5] So the trace structure of the iterable mark is open to recontextualization precisely because any given mark or singularity—me, you, the bird, the worm, the orchid, the wasp, the napkin dispenser, the North American power grid, the Earth—is not identical to itself. And that structure of universal nonidentity certainly isn't *caused* (or really in any significant way impacted) by humans and their language. Rather, this structure of the mark, the remnant, or iteration is the condition of (im)possibility for the event of being itself—human, animal, plant, planetary.

Which is to say in more prosaic terms that withering and passing away is the condition of possibility for something to come into existence in the first place; so the event that is any given entity—the emergence of everything that's come into being—necessitates that being is never fully present to itself. Which is why for Derrida, the emergence or life of a being or object is not opposed to its death or disappearance, because finitude is integral to being itself—the ability to pass from the scene inevitably and inexorably marks anything that emerges. And that law applies even to large-scale entities such as the formation of the Earth or the emergence of the human species itself—both of which will pass away eventually, taking the highly circumscribed entity of human logos with them. And such finitude is not merely an avoidable accident that befalls some existents: passing out of existence eventually happens (or at least structurally can happen) to them all; in effect, the eventuality of disappearing is the signature event that *marks* and prefigures all contextual emergence and presence. In Derrida, that necessity of finitude (the coming into being and passing away of all things, alive or otherwise) constitutes a philosophical "real"—that which far exceeds the human species, much less the arcane intricacies of human linguistic activity.

But if deconstruction is not primarily a linguistic turn discourse, if the structure of the mark is finally about a much larger field of forces than human language, how did Derrida's work get understood in the heyday of theory (and subsequently dismissed in the new materialist era) as the stern warden guarding the prison house of language, the linguistic turn discourse par excellence? Well, deconstruction caught a lot of heat from its enemies, from the very beginning, around the question of meaning's endless recontextualization and its (supposed) political upshot in a kind of shoulder-shrugging nihilism. Terry Eagleton's hugely influential 1983 primer *Literary Theory: An Introduction* summed up deconstruction like this: it "frees you at a stroke from having to assume a position on important issues, since what you say of such things will be no more than a passing product of the signifier and in no sense to be taken as 'true' or 'serious'.... Since it commits you to affirming nothing, it is as injurious as blank ammunition."[6]

As I argued over a quarter century ago, and will not belabor again here, this picture of deconstruction (as a linguistic game of showing how language strives after and inevitably fails to attain the status of univocal meaning) may in fact have been the project of American (literary critical) deconstruction associated with Yale School, though it shouldn't be confused with Derrida's (much different) horizons of engagement; but you don't have to take my word for it, as even Eagleton admits that the upshot of Derrida's work is more complicated than this project of revealing that all language usage is "literary" insofar as it's undecidable. As Eagleton writes, "Deconstruction in the Anglo-American world has tended on the whole to take this path" of rather monotonously "demonstrating that literary language constantly undermines its own meaning."[7] In short, deconstruction got as much help from its friends as it did from its enemies in being painted as a discourse that's wholly caught up in language—in showing the impossibility of meaning in the world as it is in the text. In the heyday of theory, both its proponents and its detractors seemed to agree that deconstruction was primarily in the business of understanding the workings of the world in terms of an understanding of language and the linguistic turn (a rendering of world-as-text that is simultaneously triumphalist in its reduction of the natural world to the human, and somehow at the same time completely impotent to change that world). As we've seen in subsequent years, and could have seen at the time had we been paying a different kind of attention, Derrida's philosophical prey lies far, far beyond these literary critical arguments about human language, reading, literature and meaning (or lack thereof).

Decades later, it may strike us with limpid mirth that differing paradigms for thinking about literature were ever thought to have had any rough and ready widespread political implications. But let's face constative facts: performing even the most faithfully Maoist reading of *Two Gentlemen of Verona* seems very unlikely to change much politically, in the past or present. But that sense of instant theory translation—from *PMLA* to the streets!—continues to live on, mostly these days in a negative way, in the endless parade of articles suggesting that poststructuralist theory (and even more specifically deconstruction) can be held responsible the "post-truth" world dominating our current political landscape. The argument, in short, is that the new global authoritarian regimes, and their endlessly recontextualized "alternative facts," are the obvious heirs to deconstruction's corrosive skepticism concerning meaning. I really don't want to engage that discourse here, with back and forths defending poststructuralism and deconstruction from those who accuse it of being responsible for nurturing neofascist liars and their spin doctors worldwide. If I were to engage that discourse, however, I might point out first of all that Donald Trump probably skipped the contemporary continental philosophy course in college, though Hungarian strongman Viktor Orban did study at Oxford with the eminent Hegelian Zbigniew Pełczyński, and I don't see anyone suggesting that Hegel or communitarian political theories of mutual recognition are responsible for Orban's brand of self-serving doubletalk.

Second, I'd simply note that political propaganda enjoyed a long, illustrious career before deconstruction became the rage in literature departments in the 1970s and 1980s, and such propaganda in the Internet era seems unfortunately well positioned to have far outlived the era of deconstruction as well. Third, it simply is the case that truth constitutes, as Foucault put it, a political question: What does the sequoia, the mosquito, or the washing machine care for "truth"? Truth is our problem, not theirs. Wishing it were not so, or newly fashionable theoretical appeals to a "really real," can hardly guarantee positive political results. Or one might note in passing that realist metaphysics, all the rage the first few thousand years of human thinking (until Kant, as the story goes), hardly stopped brutal massacres, colonialism and slavery; nor did philosophical realism bend the first 2000 years of human political regimes toward democracy, and the new realism doesn't necessarily seem likely to do so in the present or future. Like humanism, it may be that liberal democracy is a recent invention, and one nearing its end, due to structural reasons far more powerful than the reach of academic theories.

But in any case, no matter what the backs and forths on the issue of the linguistic turn and its legacy (critiques that could continue ad infinitum), I will cut the string here and agree with critics of the linguistic turn on at least one point: if Derrida's primary theoretical-political insight was in fact into the performative workings of language, a series of linguistic mechanisms that then could explain everything else (the endless, "undecidable" making and unmaking of human linguistic meaning as the fulcrum for thinking about the world, or even the universe), then there's not much "new" remaining for deconstruction to discover or shed light upon in the twenty-first century—especially around the question of exposing essentialism as social constructionism, which seems like double down on human linguistic exceptionalism, any way you slice it. It seems not only wrong but the height of humanist hubris to say that gravity, for example, needs to be demystified as a human construct: (a) because gravity is not a social construction, and (b) because such demystification of the "natural" world tends to reinforce human exceptionalism—the sense that the universe is, at its core, what we've made it.

In short, the broad outlines of the critique of the linguistic turn strike me as being correct—the general sense that human language and its workings cannot effectively serve as the linchpin for understanding the workings of everything else. So if deconstruction is or was a discourse completely subtended by the linguistic turn and the question of meaning, then I think interest in deconstruction going forward will remain largely historical. But my gambit here is to suggest that, while he did indeed write hundreds and hundreds of pages on the question of language, Derrida's core insights were never primarily *linguistic*.[8]

Nature/Culture, Language/Literature

Of all the hundreds of binary oppositions that got deconstructed over the years, probably none was more popular than the nature/culture binary—with hundreds of articles and countless classroom hours dedicated to showing over and over again that any conception of nature is at the end of the day a cultural linguistic construction, essentially a kind of fiction. To make this point in the literature classroom, you just have students read, for example, Hawthorne's "Young Goodman Brown" or Conrad's *Heart of Darkness*, and contrast the Puritans' or Victorians' menacing portraits of nature (including human nature) with today's loving embrace of all that is natural (including finding your inner child). Dutifully following Saussure, we can point out that the "referent" in the world may be the same (those "wild" spaces beyond the grid of the city), but different cultures and different historical periods bestow vastly different meanings on this thing called nature. And thereby we find that nature is socially constructed, as per the outline provided by Antitheory 1.0.

However, as many recent critics have argued, it may be that the new materialist understanding of imbricated, lively, co-constitutive life forms may make obsolete the nature-culture divide that was so central to social constructionist accounts of reality. Once you accept that lively, new materialist rewriting of the nature/culture divide, there's a kind of inversion from the 1.0 deconstruction of the nature/culture binary, which attempts to show that any appeal to nature is inexorably cultural. The 2.0 or new materialist deconstruction of that binary asks you to recognize not that nature was culture all along, but asks you to wonder, as Vicki Kirby puts it, "What if Culture Was Really Nature all Along?" Within the worldview of social constructionist Antitheory 1.0, language was thought to be the primary means by which human culture was barred from the realm of nature (on the Lacanian insight, once we fall into language, we are forever cut off from the real). But if humans are understood as inexorably part of the mix of nature, actants among other actants, then language (the thing that seemed to distinguish us from mute, "natural" entities) is re-understood as a continuous part of nature as well—a feature of one of the entities within the mesh of nature, much like the glaciers characteristic of the polar regions, the plumage of the peacock, or the acorns of the oak tree.

One might offer Kirby's new materialist insight concerning language in the form of a syllogism:

Humans are part of nature (not opposed to it).
Language is a distinguishing feature of humans.
Ergo, human language is part of nature.

Or, more generally, if everything in nature is lively and connected, as we learn from new materialisms, then why must we banish language from the mix, as it is a lively form of connection, a marking apparatus that can be understood as far more generally utilized by all kinds of plants, animals, and ecosystems to "communicate" (about the existence of predators, sources of food, mating and pollination, etc.). Like Derrida's reading of intentionality in Austin, language doesn't disappear on such a rereading, but it does cease to rule the chain if you understand language as one element among a structurally more powerful set of others. Likewise, following everyone from Deleuze and Guattari through Latour to the physics of Karen Barad, once we realize that inert matter isn't so inert after all—that flesh and rocks and trees are lively and are part of a network of interconnection where they co-evolve with each other (the way we tend to describe "culture")—then it begins to look like a broad, posthuman sense of language or culture is integral to the workings of nature and the very physiology of our bodies. As Kirby writes, "the meat of the body *is* thinking material. If it is in the nature of biology to be cultural—and clearly, what we mean here by 'cultural' is intelligent, capable of interpreting, analyzing, reflecting, and creatively reinventing—then what is the need to exclude such processes of interrogation from the ontology of life?"⁹ In short, a certain Derridean understanding of iteration and marking beyond the human can I think help to rescue deconstruction from its exile as a hopelessly linguistic turn discourse that understands everything else in the universe on the world-building paradigm of human language.

What I'm not so sure about is the future of literature (those worlds built largely of human language) within the realist ontological world of Antitheory 2.0. If human language is not anymore the structuring linchpin of everything else, and if the socially constructed stories we tell ourselves about things can no longer be easily (mis)taken for the way things actually are, coupled with rapid changes in technology that bring forms of media far beyond the written page to the forefront, then why is literature centrally important (anymore)?

Relatedly, and a bit more empirically, I wonder what the new realisms have to say about the fate of literature in the undergraduate classroom? I remember J. Hillis Miller telling me that all the material for his essays got worked out in the classroom, and that makes sense: because back in the day, whether it was new criticism, or deconstruction, or new historicism, or feminist or postcolonial or critical race theory (even if it's Against Theory 1.0, as in Walter Benn Michaels and Steven Knapp's 1982 intervention), it's still about various ways to interpret the meaning of literature. Once that critical reading project goes, theory (the stuff that circulates through journals and university presses) certainly can and will survive—mostly by turning its attention to things other than literature and the question of interpretation.

But whither goes the undergraduate classroom in literature departments? Do we stick with the problems of literary meaning and the hermeneutics of suspicion, even though we know they're not vanguard problems anymore? Or do we go right to non-hermeneutic forms of reading in the Milton class? If so, I'm not sure having them run rudimentary computer programs on *Paradise Lost*, or asking students to surface-read it, is going to bring our sagging majors back, or garner us much respect among our increasingly skeptical colleagues.

It's also worth remembering another decisive historical difference between the era of Antitheory 1.0 and 2.0: almost no one within a humanities discipline was talking about the end of the literature departments in the mid-1990s; whereas today, it's just about all anyone talks about at English department meetings and professional society gatherings. And it was likewise taken as axiomatic in the heyday of linguistic-turn theory that the making and unmaking of literary meaning was a—if not *the*—decisive pivot for understanding the world more generally, and the steady flow of students into the English major was taken as decisive proof of that generalization. Today, I think we have (yet) to come to terms with the fact that literary hermeneutics is no longer seen as a widely decisive factor in people's everyday lives; the ins and outs of interpretation theory begin to look, to many students and the general public, like either an expensive hobby or an antiquarian curiosity. Even the novel, by far and away the most popular literary form, has I think ceased to matter decisively when it comes to widespread cultural impact today.

Perhaps as a consequence of that decline in importance for reading the written word—the displacement of endless interpretation as the ultimate horizon of human endeavor in the humanities and arts all the way to the social and physical sciences—it seems clear to me that the scientism of the new realisms is their primary drawing point, and this is both a continuity and an important difference in terms of prior theory wars. Of course, theory got off the ground as an attempt to make more "sciencey" the project of interpretation; at a historical moment when the humanities was being research-benchmarked with the sciences, theory's explosion was the thing that launched a thousand successful tenure cases by making literary interpretation seem less like "my opinion" and more like a science of meaning. But of course it's precisely the project of the new realisms to abandon language, and abandon the question of hermeneutics, for a whole series of reasons that I think we'd want to think about in a book like this one. Is literature no longer about exploring the imaginative powers of the false, but about confirming the true? Does literary study become a branch of social science, in that case? And if so, does humanities theory thereby come into its own, on a par with the social sciences? Or does that finally confirm that all that the humanities can do is be a handmaiden to the sciences, the real purveyors of truth?

And surely second-order, demystifying or critical reading is not what students are good at in the early days of what unfortunately looks like the Trump era, so I'm happy to think about retooling it. But for the sake of what? What does the postcritical literature classroom look like? And if it is a matter of teaching undergraduates postcritical reading as affective connecting tissue (or reading as a kind of slowing-down bulwark against the superfast dictates of attention capitalism) or as a therapeutic or reparative practice, then I wonder why literature remains a crucial pivot at all in the contemporary world—binge-watching long-form television is better at working through affective narrative. In fact, your iPod mixes or Spotify streams, or simply learning how to meditate, are all much better bulwarks against punishing dictates of attention capitalism than reading a book on the bus will ever be. Literature, at least in the greater part of my *teaching* lifetime, was tied to the critical hermeneutics of suspicion; and I wonder whether as one goes the way of historical anachronism in the journals, so goes the other in the classroom?

It's worth noting that the genre of Antitheory has long been enamored of declaring the death of theory, or at least the death of this or that theory. However, I've not seen many people over the years worrying over the death of literature itself as an area of academic endeavor. In most discussions, it has seemed as if the centrality of literature is safe and enduring, and the only worries are about the shifting theoretical tools necessary to access or talk about literature with new generations of colleagues, administrators, and students. But what if the academic study of literature itself is going the way of the Pony Express?

As I intimate above, I'm pretty sure this thing called theory can survive without literary hermeneutics—as theory has strong portfolios of investment outside literature and literature departments. However, concerning the academic study of literature itself as an area of robust research innovation, I'll have to say I have my doubts. Just think of it this way: Antitheory has been very good to theory, in both its 1.0 and 2.0 manifestations; a quick glance at any university press catalog will show you there's certainly more "theory" today than there was twenty-five years ago, and twenty-five years before that. But unfortunately I don't think that "antiliterature" (increasing doubts about the relevance of studying literary production in the first place) will have the same invigorating effect on the academic study of literature. English departments won't disappear, at least not overnight. But these courses in the history of literature will in the future look a lot less like the central core of the humanities and a lot more like art history or classics—either antiquarian concerns (akin to classics, in a fast turnover world where Gertrude Stein's Paris is about as foreign to our students as Thales's pre-Socratic Miletus) or poor stepchildren to sibling subdisciplines that are already producing new biopolitical capital rather than studying the past: As art history is to painting or sculpture production classes, so will historical literature classes be to production classes like creative writing and rhetoric and composition?

Finally, I've heard it said over the years that theory killed the study of literature—Antitheory 1.0's hermeneutics of suspicion ruined the appreciation of literary mastery, and it was all downhill from there. It seems to me the opposite: theory extended literature's life considerably, gave this resolutely analog form another quarter century of disciplinary centrality in a world that had long since gone digital. In the end, we don't need Derrida to remind us that finitude is coming for us all, but maybe this time it's not just the displaced name for a linguistic predicament.

Notes

1 Ferdinand de Saussure, *Course in General Linguistics*, trans. Wade Baskin (New York: McGraw, 1966), 120.
2 Rita Felski, *The Limits of Critique* (Chicago: University of Chicago Press, 2015), 151–185.
3 Jacques Derrida, "Living On/Border Lines," trans. James Hulbert, in *Deconstruction and Criticism*, ed. Harold Bloom et al. (New York: Seabury Press, 1979), 75–176, 81.
4 Jacques Derrida, *Limited Inc.*, trans. Samuel Weber (Evanston: Northwestern University Press, 1988), 116.
5 Ibid., 134.
6 Terry Eagleton, *Literary Theory: An Introduction* (Minneapolis: University of Minnesota Press, 1983), 125.
7 Ibid.
8 For recent related attempts to further this line of reasoning concerning Derrida, see Michael Marder's *The Event of the Thing: Derrida's Post-Deconstructive Realism* (Toronto: University of Toronto Press, 2011) and Clayton Crockett's *Derrida after the End of Writing: Political Theology and New Materialism* (New York: Fordham University Press, 2017).
9 Vicki Kirby, "Natural Convers(at)ions: Or, What if Culture Was Really Nature All Along?" in *Material Feminisms*, ed. Stacy Alaimo and Susan Hekman (Bloomington: Indiana University Press, 2008), 221.

Works Cited

Crockett, Clayton. *Derrida after the End of Writing: Political Theology and New Materialism.* New York: Fordham University Press, 2017.

Derrida, Jacques. "Living On/Border Lines." Trans. James Hulbert. In *Deconstruction and Criticism.* Ed. Harold Bloom et al. New York: Seabury Press, 1979.

Derrida, Jacques. *Limited Inc.* Trans. Samuel Weber. Evanston: Northwestern University Press, 1988.

Eagleton, Terry. *Literary Theory: An Introduction.* Minneapolis: University of Minnesota Press, 1983.

Felski, Rita. *The Limits of Critique.* Chicago: University of Chicago Press, 2015.

Kirby, Vicki. "Natural Convers(at)ions: Or, What if Culture Was Really Nature All Along?" In *Material Feminisms*. Ed. Stacy Alaimo and Susan Hekman. Bloomington: Indiana University Press, 2008. 214–235.

Marder, Michael. *The Event of the Thing: Derrida's Post-Deconstructive Realism*. Toronto: University of Toronto Press, 2011.

Saussure, Ferdinand de. *Course in General Linguistics*. Trans. Wade Baskin. New York: McGraw, 1966.

2

Crisis Theory after Crisis

Peter Hitchcock

Antitheory, as theory, is unimpeachable. It could be, for instance, simply a position about theory and its relative role in cultural and literary critique. Antitheory as a philosophical dispute over the role of theory in ethics is of more significance because it concerns the relationship of rules to ways of living, principles to modes of socialization. However antitheory is characterized, there are politics at stake and certainly institutional implications. Here I am chiefly concerned with the meaning of crisis for particular kinds of theory and how crisis can produce new imperatives that may, in their own way, defy theorization. Theory is an injunction, not a specialization and certainly not a discipline (of course, theory might be read as at base profoundly inter- or transdisciplinary). I do not believe there is a before or after theory if by theory we mean what is coterminous with thinking as such (temporal markers must be thought—the experience of death is timeless, the Real is unrepresentable, etc.). Still, since thinking is situated (the thinker is mediated even if the thought itself imagines otherwise), the situations of theory are not coeval and at that level antitheory is about the struggle over combined and uneven developments, in theory and otherwise. If theory is a practice, perhaps even a theoretical practice, would crisis reveal or mystify that function? Obviously, it also depends on how crisis is theorized, and in what follows, I want to indicate why it is important to think the difference of crisis across its disciplinary decrees. The chief enemy of theory today is the parochialism of arch specialization: each specialty is blessed by a paradoxical imperial insularity that can produce excellent mythological fiddle playing while the world somewhat more literally burns. Crisis, what crisis?

One of the advantages of theorizing crisis is, for Marxism, that there is always a crisis to theorize. Capitalism lives on crisis—it is its *sur-vivre*. It can no more eradicate crisis than it can redistribute all private property as free public goods (it cannot decide to be communist therefore). In general, capitalism does not try to hide crisis—it is often passed off as an unfortunate by-product of the business cycle: overproduction, underconsumption, overconsumption, inflation, credit squeeze, stagnation, negative interest rates, print money, speculation, overproduction, and so on. There is a theory of crisis devoted to each element, and these are just the beginning. There is no space here to recapitulate the rich critical genealogy from Marx, but some indicative texts might include, Clarke's *Marx's Theory of Crisis*, Mirowski's *Never Let a Serious Crisis Go to Waste*, Berg's *Making Money—The Philosophy of Crisis*, Streeck's *Buying Time*, and Lapavitsas's edited collection on financialization. But the repetition of business cycles does not mean each crisis is a version of another, or even that the normative claims of business cycles can explain the crisis at issue. This is a warning about the texture of crisis and specific dialectical constraints. There is a singularity to crisis that is not simply uniqueness but is directly connected to the dynamism of capital as relation. Marxists are compelled to theorize conjunction and extension in considering such vigor. A crisis might be simply described or rendered an empiricist or positivist truth. A crisis can indeed be mapped, or figured by a data set. Yet crisis is never only a caesura or event, rupture or a cathartic return to a settled predisposition. It is part of a pattern of persistence, a logic of confounding universalism whose concrete particulars are beyond a doxic attention to the way of the world, the way of things, the way that is given in centuries of modernity. The maddening aspect of capitalist contradictions is that they are never only auguries of doom and transformation but also produce trenchant tinctures of comfort and recovery. Smith, Ricardo, Keynes, Friedman, and Hayek all understood this, although they might not have called it a structural antinomy and certainly not a Pharmakon in Derrida's deployment of the term. Thinking crisis is always already to theorize it at some level, but what is the crisis we are "after"?

In many ways, the crisis of 2007–2008 plays out as if its inner logic had no precedent or if it was only a specter of one. Never have so many invisible hands made such an economic mess in such material ways, chiefly from a long-standing class desire to put privatization front and center. Often, however, one was fed the insight that crisis is forbiddingly complex and that the entire capitalist system should therefore restrict itself to three letter acronyms: CDO, CDS, CMO, SPV, MBS, and so on. The major factors, a subprime mortgage bubble underwritten by key acts of deregulation in national and transnational finance (the repeal of Glass-Steagall in 1999 under President Clinton was key, but this was one of several regulatory changes that girded neoliberalism all the way back to Reagan) coupled with common or garden fraud ("alternative facts" produced by pay to play ratings agencies for instance), brought the credit infrastructure of the banking industry across the globe to the brink of collapse. In his trenchant book on the meaning of this crisis for the future, or not, of capitalism, *Seventeen Contradictions*, David Harvey outlines key elements of the debacle but does not exclude the Left from its implications:

> It is not only the capitalist elites and their intellectual and academic acolytes who seem incapable of making any radical break with their past or defining a viable exit from the grumbling crisis of low growth, stagnation, high unemployment and the loss of state sovereignty to the power of bondholders. The forces of the traditional left (political parties and trade unions) are plainly incapable of mounting any solid opposition to the power of capital.[1]

Harvey then extends the critique to what he sees as a theoretical malaise combined with a structural impasse:

> What remains of the radical left now operates largely outside of any institutional or organized oppositional channels, in the hope that small-scale actions and local activism can ultimately add up to some kind of satisfactory macro alternative. This left, which strangely echoes a libertarian and even neoliberal ethic of anti-statism, is nurtured intellectually by thinkers such as Michel Foucault and all those who have reassembled postmodern fragmentations under the banner of a largely incomprehensible post-structuralism that favors identity politics and eschews class analysis. Autonomist, anarchist and localist perspectives are everywhere in evidence. But to the degree that this left seeks to change the world without taking power, so an increasingly consolidated plutocratic capitalist class remains unchallenged in its ability to dominate the world without constraint.[2]

Readers of Harvey will know that the empiricism of his dialectics does not smile kindly on theoretical abstraction as its own reward, and, while he has nodded positively in Foucault's direction on more than one occasion, Harvey has been "antitheory" whenever theory might become a self-congratulatory code for seizing salary or the signifier rather than power. When it comes to Marx, of course, Harvey has been deeply theoretical, but the point is the complexity of the financial crisis is a prompt for theory alive to the challenge of political economy as a global critique.

When you have diagnosed the elements of crisis in the way Harvey has done, and admonished the couture critique of the theorati for its studied complicity, you have to come up with an alternative that masks all hint of abstract theoretical nuance for barricade building practicality and snub-nosed transformation. Most of the seventeen mandates Harvey devises to match or overcome the contradictions he registers are central to the production of socialism and communism and are a framework for anticapitalism rather than a blueprint for the actual practices that might secure its success. Harvey knows his Hegel and separates the slogan "smash capitalism" from any trace of teleological exclusion and order of time. On the plus side, if revolution were a constitution, its amendments would now stretch to infinity, each one designed to include the exclusion and the excluded and remain open to modification by all other amendments. On the negative side, revolution is exigential rather than exegetical, which is to say that transformation is always one moment of theoreticism away from paralysis, stasis, and torpor. The success of revolutionary humanism, as Harvey calls it, will be discerned in a number of ways, including the idea that "daily life is slowed down ... to maximize time for free activities conducted in a stable and well-maintained environment protected from dramatic episodes of creative destruction."[3] The academic cynic may simply call this "tenure," but the point would be to press the idea that aspects of the revolution already animate the everyday beyond the reflex of enthusiastic abstraction. Part of the provocation of crisis theory after crisis is the extent to which the antinomies that produce social change remain active in inhibiting it, as if even itemizing the contradictions is an element of the narrative extending them. Surely the promise of revolutionary humanism is a path beyond this crushing inertia, that it has the potential to break the cycle of crisis and displace all of the phantasmagoria of financialization in favor of something that is ethically true. Harvey quotes from Gramsci to the effect that the "absolute humanism of human history does not aim at the peaceful resolution of existing contradictions.... But is the very theory of these contradictions."[4] Could it be that the exigential theory of crisis exists in the theorization of humanism? Or, to put it in a slightly different way, what if crisis theory is the ward of those who have built a tradition of humanism within the modern state? What if the exigential crisis of capitalism is legible within the existential crisis of theorizing humanism?

This question spurs a second reading of crisis, the crisis of the humanities which, like crisis for Marxism, is not just an object of analysis but something of a way of life. What is there in the humanities that we can depend on? The short answer and the one that is yet so voluminous in the history of the humanities is "crisis" itself. No, some might say, there can be no crisis in the humanities unless Stanley Fish or Martha Nussbaum or Christopher Newfield has declared as much but, while I will have cause to mention their individual emphases (and especially Newfield's in my conclusion), the crisis of the humanities is coterminous with its substance and in large part is secreted inside the logic of the capitalist state that, since it is an organically constituted measure of socialization, must live and die with it. The solution in one is the sublation of the other for which crisis is merely an ontological name. But, and this may be counterintuitive, what has to die in the humanities threatens to occlude the theorization of humanism in Harvey's sense that would, for any transformation of capitalism, constitute the vital remainder. Is this ever how crisis is defined in the humanities? Certainly, crisis can be found everywhere in its constitutive discourses: "There is a general crisis in the humanities, there is a particular and more acute crisis in modern foreign languages" (Hans W. Rosenhaupt, 1940). "We have tended to lose the sense of delight and newness all good literature gives. This, I would say, is one aspect of the crisis in the humanities" (Germaine Bree, 1949). The Southern Humanities Conference devoted its 12th get-together to the subject of "The Crisis of the Humanities in the South" (in 1959). These examples are drawn from a brief timeline provided by Wayne Bivens-Tatum, who notes, in true materialist mode, "Throughout the 1960s, the Humanities stayed in crisis" (the centerpiece was a 1965 book by Plumb, *The Crisis in the Humanities*). Indeed, Bivens-Tatum's JSTOR investigation yields 217 hits from 1922 to the present, or roughly from about Eliot's "Wasteland" to Harpham's *The Humanities and the Dream of America*, a longer American century than research like Giovanni Arrighi's would countenance, but then hegemony cannot adjudicate its own aphanisis. One could argue that the permanent crisis of the humanities is the proof of its concern, that its value in cultivating our general species-being is precisely that it attends to the insistent problems of that endeavor (this is something of Peter Brooks's position in his introduction to the collection *The Humanities and Public Life*). Harpham suggests that for many in the humanities the crisis has become the rationale, a place of endless exercises in self-doubt rather than a process of "exposing students to the wisdom of the ages." But this is a different tack because the "humanitists" (which I use to resist the simple equivalence of the work of people in the humanities with the broader projects of humanism and humanitarianism) do not make the history of their concern, or at least the conditions of the humanities are not those of their own choosing. This is not an apology for handwringing but a hint that I favor a more state-centered understanding of the form of crisis within capitalism than one that sees it as some kind of obsessive-compulsive disorder or one that limits it to its institutional valence, the academy.

The permanence of crisis in the humanities is a specific antinomy of the modern capitalist state. This does not mean that analyses of core content, whether in textuality, humanity, and self-understanding, are irrelevant; far from it, but it does place special emphasis on the infrastructure of the state in which the humanities is manifest. One can have a state without humanities, but the lineages of the modern capitalist state suggest they are mutually and significantly implied. There can be more radical or conservative versions of the humanities, more technological and antiquarian aspects to its project but they nourish and are nourished by the logic of state which gives to them less a patina of respectability but an aura of crisis that is the very Pharmakon of its (the particular state's) existence. There is no life beyond crisis for the humanities in this regard. To be clear, "humanities and the capitalist state" does not describe the crisis; the crisis exists in their necessary imbrication, in the passion of their formation, in the texture of their modernity. If the fortunes of one are tied to the health of the other, one might surmise that the decline of the humanities is the atrophy of the state itself, but causality is never that simple, although what is symptomatic can be revelatory in the differences between state concepts and what is extant in particular states and state forms (the nation-state most prominently). Harpham links the fate of the humanities to its formation in the United States—that the structure of the field in the United States is its most influential and recognizable form (in Chapter One he writes, "the humanities are something like North America," which, in fairness to Canada, is not where the fault line necessarily lies in his argument. In Chapter Six he notes, "the modern concept of the humanities is truly native only to the United States"[5]). I agree with Harpham that the crisis in the humanities is its strength but, unlike Harpham, I do not see the demise of humanistic learning in the fields of philosophical, literary, and historical inquiry outside a concomitant collapse of a specific state form (again, not the state as such but a specific state form). The instrumentalization of knowledge is not in itself the death knell of the humanities; economic prioritization is an intensification of crisis in state viability that must, perforce, reshape the internal dynamics of institutions of knowledge. A version of the humanities, renamed as Jonathan Culler suggests, will persist but its very diminution will further weaken the state that starves it. We could argue, in Foucauldian fashion, that the crisis is about the weakening of the human as subject in intellectual inquiry, that it is a used-up ideology of anthropocentrism that fails to address a competent register of contemporary existence. But this ideology itself entails an apparatus, a field and logic of intelligibility that has proved remarkably resistant in several declensions. One must ask whether the idea of Man [sic] could disappear without its apparatus; or, to put it differently, whether state structures can remain without their epistemological guarantees? This is surely one of the challenges, for instance, of decoloniality to modernity. Certainly the interaction of humanistic with nonhumanistic disciplinary fields is getting the humanities to challenge its presuppositions. But this is a reformation of knowledge in the shadow of the state, not its transformation in the efflorescence of thinking beyond its specific state. To think through thinking at this level, I want to return briefly to Schiller's thoughts on the aesthetic education of mankind.

Friedrich Schiller is being read again and possibly more so thanks to Gayatri Spivak adapting the title of his "Letters upon the Aesthetic Education of Man" for her book, *An Aesthetic Education in the Era of Globalization*. Since her last major essay collection riffed on Kant's *Critique of Pure Reason*, it is somewhat apposite that Schiller's text is invoked in the introduction of the more recent tome since, besides Rousseau, Kant is a major inspiration in Schiller's work. Schiller, of course, resists Kant (as Spivak resists both—she professes to "sabotage Schiller"—a true spirit of antitheory on behalf of theory) and Schiller prefers the inclination or sentiment of real humans in their individuality to Kant's duty-bound and reason-centered idea of state. The natural state of the human is not idealized, but Schiller is clearly trying to think how a transition to moral fulfillment can be achieved that would overcome this natural state without destroying the society that is the basis of the rational fulfillment of the species, "a pledge in the sensible world of a morality as yet unseen."[6] Schiller suggests,

> One can ... imagine two different ways in which man existing in time can coincide with man as idea and in consequence just as many ways in which the state can assert itself in individuals: either by the ideal man suppressing empirical man and the state annulling individuals; or else by the individual himself becoming the state, and man in time being ennobled to the stature of man as Idea.[7]

The tension or antagonism here is clear although the state in play is a philosophical concept, much more than a political economy, that is, its expression or condensation. In reconciling unity in reason with the multiplicity of natural law, Schiller suggests, "The state should not only respect the objective and generic character in its individual subjects: it should also honor their subjective and specific character."[8] The obvious question is what faculty or process would enable the emergence of such a state without one force "suppressing" the other?

The restoration of the totality of our nature that the arts themselves have helped to destroy, as Schiller describes it, can be achieved only by a "higher art." The state, in this reading, cannot achieve the desired effect because the state must first be founded on a humanity that higher art can foster. Art and beauty constitute the medium for uniting reason and nature. Beauty itself is differentiated into energizing and melting forms, but neither alone can produce the necessary aesthetic for education. Energizing beauty is tensile and more wanton for the power that drives it; melting beauty is relaxing and counters the deleterious over exuberance of its other mode. The antinomy in beauty is only matched by a corresponding and coterminous antinomy between beauty's joy and its role as knowledge in the education of "man." The pleasures of beauty may found an aesthetic, but how can this be a knowledge that permits the state to integrate nature and reason in its very form? Beauty's role in the aesthetic only provides a sense of totality as potential—not the *form of action* in its state that would guarantee its truth. But this is only one reason why we might cast a jaundiced eye on Schiller's declaration that "if man is ever to solve that problem in politics in practice he will have to approach it through the problem of the aesthetic, because it is only through beauty that man makes his way to Freedom."[9]

The acknowledgment of beauty, however contested, is a basic human virtue, even if those of us in literature and arts, if not for humanities as a whole, might appear more professionally predisposed to extol the virtues of beauty's role in fulfilling our lives, in appreciating a faculty central to what makes a human, human. Indeed, among the classic defenses of the humanities, the Schillerian gambit is not uncommon (while often divorced from the lineages of German Romanticism that are immanent to its protocols, the "*Sturm und Drang*" of beauty's basic division). One may say aesthetic knowledge is useless, but it is in its uselessness that our total capacities are realized, not in knowledge's instrumentalization, which places reason's need above and beyond all others (uselessness is not the negative of practice but its aporia). Yet before we get to reality and the real, we must say more about the extent to which Schiller's schema demonstrates the very antinomy his vaunting of beauty seeks to abolish. The problem begins not so much with Schiller's anthropocentrism (with an attendant and insistent Eurocentrism), which of course cannot be explained away, but with the framing, the parerga once more, of Schiller's passionate claims for aesthetic education. In part, the theory masks the importance of theorization itself.

As the French Revolution began, Schiller gave a lecture at Jena to a packed audience with the title, "To what purpose and to what end do we study universal history?" The French masses, he conjectured, suffered from an experiential deficit: they did not understand the place of the public in the structure of the historical event they were living. Despite all the talk of liberty, for Schiller, an avatar of liberty, there was too much gesture and not enough gestation. Freedom could not take root in a public so easily swayed. As he began his letters on beauty, he also wrote to the French Chamber of Deputies to spare the king's life. Clearly the state could not survive extremes of passion or reason; the sense and form drives had to be mutually correcting or transformation could only dissolve in terror. Kantian categories can be illuminated by the circumstances of their thought; but Schiller's revolutionary hesitancy is demonstrably symptomatic of his aesthetic logic. One would have to undo, for instance, the inexorable slide between what governs man's state and the state that purports to govern man. In politics and philosophy, this is not just a problem of scale but of matter's matter. It is much more than slippery sophistry: it is about the form of state appropriate to a more radical social architectonics. The power of a state of beauty is not to be at once disparaged, but its mediating power does not enter what is extant in the state according to its own devices, or at least not by that practice alone. The difference in states is also a matter of ideology, for instance, which, in order to constitute itself as ideology, cannot nominate itself as such. This does not mean it has no moral purchase, only that it is mediated as it mediates by more than it can know, which is how ideology works, how it interpellates. When Schiller writes of the absence of determination in the aesthetic condition, he is performing an idealist metalepsis—the aesthetic has become the cause within a history in which it is its very effect. I do not think of this in accord with the repressive hypothesis as such, but the problem of justifying aesthetics often lies in adjudicating its non-said, the ways in which beauty is constrained not to speak of the conditions of its possibility as a mediating function. You can think the aesthetic in Schiller's terms by suspending the actions of concrete determination, but, like the state, the aesthetic stubbornly remains the scene of social practice and fosters morality by performing a somewhat suspect morality of covering its tracks. The more anxious the aesthetic becomes in Schiller's estimation, the more stark the statements it propels: "Taste alone brings harmony into society"[10]; or, "Beauty alone makes the whole world happy."[11] Make no mistake, such pronouncements are revolutionary, but the revolutionary state has to get down to business by attempting to reproduce the social conditions of its reproduction and tamping down expressions of disharmony and unhappiness like bread riots and tax revolts. This does not negate the aesthetic, but it is a measure of difference in emergence and emergency.

Much is made of "play" in Schiller's theorization, but what is played out is an impasse in the positive production of freedom when necessity continually rewrites its prerogatives. Schiller is clearly aware of this—part of his intervention is to suggest that in the midst of developing social life, we have enacted false divisions: we have expanded technical and empirical knowledges as he calls them, so that the unity of human nature is fragmented and we live as this "single little fragment of the whole," a kind of ruined capacity and division of labor that Marx would develop into a theory of alienation. Marx, while composing his searing investigation of political economy, always seemed to be writing about art, which to some at least has suggested that the arc of art has more solid and not just social foundations. But since we know that every hegemony needs its aesthetic, we should not be surprised that the truths of Schiller are subject to creative reaccentuation across the political spectrum. Roger Kimball, for instance, finds in Schiller a stalwart of the classics and the Western tradition. Of course, he has to clear the page of all insurgent imprint and begins by dismissing Marx's interpretation of Schiller as "fantasy." Still, Kimball cuts to the chase by noting that Schiller hoped his aesthetic education would "establish the freedom that political revolution had conspicuously failed to achieve." In my interpretation, the failure to resolve the crisis is the aporia in what the humanities represent for the state under capitalism. Schiller believes that aesthetics could mediate the antinomy of inclination and reason redolent in the revolution Kimball rightly invokes. The problem is that this aesthetic reflex is always already inclined to reproduce the contradiction Schiller seeks to solve. This is not a confirmation of the deficit announced in Marx's Eleventh Thesis on Feuerbach about the interpretation of the world versus changing it, but a point about the constitutive gap the modern state attempts to bridge between autonomy (inclination) and universal harmony (reason). Schiller argues aesthetics can negotiate this space, that beauty can save modernity from the conflagrations endemic to the desire to produce the democratic ideal. What Kimball recognizes is that aesthetics is responding to two crises simultaneously: the *ratio* of the modern state and the immediacy of the revolutionary event. These crises are articulated within two different modes of temporality: one corresponding to the abstract conditions of the state's self-identity—the longue durée of logos, if you will—and the other that attempts to face down irruptions in which the state suffers the prospect of its own transformation, the severe instant of ambivalence where the civilizing mission of aesthetics cannot be sure its image of freedom is the real of revolution. Paradoxically, for instance, whether through concepts of Bakhtin's "Great Time" or Benjamin's Jetztzeit, aesthetics is in these modalities, yet, as Schiller affirms, "snatched outside time" by the abstraction of aesthetic engagement, by the disinterestedness and practiced uselessness of its "higher reality." Aesthetics may well be an instance of freedom, but it is always and never free from the state in that expression. The reason to think aesthetics in this way is not because it is synonymous with humanities but because the latter lives the dilemmas of the former and tries to remedy this inconstancy in any number of creative ways—disciplinary reform, curricula change, institutional restructuring, conceptual interrogation ("What is the human in humanities?"), money, conferences, papers, etc. The labor of the aesthetic seems endless, but here it is intimately tied to the longevity of a particular state.

The reality, of course, is the "disinterested free appreciation of pure appearance," as Schiller puts it, and is a hard sell because it "appears" to require some form of social surplus to guarantee it. This means that, whatever the imaginary zeal of the aesthetic, its cultivation, in the last instance, is socioeconomically mediated. Its devotion to "ornament and play" is admirable and essential, but its ties to procurement and pay are as much a part of its predicament as they are for the human under specific historical conditions. This position is antitheory and necessarily anti-Schiller, who, by contrast, wants art to raise itself above "necessity and neediness." The plodding regularity of everyday socialization is for Schiller a sign of utility, and utility, as we have noted, is a burden for uselessness. In Kimball the specter of necessity produces a marked resignation, and he notes that Schiller's desire for a time when his mind is "wholly free and cleansed from the pollution of the world" can only be thwarted. Yet the structure of antinomy does not hinge on bourgeois disgust or elitist acrimony. The word that is insufficiently discussed in much of the discourse on Schiller is "education," and this is the primary sense in which aesthetics finds space in the humanities. That this space is conflictual is important in its own right, but here we are concerned about the meaning of that conflict in its relationship to the state under capitalism.

Halfway through his collection of letters, Schiller states, "the business of aesthetic education is to make out of beauties the beautiful." Now because, except for the title of the collection, this is the only place where Schiller uses the word "education"; beauty is the organizing principle and, whatever our fervent belief in the power of beauty, its aesthetic tenor alone is insufficient to the claims of education as simultaneously a state structure, an architecture of the architectonic in which the beautiful can be made. In the Schillerian schema, the state must make the beautiful or else be subject to extremes of inclination and reason that make of being only a chaos of chance. Could it be that the diminution of the humanities as an incubator of beauty's mediating function for education is symptomatic of the state's illegitimacy, that it has lost sight of the very stabilizing mode that would in theory be the substance of its greater *Aufheben*? Our return to Schiller signals the acknowledgment of our deficit while seeing his theorization as itself overdetermined by the paroxysm of revolution.

The instantiation of the antinomy is highly provocative; whether its meaning appears in our current conjuncture is worthy of further scrutiny.

For her part, Spivak's Schillerian gambit is as ominous as Kimball's, and she admits the double binds that structure her reading make the chapter less upbeat than the rest of the book (it is, however, more than consistent with its level of erudition, including its feminist politics). This pressing and depressing aestheticism is indeed a sign of the times I have just invoked. Spivak reiterates the consensus Schiller misreads Kant but notes appropriately that mistakes are learning experiences (it is one of the strengths of the humanities that it does not demonize error in its educational protocols). In fact, Spivak's reflections on Schiller are also a reconnection with her own education, particularly with her adviser, Paul de Man, and the inspiring influence of Jacques Derrida. To reaccentuate de Man's rather clever trope in his essay/lecture/transcription "Kant and Schiller," I would say in her chapter referring to Schiller, Spivak plays Schiller to Derrida's Kant. Schiller's mistake in his reading of Kant permits, says de Man, "a way of emphasizing, of revalorizing the aesthetic, a way of setting up the aesthetic as exemplary, as an exemplary category, as a unifying category, as a model for education, as a model even for the state." Certainly, what I offer here repeats the mistake without apology, because to return Schiller to Kant would miss the substance of Schiller's iteration, which I believe is instructive for the fate of the humanities and the modern capitalist state. De Man's assessment of Schiller's error comes, however, with a particularly chilling correlative: Schiller, says de Man, popularizes philosophy and thus, "the aesthetic belongs to the masses ... it belongs to culture, and as such it belongs to the state, to the aesthetic state, and it justifies the state." De Man then invokes Joseph Goebbels and quotes from the latter's novel *Michael* to illustrate the point, which is a brilliant move while being unnerving for his audience. If we are all Schillerians, as de Man states earlier, then we have participated in the massification and popularization of the aesthetic and prepared the state not for freedom, but for fascism. In the great chain of misreading, this is where de Man distances Schiller's aesthetic ideology by masking his own. De Man is in fact playing Schiller by differentiating his (de Man's) position from Goebbels's novel. In his reading of *Aesthetic Education*, de Man notes the central trope in Schiller is chiasmus (for Spivak, it is the double bind, for M. H. Abrams, in his spirited response to de Man's lecture, it is the dialectic), and, by attempting to displace Schiller (and replace Kant) through the Goebbels gesture, de Man's chiastic position in relation to a specific form of state is perhaps less than undecidable. But that is not the point: here the issue is the impossible position of aesthetics for the humanities' relationship to the state.

To make it an active part of education risks a kind of authoritarian populism; to shrink aesthetics in its uselessness renders the state unstable and ugly, unable to harmonize inclination and reason in the service of human fulfillment, beauty.

By sabotaging Schiller, Spivak is not agreeing with de Man—far from it; instead, she wants to affirm a Gramscian insistence on the intellectual's active participation in practical life: that Schiller does not prepare the ground for fascism, but for the radical democratization of intellectual practice with aesthetics not as a frivolous excess but as a vital constituent of perfecting our abilities to be, with each other and with our otherwise forlorn planet. Although Spivak references the Peace of Westphalia, the relationship of aesthetic education to the state is largely untheorized, except to point out that under actually existing globalization, the nation idea lives on as an alibi for "rogue capitalism." Spivak's suggestions for education are more than aesthetic and reflect her long-standing commitments to comparatism and subaltern schooling. She notes, nevertheless, that the humanities are no longer a moving epistemological force and will serve, like opera, a peripheral function in society. Spivak does not defer to de Man on Schiller, especially given the patriarchal assumptions that govern both (Schiller, in particular, fostered the tired division that feminizes aesthetics while masculinizing reason), but the double bind of de Man's own reading seems to disable Spivak's own. Thus, in a 600-page book that sports an adaptation of Schiller's title, Schiller only appears in one other place outside the introduction, interestingly in a chapter called "What's left of theory?" reprinted from a book of the same name. The Schiller reference does not feature in the original essay (whose title was actually different) so I find his trace somewhat compelling: the original reads, "After 1989, capitalism triumphant has led through to globalization—nearly complete abstraction, finance capital," to which is later added, "and the attendant damage control, of which Schiller is the specific, hopeless, final and persistent remedy."[12] On one level, the "last of man" is Schiller, beyond whom the very category Man would be superfluous; on another, the remedy is clearly poisonous, the Pharmakon once more, and philosophy, aesthetic education, offers only the prospect of marking time, of disabling hesitancy, of "damage control."

In Nussbaum's *Not for Profit*, the rhetoric of damage control proceeds not through Schiller, but via one of his key influences, Rousseau (Tagore's strong commitment to education that Nussbaum also foregrounds might usefully be compared and contrasted to Spivak's). The argument is by turns persuasive and breathless. Nussbaum, in the Division of Humanities at Chicago, is a vibrant booster for the humanities not least because she continually cleaves to institutional practicality in her response, a plan, if you will. Interestingly, Nussbaum notes that as a young woman, she wrote a tragic play in French on the life of Robespierre, so one hopes she entertains Schiller's sense of revolutionary contradiction. As a critical humanitist, Nussbaum sounds a somewhat familiar tune as the book opens: "We are in the midst of a crisis of massive proportions and grave global significance."[13] Despite the button-pushing hyperbole, the situation Nussbaum describes is the one that animates my discussion, but I would note that although the globality invoked is germane, the structure of the humanities she details is, as Harpham would aver, avowedly American. Of the five examples she provides in her opening chapter of the impending doom of the humanities, four are American and the fifth concerns a Tagore conference which Americans attended (the location is not mentioned). Given the argument I have made so far, two aspects of Nussbaum's analysis are striking. First, at every opportunity Nussbaum recoils from the nuance of the philosophy she invokes. This is true both of her critique of Rousseau (where Nussbaum focuses on *Emile*) and of Dewey, who is a key figure in the nexus of the humanities and America. She notes *Emile* is a "profoundly non-practical work" that is philosophically deep so she prefers to focus on "real educational experiments" based on it. Dewey, of course, was highly resistant to a notion of education where its substance was conceived only as it served capital. One can imagine Dewey saying, "Not for profit" a hundred years ago, so in that sense, Nussbaum must fight the anachronism her general thesis presents. The second question concerns the concrete divisions in America's embodiment of liberal arts education and its framework, the humanities. Nussbaum addresses the specificity of the American state form on several occasions in her text, but when she notes, laconically, that "the U.S. system of public education contains huge inequalities," she does not explore how American humanities have evolved through, rather than in spite of, the production of a public/private binary. Dialogic on so many other levels, there is a distinct lack of reflexivity in the following comment: "We in the United States should pause at this point to be thankful for our traditions, which combine a liberal arts model with a strong cultivation of humanistic philanthropy and a basically private-endowment structure of funding." She continues, "At my own university we do not have to go hat in hand to bureaucrats who lack all sympathy with what we do. Instead we go to wealthy alums whose educational values pretty well match our own."[14] Empirically, most humanists in the United States cannot depend on the sympathetic coexperiencing of this class fraction. Indeed, while it is absolutely the case that, for instance, the private liberal arts college has been pivotal in the production and reproduction of the humanities in the United States, the democratic ideals embodied in the humanities have been extended and realized in its public expression. It is the state's retreat from this answerability to beauty that now assumes a critical valence. The beneficence of "wealthy alums" is laudable especially when your endowment is measured in the billions (over seven billion at Nussbaum's institution, the University of Chicago), but as Newfield points out (in both *Unmaking the Public University* and *The Great Mistake*), every tax break concerning private school endowments and every tax deduction of donating alums further contribute to the tax levy fiasco at state schools that are in a race to privatize (by including, paradoxically, the use of endowments) to stave off dissolution. Under such circumstances, the only thing that is certain for humanities in the public university is, to rephrase Benjamin Franklin, death without more taxes. But taxes, as the example of France in 1789 reminds us, can be problematic.

Since tax only appears once in Nussbaum's understanding of profit, and then only under the rubric of incentives for charitable contribution, we will have to look elsewhere to fathom the relationship of the fiscal policy of the capitalist state and the possibilities of beauty. This is not a comment on Nussbaum's philosophy, her keen understanding of the social and psychological components of educational answers, nor on her politics, which, something like Dewey's, are liberal humanist if not democratic socialist (Dewey's brand of democratic socialism, like that of Bernie Sanders, is a rare animal outside the United States, but any hint of sympathy for it by Nussbaum is roundly criticized by her detractors, see, for instance, Gary Saul Morson in the *New Criterion*). Meanwhile, Stanley Fish begins a report titled "The Crisis in the Humanities Officially Arrives" with a reader's question: "What happened to public investment in the humanities and the belief that the humanities enhanced our culture, our society, our humanity?" In other words, he begins from the place where Nussbaum will not tread. Fish does not address the structural inequalities that produce American public education, a topic covered by Newfield in *Unmaking the Public University*, which itself is a materialist engagement with the tub-bashing of Bill Readings in *The University in Ruins* (the crisis reveals the political spectrum rather than a particular hue according to the logic of temporality in play). Fish thinks the "culture is good for you" line of argument is a nonstarter, as are appeals to the humanities' economic benefit to the state, and kind requests to the cash happy sciences to donate any leftovers in their appropriations. Fish's answer to the contemporary schisms in humanities and the state is politics, but by this Fish means the ability of senior academic administrators, presidents, chancellors, and the like, to persuade the state and the public that the liberal arts needs no economic justification, that humanities professors are not lazy, and that those who wish to bring the university to heel often do not have sufficient knowledge of its workings to do so. Fish's position provoked a good deal of response, so intense indeed that a second article was required, at which point his rather denuded sense of politics was replaced by a nod to Newfield's panacea: a restoration of strong public funding. But this basic point, that in order for the humanities to do what it does in the university, the state must be willing to levy taxes for it, is not my main argument and indeed is not Fish's, who quickly qualifies his assessment by opining that academics should justify themselves to each other, and that college presidents should make of humanities professors' uselessness a banner not a barrier. This, of course, is the Schillerian trace that I invoked earlier and remains largely undertheorized in the current conjuncture.

But how can we possibly relate this sad affect narrative of humanities in distress with our earlier assessment of the 2007–2008 crisis? Surely there is an unbridgeable chasm between the chance to teach the Karamazov Brothers and the demise of Lehman Brothers? Smerdyakov admits to killing Fydor with a pestle; Geithner admits nothing, and for most people, Lehman killed itself. In *The Great Mistake*, Chris Newfield identifies the price of privatization in the wake of the 2008 financial crisis. To be sure, like me, he detects a longue durée of crisis that affects how the public university can possibly mediate the humanities in its mission. Yet he is also at pains to read the crisis in terms of specific roles for the university, particularly the macro-structural emphasis on mass commodity learning over creative learning. There is also a synergy, however, between the function of creative learning, here what I have been discussing as aesthetic education, and the systemic crises of the capitalist state and its knowledge base. The commodity logic of one saturates the commodity learning of the other not as a real claim on productivity but, paradoxically, as an intensification of a kind of speculative reality principle. On one level, this refracts the withdrawal of the state from its own reproduction, subcontracting its existence through the vagaries of a veritable subprime subsistence. Public schools only become rich in facilities and staff according to their portfolios, endowments, and corporatism (they also accumulate, of course, on the backs of students through increases in tuition and fees and through basing instruction on contingent labor). Private schools still depend on state subsidies but have reserves to play speculative bubbles at a much larger scale (Harvard's endowment is an objective correlative of derivatives and the Dow in this respect). You would think that using the Federal Reserve as a bailout mechanism for public education as it was used for the banking sector would instantly return the humanities to its critical role in the formation of the modern state. But this is not going to happen, not just because of the Federal Reserve's structural role but because it would depend upon a different understanding of crisis in its state-centered synergies. I agree with Newfield that public education would be better if it was free and free of debt, and it is commendable he has found examples of states in which that is possible. The vortex of decline read into the fate of the humanities is not outside the liquidity crisis signaled in 2007–2008. The difference in scale, of course, requires sublime calculation. At the end of 2007, outstanding OTC derivative contracts had a notional value of 597 trillion dollars with a settlement rate between 2 and 3 percent, or approximately 30 percent of all known realizable value globally at the time. Part of the reason the Federal Reserve stepped in the next year was to cover derivative obligations when debt returns could not offset minimal asset requirements (Lehman and Bear Stearns had to be sacrificed to make the sums work; AIG, on the other hand, despite even greater malfeasance in the credit default swaps market, got a pass). The restitution tab came to about 13 trillion dollars, and the banks were slapped with larger reserve requirements, stress tests, and the Volcker rule. Problem solved. Not so much. The banks opened their coffers to quantitative easing and then repurposed the liquidity into the stock market (now at well beyond three times its low in the Great Recession), let go nasty speculators to form their own hedge funds (the 0.001 percent) but kept enough of them to sustain predatory lending, particularly around auto loans. This is another definition for speculative realism. The derivative market? The math has certainly changed, but by 2013, the OTC market hit 700 trillion dollars so we should all be glad that the problem of fictive capital has gone away (to be sure, central clearing shows more responsibility). When the decline cycle Newfield tracks would need less than 0.1 percent of this market to settle public education for a lifetime, however, the obscenity of financialization (its representative crisis beyond crisis) comes clearly into view. But this is not the point.

Whereas the ongoing crisis of the humanities has here been primarily linked to the fate of the state, the intercession of capitalist crisis appears to foreclose rather than favor its reemergence. The constitutive gap between two modes of crisis is the *Seinsvergessenheit*, the forgetfulness of being in Heidegger's parlance, between the shape of crisis and its theorization, between the "is" of humanities in this discussion and the capacity to read its imbrication with the idea of crisis as such. The crisis of 2007–2008 teaches us that the role of theory in the crisis has shifted in favor of the logic of financialization, rather than pivoting on either the *ratio* of the state or the humanities' dependence on the public university as the crisis mode of thinking humanism. To this extent, it is not the extravagance of theory that proves the irrelevance of the humanities but its relative paucity in measuring crisis as a specific socioeconomic form. The latter does not eschew the aesthetic—indeed, it is remarkable how much finance theory mediates aesthetic categories. The argument is not that humanists should be better Marxists—there is more than enough evidence that variegations in Marxism have participated in this margin as much as challenged it. The crisis after crisis tells us that returning better theory to the public university to temper the humanities is salutary. The challenge, however, is to see crisis in the humanities as crisis theory itself, an uneven development that yet thinks the end of a particular form of crisis. There is a necessary dissolution at stake, but better to theorize it from within the crisis in order to fathom the lineaments than survive it. If antitheory positions believe they are defending the humanities, crisis theory after crisis accentuates a rather more troubled braiding in its prospects. The danger remains the reproduction of the "largely incomprehensible," as Harvey put it, especially if theory does not link its uselessness to a critique of instrumentality. For his part, Newfield's emphasis on mass quality is an eminently appreciable goal, but can such aesthetic education prosper in the endgame of late neoliberal capitalism? In theory, first, although never last. We can pretend theory will help defend the humanities against the barbarism of the capitalist state or its kinder, gentler manifestations (e.g., "conscious capitalism"), but if the substance of the humanities is historically secreted within that state, one might turn theory and revolutionary humanism to the aesthetics and state that people will make beyond its crisis—and there is beauty in such freedom.

Notes

1 David Harvey, *Seventeen Contradictions and the End of Capitalism* (Oxford: Oxford University Press, 2014), xii.
2 Ibid., xiii.
3 Ibid., 295.
4 Ibid., 293.
5 Geoffrey G. Harpham, *The Humanities and the Dream of America* (Chicago: University of Chicago Press, 2011), 147.
6 J. C. Friedrich Von Schiller, *The Aesthetic Education of Man*, trans. Reginald Snell (London: Dover Books, 2004), 30.
7 Ibid., 31–32.
8 Ibid., 32.

9 Ibid., 9.
10 Ibid., 138.
11 Ibid.
12 Gayatri Chakravorty Spivak, *An Aesthetic Education in the Era of Globalization* (Cambridge: Harvard University Press, 2012), 196.
13 Martha Nussbaum, *Not for Profit: Why Democracy Needs the Humanities* (Princeton: Princeton University Press, 2010), 1.
14 Ibid., 132.

Works Cited

Arrighi, Giovanni. *The Long Twentieth Century: Money, Power, and the Origins of Our Times*. London: Verso, 1994.

Berg, Ole. *Making Money: The Philosophy of Crisis Capitalism*. New York: Verso, 2014.

Bivens-Tatum, Wayne. "The 'Crisis' in the Humanities." *Academic Librarian* (November 5, 2010). https://blogs.princeton.edu/librarian/2010/11/the_crisis_in_the_humanities/.

Brooks, Peter and Hilary Jewett, eds. *The Humanities and Public Life*. New York: Fordham University Press, 2014.

Clarke, Simon. *Marx's Theory of Crisis*. London: Palgrave, 1994.

Culler, Jonathan. "In Need of a Name? A Response to Geoffrey Harpham." *New Literary History* 36.1 (2005): 37–42.

de Man, Paul. "Kant and Schiller." In *Aesthetic Ideology*. Minneapolis: University of Minnesota Press, 1996. 129–162.

Fish, Stanley. "The Crisis in the Humanities Officially Arrives." *The New York Times* (October 11, 2010).

Harpham, Geoffrey G. *The Humanities and the Dream of America*. Chicago: University of Chicago Press, 2011.

Harvey, David. *Seventeen Contradictions and the End of Capitalism*. Oxford: Oxford University Press, 2014.

Kimball, Roger. "Schiller's 'Aesthetic Education.'" *The New Criterion* (March, 2001): 12–19.

Lapavitsas, Costas, ed. *Financialisation in Crisis*. Boston: Brill, 2012.

Mirowski, Philip. *Never Let a Serious Crisis Go to Waste: How Neoliberalism Survived the Financial Meltdown*. New York: Verso, 2013.

Morson, Gary Saul. "Empathy with Us." *The New Criterion* (June 2010): 69–72.

Newfield, Christopher. *Unmaking the Public University: The Forty-Year Assault on the Middle Class*. Cambridge: Harvard University Press, 2011.

Newfield, Christopher. *The Great Mistake: How We Wrecked Public Universities and How We Can Fix Them*. Baltimore: Johns Hopkins University Press, 2016.

Nussbaum, Martha. *Not for Profit: Why Democracy Needs the Humanities*. Princeton: Princeton University Press, 2010.
Readings, Bill. *The University in Ruins*. Cambridge: Harvard University Press, 1997.
Schiller, J. C. Friedrich Von. *The Aesthetic Education of Man*. Trans. Reginald Snell. London: Dover Books, 2004.
Spivak, Gayatri Chakravorty. *A Critique of Postcolonial Reason*. Cambridge: Harvard University Press, 1999.
Spivak, Gayatri Chakravorty. *An Aesthetic Education in the Era of Globalization*. Cambridge: Harvard University Press, 2012.
Streeck, Wolfgang. *Buying Time: The Delayed Crisis of Democratic Capitalism*. Trans. Patrick Camiller. New York: Verso, 2014.

3

Epic Fail: Prolegomenon to Failing Again, Finally

Irving Goh

What follows is a prolegomenon to a reconsideration of failure. It is strictly a "reconsideration" because, as we all know, failure is certainly not a new topic in intellectual discourse. The twentieth century had generated enough manmade catastrophes for writers and scholars to not only highlight the failure of mankind but also make failure a subject of thought. Just to cite a few well-known examples here: there has been Beckett, who, apart from his dramatic works that outline the apocalyptic horizons of those failures, has nonetheless encouraged us to "fail again," to "fail better;"[1] then there is Derrida, who, in what seems to be a riff on Beckett, but writing in a context of mourning, has also advised us to "fail well" (*bien echouer*)[2]; and there is Jameson, who has pronounced the failure of "postmodernism" to account for new aesthetic experimentations that emerge at the contemporaneous moment. Yet we are clearly not done with failure. Failure continues to plague us. Or, we continue to fail, and not necessarily "better" or "well." On the contrary, we might even appear to be doing worse, as if fulfilling Beckett's prophecy of us heading only "worstward." Ever since the turn of the century, we have seen nation-states—mighty ones at that—failing to protect homelands from terrorism, failing to come up with effective measures that could short-circuit the spread of global terrorism, except those that curtail civil and private liberties of their own political subjects and further incurring the wrath of those whom the policies target; we have seen capitalist economies, while still far from adequately addressing poverty, labor exploitation, or the unequal distribution of goods and wealth, allowing dubious banking and financial practices to precipitate into global economic and housing crises; more recently, we are witnessing not just apathy but also violent backlashes against migrants and migrant labor, putting to waste no doubt all those decades of efforts to establish the universal right to live and work; not unrelated to that violent reaction against migrants, there is the new hatred of others and differences, manifesting itself not just through the rise of hate crimes (Orlando, Portland, just to name a few) but also of police brutality (Chicago, Baltimore, just to name, again, only a few); and then there are the shocking results in 2016 of the Brexit vote in the UK and the US presidential elections, which many consider to be major failures of political institutions, and which have also seen to the resurgence of right-wing and/or alt-right, if not worse, "white supremacist," political parties and movements both in Europe and the United States.

Evidently, then, we fail. Or, to reflect more honestly (on) our human existence, efforts, and actions, perhaps we could say: We. Fail. That is to say, both the very idea of "we" as a human collective capable of improving the lot of humanity and what this "we" has accomplished so far, if we dare to admit, would receive a "fail" grade. Or, to put it yet another way in the rhetoric of millennials: "epic fail." I would not go so far to say that there is actually critical thought involved when millennials enunciate this phrase. In fact, the situations to which they make that pronouncement are actually mostly trivial or banal, in other words, those that are barely causes for concern. Yet I would say that the widespread use of that phrase, which I perceive to have been on the upward trend as we enter the second decade of this twenty-first century, may be symptomatic of something more significant. It seemingly bespeaks of the phenomenon of more failures everywhere, more than ever. That is to say, with rampant failures pervading almost all aspects of human activity, failure is not spectacularly exceptional to events bearing geopolitical proportions or those deemed worthy of the scale of the historical or of a "grand narrative," the effect of which will only be registered by an aesthetic or critical work. "Epic fail" articulates how common failure is today, and only common parlance such as itself can be close enough to capture the frequency and prevalence of failure. Of course, failure articulated in terms of such common parlance does run the risk of promulgating the reductive statement: "everything is failure." That, in turn, risks not only homogenizing everything (as failure) but also, along with "epic fail," because of the speed (and spread) of its enunciation, naturalizes failure as part of the human psyche, leaving failure largely outside the concern of critical thought, not to mention the task of its historicization (which lies, unfortunately, beyond the scope of my intervention here). Putting aside the phrase "epic fail" for now and to turn to this present volume's concern with theory, let it be said that the failures mentioned earlier are not just the failures of economic, political, and sociocultural institutions. It is also a certain failure of theory, and I mean theory in the structuralist or "deconstructivist" mode, typically associated with names such as Derrida, Cixous, Foucault, Deleuze, Blanchot, Bataille, Irigaray, and Nancy. This brand of theory has always been calling for the freedom of all existences, the affirmation and respect of others and differences, the revolutionizing of politics to accommodate the idea of "unconditional hospitality" where none would exclude another, and the complete overhaul, if not sidestepping, of capitalist principles and practices in order to end exploitation or to even entertain the possibility of the "an-economic." When what we have in the world today largely goes against these theoretical propositions, we are witnessing not only some form of regression from decades of such theoretical work but also, admittedly, the failure of theory to effectuate a real paradigm shift in thinking and acting in the world.

In a way, then, theory is somewhat implicated in our real, contemporary failures. However, theory at large is in fact not immune to failures, especially pronouncements of *its* failures. As seen across the recent decades, articulations such as "against theory," "the death of theory," "theory's empire," "theory aside," or even "dead theory," or the more explicit "failed revolt," have all either pronounced or hinted at certain failures of theory: its failure to communicate in ways others would regard as clear or logical, its failure to deliver its supposed promises, or its failure to be what it is thought to be, for example, thoroughly transformative, revolutionary, "canon"-demolishing, and so on. In short, theory has been considered to fail at not only establishing itself as some "legitimate" mode or form of thought but also at convincing or persuading others of its validity and/or soundness. Put otherwise: theory is plagued with, or haunted by, a failure to find general acceptance, endorsement, or validation within the wider intellectual community, academic institutions, and even the larger reading public. And "antitheory"—the topic about which we have been asked to critically think here—is undoubtedly an echo of those pronouncements of theory's failures. Theory, to paraphrase Latour, has become a mere object that can be left at the wayside rather than made itself a Thing in the Heideggerian sense, that is, a Thing that inscribes all the worldly and heavenly folds into which it enters, precisely because theory in or by itself as "a gathering has failed."[3]

Nonetheless, as we have all witnessed too, theory has more or less stood its ground in the face of all those pronouncements. Theory has either resisted those judgments, arguing against the judgments of failure pronounced upon them, or else remained indifferent to them, in this case seemingly unconcerned with whether it fails or not, not especially when these pronouncements of failure are made by others. There is a resilience about theory, in other words. It is resilient in the face of those death sentences as it proceeds, carries on, or lives on (or *sur-vivre*, to use Derrida's term), and the present investment in the idea of "antitheory," which effectively follows a prior interest in "dead theory," not to mention other articulations such as "theory after 'theory'" are testimonies to that. But it also seems that theory is resilient to the notion of failure, and this particular resilience interests me here. Now, I am not saying that theory has never taken into account, or thought about, failure. I have mentioned Derrida's notion of "failing well." Other than that, Deleuze and Guattari's "abstract machines" that break down, and Blanchot's and Nancy's respective *désœuvrement* or "unworking"/"inoperativity" all also deal with failure in one way or another. Nevertheless, there seems to be some sort of recuperative horizon with those articulations of failure: for example, the retrieval of community as made manifest by the fact of one and the other coming together *and* departing freely through the *désœuvrement* of all calculated projects of a totalizing, fusional community; the liberation of all desires or even a libidinal economy through "abstract machines;"[4] and the inscription of a possible eternal remembrance as long as mourning "fails well." In other words, worked into theory's rhetoric of failure is a certain teleology of perfectibility, some sort of progress narrative, if not success story, through which failure will be overcome; with, or in, theory, there is an undeniable optimism that things will, slowly but surely, work out.

What I am implying, then, is that theory has not dared to dwell further and longer with or in failure, particularly its failure, including dwelling in all the accompanying affective states of shame, anguish, hopelessness, and humility.[5] It has not thought radically enough of failure in a way that does away with all hopes or possibilities of a positive outcome. Or, it does not see to its failure; it does not see through its failure to its end, that is, to stay with failure as long as failure endures, rather than seeking to elevate it into something other than failure. Perhaps that is what remains for theory: to say it fails, and to stay or even wallow in the state of failure, rejecting the binary structure to which failure seems to be tied,[6] through which failure seems compelled to choose either a recuperative teleology or a nihilistic, eschatological abjection. For that, one must resist any aestheticization of failure, as Beckett has already done. One must also resist the question of "to what ends" as theory dwells in failure. To fail, or to wallow in failure, is simply *to fail*, and nothing else, nothing to be done. Yes, it is circular, but only so as to resist the impulse for theory to lead somewhere, to get out of failure. That is perhaps what theory has yet to do, if not failed to do so far.

Theory's saying to itself that it fails, it's seeing itself as a failure or as failed, or it's dwelling in failure, has to be done *now*. And why not? As suggested at the beginning, all the apparent failures of our current century seem to reflect a certain failure of theory: its failure to convince that its political and ethical propositions would be for the better for our coexistence with others in this world. Thus, when the current sociopolitical and political economic situations seem to bespeak a certain disenchantment with theoretical propositions, why should theory insist on plodding and prodding on, in order to critique the current state of affairs, if not to even try to effectively change things? For theory to see itself fail now, perhaps, contrary to Latour's concern, is for theory to let itself run out of steam, instead of pushing ahead. Besides, we have also seen the problematic of pushing ahead with the times via a particular idea and then retroactively recognizing its failure. That is undoubtedly the case of Heidegger's *Black Notebooks*, where Heidegger justifies his disastrous political choice as but being faithful to the an-archic freedom of *Dasein*, faithful to *Dasein*'s "freedom to fail" according to Peter Trawny's reading.[7] This belated failure, or acknowledgment of failure after the fact, is not true failure, in my view, not to mention that such pronouncement of failure only serves to recuperate or save the thought of *Dasein*, hence giving, again according to Trawny's analysis, *Dasein* a tragic quality. It is in opposition to that almost heroic and redemptive quality of tragic failure that I propose the lesser, and perhaps absurd, or even banal, notion of "epic fail." This is also not to forget that theory as "a fail," to use millennial-speak once again, has after all taken on an epic proportion. Some of the pronouncements of theory's failure mentioned above have been made as long ago as in the 1980s; and François Dosse's insightful history of structuralism has in fact shown that theory's failure to capture the imagination of young French intellectuals or French intellectual culture in a sustained manner was already apparent even before the May '68 revolution. So, again, there should be no further delays for theory to say it fails, to see to its failure, to see through its failure. It must not be done any later.

How does theory articulate, or narrate, this "epic fail"? Do we have an instance of such articulation or narration of "epic fail" in theory, which theory nevertheless hesitated or failed to elucidate? I would argue yes, even though the example I am going to cite is not exactly epic, hence not exactly a perfect example—and yet perhaps that paradoxically makes it a fitting candidate for an exposition on failure. The instance or example I have in mind is the Aztec myth cited by Bataille in *La Part maudite*. Let me quote the passage in question in its entirety:

> It is said that before the light of day existed, the gods assembled at the place called Teotihaucan ... and spoke among themselves, saying: "Who will take it

upon himself to bring light to the world?" On hearing these words, a god called Tecuciztecatl presented himself and replied: "I will be the one. I will bring light to the world." The gods then spoke again and said: "Who else among you?" They looked at one another then, wondering who this would be, and none dared accept the charge; all were afraid and made excuses. One of the gods who usually went unnoticed did not say anything but only listened to what the other gods were saying. The others spoke to him, saying, "Let it be you, bubosito." And he gladly accepted, replying: "I receive your order gracefully; so be it." And the two that were chosen began immediately to do penance, which lasted four days. Then a fire was lit in a hearth made in a rock.... The god named Tecuciztecatl only offered costly things. Instead of branches he offered rich feathers called quetzalli; instead of grass balls he offered gold ones; instead of maguey spines he offered spines made with precious stones; and instead of bloodied spines he offered spines of red coral. And the copal he offered was of a very high quality. The buboso, whose name was Nanauatzin, offered nine green water rushes bound in threes, instead of ordinary branches. He offered balls of grass and maguey spines bloodied with his own blood, and instead of copal he offered the scabs of his bubas.

A tower was made for each of these two gods, in the form of a hill. On these hills they did penance for four nights.... After the four nights of penance were completed, the branches and all the other objects they had used were thrown down there. The following night, a little before midnight, when they were to do their office, Tecuciztecatl was given his adornments. These consisted of a headdress of aztacomitl feathers and a sleeveless jacket. As for Nanauatzin, the buboso, they tied a paper headdress, called amatzontli, on his hair and gave him a paper stole and a paper rag for pants to wear. When midnight had come, all the gods gathered round the hearth, which was called teotexcalli, where the fire had burned for four days.

They separated into two lines on the two sides of the fire. The two chosen ones took their places near the hearth, with their faces to the fire, in the middle of the two lines of gods. The latter were all standing and they spoke to Tecuciztecatl, saying: "Go on, Tecuciztecatl. Cast yourself into the fire!" Hearing this, he started to throw himself into the flames, but the fire was burning high and very hot, and he stopped in fear and drew back. A second time he gathered his strength and turned to throw himself into the fire, but when he got near he stopped and did not dare go further; four times he tried, but could not. Now, it had been ordered that no one could try more than four times, so when the four attempts had been made the gods addressed Nanauatzin, saying: "Go on, Nanauatzin. It is your turn to try!" As soon as these words were said, he shut his eyes and, taking courage, went forward and threw himself into the fire. He began at once to crackle and sizzle like something being roasted. Seeing that he had thrown himself into the fire and was burning, Tecuciztecatl also cast himself into the flames and burned. It is said that an eagle went into the fire at the same time and burned, and this is why the eagle has scorched-looking and blackened feathers. An ocelot followed thereafter but did not burn, only being singed, and this is why the ocelot remains spotted black and white.

A short while later, having fallen on their knees, the gods saw Nanauatzin, "who had become the sun," rising in the East. "He looked very red, appearing to sway from side to side, and none of them could keep their eyes on him, because he blinded them with his light. He shone brightly with his rays that reached in all directions." The moon in turn rose up over the horizon. Because he had hesitated, Tecuciztecatl shone less brightly. Then the gods had to die; the wind, Quetzalcoatl, killed them all: The wind tore out their hearts and used them to animate the newborn stars.[8]

This myth clearly deals with sacrifice, and according to Bataille, sacrifice sees to the dilapidation of both objects and humans, such that both, when treated as sacrificial ornaments and human sacrifice, are liberated from their utilitarian value with regard to the real world of productivity; and after they are thrown into the sacrificial fire, only nothing remains, if not nothing really effective or material is produced. For Bataille, this is pure, unproductive expenditure. Given Bataille's praise for sacrifice, it would not be wrong to think that Nanauatzin, considering Bataille's emphasis on Nanauatzin's "voluntary sacrifice,"[9] stands for Bataille's figure *par excellence* of unproductive expenditure, if not the high priest of pure expenditure theory. That is all fine for a theory of expenditure, which does have a recuperative or redemptive horizon no less, since, according to Bataille, pure expenditure returns the world to the cosmic order of flows, rather than submit it to the accumulative impulse of modern labor and industry. To think of failure, however, it is not to Nanauatzin whom one should turn, but Tecuciztecatl. Tecuciztecatl, after all, fails the sacrificial ritual, even though he was in fact the one who first volunteered for the sacrifice, and even though he was the one others expected to succeed, given the ostentatious sacrificial ornaments they lavish on him. Yet, as said, he fails. Furthermore, he fails not only the sacrificial process, in not daring to throw himself into the fire, but also the sacrificial structure itself, since, despite the interdiction against trying again after four attempts, he violates that commandment and hurls himself into the blazing pit, which effectively achieves nothing, since the sacrificial rite by now has already been completed by Nanauatzin's "voluntary sacrifice."

Evidently, because of his failings before and against the sacrificial order, Tecuciztecatl gets passed over in Bataille's reading and analysis. For my part, though, I would like to stay a little with Tecuciztecatl. To be sure, I do this *not* to glorify him but to give some time to the articulation of some of the affective states that could have been in effect as Tecuciztecatl experiences failure. There is no doubt desperation, as he finds himself failing at the first attempt, something that must be quite unexpected on his part and others, and this desperation surely endures throughout all the remaining attempts. Then, there is probably shame too, since it has been made rather spectacularly by others as well that he is thought to most likely succeed, and this shame is surely accompanied by the sense of abandonment, as the other gods turn away from him and toward Nanauatzin to complete the task. And at the height of this desperation–shame–abjection confluence, mixed with anguish no doubt, it is possible too that Tecuciztecatl finds himself in a state of what Bataille would call "non-knowledge," the state of not knowing what to do, after failing all four attempts. Perhaps that would be the point where everything breaks down, where one starts to fumble, to lose one's hold on things, to unconsciously or even consciously do things that disrupt the general order of things, and that is how I would read Tecuciztecatl's final leap. That does not mean that there might not be some perverse inner glee as well while everything around breaks down because of one's failures, or even a burst of laughter, as Bataille would want it, which could also signify not taking oneself and everything else seriously, the kind of laughter that will seal failure as failure.[10]

Now, more faithful to Nancy's philosophy than to Bataille's, that is, a philosophy that believes that no existence can be made sacrificial, I am not advocating Tecuciztecatl's final fumbling act of hurling himself into the sacrificial pit. (In a somewhat related way, I am neither espousing Socrates's resolution to drink the hemlock when (his) philosophy shows itself to be something of an "epic fail" in Athens.) As mentioned above, I just want to stay with all those senses of desperation, abandonment, shame, anguish, abjection, and humility even, all of which might be communicated through a burst of laughter.[11] Given time too, there is no stopping these senses or affects in sending the failed subject precipitating into a depressive zone. As Mark Fisher has suggested, depression is in fact theoretical: "Depression is, after all and above all, a theory about the world, about life."[12] He will go on to say: "Depression is not sadness, not even a state of mind, it is a (neuro)philosophical (dis)position."[13] Through his lucid *Ghosts of My Life*, I am convinced by Fisher's argument that depression is "a (neuro)philosophical (dis)position." However, I cannot see why it cannot be sadness (even despite a Bataillean laughter) or a state of mind as well. Perhaps Fisher fears that that state of mind or sadness might just suspend or render inoperative the "(neuro)philosophical (dis)position." Or, and if I may put it in relation to the Aztec myth, the interdiction against sadness and state of mind might only betray Fisher's fear of the state in which Tecuciztecatl finds himself when he fails the sacrificial ritual, the state where Tecuciztecatl knows not what to do or think, or how to act. To put it in psychiatric terms, this state could be close to catatonia, particularly motionless catatonia, where motor activity is almost nonexistent, or where the body is mute, motionless, and rigid, indifferent to external stimuli and almost moribund. Otherwise, it could even degenerate into catatonic excitement, where one becomes agitated and excited without purpose, or else delusional and hallucinatory; such catatonia perhaps resonates more with Tecuciztecatl's subsequent actions in his flustering or floundering as, in an apparently senseless gesture, he throws himself into the fire in defiance of the rules of the sacrificial ritual. And to put it in theoretical terms, catatonia, for Deleuze and Guattari, is one of the ways by which we approximate ourselves to a "body without organs," where the body loses, if not frees itself from, all rigid, delimiting, or restrictive senses of organization. That, however, might once again betray theory's desire to overcome failure, to give failure an optimistic spin. Let resound, then, against the grain of Nietzsche's philosophy and Deleuze's echo of it, *ressentiment* in the pessimistic key of Jean Améry, *ressentiment* that bears an "immunity to self-pity."[14] Or else, and to use Fisher's term but deviating from it at the same time, dwell in melancholia, that is to say, immerse oneself purely in, or let oneself be haunted by, the sense of loss without any knowledge, and without any desire of the knowledge, of what the lost object is.[15]

In any case, I have yet to see theory explicitly in all these states of desperation, abandonment, shame, anguish, abjection, humility, depression, catatonia, *ressentiment*, and melancholia. And perhaps for theory to say that it fails, for it to "fail well," those are the states that theory must acknowledge, endure, and not repress, especially when others have pronounced its failures. To "fail well," it must abandon itself to those states, or rather abandon itself simply. Perhaps that is what Bataille considers the "anguishing/incomplete, explosive loss of self [*perte de soi partielle, explosive*] as unproductive expenditure/dissipation [*détente*], etc." trajectory, a trajectory no less epic as marked by the "etc.," and which Bataille opposes to the "real-world worry [*souci réel*]/action or channeling of productive energy [*dépense d'énergie productive*]/resolution [*détente*]" sequence.[16] Otherwise, still staying with a Bataillean imagery, it would be like the extravagant, absurd gesture of throwing a cup of coffee into the sea, through which nothing of the coffee would be saved (for human consumption).[17] Any why not, given that theory—or rather "high" theory, that is, theory regarded as some sort of luxury because of the prejudiced image of it only engaging in thinking as if from some lofty position, away from the practical concerns and conditions of the real world—has faced enough mounting pressure that only signals its rejection?

To abandon itself to the state of failure, to abandon itself: perhaps that is what it means to be "antitheory" today (at a time when it seems impossible to be "antitheory"[18]), that is to say, theory to be "anti-" itself, rejecting any recuperation, on the one hand, and refusing the self-annihilating position, on the other. That is perhaps theory in its true form, that is, as "anti-" through and through, theory bringing the "anti-" gesture to its final domain, to itself, after it has enacted this "anti-" force on almost everything else. That could no doubt mean the extinction of theory or even "extinct theory" as Colebrook sees it, through which the thought of "the tomorrow of its non-existence" sets in,[19] or else a new dawn for a totally different world or cosmic order as is the case in the Aztec myth. And yet, as said earlier, the question of the ends of failure would be to fail failure, and so, for theory to "fail well," whether it be extinction or a new dawn should not be a matter of concern at all. Nothing more to do. Nothing more to say either, except, maybe: fail.[20]

Notes

1 See *Worstward Ho!* Samuel Beckett, *Company/Ill Seen Ill Said/Worstward Ho/Stirrings Still* (New York: Faber and Faber, 2009).

2 "By Force of Mourning," in Jacques Derrida, *The Work of Mourning*, ed. and trans. Pascale-Anne Brault and Michael Naas (Chicago: University of Chicago Press, 2001), 144.

3 Bruno Latour, "Why Has Critique Run Out of Steam? From Matters of Fact to Matters of Concern," *Critical Inquiry* 30.2 (2004), 246. Of course, Latour is concerned more specifically with "critique" rather than "theory," and I agree that there is a difference between both terms and that difference should be articulated (something I am unable to do here). However, Latour does throw Derridean deconstruction into the mix when he discusses "critique" in the same essay, hence my paraphrasing Latour here.

4 In addition, one could also say that Deleuze and Guattari, in their philosophy, do not allow failure to arrive in its eventfulness or as an event, that is to say, as a pure surprise, the arrival of which is never programmed, calculated, or anticipated. As they say of becoming, "even failures are part of the plan" (Gilles Deleuze and Félix Guattari, *Mille plateaux* [Paris: Minuit, 1980], 312).

5 To my knowledge, Costica Bradatan at Texas Tech is currently writing a book praising failure and explicating the notion of humility that follows from failure.

6   I am indeed seeking a deconstruction of failure, if not to dwell in the *différance* of failure, that is, in its difference from its *other* term such as "success," and in its deferral from any resolution or (its) dissolution, or even sublation into something else (such as, again, success).
7   See of course Peter Trawny, *Freedom to Fail: Heidegger's Anarchy*, trans. Ian Alexander Moore and Christopher Turner (Cambridge: Polity, 2015).
8   Cited in Georges Bataille, *Le Coupable, suivi de L'Allehuiah* (Paris: Gallimard, 1961), 46–49.
9   Ibid., 98.
10 See especially Bataille's *Le Coupable*, 155.
11 To make the move away from sacrifice, perhaps one could also think of intoxication [*ivresse*] according to Nancy (which, Nancy does not fail to note, nonetheless has some links to sacrifice; see Jean-Luc Nancy, *Ivresse*, [Paris: Rivages, 2013], 28–29). In the state of intoxication, the following questions may be posed and answered: "What is proper? What is proper to me? To be susceptible to be seized, to stumble, to not follow my way or to even not have one: that is more proper to me than any other supposedly distinct mark" (Nancy, *Ivresse*, 81).
12 Mark, Fisher, *Ghosts of My Life: Writings on Depression, Hauntology, and Lost Futures* (London: Zero Books, 2014), 59.
13 Ibid., 59.
14 "Resentments," in Jean Améry, *At the Mind's Limits: Contemplations of a Survivor on Auschwitz and Its Realities*, trans. Sidney Rosenfeld and Stella P. Rosenfeld (Indianapolis: Indiana University Press, 2009), 68. Here, I share with both Agamben's reading of Améry's writing as "a genuine anti-Nietzschean ethics of resentment" (Giorgio Agamben, *Remnants of Auschwitz: The Witness and the Archive*, trans. Daniel Heller-Roazen [New York: Zone, 2002], 104) and Sebald's, which follows Améry in calling for "the *right* to resentment" ("Against the Irreversible," in W. G. Sebald, *On the Natural History of Destruction*, trans. Anthea Bell [New York: Modern Library, 2004], 158). I do not, however, agree with the thought of revenge in Améry's *homme du ressentiment*, since that could lead, once again, to a sublation of *ressentiment*.
15 I am deviating from Fisher because melancholia for him involves nonetheless a gesture of overcoming, for example, "a refusal to give up on the desire for the future," or "refusing to yield," "a refusal to adjust to what current conditions call 'reality'" (Fisher, *Ghosts of My Life*, 21, 24). Like Fisher, I am arguing against any reorientation toward current conditions, for example, those that call for the eradication of failures. However, I do resist the "desire for the future," which might tempt one to suppress and repress all senses of failure in view of a "better" future. In attempting to give due thought to failure, I would prefer to yield, as said above, to all the affective states implicated in failure.

16 Bataille, *Le Coupable*, 142.
17 In invoking the word "absurd," I do not forget Camus's philosophy here. There is no doubt something of the absurd in Camus's sense in what I say above, that is, to accept and endure all the affective states of failure and to reject the sacrificing of existence. After all, Camus has said: "To live is to let live the absurd [*Vivre, c'est faire vivre l'absurd*]" (Albert Camus, *Le mythe de Sisyphe* [Paris: Gallimard, 1985], 78). (In the wake of Camus's statement, I would add: *to live is to let live failure*.) This is also not to mention his philosophical refusal of suicide. A more detailed discussion of Camus in relation to failure lies beyond the scope of this prolegomenon, regrettably.
18 It is Claire Colebrook who argued that it is impossible to be "antitheory" today, because of a "failure of theory" in terms of its having "taken institutional hold" not only in a prevalent but also totalizing manner, in the sense that no study in the field of humanities can do without some reference to theory (Claire Colebrook, *Death of the Posthuman: Essays on Extinction, Vol. 1* [Michigan: Open Humanities Press, 2014], 33). In a somewhat similar line of thought, Ian Balfour has also made the observation that "to be antitheory is to be anti-intellectual" (Ian Balfour, "Needing to Know (:) Theory/Afterwords," in *Theory Aside*, ed. Jason Potts and Daniel Stout [Durham and London: Duke University Press, 2012], 80).
19 Colebrook, *Death of the Posthuman*, 43.
20 For Yanbing Er.

Works Cited

Agamben, Giorgio. *Remnants of Auschwitz: The Witness and the Archive*. Trans. Daniel Heller-Roazen. New York: Zone, 2002.

Améry, Jean. *At the Mind's Limits: Contemplations of a Survivor on Auschwitz and Its Realities*. Trans. Sidney Rosenfeld and Stella P. Rosenfeld. Indianapolis: Indiana University Press, 2009.

Balfour, Ian. "Needing to Know (:) Theory/Afterwords." In *Theory Aside*. Ed. Jason Potts and Daniel Stout. Durham and London: Duke University Press, 2014. 280–286.

Bataille, Georges. *Le Coupable, suivi de L'Allehuiah*. Paris: Gallimard, 1961.

Bataille, Georges. *The Accused Share*. Trans. Robert Hurley. New York: Zone, 1991.

Beckett, Samuel. *Company/Ill Seen Ill Said/Worstward Ho/Stirrings Still*. New York: Faber and Faber, 2009.

Camus, Albert. *Le mythe de Sisyphe*. Paris: Gallimard, 1985.

Colebrook, Claire. *Death of the Posthuman: Essays on Extinction, Vol. 1*. Michigan: Open Humanities Press, 2014.

Deleuze, Gilles and Félix Guattari. *Mille plateaux*. Paris: Minuit, 1980.

Derrida, Jacques. *The Work of Mourning*. Ed. and trans. Pascale-Anne Brault and Michael Naas. Chicago: University of Chicago Press, 2001.

Fisher, Mark. *Ghosts of My Life: Writings on Depression, Hauntology, and Lost Futures*. London: Zero Books, 2014.

Latour, Bruno. "Why Has Critique Run Out of Steam? From Matters of Fact to Matters of Concern." *Critical Inquiry* 30.2 (2004): 225–248.

Nancy, Jean-Luc. *Ivresse*. Paris: Rivages, 2013.

Sebald, W. G. *On the Natural History of Destruction*. Trans. Anthea Bell. New York: Modern Library, 2004.

Trawny, Peter. *Freedom to Fail: Heidegger's Anarchy*. Trans. Ian Alexander Moore and Christopher Turner. Cambridge: Polity, 2015.

4

Antitheory, Positivism, and Critical Pedagogy

Kenneth J. Saltman

Across social institutions, an imperative for positivism demands data accumulation, data display, data-driven leadership, and data-driven accountability regimes. In the tradition of positivist rationality, facts are alienated from the conditions of their production and appear to speak for themselves, to be meaningful on their own, requiring no interpretation. A number of fields have succumbed to "data-driven" rhetoric. Police departments use CompStat to aggregate and crunch crime statistics and then orient their policing activities to "juke the stats." Journalism remains bound to the guise of disinterested objectivity. Perhaps more than any other field, the imperative for positivism pervades education. Public schooling uses test-based accountability in which learning is equated with numerical test scores and changes to teaching and administrative practice are to be guided by the numerical outcomes. Superintendents, principals, and teachers are, according to educational rhetoric and doxa, to be driven not by theorizing educational situations but rather by data. "Data-driven" discourse presumes that the data are not collected with underlying theoretical assumptions or interpreted with theoretical assumptions.

All of the major recent educational policies such as the revised teacher education accreditation body CAEP (Council for the Accreditation of Educator Preparation) formerly NCATE (National Council for Accreditation of Teacher Education), the Pearson-run student teaching assessment platform edTPA, and the Common Core State Standards have underlying assumptions. These policies assume that knowledge is a deliverable commodity, that teachers are delivery agents, and that students are knowledge consumers. These policies share an approach to learning and knowledge characterized by an active denial of how knowledge relates to the experience and subjectivity of students and teachers. As well, these policies refuse to take into account how learning and knowledge relate to the world and the capacity of subjects to use knowledge to shape it. That is, dominant educational policies presume a conception of agency in which the social power of the individual derives from the acquisition and exchange of socially consecrated knowledge. Agency in this view does not stem from the use of knowledge to interpret, judge, act on, and shape the social world while reflecting on what one does. Instead, agency appears as consumption and display of knowledge for academic promotion and later material consumption.

The expansion of radical empiricism coincides with a crisis of truth, evidence, knowledge, information, and education. This crisis of truth appears in educational discourse as particularly market-based educational policy and practices are promoted and implemented regardless of a lack of evidence for them or even despite counter evidence. For example, vouchers, charters, school turnarounds, and urban portfolio models are all privatization schemes that are unsupported by empirical evidence and are undermined by empirical evidence or for which empirical evidence is impossible to obtain.[1] Nonetheless, all of these schemes are promoted by rightist think tanks. Departments of Education under both parties have embraced unsubstantiated policies swayed by advocacy organizations. Both conservative and liberal think tanks largely remain with the radical empiricist model, bickering back and forth in policy briefs over numbers and measurement methodologies and seldom going beyond disputes over efficacy. Do, for example, charter schools raise or lower test scores? The focus on positivist measures of numerical efficacy elides questions as to economic, political, and cultural purposes and roles of schooling. Implicit in the efficacy debates is an assumption that schools assimilate people for the existing social order—that is, make productive future workers and citizens who will accept electoral republican democracy in its corporate-managed form.

Similarly, value-added modeling calls for K12 administrators to measure teacher performance by standardized test outputs and links compensation and job security to the numbers. Universities defund the interpretive humanities and expand fields not just with commercial application but also with empirical orientation, while theory is replaced by a renewed archival research and emphasis on data collection. Higher education is regularly being subject to calls for quantifying student learning through tests and then tying financing to the outputs. Student income loans make this explicit as private tuition lending is tied to the expected future earnings of the student. Under the pretext of consumer protection from the predatory for-profit higher education sector, the US Department of Education under Obama began measuring the value of universities based on the future earnings of students relative to the costs of the education. Of course, these projects belie not only an instrumental rationality in which interpretive forms of learning have no place but they also lend themselves to being linked to commercial exchange and commercial competition. These assumptions have become only more overt under the Trump administration's educational initiatives that include aggressive promotion of for-profit education at all levels.

This chapter explains the central role of radical empiricism and the hostility to theory in education and journalism. In the contemporary crisis of truth, in place of theory, argument, and evidence people are seeking foundations for assertion in forms that offer a false promise of certainty—numbers and bodies. I focus on the contradiction between the simultaneous *faith in fact* for public, academic, and policy discourse and yet the widespread *disregard for fact*, evidence, argument, and truth in these domains. The first sections take up this contradiction in education historically and at present. The second part addresses journalism, and the third discusses how both can be understood as the alienation of fact, the replacement of fact with dogma. This problem of knowledge, evidence, and fact is driving a dangerous turn toward not just decontextualized numbers and a frenzy for empty displays of efficacy to ground assertion but worse yet, essentialized identitarian forms of politics that seek to ground truth in allegedly good and bad bodies. As I explain below, the crisis of truth, fact, evidence, and theory is profoundly wrapped up with the recent resurgence of white supremacy, anti-Semitism, xenophobia, and sexism as well as rampant conspiracy and political authoritarianism. As Zygmunt Bauman contends, material precarity produced through growing inequality and the upward amassing of wealth drives people to seek security in the Strongman.[2] My argument here is that the estrangement of fact compels a similar frenzied pursuit of security in the false promise of material grounding found in numbers and bodies.

The neoliberal restructuring of public education and its revival of positivism is historically implicated in the current crisis of truth, fact, and politics. As well, the crisis of truth and the alienation of fact must be addressed in part through critical pedagogical projects that reject the culture of positivism and its antitheoretical tendencies and instead can foster critical consciousness, reflective action, and democratic identifications.

The Persistence of Positivism in Education

The practices of K12 schooling and the field of education have a long history with radical empiricism. Empiricist theories of learning date back to Locke and Rousseau with a conception of the student as an empty vessel needing to be filled with knowledge or a blank slate upon which to be written. While August Comte conceived of positivism in the nineteenth century, it was not until the early twentieth century that positivist models of teaching and learning were developed from the ideals of industrial efficiency and Frederick Taylor's scientific management. The school was reconceptualized as a factory. Across the United States, the Gary Plan was implemented in which the time and space of school were organized to model a factory with shifts and bells. Knowledge was imagined as an industrial product that needed to be ever more efficiently produced and transmitted and be consumed by the student. Teachers' work within this view ought to be seen like factory work and could be broken down and made more efficient, speeded up, and measured. From the 1930s to the 1960s, scientific management surged in education. It was bolstered by the rise of educational psychology and its eugenic legacy that sought to establish an empirical science of intelligence, learning, and ability.[3] The eugenics legacy of testing and standardization of knowledge and the learning process merged with the industrial manufacturing promotion of standardization of knowledge as product and process needing to be made ever more efficient.

By the 1970s and 1980s, a growing body of liberal and radical educational scholarship pushed back against radical empiricism. This literature drew on the earlier progressive and radical educational theory of Dewey and George Counts. Social and Cultural Reproduction theorists and proponents of critical pedagogy also appropriated from Marx, Gramsci, the Frankfurt School of Critical Theory, and critical sociology as well as from feminist theory, pragmatism, black studies, and poststructuralism. Unlike the dominant positivist discourses, radical education theory emphasized the inherently political nature of teaching and learning, the politics of knowledge and curriculum, the assumption that all educational practices are undergirded by theories whether recognized or not. Against the assumption of a universally valuable and disinterested view of schooling, radical educational theorists drew on Gramsci to emphasize the extent to which the school and the curriculum are sites and stakes of class and cultural struggle. Against the positivist view of the subject as a receptacle for commodified units of knowledge, radical education theory such as that of Paulo Freire and Henry Giroux emphasized that theory is always behind educational practices and that the question is really whether teachers are aware of the theories that they employ.[4] Radical educators pushed back against the tendency of psychological and developmental radical empiricist approaches to biologize, naturalize, and individualize educational practices. Instead, they emphasized the social, political, and cultural aspects of pedagogy and curriculum.

While critical educational studies drew on a broad array of critical theories in the social sciences and the humanities, the majority of subdisciplines in education in the later half of the twentieth century were predominantly influenced by empirical psychology. By the late 1990s, economics became the dominant trope through which educational studies were framed. Economic framings of educational problems and solutions from the early 1980s to the present owe in no small part to the expansion of neoliberal ideology in education and the related accountability movement.

From the 1980s to the present, radical empiricism has played a central role in the radical restructuring of public education by bringing together two key trends: (1) neoliberal privatization in its various forms paired with (2) the radically empiricist accountability and standards movement. Neoliberal privatization involved public sector defunding, privatizations like charters and vouchers, commercialism, managerialism, and the ideology of corporate culture. The accountability and standards movement involves heavy standardized testing, high stakes testing in which funding depended on raised test scores, standardization of curriculum, and the expansion of technologies for tracking, testing, and homogenizing. Privatization and accountability are two mutually reinforcing trends with radical empiricism at their centers. Neoliberal privatization has been justified since the early 1980s by incessant declarations of the failure of public education. Such declared failure has been framed through the register of market and military competition, but it has drawn most heavily on selective claims as to numerical standardized test score failures. Test-based failures have been claimed through reference to international and domestic comparisons such as the OECD's PISA scores as well as to the low test scores of urban schools.[5] Public school failure declarations erase how the tests represent the class position of students, their cultural capital, and the radically different histories of investment in schools and communities. Working-class and poor schools that were deemed "failed" in part through reference to the scores were deemed ripe for experimentation, especially with the market. Hence, urban and rural poor schools were targeted for privatization in the form of chartering, vouchers, for-profit contracting, and corporate managerial reforms.

The accountability and standards movement has itself been a massive for-profit industry in test, textbook, and electronic curricular products. The standardization of curriculum has been promoted as allowing greater control over the delivery and consumption of knowledge. Standardized testing and prescriptive standardized curriculum products have come to dominate public school curriculum. Standardized tests erase the process of knowledge making by disappearing the people who make the tests as well as their social positions, interests, and ideological commitments. Facts in this view come from nowhere, are delivered, and are either properly or improperly consumed. Standardized tests evacuate the necessary act of interpretation of fact that is foreclosed by the prescribed choices of four or five possible answers. Such practices make learning seem mechanical, as though one collects little pieces of knowledge along a path that is there before one encounters it.

Venture philanthropists such as Gates and Broad have spent millions to promote educational administration and leadership that are "data-driven." They have funded database-tracking projects that aim to align numerical measures of test performance to behaviors and then use the data to inform and control behaviors of teachers. More recently, philanthrocapitalists such as Chan Zuckerberg Initiative (CZI) and major technology companies are promoting the replacement of teachers and dialogic forms of learning with mass-produced corporate knowledge products that can be quantified and standardized. These digital technologies that include adaptive learning software and biometric pedagogy technology put students to work generating data that is a lucrative commodity in surveillance capitalism. In this case, the disregard for the specificities of subjectivity and context is sold as their opposite, "personalized learning."[6] As I discuss in my recent book *Scripted Bodies*, there are a number of radically empiricist projects that now pair positivism with the use of various technologies that control bodies. For example, nootropic drugs or smart drugs, typically amphetamines, are used to drug kids into attention for standardized test performance or to drug kids into controlling themselves to not disturb other kids' testing. Grit pedagogy revives behaviorism through tactics for learned bodily self-control—a new corporeally targeted neoliberal character education. Psychologists and the OECD are promoting the quantification of "social emotional learning" through allegedly objective disinterested standards and measures. The business of making commodified data out of normalized student behavior is booming and merging with the banking industry's profiteering through social impact investing.

So, on the one hand, educational policy and practice has become thoroughly dominated by the assumption that what matters most is just the facts. On the other hand, there is an incredible disregard for facts, information, evidence, or reasoned argument when it comes to the most dominant educational policy pushes. For example, Donald Trump's Secretary of Education Betsy Devos spent twenty years promoting educational privatization in Michigan. Devos promoted for-profit chartering and vouchers. Both policies have an empirical record of poor performance in test-based achievement.[7] However, there is a long legacy of right-wing promotion of failed market-based reform. There is an extensive empirical record of the disaster of vouchers internationally—a record of gutting the public education system, of vastly exacerbating unequal quality schools, and causing the proliferation of cheap, bad, for-profit schools for the poor.[8] Vouchers in the United States have long been promoted as a way to get a foot in the door for educational privatization. Once a single market-based scheme can be launched, then right-wing think tanks can call for more studies, more experiments.

Another clear case in point of a complete disregard for evidence is the right-wing promotion of charter schooling as a catalyst to replace public schooling with a private industry. Andy Smarick in the Hoover Institution's magazine *Education Next* was quite explicit that the right should champion charters in the short run in order to justify declaration of charters as a public failed experiment and to justify more widespread privatization.[9] Paul T. Hill, like Smarick, calls for "churn" or "creative destruction." Hill, of the neoliberal Center for Reinventing Public Education, relentlessly promoted "urban portfolio districts" in order to expand charter-based privatization and admitted in his advocacy work that there would be no way to empirically ascertain whether or not the urban portfolio model of "churn," opening and closing schools and chartering, would result in improvements of academic performance.[10] However, Hill insisted that the privatizations afforded by the model justify it. Smarick, Hill, and other market fundamentalists aim to replace public education with a private for-profit industry in education.

The thinking of such ideologues was behind the radical privatization of public education in New Orleans after hurricane Katrina and Chicago following the razing of its public housing projects. Following the storm, the New Orleans public schools and the teachers union were dismantled and replaced by a network of four charter districts. Chicago closed a significant portion of its neighborhood public schools and replaced them with charters. Recently scholars, such as Sean Reardon at Stanford, and journalists, such as David Leonhardt of *The New York Times*, have promoted claims that New Orleans and Chicago represent evidence of school improvement following radical neoliberal restructuring (school closures, privatizations, and union busting) pointing to small increases in standardized test scores.[11] While New Orleans by 2017 saw a three-year decline in test scores most studies of Chicago charters find nearly identical test scores as neighborhood schools. Meanwhile, those making these claims of improvement are being sure to ignore the massive displacement of working-class and poor students and families from these cities combined with rising family incomes. Standardized tests consistently correlate with family income.[12] Following Katrina in New Orleans, the poorest families were dispossessed of their communities. The new four charter districts represent a different population than the one prior to the storm. Similarly following massive planned gentrification/public housing and neighborhood school closure coordinated by the Commercial Club of Chicago and more than a decade of steadily rising family income in the city, the tests are measuring different students and most importantly richer students. As sociologist Pierre Bourdieu explained, the reason that test scores correlate to family income is because the tests measure the knowledge, tastes, and dispositions of professional and ruling-class people who also happen to be the ones who commission and make the tests. So what we have is a situation where rich investors are pushing the poorest people out of cities, putting in place market-based school reforms, testing the new population, and claiming that it was the reforms rather than the dispossession causing the alleged change. These empirical studies not only misrepresent positivist standardized tests as definitive evidence of meaningful learning but they also fail to account for epidemic cases of charters pushing out the students who are the hardest to educate, including special education, English language learners and those identified as discipline problems. These claims of neoliberal restructuring working are examples of ideological uses of evidence for justifying a privatization agenda.

Mark Fisher described in his book *Capitalist Realism* this fictive performance of quantifiable efficacy as "market Stalinism." The contradiction between the imperative for radical empiricist approaches to policy and practice and the abandonment of evidence and argumentation is playing out in media culture and more specifically news and journalism as well.

What Antitheory Has to Do With Fake News, Bad Journalism, and Conspiracy

Following the election of Donald Trump, numerous essays in the popular press have offered explanations for how a flagrant and compulsive liar with no regard for truth or evidence could garner widespread support. While a lot of politicians lie, the quantity and brazenness of Trump's lies represent broader disregard for empirical evidence and for education. As of June 10, 2019 (not that anybody's counting, but …), Trump publicly lied or made misleading statements 10,796 times.[13] Examples of the disregard for evidence range from insisting that Obama was not born in the United States to a rejection of the scientific consensus about human-caused climate change, to scapegoating undocumented immigrants by accusing them of rape and murder, to the making of impossible claims about financing a border wall, to describing his loss of the popular vote as winning by a landslide, to nominating figures such as Mike Flynn to head the NSA (Flynn falsely claims that Sharia Law is being built in the United States and his reputation for untruth got his statements in the military derided as "Flynn Facts"). Examples of his disregard for education include stating that he "likes the uneducated" and appointing Education Secretary Betsy Devos, who remains committed to expanding vouchers and for-profit charter schooling even as her efforts in Michigan have resulted in overwhelming empirical evidence that these policies worsen schools and lower test scores.[14] Devos has also financially supported organizations dedicated to expanding the use of public money for private religious education. As Devos' nomination moved forward, additional statements and actions raised questions as to her commitment to truth, fact, and evidence. These ranged from defending guns in schools to protect against grizzly bears, as she stated in her Senate confirmation hearing, to her investments in a sham brain treatment center that shows children with autism and ADHD movies and interrupts them when they stop paying attention.[15] In fact, getting more guns in schools does not make schools safer: guns appear not to be the best defense against the scourge of grizzlies (pepper spray does work). There is no empirical evidence either for the movie-based brain treatments.

Popular press explanations for the acceptability and even widespread embrace of un-truth include varieties of "blame the internet." One version of "blame the internet" offers the "fake news" narrative, in which the abundance of ersatz news stories rendered the population incapable of distinguishing real from fake news. The stories about "fake news" imply that "real news" could allow citizens to make informed choices just as such "real news" covered the 2016 election with nearly no investigative journalism or dissection of the untruths spoken by politicians let alone minimal analysis of policy proposals. However, "real news" suffers from saturation by commercial promotional content.

Media theorist Robert McChesney has demonstrated that the decline of investigative journalism must be understood as the result of corporate media consolidation rather than Internet competition for news outlets.[16] The decline of investigative journalism has resulted in news content consisting of about 90 percent public relations content. As corporate media venues covered fake news and its role in the election, right-wing media outlets propelled by Trump's claims began characterizing mainstream media news itself as fake news. Outlandish fake news stories were generated in part in order to drive internet click-through profits, especially during the 2016 presidential election. Web entrepreneurs wrote sensational stories such as the one about Hillary Clinton operating a pedophile prostitution ring out of a pizza parlor: "Pizzagate." An armed vigilante intent on saving the victims fired his rifle in the restaurant only to discover that Hillary Clinton and the children she was pimping were not there.

The problem of the news media involves not only the extent to which content production has been compromised by commerce but also the extent to which educative institutions have failed to provide citizens with the tools to interpret the quality of sources and veracity of claims. For example, most Americans have not learned about the standards and varieties of editorial review such as journalistic and scholarly review and the differences between these and an internet posting. Functional literacy now requires the capacity to distinguish sources of information lest we all heroically invade pedophile prostitution pizza parlors. Yet, functional literacy is not enough.

One crucial element missing from the discussion of fake news is the way that both professional journalism and fake news disavow the politics of knowledge behind claims to truth. Mainstream journalism effaces its own framing assumptions and theoretical presuppositions behind the framing of narratives, the collection of facts, and the interpretation of the meaning of those facts. Rightist critics of media began describing mainstream journalism as fake news, alleging mainstream journalism is a collection of false facts, rather than criticizing the underlying values, assumptions, and positions that underlie the narratives. Following allegations that fake news was involved in Trump's election, Trump himself declared CNN "fake news," and he has been repeating and expanding this accusation. Trump got this right but for the wrong reasons. The problem of CNN most of the time is not ludicrous made-up stories but rather the failure to provide examination of competing values, assumptions, and ideologies behind claims to truth as well as the relationship between these symbolic contests and material ones. The lie built into mainstream media is the guise of disinterested objectivity in which ruling class and dominant cultural group interests are obscured and universalized, as *The New York Times* motto puts it, as "All the News That's Fit to Print." Corporate media juxtaposes falsehoods in the fake news with its own allegedly disinterested and neutral "true" news coverage. The missing element from both perspectives is consideration of the theory behind the organization of and interpretation of fact. The lie of disinterested objectivity is the same lie built into standardized tests and curriculum.

News media could draw on an endless pool of free scholarly experts to analyze and theorize current events. Instead, the prevalence of vapid news media punditry, yelling heads making unbacked assertions, in place of investigative journalism or scholarly analysis has both a financial and an ideological dimension. Advertising drives content. Amplifying volume and spectacle delivers emotionally stimulated viewers to ads. Keeping scholarly experts off of news programming avoids the introduction of ideologically dangerous questions about power, politics, and history that might raise doubts about ruling class and ruling cultural group priorities.

Another popular press explanation for the crisis of truth has to do with the alleged nature of the Trump supporters. Rebecca McWilliams writing in *The Nation* magazine provides the "Hunter Thompson Hell's Angel's Revenge Theory" of the angry white working-class male.[17] In this explanation for the affirmation of untruth by the electorate, decades of alienation driven by neoliberal globalization have resulted in an economically and politically excluded population of white men who are driven primarily by revenge against political and educated elites. In this narrative, Trump's rejection of fact, evidence, and truth is not a problem for supporters because they are well aware that politics is a show and, most importantly, believe that Donald Trump the showman will stick it to elites (of course, after the election he proceeded to stock the government with Wall Street and billionaire elites who have aggressively redistributed wealth upward while targeting the caregiving social state). This perspective suggests that the real promise of Trump was one of subverting the elite establishment. In fact, the more transgressive Trump's statements became, the more credence they gave to the perception that he was a true threat to the ruling establishment and not beholden to the rules of a game that elites had rigged against most of the population. Hence, Trump provided a point of identification for citizens in which his lies were a catalyst to a greater truth that the mainstream media, political class, academics, and the economic elites largely didn't want to admit—that an ostensibly fair system is in fact a system rigged by and for elites at the expense of most. Like critical theorists, the Trump voter is deeply suspicious of appearances. However, the critical theorist wants to take experience, appearance, and claims to truth on a detour through theory.

Theory provides an examination of the values, assumptions, and ideologies that undergird claims to truth. It allows facts to be interpreted and situated in terms of broader structural and systemic patterns, history, and context. Theory also allows one to comprehend how the interpretive scaffold of the subject is formed by the social and how the social is formed of subjects. Theory allows one to reflect upon one's action, and it expands the language to mediate experience and to interpret facts. Theory expands political agency, and political agency is crucial for a democratic society.

The Trump voter employs conspiracy rather than theory. Conspiracy imagines that there are superagents endowed with the ability to secretly determine outcomes. Within the logic of conspiracy, those on the outside of the conspiracy are left with spectatorial agency—able to get a glimpse of the conspiracy but without the tools to make sense of what produced a particular social phenomenon or experience. Bad superagents, the conspirators, conspire to conceal fact, propagate lies, and shape history in the shadows. Only good superagents who allegedly embody truth, such as a charismatic and strong leader, can reveal the conspiracy (i.e., fabricate it) and then shape history on behalf of the victims of the conspirators. The conspirators, on the other hand, do not simply speak untruth; they embody untruth. The problem for the Nazis wasn't that the Jews believed the wrong thing and needed to be reeducated to the right views. It was who they were, their essence, their nature. The problem for Trump and the alt-right is not radical Islam but Muslims themselves. Hence, the ban on travel from Muslim majority countries under the pretext of security, in spite of the fact that since before September 11, 2001, there has not been a terrorist attack by any individuals from these nations. For conspiracy, the identity-based grounding of the enemy is not a coincidence but rather is consistent with the need to give a material grounding to anchor the accusation. The body functions like numbers in the world of alienated fact, providing an aura of foundation to scapegoating and lies.

From vaccines causing autism to fluoride in drinking water, birtherism, chem-trails to 9/11 conspiracy, Holocaust denial, QAnon, and so on, a frenzy of irrationalism belies a deep distrust of facts and yet a faith in fact unmoored from the history and context that gives fact its meaning. In a culture in which positivism suggests the supremacy of the fact, fact is decontextualized and dehistoricized, appearing to come from nowhere—to be all powerful and yet deeply suspicious. In such a context, the repetition of baseless assertion, and lies, flourishes. The positivist legacy provides the conditions of possibility to authoritarians who are hostile to democratic cultures of free exchange of knowledge, the value of which is established by superior argument and evidence. Positivism supports those who prefer knowledge to be grounded by the social authority of the claimant.

Another popular explanation for the embrace of untruth could be called the "mainstreaming of postmodernism" position. This view suggests that we are now living in a "post-truth" era, in which most people recognize that uncertainties about facts, spin, or partial narratives are the new norm. Such a view can be seen in popular discourse when George W. Bush's chief of staff Karl Rove derided journalists in the "reality-based community," who criticized the president for ignoring reality. Rove claimed that, by acting, those in power make a new reality. Stephen Colbert named the tendency to ignore facts in making assertions "truthiness." Oil and tobacco companies have long embraced postmodern truth by hiding their own empirical studies of lung cancer and human-caused climate change and insisting that there are a multitude of competing narratives and bodies of evidence and hence these dangers cannot be grounded. In the absence of definitive proof, let's keep burning fossils and cigarettes. Critics of this mainstreaming of postmodern truth view refer to the material limits of epistemological uncertainty. Facts matter like the fact of gravity when jumping out of a window. However, Trump's open and irrational rejection of empirical evidence is very different from antifoundationalism in its pragmatist, postmodern, or critical theory forms in which competing narratives, arguments, and evidence call into question the possibility of access to certain knowledge of objective reality. As in science, these positions share a comfort with truth being provisional, antifoundational, and fallible and with the best theoretical assumptions, arguments, and evidence winning until better ones can displace them.

From the Alienation of Fact to Critical Pedagogy

How do we make sense of this glaring contradiction between, on the one hand, the imperative for positivism in which the fact is positioned as the supreme self-evident value, and, on the other hand, the abandonment of fact, evidence, or even truth itself when it comes to speech and policy? What explains these contradictions playing out in both educational and media discourse is (1) the alienation of fact and (2) the related replacement of reasoned argument with faith/dogma.

Critical theory has a long tradition of analyzing how dogma sediments in social consciousness. German social theorist Theodor Adorno, for example, drew on the sociological analysis of George Simmel to offer an explanation for the allure of positivism. Adorno explained that in a capitalist world in which everything is for sale, everything loses its value other than as a means of abstract exchange.[18] This loss of value renders all things abstract, and everything in the social world is experienced as floating and ephemeral. Numbers promise to restore the solidity and certainty lost through alienation. We can think about this with regard to standardized testing. Standardized testing has now been dominating public education for nearly twenty years, since No Child Left Behind was launched in 2001. Knowledge is decontextualized, and truth claims are delinked from their conditions of production in the standardized test. Yet, the attachment of numbers to the test performance provides a scientistic aura of certainty that recontextualizes knowledge and the test taker within a system of educational exchange that leads through academic promotion to a promise ultimately of economic exchange. The attachment of numbers to truth claims and their false promise of certainty and solidity has resulted in a now-dominant way of thinking about learning as earning. It has transformed a generation's way of thinking about learning as instrumental, grade motivated, equated knowledge with authority, and evacuated curiosity that is not contextualized through numerical reward.

Numerical quantification applies not science but a guise of science or scientism, invoking a careful and systematic process of measurement. It also suggests disinterestedness, objectivity, and universality. It provides a feeling of control by invoking abstract objectivity and universality. While numbering things offers a response to the alienation of market exchange everywhere, it is also alienating in its tendency to delimit the relationship between subjectivity and the objective world.

To extend Adorno's insight, we might consider those activities to which the attachment of numerical quantification is anathema. Numbers do not promise certainty and solidity in certain contexts. Think about your closest relationships, the people you care most about. Imagine those you love providing a numerical rating for your affections. "Dinner with you was an 8.5." Imagine telling a joke with a friend and getting a numerical rating in return. What these examples highlight is that our pleasures for human intimacy and intersubjective connection are contrary to the promise of numerical control offered by positivism. Quantification as a remedy for alienation simultaneously offers a guise of control while creating more alienation. Those suffering from obsessive compulsive disorder (OCD) often have a need to apply numerical rituals to experiences. For example, to leave a room, someone with OCD may need to open and close the door a certain number of times or count the number of steps to the door. The counting provides a temporary feeling of control otherwise experienced as lacking in these individuals. The numbers do not fix the obsession; they just briefly sooth the anxiety. Is not the ideology of positivism a kind of collective obsessive compulsive disorder, offering a soothing yet false promise of control over a physical world experienced as slipping away, melting in air? The alienation of fact involves the disappearance of the conditions of production of fact, the mystification of fact, and the treatment of fact as dogma to be transmitted and received.

What stands behind the absence of evidence and reasoned argument in educational policy and practice is faith—a faith in markets. The faith in markets is not only the result of decades of neoliberal ideology and the promotion of the TINA thesis (There Is No Alternative—to the market) but also the result of decades of schooling in which knowledge has been positioned as true by virtue of the authority of the claimant. The era of standardized testing has effectively accomplished this equation of truth with authority by alienating truth claims, making them appear to come from nowhere, and having authority by virtue of their anonymous authorship. Standardized tests do not come with the tools to question or dispute; they defy dialogue and follow the logic of monologue.

In my book *The Failure of Corporate School Reform*, I discussed the relationship between the new uses of positivism in education and market fundamentalism or capitalist dogma. What I termed "the new market positivism" is typified by the reinvigorated expansion of long-standing positivist approaches to schooling: standardized testing, standardization of curriculum, the demand for policy grounded exclusively in allegedly scientific (really scientistic) empirically based pedagogical reforms, the drumbeat against educational theory and in favor of practicalism. The new market positivism signals the use of these long-standing approaches toward the expansion of multiple forms of educational privatization.

In the fordist era, positivism neutralized, naturalized, and universalized social and cultural reproduction under the guise of the public good, the public interest, but also individual values of humanist education. Critical educational scholars of the 1970s and 1980s referred to this obscuring of the capitalist reproduction function of the public school as "the hidden curriculum." The economic role of schooling as a sorting and sifting mechanism for the capitalist economy was largely denied. As Pierre Bourdieu and Jean Passeron pointed out, mechanisms such as testing and grades simultaneously stratify based on class while *concealing* how merit and talent stand in for the unequal distribution of life chances.[19] Reproduction in the new market positivism still neutralizes and naturalizes the unequal distribution of life chances through the unequal distribution of cultural and social capital. Class mobility in the United States is far less possible today. But the new market positivism also openly naturalizes and universalizes a particular economic basis for all educational relationships while justifying a shift in governance and control over educational institutions. Testing—database projects designed to boil down the allegedly most efficient knowledge delivery systems and reward and punish teachers and students—these are not only at the center of pedagogical, curricular, and administrative reform but they are also openly justified through the allegedly universal benefits of capitalism. The new market positivism subjects all to standardization and normalization of knowledge, denying the class and cultural interests, the political struggle behind the organization, and the framing of claims to truth. The new market positivism links its denial and concealment of the politics of knowledge to its open and aggressive application of capitalist ideology, that is, the faith in the religion of capitalism, to every aspect of public schooling.

In *Escape from Freedom*, Erich Fromm suggests that the very possibility of modern rationality comes from disobedience, dislocation, and estrangement. The child's "no" introduces a separation from parental authority. For Fromm, the social and historical conditions for self-reflection come from the alienating effects of capitalism. Only by being estranged from the land and labor and social relations can one make an object of analysis of oneself and society. Paulo Freire, Henry Giroux, and others followed Fromm's thought in advocating the making of both subjective experience and analysis of the objective social world objects of critical analysis. In the tradition of critical pedagogy, the process of theorizing self and society creates the conditions for humanization and agency by countering capitalist objectification in its many forms.

As both liberals and conservatives continue to embrace positivist forms of education and journalism, they contribute to the alienation of fact and the crisis of truth it makes. Against the "bad alienation of fact" of radical empiricism that decontextualizes and dehistoricizes truth claims, critical pedagogy puts forward what we could call a "good alienation of fact" that seeks to contextualize and comprehend not only the theoretical assumptions and ideological underpinnings but also the broader material interests, social forces, and symbolic contests that are imbricated with claims to truth. Critical pedagogy estranges experience and truth claims by denaturalizing them and treating them as an object of analysis. Critical pedagogy reinvests claims to truth with the conditions of their production—that is, the history, context, and social contests that give truth claims meaning. It provides an approach to knowledge that emphasizes how acts of interpretation of fact can form the basis for social intervention. Critical pedagogy fosters democratic dispositions, including linking the process of learning to engagement with public problems and the commitment to dialogic forms of learning and public life. As such, critical pedagogy asserts the potential for fact, when theorized and interpreted, to be a source of agency rather than an oppressive, alienated force.

Notes

1. Three major new studies of vouchers were released at the start of 2017 that joined with other studies and international studies from Chile and India to paint an utterly damning picture of the empirical case for vouchers. See Martin Carnoy, "School Vouchers Are Not a Proven Strategy for Improving Student Achievement," *Economic Policy Institute* (February 28, 2017). http://www.epi.org/publication/school-vouchers-are-not-a-proven-strategy-for-improving-student-achievement/.
2. Zygmunt Bauman, *Strangers at Our Door* (New York: Polity 2016).
3. See, for example, *The Mismeasure of Man* (New York: Norton, 1996) or a contemporary dissection of the application of these ideas in Mark Garrison, *A Measure of Failure* (Albany: SUNY, 2009).
4. See Paulo Freire, *Pedagogy of the Oppressed* (New York: Continuum, 1972) and Henry A. Giroux, *Theory and Resistance in Education* (Westport: Bergin & Garvey, 1983).
5. See David Berliner and Bruce Biddle, *The Manufactured Crisis* (New York: Basic Books, 1996) and more recently Gene Glass and David Berliner, *50 Myths and Lies that Threaten America's Public Schools: The Real Crisis in Education* (New York: Teachers College Press, 2014).
6. See the discussion of the Chan Zuckerberg Initiative, philanthrocapitalism, and personalized learning in Kenneth Saltman, *The Swindle of Innovative Educational Finance* (Minneapolis: University of Minnesota Press, 2018).
7. Caitlin Emma et al., "Devos' Michigan Schools Experiment Gets Poor Grades," *Politico* (December 9, 2016). http://www.politico.com/story/2016/12/betsy-devos-michigan-school-experiment-232399. For a review of the educational policy scholarship situated in terms of a broader advocacy of critical education, see Kenneth Saltman, *The Failure of Corporate School Reform* (New York: Routledge, 2012).
8. Carnoy, "School Vouchers Are Not a Proven Strategy for Improving Student Achievement."
9. Andy Smarick, "The Turnaround Fallacy: Stop Trying to Fix Failing Schools. Close Them and Start Fresh," *Education Next* 10.1 (Winter 2010). http://educationnext.org/the-turnaround-fallacy/.

10 Paul T. Hill et al., "Portfolio School Districts for Big Cities: An Interim Report," *Center on Reinventing Public Education* (October 2009). Kenneth Saltman, *The Failure of Corporate School Reform* (New York: Routledge, 2012).
11 David Leonhardt, "A Plea for a Fact-Based Debate about Charter Schools," *The New York Times* (July 22, 2018). Sean F. Reardon and Rebecca Hinze-Pifer, "Test Score Growth among Chicago Public School Students 2009–2014," *Stanford Center for Education Policy Analysis* (November 2017).
12 See the NAEP National Assessment of Educational Progress, NAEP National Assessment of Educational Progress. "How Did U.S. Students Perform on the Most Recent Assessments?," *The Nation's Report Card*, https://www.nationsreportcard.gov/.
13 Glenn Kessler, Salvador Rizzo, and Meg Kelly, "President Trump has made 10,796 False or Misleading Claims over 869 Days," *The Washington Post* June 10, 2019. https://www.washingtonpost.com/politics/2019/06/10/president-trump-has-made-false-or-misleading-claims-over-days/?noredirect=on&utm_term=.7f326aa0d08c.
14 Emma et al., "Devos' Michigan Schools Experiment Gets Poor Grades."
15 Ulrich Boser, "Betsy Devos Has Invested Millions in This 'Brain Training' Company. So I Checked It Out," *The Washington Post* (May 26, 2017). https://www.washingtonpost.com/posteverything/wp/2017/05/26/betsy-devos-neurocore/?utm_term=.366a865e3c3d.
16 See Robert McChesney, *Digital Disconnect* (New York: The New Press, 2013).
17 Susan McWilliams, "This Political Theorist Predicted the Rise of Trumpism: His Name Was Hunter S. Thompson," *The Nation* (December 15, 2016).
18 Theodor Adorno, *Introduction to Sociology* (Stanford: Stanford University Press, 2002).
19 Pierre Bourdieu and Jean Passeron, *Reproduction in Education Society and Culture* (Thousand Oaks: Sage, 1990).

Works Cited

Adorno, Theodor. *Introduction to Sociology*. Stanford: Stanford University Press, 2002.
Bauman, Zygmunt. *Strangers at Our Door*. New York: Polity, 2016.
Berliner, David and Bruce Biddle. *The Manufactured Crisis*. New York: Basic Books, 1996.
Boser, Ulrich. "Betsy Devos Has Invested Millions in This 'Brain Training' Company. So I Checked It Out." *The Washington Post* (May 2, 2017). https://www.washingtonpost.com/posteverything/wp/2017/05/26/betsy-devos-neurocore/?utm_term=.366a865e3c3d.
Bourdieu, Pierre and Jean Passeron. *Reproduction in Education Society and Culture*. Thousand Oaks: Sage, 1990.

Carnoy, Martin. "School Vouchers Are Not a Proven Strategy for Improving Student Achievement." *Economic Policy Institute* (February 28, 2017).

Emma, Caitlin et al. "Devos' Michigan Schools Experiment Gets Poor Grades." *Politico* (December 9, 2016). http://www.politico.com/story/2016/12/betsy-devos-michigan-school-experiment-232399.

Freire, Paulo. *Pedagogy of the Oppressed*. New York: Continuum, 1972.

Garrison, Mark. *A Measure of Failure*. Albany: SUNY, 2009.

Giroux, Henry A. *Theory and Resistance in Education*. Westport: Bergin & Garvey, 1983.

Glass, Gene and David Berliner. *50 Myths and Lies that Threaten America's Public Schools: The Real Crisis in Education*. New York: Teachers College Press, 2014.

Gould, Stephen Jay. *The Mismeasure of Man*. New York: Norton, 1996.

Hill, Paul T. et al. "Portfolio School Districts for Big Cities: An Interim Report." *Center on Reinventing Public Education* (October 2009).

Kessler, Glenn, Salvador Rizzo, and Meg Kelly. "President Trump has made 10,796 False or Misleading Claims over 869 Days." *The Washington Post* (June 10, 2019). https://www.washingtonpost.com/politics/2019/06/10/president-trump-has-made-false-or-misleading-claims-over-days/?noredirect=on&utm_term=.7f326aa0d08c.

Leonhardt, David. "A Plea for a Fact-Based Debate about Charter Schools." *The New York Times* (July 22, 2018).

McChesney, Robert. *Digital Disconnect*. New York: The New Press, 2013.

McWilliams, Susan. "This Political Theorist Predicted the Rise of Trumpism: His Name Was Hunter S. Thompson." *The Nation* (December 15, 2016).

NAEP National Assessment of Educational Progress. "How Did U.S. Students Perform on the Most Recent Assessments?" *The Nation's Report Card*. https://www.nationsreportcard.gov/.

Reardon, Sean F. and Rebecca Hinze-Pifer. "Test Score Growth among Chicago Public School Students, 2009-2014." *Stanford Center for Education Policy Analysis* (November 2017).

Saltman, Kenneth. *The Failure of Corporate School Reform*. New York: Routledge, 2012.

Saltman, Kenneth. *The Swindle of Innovative Educational Finance*. Minneapolis: University of Minnesota Press, 2018.

Smarick, Andy. "The Turnaround Fallacy: Stop Trying to Fix Failing Schools. Close Them and Start Fresh." *Education Next* 10.1 (Winter 2010). http://educationnext.org/the-turnaround-fallacy/.

5

Down with Theory!: Reflections on the Ends of Antitheory

Jeffrey R. Di Leo

> "Down with philosophy!" is the cry of innumerable scientific minds. "Give us measurable facts only, phenomena, without the mind's additions, without entities or principles that pretend to explain." It is largely from this kind of mind that the objection that philosophy has made no progress, proceeds.
> —William James[1]

The linguistic turn of the late 1960s announced the entry of *theory* into the academy. While Greek philosophers from Xenophanes to Aristotle coined its historical role in Western thought, late-twentieth-century theory was not the *theoria* of antiquity.[2] *Theory* generally referred to the structuralist and poststructuralist thought that was having a revolutionary impact on the human sciences, including literary studies and philosophy.[3] Not only did theory challenge the critical model of the New Criticism then fashionable in English departments, it also had a ripple effect in philosophy departments, which were then largely divided along analytic and continental lines.

Whereas English departments were relatively quick to absorb the fruits of the linguistic turns of structuralism and poststructuralism into their curriculums and scholarship, philosophy departments had the opposite reaction. Instead of widely embracing the linguistic turn, the roots of which lay deep in the philosophical tradition, they used it as an opportunity to further widen the analytic and continental divide in philosophy.[4]

Whereas prior to the linguistic turn, continental philosophy from the perspective of the American philosophy department largely involved phenomenology, existentialism, and the Frankfurt school, after the linguistic turn, it expanded to include structuralism and poststructuralism. By the close of the twentieth century, though the continental philosophies of Jacques Lacan, Julia Kristeva, Hélène Cixous, Jean-François Lyotard, Gilles Deleuze, Michel Foucault, Jacques Derrida, and others were an important part of the American higher educational curriculum, with many professors producing scholarship in this area, it was largely not due to the efforts of its philosophy departments, which widely refused to teach the work in this area or even to recognize it as "good" philosophy. Instead, the rise of theory in the academy was largely due to its adoption by English, comparative literature, and foreign language departments.[5]

The reason for this is that philosophy in America was still on a course laid out a century earlier when it came to be bitten by the scientific progress bug. The irony here is that this "bug" came to American philosophy in the late nineteenth century via developments on earlier work from the continent by English philosophers, such as Francis Bacon, William Whewell, and J. S. Mill, and by American philosophers, such as Charles S. Peirce and William James, for whom the scientific method came to mean experimental empiricism.[6] This was occurring while other important American philosophers, such as Henry David Thoreau and Ralph Waldo Emerson, the latter of whom famously called for a break from the continental traditions as early as 1837,[7] were starting to be ignored by mainstream philosophers and philosophy departments—a course that would intensify such that by the close of the twentieth century, their work was primarily relegated for study only in English departments, which were also home to much of the work of theory.[8]

Analytic philosophy found in the conceptual analysis of G. E. Moore and logical atomism (and logical-analytic pluralism) of Bertrand Russell a methodology that could mirror the exactitude and certainty of the sciences. Logical empiricism, as you will recall, rejected metaphysics as unverifiable and focused instead on perfecting conceptual analysis.[9] Moreover, analytic philosophers had their own "linguistic turn." It was not one that revolved around the work of structuralism and poststructuralism, but rather one that involved the aforementioned logical empiricism in addition to American pragmatism and ordinary language philosophy. However, before the rise of logical empiricism, philosophy found itself in a similar position to theory today: namely cast aside for the new shiner areas of inquiry that were emerging from its own efforts.

I'd like to begin by revisiting the "down with philosophy" moment at the turn of the twentieth century noted by James in the epigraph above and use it to provide some insight on our current "down with theory" moment that now seems to be growing into a movement. It is ironic that philosophy not so long ago found itself in a situation similar to the one that theory finds itself today though with a fatal twist: whereas the antiphilosophy of the early twentieth century did not destroy academic philosophy, twentieth-century antitheory has the potential not only to bring down its home departments, but also to destroy the humanities, if not bring down the academy itself.

A One-Sided Arch

James noted the "Down with philosophy!" cry in a textbook on metaphysics that he never saw to publication. Posthumously published in May of 1911, *Some Problems of Philosophy* was meant to be an "introductory text-book for students in metaphysics,"[10] which he "hoped by it to round out [his] system, which now is too much like an arch built only on one side."[11] Ralph Barton Perry, himself a noted philosopher as well as a celebrated James biographer,[12] says that in his last days, James devoted himself very seriously to the "philosophical enterprise." It was, in Perry's estimation, "the most technical and carefully reasoned of all his books," and "represent[ed] a definite turning away from polemics, popular and literary appeal, mysticism, and flights of imaginative speculation."[13]

Some Problems of Philosophy "grew out of introductory courses at Harvard and Stanford," and, according to Perry, "was designed to serve as a college textbook having a wide circulation."[14] Moreover, "it was written for readers, and not for an audience" of listeners. In this way, it was different from all of his other philosophical works, says Perry, except *The Meaning of Truth: A Sequel to "Pragmatism"* (1909) and the posthumously published *Essays in Radical Empiricism* (1912). But here too *Some Problems* also differed from these two books as it was "conceived as a unified treatise rather than a volume of independent articles."[15]

In short, in his last days, James was hard at work on his first unified philosophical treatise. In a memorandum dated July 26, 1910, just a month before his death, James acknowledged that though his treatise is "fragmentary and unrevised," it should nonetheless be published with the subtitle "A Beginning of an Introduction to Philosophy."[16] His brother, Henry James, who wrote a prefatory note for the book, comments that the philosopher "cherished the purpose of stating his views on certain problems of metaphysics in a book addressed particularly to readers of philosophy."[17]

For those unfamiliar with his work, James may seem an unlikely to place to begin reflection on the ends of contemporary antitheory. However, as we shall see, he too was concerned with the fate of theory—and his situation offers a useful and sobering perspective on the contemporary one. At the time of his death on August 26, 1910, James was pronounced in his *New York Times* obituary as "America's foremost philosophical writer, virtual founder of the modern school of psychology and exponent of pragmatism."[18] Though he retired from teaching a few years before his death, James had been an active member of the Harvard University faculty from 1872 to 1907. When he met with his advanced students in philosophy for the last time on January 22, 1907, they gave him a silver loving cup.

His first book, the classic *Principles of Psychology*, was published in 1890 "after twelve years of introspective experimentation upon the physiology of the mind."[19] It would become the standard textbook for university use and is claimed to have "practically founded the modern science of psychology in America," although it is usually duly noted in histories of psychology "some experimental work had been done along the same line [as James's work] in Europe."[20] Until 1880, James worked as a faculty member in Comparative Anatomy and Physiology at Harvard. He then was on the philosophy faculty at Harvard from 1880 to 1889, but moved to the psychology faculty from 1889 to 1897—and then back to the philosophy faculty from 1897 to 1907.

James opens *Some Problems of Philosophy* by commenting "every generation of men produces some individuals exceptionally preoccupied with theory."[21] "Such men," he continues,

> find matter for puzzle and astonishment where no one else does. Their imagination invents explanations and combines them. They store up the learning of their time, utter prophecies and warnings, and are regarded as sages.[22]

For James, this theoretical work is the work of philosophy, something he regards as an essential part of a liberal education:

> To know the chief rival attitudes towards life, as the history of human thinking has developed them, and to have heard some of the reasons they can give for themselves, ought to be considered an essential part of liberal education. Philosophy, indeed, in one sense of the term is only a compendious name for the spirit in education which the word 'college' stands for in America.[23]

For James, in agreement with John Dewey, "philosophy expresses a certain attitude, purpose, and temper of conjoined intellect and will, rather than a discipline whose boundaries can be neatly marked off."[24]

Nevertheless, in spite of its many advantages, "the study of philosophy has systemic enemies, and they were never as numerous as at the present day."[25] For James, these enemies, in part, stem from the "definite conquests of the sciences and the apparent indefiniteness of philosophy's results."[26] They can also be found in "man's native rudeness of mind, which maliciously enjoys deriding long words and abstractions."[27] Says James, the critics of philosophy liken "the philosopher to 'a blind man in a dark room looking for a black cat that is not there.'"[28] They also describe philosophy "as the art of 'endlessly disputing without coming to any conclusion.'"[29]

James finds the "hostility" of his time toward philosophy "reasonable," but "[o]nly to a very limited degree,"[30] and makes some effort to reply to the critics of philosophy. To the objection that philosophy "makes no progress and has no practical applications," whereas "the sciences make steady progress and yield applications of matchless utility," he reminds us "the sciences are themselves branches of the tree of philosophy."[31] "As fast as questions got accurately answered," continues James,

> the answers were called "scientific," and what men call "philosophy" to-day is but the residuum of questions still unanswered. At this very moment, we are seeing two sciences, psychology and general biology, drop off from the parent trunk and take independent root as specialties.[32]

Indeed, James's prognostications about psychology and general biology were prescient. Today they are major disciplines unto themselves whose relationship to philosophy just a century earlier is largely ignored by their denizens. As sciences, both would rather we forget the way in which they were initially the products of *theory*, that is, the imagination inventing explanations for puzzling matters. But this relationship is nevertheless important to recall when attacks are made upon theory by branches that fell off its tree and took deep root in the fertile scientific soil of academe. Subsequently, at least one other major discipline has resulted from a similar path. Namely, computer science and its subfield, artificial intelligence, which both "dropped off from the parent trunk" of philosophy in the twentieth century and took independent root as specialties. In addition, the growing subfield of cognitive science needs also to be noted as a field of study which brings together the disciplinary work of biology, psychology, and computer science, each of which, again, has theoretical and institutional roots in philosophy.

The Tree of Theory

The situation of theory at the turn of the twenty-first century is not unlike the situation of philosophy at the turn of the twentieth century. Both have vocal critics and systemic enemies,[33] some of whom were also formerly proponents.

The difference though is that unlike philosophy, which has been part of the academy since its origins in ancient Greece, theory as it has come to be known since the late 1960s is a relatively recent addition to the academy. Also, unlike philosophy, which is institutionally situated as its own discipline within the academy, theory has never been its own discipline within the academy. Though the division of the faculty has included and still includes many who self-identify as "theorists," the division of the academy has not afforded theory its own discipline.

Theory functions in the academy primarily at the service of literary and cultural studies. While it has twentieth-century historical roots in many different disciplines, including philosophy, English, comparative literature, psychology, anthropology, sociology, foreign languages, and linguistics, it is ultimately at home in none of these areas. Moreover, the birth of theory in the academy arguably came at the same time as the birth of antitheory. Their histories are tied together like the two sides of a coin—or, following James, the two sides of an arch.

For James, the scientific minds of his time that were embracing the nascent fields of psychology and biology were turning their backs on the work of philosophy—which James also prophetically calls "theory"—that had brought about the creation of these new areas of inquiry. The cry "Down with philosophy!" he notes could have just as well been calls for the "death of philosophy." The objection to philosophy that James is mentioning was not that it was not historically important, but rather that at the turn of the century, philosophy was not making the kind of "progress" found in some of the newer, "scientific" areas of inquiry.

The "progress" of philosophy though in twentieth century has been markedly different than the "progress" of theory in the late twentieth and early twenty-first centuries. Whereas philosophy served as the tree from which different branches took root as their own disciplines, with biology and psychology being the major branches from philosophy in James's own time, and computer science and cognitive science being the major branches coming into their own from philosophy in the mid-to-late twentieth century, theory has had a somewhat different relationship with its own branches.

The short version of this story of the relationship of theory to its branches is that from the early "high" theory of structuralism and poststructuralism came various "low" theories, such as cultural and area studies as well as posttheory and antitheory. The "branches" of the theory tree include feminism, race and gender studies, cultural studies, globalization studies, queer theory, postcolonialism,

Marxism, and new historicism. For some, they represent "progress" in theory, though for others, particularly antitheorists, their relationship to theory is more like the one James describes as the relationship of psychology and biology to philosophy. Namely, these branches from the theory tree that have taken independent root in academe obviate the need for their progenitor: theory. The difference here of course is that whereas it is common now to find "professors of" biology or psychology in the university, it is very uncommon to find "professors of" new historicism or feminism. But, more to the point, it is rare too to find "professors of theory" or "antitheory."

To make matters even more complicated, as I have pointed out elsewhere:

> Theory in the new millennium is a multi- and interdisciplinary endeavor that operates within and among the humanities (particularly, history, languages, linguistics, the arts, philosophy and religion, in addition to literature), the social sciences (including anthropology, ethnic and cultural studies, economics, political science, psychology, and sociology), and many of the professions (for example, architecture, business, communication, education, environmental studies, journalism, law, museum studies, media studies, military science, public policy, and sport science, among others). In addition to its now somewhat more standard-fare work in these areas ... it has also made some substantial inroads into the natural sciences (for example, biology, physics, the earth sciences, and the space sciences) and the formal sciences (especially mathematics, computer science, and systems science).[34]

Thus, while the tree of theory has produced many new branches, none of them has taken root as a new tree or discipline in the way psychology or biology has taken root. Moreover, for the purposes of the academy, theory is not, nor has it ever been, one of its trees. It is not a discipline in itself like philosophy or psychology even though it arguably today operates in every discipline in the academy—including philosophy and psychology.[35]

Arguments as to whether the branches of theory are signs of progress or merely growth are moot if the most progressive and fastest growing area of inquiry in the university is both not recognized as a discipline and is under continuous challenge from antitheorists. Making matters even more complicated is the presence of theorists who are not pluralistic about theory.[36] These theorists resist the model of theory as differing "approaches" or "methods." For them, there is only one way to teach and research in their chosen field be it literature or some other area of inquiry. To call their chosen manner of teaching and researching an "approach" or "method" presents the false illusion that there are other competing ways to teach and research that are just as legitimate. Some consider this theoretical "dogmatism"—a dogmatism of the type that leads to remarks like "Down with [every] theory [other than my own]!"

Such dogmatism about competing visions of theory recalls a similar situation in philosophy. One of the things that made James such a respected scholar and popular theorist was the pluralism at the heart of his approach to education. As quoted earlier, James regarded knowledge of "the chief rival attitudes towards life, as the history of human thinking has developed them" as well as "some of the reasons they can give for themselves" as "an essential part of liberal education."[37] He then linked this pluralistic "spirit of education" to the term "philosophy" going so far as to say that it is what "the word 'college' stands for in America."[38] A century later, can we say the same of "theory," namely, that it captures the "spirit of education" in our time and that it is what "the word 'college' stands for in America?"

Given the insight that theory provides on education, society, and the world, it should be the case it does. Unfortunately, however, it doesn't. The fault is not with the tree of theory and its branches—antitheory and otherwise. Rather, the fault is with the immodesty and arrogance of many theorists and antitheorists today. Some might blame it on the neoliberal university that pushes professors to produce original research. The argument here is that pluralism regarding theory results in embracing a wide range of theory, and this is not what the university demands of its most distinguished members. Rather, it demands that they either carve out new areas of inquiry, shut down old areas of inquiry, or both.

Announcing the "death of theory" at the same time the tree of theory continues to grow new branches is one of the absurd realities of scholarship in the neoliberal university.[39] The heights of it are reached by those like the proponents of postcritique who dismiss critique and the hermeneutics of suspicion *in toto* simply because this is not what students would prefer to do in the classroom. Rather than approaching the situation like James, who chose the production of textbooks even in his final days as a way to *educate* students on the varieties of philosophical approach to metaphysics, antitheory today chooses to dismiss theory *as a whole* in the pursuit of a more affective approach.

After a long and distinguished career in both psychology and philosophy, and knowing that because of recurring health issues, it would probably be his final project, James chose to work on a philosophy textbook. It aimed to be a book not for a general audience, but for students of and readers in philosophy in particular. It was to be a component of a liberal education, not a rejection of philosophical pluralism. James did not want to give the next generation of students who might follow in his footsteps the misguided notion that they should abandon philosophy (or theory) for the "progress" of psychology and biology—fields that his own work played a role in developing. In specific, James's textbook aimed to not just announce his commitment to theory but to prove it through the development and defense of his own metaphysics. *Some Problems of Philosophy* aimed to provide the metaphysical side of the pragmatist arch that he felt was being lost or forgotten in assessments of his philosophical contribution.

Perry describes well James's philosophical temperament by comparing it to that of the philosopher Charles S. Peirce, the person James introduced "in 1898 as the originator of pragmatism"[40]:

> Peirce, both by aptitude and by training, was an exponent of exact science, where a man might be sure of his ground, and where inaccuracy was the deadliest of sins; whereas James was at home in literature, psychology, and metaphysics, where accuracy is likely to be pretentious or pedantic, and where sympathy, insight, fertility, and delicacy of feeling may richly compensate for its absence.[41]

Perry adds to this: "James most eagerly desired to be understood, while Peirce was sometimes playfully or maliciously obscure."[42]

Though it is debatable as to whether Peirce was ever *deliberately* obscure, it seems to me to be uncontroversial that James "eagerly desired to be understood" as well as to help others including his students to "understand." As an active university professor who took his classroom duties seriously as well as someone who wrote textbooks and aimed a great amount of his work toward a general audience, James can never be accused of not striving to be understood. However, the trade-off here seems to be that in striving to be understood, he ended up producing philosophical work less attuned to the rigorous standards of twentieth-century analytic philosophy than that of his less well-known contemporary, Peirce. Moreover, the contributions of Peirce arguably came to be much more influential to both philosophers and theorists in the twentieth century than those of James.

While I am not calling for us to reject rigorous standards in philosophy or any other field, I am suggesting that to approach theory today as a series of rejections of failed theories not only kills theory (or philosophy) but also further destroys liberal education in America. James understood this when he stood in opposition to the powerful fields of psychology and biology that he had helped to develop and counterintuitively called for us to continue work in philosophy. In fact, his own effort to develop a metaphysics in his final days was not only his last philosophical contribution but probably his most rigorous one.

The notion of denizens of the nascent fields of psychology and biology looking down their noses at philosophy gives us some needed perspective on the recent work of antitheorists who are today looking down their noses at theory. While speculative realism and postcritique may be the shiny new intellectual achievements of our day, their rejection of theory echoes the rejection of philosophy by psychology and biology in James's day. But unlike complaints about philosophy such as it "makes no progress and has no practical applications,"[43] "is dogmatic, and pretends to settle things by pure reason, whereas the only fruitful mode of getting at truth is to appeal to concrete experience,"[44] and "is out of touch with real life, for which it substitutes abstractions,"[45] all objections that James directly addresses in *Some Problems of Philosophy* before developing and defending his own philosophical conclusions regarding metaphysics, theory has no long institutional history for it to bend back upon when dealing with complaints about it by antitheorists. When antitheorists yell, "Down with theory!" it has the effect of taking an ax to the relatively young trunk of theory, whereas the "Down with philosophy!" has never meant anything more than acknowledging and recognizing the developments of a few of its branches.

Moreover, if we look at the academy today, and situate antitheory and its "Down with theory!" cries within the context of the rise of the neoliberal vision of the university, one that has decimated its academic ideals and replaced them with the protocols of debt culture and market economics, one finds in antitheory echoes of the attack on the liberal education spoken of by James.

While it may have been possible once to make the utilitarian case that studying theory provided the skills needed to be successful in your life and career, this can no longer be achieved. The professional training model of higher education which places a high value on curricular efficiency and educational instrumentality now runs deep in the veins of the public imagination. To be sure, a trade imbalance regarding theory exists in the university today. It has come about because far too many students, faculty, and administrators have chosen to trade theory and the higher aims of education away. Similar shameful trade-offs too have been made in other areas of inquiry such as philosophy and rhetoric. To trade away work that has been a central part of the academy since its origins in ancient Greece is ultimately to trade away higher education for a much lower and inferior version. Antitheory, which calls on us to denounce theory, in the end only works to bolster the ends of neoliberal academe.

The ends of antitheory are very different though from the ends of what we might call "antiphilosophy." James is correct in pointing the finger at the sciences as the source of antiphilosophy. Whereas the sciences claim to be more in touch with the "facts" of the "real" world than philosophy, seem to provide a better sense of "progress" than philosophy, and do not appear to rely on dogmatism as much philosophy, this ultimately is one of the dogmas of science—not philosophy. But as much as science and philosophy duel with each other for academic supremacy, there are philosophers who are not antiscience, and many scientists who are not antiphilosophy.

However, the situation of antitheory with respect to theory is very different. While it is possible to be both a scientist and a philosopher, it is not possible to be both a theorist and an antitheorist. The very notion of antitheory forces its practitioners to take a stand on theory. "Down with theory!" for the antitheorist is not about the relationship of the tree of theory to its branches; rather, it is about which tree one chooses to climb. By denouncing theory, one is not simply making a disciplinary preference but rather rejecting the entirety of the work of theory.

The academic move of one upping the work of prior theorists thus becomes a dangerous game when it involves the rejection of theory. While some contend that antitheorists are not actually antitheory, this is not always evident to observers (and funders) who take antitheorists at their word. Just as the internal squabbles among philosophers are the modus operandi of philosophy, so too are they among theorists. However, you do not find philosophers rejecting philosophy. But we have seen and do see antitheorists who play the dangerous game of appearing to "reject" theory—when in fact, they are merely theorists expressing disagreement about the work of other theorists through antitheory.

Conclusion

At the turn of the twenty-first century, both philosophy and theory are still struggling for institutional life against the efforts of their doubters and enemies. Philosophy has the distinct advantage here, though, in prevailing institutionally against its doubters because of its long history as a central discipline in the academy. Theory, however, as a recent addition to the academy, is not in as secure a position.

With no central or singular disciplinary home, theory is everywhere and nowhere in the academy today. This is both one of its strengths and one of its weaknesses. It is a strength because of the transformative impact it has in so many different disciplines. Many different points of contact with theory mean many different ways for it to be influential and relevant throughout the academy. However, this lack of disciplinary center makes it more vulnerable to the attacks of those who seek to eliminate it from the curriculum and replace it with more a vocationally oriented area of study. Some of these critics of theory are disciplinary purists who resent its encroachment on their discipline and use the neoliberal vocational-telos of education as an excuse to purge theory from their curriculum.

Moreover, *both* philosophy and theory still remain vulnerable to threats from the sciences who still claim as they did a century ago in James's day that the certainty of their work makes the speculative work of philosophy and theory of secondary intellectual significance. In this regard it is important to recall the sciences whose existence was largely made possible by the work of speculative thinking. It took philosophy over two thousand years to bring about the psychological, biological, and computational sciences. If we put theory in the same league as philosophy, that is, regard it as a speculative rather than scientific endeavor, then why not at least allow it more time to mature as an area of inquiry before summarily dismissing it through antitheory?

But what is forgotten here too is that despite its long history going back to Greek antiquity, the central role of philosophy in the academy was not always a given—even thousands of years after its birth. One needs only to recall, for example, its famous struggles for institutional support and prestige in late-eighteenth- and early-nineteenth-century Germany.

Immanuel Kant published *The Conflict of the Faculties* in 1798 in part as an effort to "liberate the philosophy faculty within the academy from its subordinate position in relation to the 'professional' faculties of law, medicine, and theology."[46] But he was not the only philosopher at the time to advocate for a greater role for philosophy in the academy. So too did other major German philosophers, including F. W. J. Schelling in lectures delivered in Würstburg in 1802, Friedrich Schleiermacher in *Occasional Thoughts on Universities in the German Sense* (1808), and J. G. Fichte in *Lectures on the Theory of Ethics* (1812). These philosophers were part of the radical reformist spirit for the German university, which resulted in a much better place for philosophy in the university.[47]

So given philosophy's historical battles for institutional prestige and disciplinary centrality, it is not surprising that theory has faced and continues to face similar challenges in the academy. Antitheorists who are throwing in the towel on theory are at the same time casting off the many accomplishments of theory in the academy. Critical citizenship, democratic values, social justice, and identity politics have all flourished as areas of concern of late in the academy through the efforts of theory. Where respect for others wanes, theory has provided intellectual resources to push back; when an economy that values market growth over human need takes rise, theory has been there to call it out; when the university ceases to be about education and becomes a job-training center, theory calls for its reform. In each of these cases, theory pushes the local perspectives of its host disciplines into a wider institutional chorus that says we in the academy need to do better by our students lest our society and world become one that we and they abhor.

When James says that one sense of the term "philosophy" is "only a compendious name for the spirit of education which the word 'college' stands for in America," one can see how in only a century our own educational spirit has changed. "College" today stands more for "vocational training" and the development of docile neoliberal subjects to serve in its economy than "philosophy."[48] If anything, "theory" represents the *rejection* of the neoliberal spirit of education. This, perhaps, more than any other reason is why the neoliberal academy seems so invested in eliminating every last vestige of theory from the academy.

Antitheorists who worry about the fate of literature in the academy forget that without the resistance that theory provides against the neoliberal university, the fate of literature in the academy becomes moot when a liberal education is no longer valued. Moreover, antitheorists who call for the rejection of critique and its "hermeneutics of suspicion" are as well calling for the rejection of the very instruments that are central from keeping the university from becoming a vocational training center. Ultimately, the greatest proponent of antitheory is the neoliberal university. Its aim is to eliminate critique and to repress the voices of those who believe that a key element of the spirit of education is *theory*.

The ends of antitheory are not the same ends of the sciences that were once branches of the tree of philosophy. The end of antitheory is always to cut down and burn the tree of theory regardless of whether it regards itself as a branch of theory or not. The sciences may frown upon philosophy from time to time, but even in their most hubristic moments, they do not call for its elimination as an area of inquiry. Why some theorists have become antitheorists is perhaps more a sign of our neoliberal academic times than anything else. Announcing the newest, shiniest, most novel theory provides one with a level of prestige in the academy that is hard to come by in the liberal arts today—and it unfortunately makes some all too quick to ride rough-shot over alternative theories on their path to academic glory. But by rejecting the spirit of theoretical pluralism, they are promoting a form of antitheory that works against the institutional interests of theory—and winds up supporting the ends of neoliberal academe, which, again, would like nothing more than to have theory disappear entirely from the academy. In short, antitheory that works against the interests of the humanities and the academy may be theory, but it is "bad" theory.

Theory is not, nor should it be, simply the product of an individual rejecting or opposing the views of others just because they can. Rather, theory involves the *shared pursuit* of values[49] that ultimately have the potential to make the academy a better site of education—and give it the best chances to have a positive and transformative impact in the world. As theory was born in the academy and is primarily the province of academic publishing, it should not be surprising that its first goal seems at times to be innovation for the sake of boosting individual academic careers and the marketplace for theory.

Rather, theory's primary aims should be to make the academic community a stronger and more vibrant place, to provide resistance to injustice and violence of all forms, and to promote critical citizenship and democratic values. As such, when we consider the role of theory versus antitheory in overcoming some of the problems facing the humanities and the academy, the progressive potential of theory trumps the innovative potential of antitheory. Ultimately, the best way to destroy the humanities and the academy is to become an antitheorist who categorically rejects theory. This, of course, is a counternarrative to the antitheorists who claim that they are *saving* the humanities and the academy by rejecting the mandates of theory. But theorists know better.[50]

Notes

1 William James, *Some Problems of Philosophy: A Beginning of an Introduction to Philosophy* (New York: Longmans, Green, and Co., 1916), 22.

2 For an historical introduction to theoria, see, for example, Scott M. DeHart, "The Covergence of Praxis and Theoria in Aristotle," *Journal of the History of Philosophy* 33.1 (1995): 7–27.

3 There are of course a couple of other senses of theory in addition to the somewhat narrow structuralist and poststructuralist high-theory notion. They include but are not limited to the idea that theory is the "methods" of literary studies; that theory is a collection of schools or movements that include but are not limited to structuralism and poststructuralism such as Marxism, psychoanalytic, and gender theory; that theory is a flexible toolbox of concepts; and that theory is just what every specialist knows. For a recent survey of the major senses of theory, see Vincent Leitch, *Literary Criticism in the 21st Century: Theory Renaissance* (London: Bloomsbury, 2014).

4   It should be noted that analytic philosophy also had its own "linguistic turn" albeit one very different than the one in structuralism and poststructuralism. If Ferdinand de Saussure's *Cours de Linguistique Générale* (1916) is considered the foundational text of theory's linguistic turn, then Ludwig Wittgenstein's *Tractatus Logico-Philosophicus* (1921) is the foundational text of philosophy's linguistic turn. According to P. M. S. Hacker, the expression "the linguistic turn" was first introduced in a review of Peter Strawson's book *Individuals* in 1960 by Gustav Bergmann. Richard Rorty popularized the name among philosophers when he edited the book *The Linguistic Turn* in 1967. The first part of the book contains classic statements on the thesis that philosophical questions are questions of language with contributions by Moritz Schlick, Rudolph Carnap, Gustav Bergmann, Rudolf Carnap, Gilbert Ryle, John Wisdom, and Norman Malcolm. The book also has major sections on the problem of ideal language philosophy (including essays by Irving Copi and W. V. O. Quine) and ordinary language philosophy (including essays by Roderick Chisholm and Stanley Cavell). In short, this group of philosophers and approach came through Bergmann and Rorty to be analytic philosophy's "linguistic turn," one very different than the project of structuralism and poststructuralism. For a survey of the linguistic turn in philosophy, see Richard Rorty, ed., *The Linguistic Turn: Essays in Philosophical Method* (Chicago: University of Chicago Press, 1967), and P. M. S. Hacker, "The Linguistic Turn in Analytic Philosophy," in *The Oxford Handbook of The History of Analytic Philosophy*, ed. Michael Beaney (Oxford: Oxford University Press, 2013), 926–948.

5   This situation presented a particular set of institutional challenges for philosophy students in the United States who were interested in the intersections of literature and philosophy as presented through continental theory. See Jeffrey R. Di Leo, "On Being and Becoming Affiliated," in *Affiliations: Identity in Academic Culture*, ed. Jeffrey R. Di Leo (Lincoln: University of Nebraska Press, 2003), 101–114.

6   See, Horace Fairlamb, "Scientific Method," in *The Bloomsbury Handbook of Literary and Cultural Theory*, ed. Jeffrey R. Di Leo (London and New York: Bloomsbury Academic, 2019), 677–678.

7   I'm referring here, of course, to Emerson's famous 1837 divinity school address, "The American Scholar," which is collected in *The Essential Writings of Ralph Waldo Emerson*, ed. Brooks Atkinson (New York: The Modern Library, 2000), 43–62. For discussion of its role in the formation of an American literature and philosophy, see Jeffrey R. Di Leo, "Who Needs American Literature? From Emerson to Marcus and Sollors," in *American Literature as World Literature*, ed. Jeffrey R. Di Leo (New York and London: Bloomsbury, 2018), 65–86.

8   If not for the influential contributions of the late-twentieth-century Harvard philosopher Stanley Cavell, whose work brought Emerson and Thoreau into

conversation with Wittgenstein, J. L. Austin, and others, these philosophers would probably have an ever smaller role in US philosophy departments today, who, for the most part, relegate their work merely to surveys of nineteenth-century American philosophy. See, for example, Stanley Cavell, *This New Yet Unapproachable America: Lectures after Emerson after Wittgenstein* (Albuquerque, NM: Living Batch Press, 1989).

9 Proponents of logical empiricism include Moritz Schlick and Rudolf Carnap, who each represent different wings of thought in this direction and are fittingly the first two philosophers anthologized by Rorty in *The Linguistic Turn*. In addition to the logical empiricists, there were also the Cambridge analysts, who included C. D. Broad, G. E. Moore, and John Wisdom.

10 James, *Some Problems of Philosophy*, vii.

11 Ibid., viii.

12 Perry was also a former graduate student of James as well as later his colleague at Harvard.

13 Ralph Barton Perry, *The Thought and Character of William James: Briefer Version* (New York: Harper Torchbook, 1964 [1948]), 352. This book is a briefer version of the two-volume edition originally published by Harvard University Press in 1935, to which Henry James, not Perry, held the copyright.

14 Ibid., 352.

15 Ibid., 352.

16 James, *Some Problems of Philosophy*, vii–viii. William James died on August 26, 1910.

17 Ibid., vii.

18 "William James Dies; Great Psychologist," *New York Times* (August 27, 1910). movies2.nytimes.com/learning/general/onthisday/bday/0111.html.

19 Ibid.

20 Ibid.

21 James, *Some Problems of Philosophy*, 3.

22 Ibid., 3.

23 Ibid., 6.

24 Ibid., 6.

25 Ibid., 8.

26 Ibid., 8.

27 Ibid., 8–9. Note the similarity of these comments of these critics of philosophy to those of antitheorists who aim to rescue literary criticism from theory's "esotericism, jargon, and delusions." See my introduction to this volume.

28 Ibid., 9.

29 Ibid., 9.

30 Ibid., 9.

31 Ibid., 10.
32 Ibid., 10.
33 For a collection of complaints about theory by some of its major critics, see Daphne Patai and Will H. Corral, eds., *Theory's Empire: An Anthology of Dissent* (New York: Columbia University Press, 2005).
34 Jeffrey R. Di Leo, "Introduction: Theory in the New Millennium," in *The Bloomsbury Handbook of Literary and Cultural Theory*, ed. Jeffrey R. Di Leo (London and New York: Bloomsbury Academic, 2019), 2.
35 In philosophy, the work of Jacques Derrida and Michel Foucault are representative; in psychology, the work of Jacques Lacan is of singular importance.
36 One of the most significant rebellions in the history of the American Philosophical Association (APA) was called the "pluralist movement." Led by Bruce W. Wilshire, a group of metaphysicians, continental, and pragmatic philosophers in the early 1970s demanded that the APA not treat their work as second-rate to the dominant analytic philosophy and include more of it in their conference programs. The work of this "pluralist movement" eventually changed the APA to be more inclusive of "non-analytic philosophy" in the conference program and laid the course for the inclusion as well of the work of women and racial and ethnic minorities in APA conference programming. I invoke the term here in both the spirit of Wilshire's "pluralist movement" and its achievements as well as William James, whose thought Wilshire greatly admired. See, Edward S. Casey's "Foreword" to Bruce W. Wilshire, *The Much-At Once: Music, Science, Ecstasy, the Body* (New York: Fordham University Press, 2016), x, and Bruce W. Wilshire, "The Pluralist Rebellion in the American Philosophical Association," in Bruce W. Wilshire, *Fashionable Nihilism: A Critique of Analytic Philosophy* (Albany: State University of New York Press, 2002), 51–64.
37 James, *Some Problems of Philosophy*, 6.
38 Ibid., 6.
39 Related to the death of theory is the legacy of theory after the death of so many of its leading lights, from Roland Barthes to Jacques Derrida. Not only has the question of the death of theory haunted theory from its beginnings but so too has the specter of death. See Jeffrey R. Di Leo, ed., *Dead Theory: Derrida, Death, and the Afterlife of Theory* (London: Bloomsbury, 2016).
40 Perry, *The Thought and Character of William James*, 129.
41 Ibid., 131.
42 Ibid., 131.
43 James, *Some Problems of Philosophy*, 88.
44 Ibid., 96.
45 Ibid., 97.

46 Benjamin D. Crowe, "Editor's Introduction," in J. G. Fichte, *Lectures on the Theory of Ethics* (1812), trans. and ed. Benjamin D. Crowe (Albany: State University of New York Press, 2015), ix.
47 In addition to Crowe's introduction to J. G. Fichte's *Theory of Ethics,* see Theodore Ziolkowski, *German Romanticism and Its Institutions* (Princeton: Princeton University Press, 1990) and Charles E. McClelland, *State, Society, and University in Germany 1700-1914* (Cambridge: Cambridge University Press, 1980), for further background on philosophy and German university reform in relationship to the discipline of philosophy.
48 The notion of the docile subjects of neoliberal academe is established in some depth in my book *Corporate Humanities in Higher Education: Moving beyond the Neoliberal Academy* (New York: Palgrave Macmillan, 2013) as is a critique of the neoliberal crusade in higher education to reduce the pursuit of knowledge in favor of an increase in vocational training.
49 For a defense of the role of community in theory, see Jeffrey R. Di Leo, "Running with the Pack: Why Theory Needs Community," *Intertexts* 20.1 (2017): 65–79.
50 This chapter is dedicated to the late Bruce W. Wilshire, who I had the good fortune to have as my academic adviser as an undergraduate philosophy major, and whose philosophically rebellious spirit and passion for American philosophy, particularly the work of Ralph Waldo Emerson and William James, left a deep impression on me.

Works Cited

Casey, Edward S. "Foreword." In Bruce W. Wilshire, *The Much-At Once: Music, Science, Ecstasy, the Body*. New York: Fordham University Press, 2016. vii–xii.

Cavell, Stanley. *This New Yet Unapproachable America: Lectures after Emerson after Wittgenstein*. Albuquerque, NM: Living Batch Press, 1989.

Crowe, Benjamin D. "Editor's Introduction." In J. G. Fichte, *Lectures on the Theory of Ethics* (1812). Trans. and ed. Benjamin D. Crowe. Albany: State University of New York Press, 2015. vii–xxix.

DeHart, Scott M. "The Covergence of Praxis and Theoria in Aristotle." *Journal of the History of Philosophy* 33.1 (1995): 7–27.

Di Leo, Jeffrey R. "On Being and Becoming Affiliated." In *Affiliations: Identity in Academic Culture*. Ed. Jeffrey R. Di Leo. Lincoln: University of Nebraska Press, 2003. 101–114.

Di Leo, Jeffrey R. *Corporate Humanities in Higher Education: Moving beyond the Neoliberal Academy*. New York: Palgrave Macmillan, 2013.

Di Leo, Jeffrey R. ed. *Dead Theory: Derrida, Death, and the Afterlife of Theory*. London: Bloomsbury, 2016.

Di Leo, Jeffrey R. "Running with the Pack: Why Theory Needs Community." *Intertexts* 20.1 (2017): 65–79.

Di Leo, Jeffrey R. "Who Needs American Literature? From Emerson to Marcus and Sollors." In *American Literature as World Literature*. Ed. Jeffrey R. Di Leo. New York and London: Bloomsbury, 2018. 65–86.

Di Leo, Jeffrey R. "Introduction: Theory in the New Millennium." In *The Bloomsbury Handbook of Literary and Cultural Theory*. Ed. Jeffrey R. Di Leo. London and New York: Bloomsbury Academic, 2019. 1–14.

Emerson, Ralph Waldo. "The American Scholar." In *The Essential Writings of Ralph Waldo Emerson*. Ed. Brooks Atkinson. New York: The Modern Library, 2000. 43–62.

Fairlamb, Horace. "Scientific Method." In *The Bloomsbury Handbook of Literary and Cultural Theory*. Ed. Jeffrey R. Di Leo. London and New York: Bloomsbury Academic, 2019. 677–678.

Hacker, P. M. S. "The Linguistic Turn in Analytic Philosophy." In *The Oxford Handbook of The History of Analytic Philosophy*. Ed. Michael Beaney. Oxford: Oxford University Press, 2013. 926–948.

James, William. *Principles of Psychology*. Two vols. New York: Henry Holt and Company, 1890.

James, William. *The Meaning of Truth: A Sequel to "Pragmatism."* New York: Longmans, Green, and Co., 1909.

James, William. *Essays in Radical Empiricism*. New York: Longmans, Green, and Co., 1912.

James, William. *Some Problems of Philosophy: A Beginning of an Introduction to Philosophy*. New York: Longmans, Green, and Co., 1916.

Kant, Immanuel. *The Conflict of the Faculties* [1798]. Trans. Mary J. Gregor. Lincoln: University of Nebraska Press, 1992.

McClelland, Charles E. *State, Society, and University in Germany 1700–1914*. Cambridge: Cambridge University Press, 1980.

Patai, Daphne and Will H. Corral, eds. *Theory's Empire: An Anthology of Dissent*. New York: Columbia University Press, 2005.

Perry, Ralph Barton. *The Thought and Character of William James: Briefer Version* [1948]. New York: Harper Torchbook, 1964.

Rorty, Richard, ed. *The Linguistic Turn: Essays in Philosophical Method*. Chicago: University of Chicago Press, 1967.

Saussure, Ferdinand de. *Cours de Linguistique Générale* [1916]. Ed. Charles Bally and Albert Sechehaye. Paris: Payot, 1971.

Schleiermacher, Friedrich. *Occasional Thoughts on Universities in the German Sense: With an Appendix regarding a University Soon to Be Established* [1808]. Trans. Terrence N. Tice and Edwina G. Lawler. San Francisco: EM Text, 1991. Trans. of *Gelegentliche Gedanken über Universitäten im deutschen Sinn*. Berlin: G. Reimer, 1808.

Wilshire, Bruce W. "The Pluralist Rebellion in the American Philosophical Association." In Bruce W. Wilshire, *Fashionable Nihilism: A Critique of Analytic Philosophy*. Albany: State University of New York Press, 2002. 51–64.

"William James Dies; Great Psychologist." *New York Times* (August 27, 1910). movies2.nytimes.com/learning/general/onthisday/bday/0111.html.

Wittgenstein, Ludwig. *Tractatus Logico-Philosophicus* [1921]. International Library of Psychology, Philosophy, and Scientific Method. London: Routledge & Kegan Paul LTD, 1922.

Ziolkowski, Theodore. *German Romanticism and Its Institutions*. Princeton: Princeton University Press, 1990.

Part Two

Reading as Antitheory

6

Critique Unlimited

Robert T. Tally Jr.

In recent years, whether having to do with the generally perceived crisis in the humanities or with some more basic upheaval in education, the value and function of literary criticism have been increasingly called into question. Leaving aside the hue and cry over the decline in the numbers of humanities and literature majors, not to mention the various pronouncements of new forms of cultural illiteracy in a supposed postliterate society, criticism itself has come under fire as a somehow illegitimate or flawed practice. Academic literary critics are viewed as hopelessly out of touch with some imagined "mainstream" reading public, a view that has become a cornerstone of a cultural journalism bent on toppling university-based intellectuals from their ostensible pedestals. Some of these assaults on the Ivory Tower have been launched by academics themselves, many of whom express nostalgia for some prelapsarian moment when the study of literature was somehow unsullied by "theory," and equally academic literary critics have proposed solutions that would in one way or another help to save the humanities.

Among the more celebrated recent examples of this, Rita Felski's call for a "postcritical" approach to literature is, in her own words, "motivated by a desire to articulate a positive vision for humanistic thought in the face of growing skepticism about its value."[1] The object of Felski's polemic is something she calls *critique*, which for her is as much a rhetorical attitude or tone as a methodology or genre. As she sees it, critique is inextricably tied to the "hermeneutics of suspicion," a term borrowed from Paul Ricoeur and used to designate an approach to interpretation that seeks to unmask meanings hidden from the everyday reader. In Ricoeur's characterization, "This hermeneutics is not an explication of the object, but a tearing off of masks, an interpretation that reduces disguises."[2] Felski does not go into Ricoeur's argument beyond repeatedly citing the phrase, but she asserts that this hermeneutics of suspicion lies at the heart of the problem with literary studies as they are currently practiced. Although her target is explicitly *critique*, Felski implicitly mounts an argument against literary or critical theory as well. Even as she good-naturedly confesses to having dabbled in theory herself, she clearly sees "Theory with a capital T" as abetting the critical attitude she opposes.[3] As such, her polemic against critique and against a certain hermeneutics of suspicion offers a good example of the current widespread antipathy toward theory in the literary humanities today.

That a certain "antitheory" sensibility pervades literary studies at present is not really in doubt, and I believe that the turn away from theory in recent years has had deleterious effects for literary criticism as a whole. The current trend toward postcritical approaches to literature is itself part of the movement away from theory, inasmuch as the principal theoretical traditions imagined by the postcritical critics have tended to trace their pedigrees back to that unholy trinity of Marx, Nietzsche, and Freud, those "masters of suspicion," as Ricoeur dubbed them, whose later twentieth- and twenty-first-century legatees have included a pantheon (or is it a pandemonium?) of celebrated critical theorists, such as Walter Benjamin, Georg Lukács, Antonio Gramsci, the Frankfurt School researchers, Jacques Lacan, Michel Foucault, Gilles Deleuze, Jacques Derrida, Fredric Jameson, Gayatri Spivak, Judith Butler, the poststructuralists, the postmodernists, and so on. The writings of Marx, Nietzsche, and Freud alone represent an astonishing diversity of thought, and the idea that the wide-ranging theoretical traditions made possible by their work could be neatly encapsulated into a single critical program or agenda is absurd, but one feature these profound heterogeneous discourses share is an apparent commitment to question, to look into more deeply or to look beyond the world as it presents itself to us. In this sense, critical theory is *subversive*, not so much in terms of a political project but in the more literal or etymological sense that theory attempts to undermine and overturn the status quo.

Not surprisingly, then, an effect if not the aim of a lot of the polemics against critical theory has been to support a status quo, or in some more reactionary cases a status quo ante, that theory and critique were to have maligned. Indeed, I would argue that the postcritical and antitheoretical tendencies in contemporary academic literary studies are symptomatic of a greater capitulation to what has been thought of as neoliberalism in higher education, which has involved a consumerist ethos and a degradation of thinking in all corners of its fields of influence. By trying to appeal to a public discourse fundamentally at odds with criticism and theory—that is, a discourse wholly committed to perpetuating a certain status quo and to limiting both the critique thereof and speculation over alternatives—the postcritical and antitheoretical scholars have ceded the territory to the enemy, allowing the opponents of literature and the humanities to set the terms of the debate, which has in turn frequently presented a crassly utilitarian or pragmatist vision of literary and cultural studies. I find a curious resonance between the contemporary critique of critical theory and the jeremiads emerging from the culture wars in higher education in the 1980s, and I maintain that a robust critical theory and practice is all the more necessary to combat the forces arrayed against the humanities in the twenty-first century. Moreover, I assert that such critical theory and practice is the very *raison d'etre* for the humanities.

In discussing these matters, I have tried to succumb neither to feelings of nostalgia nor to feelings of resignation. That is, notwithstanding the fantastic critical utopias that epigones like myself might envision as existing in the heyday of our heroes and heroines of yore, it is clear that there was never really a historical Golden Age of theory to which we should strive to return. As I discuss below, there really was no heyday of theory, in academe or in the society at large, even if there had been various moments of excitement and possibility along the way. Similarly, there is not much of value in the all too commonly held sense that *plus ça change, plus c'est la même chose*, despite the nagging aura of *déjà vu* that accompanies any retrospective analysis of the phenomenon. The narrative of critical theory's rise and fall in the literary humanities does not maintain a simple or linear plot, although various versions of the story can be told with different aims and effects. Similarly, the diversity of literary criticism and theory assures the possibility that many excellent and many awful works can be produced and coexist, with an extraordinarily wide range of examples along the spectrum. In this chapter, I want to address first antitheory itself, then its current expression in what is today celebrated as a postcritical approach to literature, and finally what I suggest is our duty, as culture workers in the literary humanities, to oppose this vision.

The Persistence of Antitheory

Decrying the lingering critical attitude she associates mainly with poststructuralism, Felski points out, "While the era of Theory with a capital *T* is now more or less over, this same disposition remains widely in force, carried over into the scrutiny of particular historical or textual artifacts."[4] Felski's sense that theory's epoch has ended is quite common nowadays, even as the formal remnants of the era are everywhere to be seen. Indeed, I have often thought that the so-called death of theory was due, in part and paradoxically, to what could be thought of as theory's huge success. That is, what had once been considered somewhat arcane types of critical theory became so much an intrinsic and familiar part of the study of literature, and of other subjects as well, that it lost a great deal of its critical power, a power based to a significant degree on its fundamental alterity or strangeness as a discourse and as a set of practices. To employ an overused term these days, theory became normalized, such that it was no longer *outré*, radical, or unorthodox, but had become an ordinary aspect of literary studies, if not a new orthodoxy, to be sure.

In my own department, at a university originally founded as a regional teachers' college, our undergraduate students are required to take a course called "Critical Theory for English Majors," and our master's literature students take a similar course titled simply "Literary Scholarship." Several professors who teach these courses "do" theory in their own scholarly activities, and we have had on our faculty a professor expressly hired as a specialist in literary criticism and theory since 2002. I think that is fair to say that these are not eccentric practices at universities and English departments around the United States. Apparently, by our own reckoning, the students majoring in English must have some basic familiarity with theory, even if courses on Shakespeare, Milton, and Chaucer are not required. That a faculty like ours in a time like ours feels the need to maintain a theory requirement is, I think, a sign that yesteryear's avant-garde proponents of critical theory—the Yale Critics, Colin MacCabe, the Marxist Literary Group, or other embattled partisans from the 1970s—sort of "won."[5] But, then, I could probably argue with equal force that the addition of theory courses to a standard English curriculum is a sign of just how much theorists and theory have "lost" over the years. For while courses like these do acquaint students with names like Saussure, Derrida, Lacan, and Foucault, they could also rob such theorists of any transformative power, as they become keywords in an informal disciplinary lexicon, and their work reduced to simplistic exercises designed to be grasped by undergraduates in order to demonstrate basic proficiency. Students learn that there's no meaningful difference between performing a feminist reading of a given text, a deconstruction of it, and a Marxist analysis; these are merely different critical "lenses" one may choose to look through when reading. Notoriously, in fact, in their attention to formal features, meticulous detail, and close reading, deconstructive analyses often resemble the New Critical interpretations of old, which might help to explain its prominence among Yale critics weaned on

William K. Wimsatt and Cleanth Brooks. Students may now incorporate terms like *signifier, hegemony, the Other*, or *performativity* into vocabularies once featuring *allegory, irony*, or *symbolism* as keywords, but the basic approach to the materials remains pretty much the same.

The basic story told about the rise of theory in literary studies is widely accepted, at least judging from the many textbooks designed for use in courses such as our Critical Theory for English Majors. The narrative tells of a prehistoric time—actually, merely the pre-1960s—when a hegemonic New Criticism (especially in the United States) or a sort of Leavisite humanism (if we are talking about the UK) held sway over all approaches to literature. That these informal schools of criticism themselves represented *theories*, that they were also quite innovative and controversial, and that there was significant resistance to them within both the groves of academe and the wider literary world are seldom mentioned in the introductions to literary or critical theory.[6] The advent of "theory" is depicted as part of a general backlash against New Criticism or liberal humanism, a backlash occasioned mainly by the incursion of foreign thought and of different disciplines into literature departments in the 1960s and 1970s. French structuralism brought Saussurean linguistics to bear on not only literary texts but on everything; after all, with semiotics, everything can become a sign-system to be decoded or a text to be interpreted, as Roland Barthes displayed so elegantly with such books as *Mythologies* and *The Fashion System*. Along those same Francophone lines, works of and figures representing anthropology (Lévi-Strauss), psychology (Lacan), philosophy (Foucault, Deleuze, Derrida, Althusser, and Lyotard), history (Foucault again), sociology (Bourdieu), and other disciplinary fields insinuated themselves into the required reading lists of literature scholars.[7] Add to this a Germanic tradition, deriving from Marx, Nietzsche, and Freud, if not also Hegel and Kant, which—along with Georg Lukács, Martin Heidegger, Walter Benjamin, and the Frankfurt School, among others—led to various schools of theory mingling with or contesting these others.[8] And apart from the foreign invaders, a certain homegrown sensibility among English professors led them to develop critiques of New Criticism or old-fashioned humanism on their own, owing to a variety of political or intellectual motives.[9]

The key to the story is rebellion from a dogmatic norm, in which the proponents of theory are cast as revolutionaries, but to those who spent any time investigating the history of criticism this narrative never really rang true. For one thing, there was plenty of "theory" before the New Criticism or its detractors. A parochial focus on English, as opposed to other languages and literatures, is partly to blame, as the New Criticism was never particularly influential on French or German departments, where phenomenological and philological approaches, including "style studies," were more commonly practiced in the 1950s. As for what would come to be called interdisciplinarity, certainly T. S. Eliot or F. R. Leavis read widely in philosophy, history, and other disciplinary fields, and even the most provincial of English professors read works from different languages. To the extent that what becomes known as *theory* develops out of literary and philosophical traditions or countertraditions of the nineteenth century, even such early critics as I. A. Richards or R. P. Blackmur were already engaged in theory.[10] Moreover, major figures who do not fit neatly within this now-dominant story—I am thinking of Edmund Wilson, Kenneth Burke, or Northrop Frye, for instance—are often omitted entirely. If a study like Frank Lentricchia's *After the New Criticism* (1980) helped to establish the rise of theory as a reaction to the New Criticism's less obviously theoretical approach, the textbook history of this rise by later scholars neglected Lentricchia's emphasis on Frye, Burke, and Kermode, as well as his discussions of existentialism, phenomenology, and an American Studies that frequently eschewed any contact with the fallacies associated with the New Criticism.[11] In fact, when it came to American literature, the predominance of what came to be known as the Myth and Symbol school of criticism ensured that a very different sort of theoretical framework influenced generations of scholars in that field. The commonly understood narrative of the emergence and dissemination of theory that is presented in so many introductory guides involves a great deal of overgeneralization and oversimplification at best.

It is also the case that the resistance to theory has been part and parcel of the rise of theory, with scholars and critics pooh-poohing the various schools of theory almost as quickly as they became known.[12] A symbol of this may be found in the coincidence of Stephen Knapp and Walter Benn Michaels's notorious "Against Theory" article and Terry Eagleton's bestselling *Literary Theory: An Introduction*, both published in 1982. The latter became a classroom staple—still available now in a third edition—that has introduced more than one generation to the subject, essentially making theory an essential part of literary studies, while the former argued the literary criticism and scholarship would be better off without theory entirely.

My own experience with theory was more subtle. Influenced by my adolescent enthusiasm for existentialism, for the fiction of Jean-Paul Sartre and Albert Camus, but especially for the ideas of Marx, Nietzsche, and Freud—I was already inclined toward those "masters of suspicion" apparently—I majored in philosophy while remaining keenly interested in literature, especially nineteenth- and twentieth-century European literature. (William Faulkner was, in my sophomoric opinion, among the only acceptable US writers, but mostly because I viewed him as the American Dostoevsky.) In my first semester in college, I took a course in Comparative Literature taught by a professor from the German department and called "The Poetics of Thought," which focused on texts that combined the literary and the philosophical.[13] It was not a theory course, and Erich Auerbach was perhaps the only twentieth-century theorist directly mentioned in class, but it was this sort of mélange of philosophy and literature that excited me the most. I did not realize that such a blend, when examined critically and perhaps with more focus on language itself, was what was being called *theory*, and I was especially ignorant of what might be more narrowly understood as *literary theory*. Given the writers I was most interested in, the theory produced seemed to be far less a rejection of this or that dominant practice within a disciplinary field than a continuation of what might be considered interdisciplinary tendencies within literature and philosophy broadly conceived. I ended up focusing within my philosophy major on post-Kantian Continental thought, and I took as many courses in literature (not English, incidentally) as I did in my major: between the two departments of philosophy and literature, I took entire courses on Hegel, Marx and Marxism, Nietzsche, Freud, the Frankfurt School, Lacan, Foucault, Deleuze, and modern social theory including works by Lukács, Gramsci, Strauss, and Habermas.[14] But by the time I neared graduation and applied for graduate schools, I knew that I wanted to "do" theory.

And so I did. I arrived in a graduate program already known for its commitments to literary and cultural theory,[15] and I was thrilled to study under professors whose own work represented both the study and practice of theory. Clearly, I was in the right place at the right time! Imagine my surprise, consternation, and perhaps disappointment, then, when in my first year my own mentor published a book called *In the Wake of Theory*, whose opening line read as follows: "During the late 1970s and the 1980s, various political, cultural, and intellectual forces combined to bring the moment of 'literary theory' to an end in the United States."[16] Wait, I thought, theory is over? I just got here. And *wait*, theory was over way back in the early 1980s, before I even went to college? The "wake of theory" phrase itself suggested the dual meaning of a requiem and an aftermath or lingering influence, but whichever metaphor was preferred, theory itself was understood to be a thing of the past.

Paul A. Bové's book was a response to what he took to be a dominant, antitheory discourse in both the academy and the broader public sphere during that decade, more or less tied to a sort of generalized Reaganism (and

Thatcherism) combined with a crassly pragmatic or professionalized view of the value of higher education. Within academic literary criticism, not only had the old guard who had withstood the encroachments of Continental theory onto the territory of English literature (say, an M. H. Abrams) effectively maintained their opposition to theory but a forcefully articulated antitheory position was stressed by the some of the young Turks of literary academe as well: I have mentioned Stephen Knapp and Walter Benn Michaels's famous "Against Theory" article in *Critical Inquiry* in 1982, which made the bizarre, neopragmatist argument that meaning and intention, language and speech acts, and knowledge and belief were each inseparable.[17] The bizarreness of this "pragmatism" did not go unnoticed, as even W. J. T. Mitchell, in introducing the debate stirred up by this article, noted with irony that nobody in practice, but only "in theory," could buy Knapp's and Michaels's conclusion, since, for example, "in practice, to say I *believe* something to be the case is tantamount to saying that I do not *know* it for a fact."[18] Worse still, major theorists themselves appeared to be turning away from "theory," as when Edward Said criticized "American Left Criticism" or "Traveling Theory" in his post-*Orientalism* writings,[19] or later when such eminent figures as Lentricchia (whose *After the New Criticism* and *Criticism and Social Change* constituted major studies of, and contributions to, literary theory), Stanley Fish, Harold Bloom, Henry Louis Gates Jr., and Stephen Greenblatt all abandoned theory in favor of this or that largely antitheoretical form of rhetorical, historical, cultural studies, or, in Lentricchia's particular case, fiction writing. Outside the ivory tower, the outsized influence of William Bennett's "To Reclaim a Legacy" report—since when does a National Endowment for the Humanities report make national news?—and bestsellers like Allan Bloom's *The Closing of the American Mind* or E. D. Hirsch's *Cultural Literacy* proved that there was a market for such reactionary responses to theory. (It almost makes one nostalgic to recall that Bloom identified "the Nietzscheanization of the Left" as the chief malady of the era; if only US conservatives today prescribed reading more Plato as the cure to what ails the national culture!) Conservatives in the media, such as George Will, Lynn Cheney, Pat Buchanan, and William Safire, lapped this stuff up; as more books followed—Roger Kimball's *Tenured Radicals*, Dinesh D'Souza's *Illiberal Education*, to name just two influential ones—even the liberal media jumped in, all too eager to cherry-pick titles from the MLA convention program, for instance, to show how dangerous and out of touch humanities professors were. In most cases, the problem with those professors was related to, if not identified simply as, their embrace of theory, such that terms like *Marxist, feminist, deconstructionist,* and *postmodernist* came to serve as readymade labels with which to dismiss an academic critic. In 1992, antitheory already seemed to be mainstream, theory itself in retreat if not defeated outright, and Bové's eulogistic assessment of theory's gains necessarily included a sense that literary criticism itself was no longer critical.

This brief rehearsal merely serves to emphasize the profoundly antitheoretical intellectual and profession contexts in which many of us first came to theory. Antitheory has been dominant throughout, and yet theory's influence in a certain sort of critical discourse, as well as its value as a commodity, remains fairly strong. One of the reasons antitheory maintains its prestige, after all, is that is can so potently convince others that theory is still an enemy worthy of vanquishing. Theory may well be a straw man in these arguments, but it is a very resilient one.

The Postcritical Turn

Much like the culture warriors of the 1980s, today all manner of scholars stand heroically against theory, as if by doing so, they have already demonstrated themselves to be heroic. They are "saving" literature from the barbarians, or perhaps they are saving literature from the hegemonic elites on behalf of those unfairly dismissed as barbaric. By denouncing critical theory, it seems, they are rescuing the field from itself. One of the more celebrated challenges within the literary humanities comes from the postcritical approach to the study of literature, an approach championed by Felski in her book, *The Limits of Critique*. Felski has made the news recently as the recipient of a multi million-dollar grant, which has been awarded to her to support her investigation into various postcritical approaches to literature. The *Chronicle of Higher Education* even published an advertisement for her work masquerading as an article called "What's Wrong with Literary Studies?,"[20] in which Felski was specifically presented as the person to answer the question—the subtitle's answer: "the field has become cynical and paranoid"—and as the one to make literary studies "right." Citing with approval both the argument of her book and the notion of a postcritical approach to literary studies, the author begins and ends with references to her $4.2-million grant, almost as if the worth of the award reinforces the value of the postcritical approach to literature.

Being opposed to critique is extraordinarily lucrative, it seems, and those of us trained in "the hermeneutics of suspicion" are likely not surprised. Felski herself has hijacked this felicitous phrase normally attributed to Ricoeur, used by him to characterize the interpretative strategies of Marx, Nietzsche, and Freud, but Felski does not analyze the term or these masters of suspicion. In fact, she simply invokes the label, out of context and certainly without reference to Ricoeur's own more particular uses of the term "suspicion," as a way of characterizing the sorts of literary criticism she now opposes in *The Limits of Critique*. In *Freud and Philosophy*, Ricoeur had distinguished the interpretative strategies of the "school of suspicion" from those of what he acknowledges would be a school of "faith." (As it happens, Ricoeur does not actually use the literal phrase "hermeneutics of suspicion" in that book.) The faithful interpreter seeks to recover a lost meaning in the text, whereas the suspicious interpreter doubts the existence of the pure meaning, instead looking at the ways that the text disguises or masks the truth. Although Felski never admits it, Ricoeur's position vis-à-vis the "masters of suspicion" is largely one of admiration. Whereas Felski sees critique as being undergirded by a rhetoric and tone of cynicism, Ricoeur expressly states, "These three masters of suspicion are not to be misunderstood, however, as three masters of skepticism.... All three clear the horizon for a more authentic word, for a new reign of Truth, not only by means of a 'destructive' critique, but the invention of an art of *interpreting*."[21] This appreciative view of Marx, Nietzsche, and Freud as inventors of interpretive arts is wholly consistent with Felski's more dismissive view of these theorists; in fact, her opposition to the theoretical and critical traditions that are indebted to their writings and her since her criticism of "critique" are based on not only the apparently suspicious attitude of critical theory but also theory's commitment to interpretation itself. In this way, her interests diverge quite significantly from Ricoeur's concerns.

Felski's actual opponent, however, is not the critic who follows the school of suspicion. The reader of *The Limits of Critique* will search in vain for what surely must have been the missing section in which Felski engages with a particular work of criticism, showing how its rhetoric and tone belied its baleful project. Much as she paraphrases or imagines critics making suspicious arguments about cultural artifacts, Felski does not really present a clear example of a critic or work of criticism to support the argument. The closest thing I could find to such an example was a short paragraph, no more than half a page, summarizing Jameson's *The Political Unconscious*. As a Marxist critic who draws upon both psychoanalytic theory and Nietzschean critique of ethics to make the case for a new approach to interpreting literary texts in such a way as to reveal hidden ideological or political content in the forms, Jameson would seem to be the natural target, indeed, the poster child, for Felski's criticism, and indeed she does cite Jameson's famous text as an exemplary case. (One obvious objection to employing *The Political Unconscious* as a cautionary example of critique's hegemony within literary and cultural studies in the present is its age. Can we really say that a book published in 1981, no matter how influential, represents the dominant critical ethos of academic literary studies today?) But even so, the best Felski can muster in her critique of that work—beyond summarizing it, which I suppose counts as criticism, assuming you're preaching to the choir—is the vague suggestion that Jameson is insufficiently "respectful, even reverential" toward the texts, and that he does not make a "good-faith effort to draw out a text's implicit meanings."[22] I would argue that this is a misreading of Jameson, who makes no moral judgments whatsoever about the texts and is remarkably sensitive to the aesthetic appeal of literature, not only in *The Political Unconscious* (with its meticulous readings of novels by Balzac, Gissing, and Conrad, for example) but throughout his career,[23] but Jameson's commitments to critical theory certainly place him at odds with Felski's postcritical approach.

In fact, Felski's choice to focus on such nebulous forms as the rhetoric, tone, or mood of critique, as opposed to working through various examples of actual critical readings with which she takes issue, makes it rather difficult to grapple with her argument at a substantive level. The would-be champions of critique find themselves in a position somewhat like that of Bové in the 1980s, who lamented his inability to engage critically with Bloom's *The Closing of the American Mind* because, as he put it, "The book appears as a set of mere assertions about other books and events whose authority must simply be granted to Bloom." Bové goes on to say that "the book appears everywhere and always to be made up of gross simplifications."[24] As a critic herself and a literature scholar, Felski is much better than this, but it is also true that her book sometimes reads like a rambling polemic against largely unnamed straw men, "critics" whose rhetoric and tone, much more than their actual arguments and conclusions, are considered objectionable to her and to the field she claims to be protecting and defending.

Rather than crossing swords with any particular opponent, as noted, Felski reserves all of her postcritical criticism for a shadowy, ill-defined concept called simply "critique," which becomes queerly personified and then psychoanalyzed through a series of regrettable mixed metaphors. Consider the following passage, for example:

> Critique, it must be said, is gifted with an exceptionally talented press agent and an unparalleled mastery of public relations. Occupying the political and moral high ground in the humanities, it seems impervious to direct attack, its bulletproof vest deflecting all bursts of enemy fire. Indeed, as we'll see, even those most eager to throw a spanner into the machinery of critique—those

gritting their teeth at its sheer predictability—seem powerless to bring it to a halt. The panacea they commonly prescribe, a critique of critique, might give us pause. How exactly do we quash critique by redoubling it? Shouldn't we be trying to exercise our critique-muscles less rather than more?[25]

The metaphors shift so furiously in this paragraph that the underlying argument is fairly difficult to keep up with. First, "Critique" is the name of a person who, despite being an unparalleled master of public relations, has been given a talented press agent. Critique occupies a position of such military advantage as to be impervious to attack, yet wears a bulletproof vest that repulses enemy fire; why it has enemies at all is a good question, given its well nigh universally high approval ratings. In the next sentence, such enemies are thwarted in advance, as Critique is now imagined as a machine whose movements are so irritatingly predictable as to cause opponents to grit their teeth, but even their spanner-throwing does nothing to slow its exorable momentum. Then this Critique person or machine quickly becomes a sort of illness or epidemic calling for a panacea, which, despite the definition of the term, does not seem to cure the ailment at all. Finally, Critique is a body part belonging to all of us, like an arm or a leg, whose muscles may be flexed or relaxed at will. Felski never does explain why someone with such a good press agent, "unparalleled" PR skills, and invulnerable to attack could manage to make so many enemies, but she does imagine them not only to exist but to be extraordinarily well armed, while also gritting their teeth, developing cure-alls, and flexing their own critique-muscles. It is a rather impressive half of a paragraph, but it tells us nothing of critique other than that Felski does not like this fellow very much, wildly popular though he apparently be in her chosen field of study.

The lines quoted above appear in a chapter titled "Crrritique," literally spelled with three *Rs*, so one might assume that Felski wishes us to growl out the pronunciation of the word. I am not familiar with this convention, except in the advertisements for a brand of breakfast cereal made of frosted corn flakes, whose cartoon spokestiger assures us are "grrreat!" But then, tigers are by nature growling animals, which seems to be the point in the juxtaposition of the character with the marketing catchphrase ("They're grrreat!"). I suppose that it is possible that Felski imagines critics as growlers—we are a rather querulous tribe, as it happens—or maybe her formulation is intended to indicate the ways that postcritical scholars like herself are growling about the persistence of critique.[26] At no point in the chapter does she explain the bizarre spelling, and apart from the title, the misspelled word appears only once, in the following, rather confusing lines: "*Crrritique!* The word flies of the tongue like a weapon, emitting a rapid guttural burst of machine-gun-fire. There is the ominous cawing staccato of the first and final consonants, the terse thud of the short repeated vowel, the throaty underground rumble of the accompanying r."[27] Leaving aside the fact that weapons do not usually fly off tongues, even metaphorically, or that the machine-gun-fire of the gut might not yield a throaty "r" sound, or that the vowel sound is not, as Felski claims, "repeated" since "crit" and "tique" (phonetically, "kri" and "tēk") hardly rhyme and do not seem to "thud," Felski's choice of spelling does seem to have value as a neologism, a unique sounding name (perhaps eligible for trademark protection?) to label this mélange of metaphors that represents her enemy. Perhaps her problem is less with critics than with *crrritics*? Yet, apart from this one instance, the more commonly spelled "critique" is used throughout *The Limits of Critique*.

One might argue that Felski is not herself antitheory, and she is intelligent enough to recognize that theory, in some senses, is inescapable. That is, she knows well the old line about how those who claim to oppose theory are generally operating under another, often older theory. Moreover, she embraces a certain actor-network theory (abbreviated ANT) of Bruno Latour in making her case against critique. Like neopragmatism, this ANT represents a somewhat antitheoretical theory, one here used to undermine the so-called high theory of such masters of suspicion as Marx, Nietzsche, Freud, and their poststructuralist, Frankfurt School, and postmodern legatees. Indeed, the sort of "theory" in question is sometimes labeled *critical theory*, which Felski expressly objects to on the basis of its foundational hermeneutics of suspicion. Marx and Marxism, even more than the Nietzschean and Freudian varieties of suspicion, seem to be particularly objectionable, as Felski refers rather dismissively to Marx, who "sprinkles the word [*critique*] copiously through his book titles"; none of Marx's actual books or writings are ever cited or examined by Felski, naturally, as this offhanded dismissal without any evidence is shown consistently to be the modus operandi of Felski's polemic.[28] But even with a more restrictive vision of this material as *literary theory*, Felski's position is generally anti-interpretive, favoring mere description to any attempt to generate meaning beyond mere appearances or the status quo as it presents itself to the reader. (The reader in this vision of things will remain mercifully untheorized as an autonomously acting ego that can have an affective appreciation for the text, outside of any particular context.) Felski's celebrated postcritical approach to literature is functionally, if not always explicitly, another attack on critical theory, and in its effects the postcritical vision is far closer to the antitheory discourse of the 1980s than is perhaps recognized.

Whereas the terminology and antagonists of the old culture wars are clearly dated, the resistance to theory, antipathy toward critique, and celebration of a positive, pragmatic, and useful understanding of literature remain all too timely.

Anti-Antitheory

What is to be done?... the perennial question. In the face of this assault of theory and on criticism, which now masks or simply misunderstands its ideological position with an appeal to "positive" thinking or to the defense of the humanities, I believe that a more strident and self-consciously negative critical theory is all the more needed. Indeed, I am still inclined toward the view of the young Marx, who in his famous 1843 letter to Arnold Ruge asserted that our project should entail "the ruthless critique of all that exists," and that this critique is fueled by and grounded in a profoundly critical theory.

As a purely practical matter, the argument that a more positive or even pragmatic vision of the humanities will help to save them from their enemies in state legislatures and governor's mansions and the media more broadly is, in a word, ludicrous. As Lee Konstantinou put it in the aforementioned *Chronicle of Higher Education* article, a less politicized reading of Jane Austen will not change Governor Scott Walker's opinion about the value of the University of Wisconsin system.[29] The enemies of literature, the humanities more widely, or higher education in general are not apt to change their minds based on some postcritical readings. Moreover, as Stanley Fish has warned, presenting our work in the terms of instrumental use value will either fail in principle at once or subject us to ever more rigorous measurement of "outcomes," which will inevitably prove literary critics and scholar to be lacking in the very instrumentalized value they had claimed to offer.[30] It is a losing strategy that has proven itself a loser for some time.

The ruthless critique of all that exists strikes me as a much better approach, and there is just so much that needs to be subjected to rigorous critique these days. Similarly, I think that the need for theory is all the greater in an epoch like ours, in which fake news, truthiness, and new normals reign. To adopt a stance that is anti-antitheory also seems like a good start. This is akin to the position attributed to Sartre, who allegedly embraced the notion of "anti-anticommunism" when faced with an unacceptable Soviet-style communism, on the one hand, and an almost equally abhorrent American-led anticommunism, on the other. Jameson has revived the concept more recently in *Archaeologies of the Future*, where he affirms that, "for those only too wary of the motives of its critics, yet no less conscious of Utopia's structural ambiguities, those mindful of the very real political function of the idea and the program of Utopia in our time, the slogan of anti-anti-Utopianism might well offer the best working strategy."[31] In fact, the sort of utopian thought Jameson has in mind is of a piece with the critical theory that is still needed, since Utopia was always less a blueprint of an idealized future than a satirical critique or Great Refusal, to borrow Herbert Marcuse's phrase, of the actually existing state of things. The power of the negative, something the Frankfurt School kept emphasizing throughout the twentieth century, is all the more necessary here in the United States, where even the most motivated of social critics insist upon an optimism and positive thinking that feels like a slap in the face to those facing an unjust reality, as Barbara Ehrenreich has rightly lamented.[32]

More to my point, I think that a ruthless critique of all that exists must be undertaken from a thoroughly oppositional stance, against those who would give their support, consciously or otherwise, to an intolerable status quo. In terms of literary critical practice, this means continuing and expanding upon the projects that theoretically oriented criticism has made possible over the years, while making sure to subject one's own criticism to the scrutiny of a critical and theoretical perspective. In literary history, to borrow a phrase from Jonathan Arac, this is not "history from below," but "history from athwart," going against the grain to disclose or create novel connections.[33] It means imagining alternatives, the very conditions for the possibility of which partly require the rejection of the tyranny of "what is." But then literature, along with literary criticism and literary theory, has always excelled at that.

For all the Black Forest gloom and prison-house austerity that the postcritical and antitheory critics perceive in the writings of Adorno, Foucault, or those who read them, there is also that unrecognized joy that comes with critique. As Jameson wrote in 2008, "inasmuch as ideological analysis is so frequently associated with querulous and irritable negativism, it may be appropriate to stress the interest and delight all the topics, dilemmas and contradictions as well as jests and positions still have for me."[34] Often forgotten amid the somber lessons of history, the incisive critiques of present situations, and the tenebrous forecasts of what seems likely to come is the sheer pleasure of engaging in critical theory. This is one more reason to be opposed to the proponents of postcritical antitheory, of course: in their insistence upon pragmatic reading, their relentlessly optative mood, and a good working relationship with the powers that be, they're trying to spoil all the fun.

Notes

1. Rita Felski, *The Limits of Critique* (Chicago: University of Chicago Press, 2015), 186.
2. Paul Ricoeur, *Freud and Philosophy: An Essay on Interpretation*, trans. Denis Savage (New Haven: Yale University Press, 1970), 30.
3. See Felski, *The Limits of Critique*, 25. Against appearances, Felski asserts that her book is "not conceived as a polemic against critique," and she admits that her "previous writing (in feminist theory and cultural studies, among other topics) owes an extended debt to critical thinking. I was weaned on the Frankfurt School and still get a kick out of teaching Foucault" (5).
4. Felski, *The Limits of Critique*, 25.
5. In *Beginning Theory*, Peter Barry sketched a history of theory's rise and fall using ten signature events, including "the MacCabe Affair" (i.e., the controversial decision by Cambridge not to promote then lecturer Colin MacCabe, who was apparently tainted by his associations with structuralist theory), to mark various moments along the way. See Barry *Beginning Theory: An Introduction to Literary and Cultural Theory*, 3rd ed. (Manchester: Manchester University Press, 2009), 262–286.
6. But see Joseph North, *Literary Criticism: A Concise Political History* (Cambridge: Harvard University Press, 2017).
7. One of the early "antitheory" themes still sounded by some today—Mark Bauerlein, for instance—reflects this turf-war question, whether English literary studies ought to be influenced by thinkers from other disciplines. See, for example, Bauerlein, "Where Are the Literary Scholars/Theorists?" *Chronicle of Higher Education* (April 26, 2010). http://www.chronicle.com/blogs/brainstorm/where-are-the-literary-scholars-theorists/23481. Yet it is difficult to imagine a time when literary scholars read only other literary scholars, and all the more difficult to imagine such a thing would be desirable.
8. Peter Dews's *Logics of Disintegration* (London: Verso, 1987) remains an excellent study of the interrelations and oppositions between the German and French theorists associated with, respectively, the Frankfurt School and poststructuralism.
9. Using three Yale-educated critics (Harold Bloom, Stanley Fish, and Stephen Greenblatt) as examples, Jeffrey Williams has discussed the ways that American critics emerging from the very heart of academic New Criticism at Yale University developed approaches—psychoanalytic, reader-response, and new historicist, respectively—undermining the precepts of the New Criticism, especially the intentional and affective fallacies. See Williams, "Prodigal Critics," *The Chronicle of Higher Education: The Chronicle Review* (December 6, 2009), B14–B15.
10. See, for example, Andrew Cole, *The Birth of Theory* (Chicago: University of Chicago Press, 2014).
11. See Frank Lentricchia, *After the New Criticism* (Chicago: University of Chicago Press, 1980).

12　Forgive the pun, but Frederick Crews's *The Pooh Perplex* (Chicago: University of Chicago Press, 2003), originally published in 1963 and lampooning Marxist, Freudian, Mythic, New Critical, and other forms of literary criticism, remains a classic touchstone in this regard. Nearly four decades later, Crews published *Postmodern Pooh* (New York: North Point Press, 2001), in which he satirizes various approaches (deconstruction, feminism, postcolonial studies, etc.) to have emerged in academic literary studies since the 1960s.

13　As it happened, the professor was completing a study of Johann Gottfried Herder, using the same title. See Michael Morton, *Herder and the Poetics of Thought: Unity and Diversity in On Diligence and Several Learned Languages* (University Park: The Pennsylvania University Press, 1989).

14　In the mid-to-late-1980s, the Graduate Program in Literature at Duke University, under the direction of Fredric Jameson, had dropped the word "comparative" and developed a particularly theory-oriented curriculum, which profoundly influenced undergraduate courses in various departments.

15　The doctoral program based in the Department of English at University of Pittsburgh was then (and is now still) called the Ph.D. in Critical and Cultural Studies, a sign of the interdisciplinary emphases as well as the importance of different media, especially film studies, studied in the department's graduate programs.

16　Paul A. Bové, *In the Wake of Theory* (Hanover, NH: Wesleyan University Press, 1992), 1.

17　Originally published in *Critical Inquiry* 8.4 (Summer 1982), 723–742, it was republished as the title essay in W. J. T. Mitchell, ed., *Against Theory: Literary Studies and the New Pragmatism* (Chicago: University of Chicago Press, 1985), 11–30.

18　Mitchell, "Introduction: Pragmatic Theory," *Against Theory*, 9.

19　See Edward W. Said, *The World, the Text, and the Critic* (Cambridge: Harvard University Press, 1982).

20　See Marc Parry, "What's Wrong with Literary Studies?" *Chronicle of Higher Education* (November 27, 2016): http://www.chronicle.com/article/Whats-Wrong-With-Literary/238480.

21　Ricoeur, *Freud and Philosophy*, 33.

22　Felski, *The Limits of Critique*, 57.

23　See my *Fredric Jameson: The Project of Dialectical Criticism* (London: Pluto, 2014).

24　Bové, *In the Wake of Theory*, 69.

25　Felski, *The Limits of Critique*, 118.

26　In fairness, Felski does not appear to be opposed to growling: "Academia has often been a haven for the disgruntled and disenchanted, for oddballs and misfits. Let us defend, without hesitation, the rights of the curmudgeonly and cantankerous!" See Felski, *The Limits of Critique*, 12.

27 Ibid., 12.
28 Felski, *The Limits of Critique*, 141.
29 Quoted in Parry, "What's Wrong with Literary Studies."
30 "If the point of liberal arts education is what I say it is—to lay out the history and structure of political and ethical dilemmas without saying yes or no to any of the proposed courses of action—what is the yield that justifies the enormous expenditure of funds and energies? Beats me! I don't think that the liberal arts can be justified and, furthermore, I believe that the demand for justification should be resisted because it is always the demand that you account for what you do in someone else's terms, be they the terms of the state, or of the economy, or of the project of democracy. 'Tell me, why should I as a businessman or a governor or a preacher of the Word, value what you do?' There is no answer to this question that does not involve preferring the values of the person who asks it to yours. The moment you acquiesce to the demand for justification, you have lost the game, because even if you succeed, what you will have done is acknowledge that your efforts are instrumental to some external purpose; and if you fail, as is more likely, you leave yourself open to the conclusion that what you do is really not needed. The spectacle of departments of French or Byzantine Studies or Classics attempting to demonstrate that the state or society or the world order benefits from their existence is embarrassing and pathetic. These and other programs are in decline not because they have failed to justify themselves, but because they have tried to." See Fish, "Always Academicize," *The New York Times*, opinion online (November 5, 2006). https://opinionator.blogs.nytimes.com/2006/11/05/always-academicize-my-response-to-the-responses/.
31 Jameson, *Archaeologies of the Future* (London: Verso, 2005), xvi.
32 See Barbara Ehrenreich, *Bright-Sided: How Positive Thinking Is Undermining America* (New York: Metropolitan Books, 2010).
33 Jonathan Arac, "Nationalism, Hypercanonization, and *Huckleberry Finn*," boundary 2 19.1 (Spring 1992), 15.
34 Jameson, "Introduction," *The Ideologies of Theory* (London: Verso, 2008), xi.

Works Cited

Arac, Jonathan. "Nationalism, Hypercanonization, and *Huckleberry Finn*." boundary 2 19.1 (Spring 1992): 14–33.
Barry, Peter. *Beginning Theory: An Introduction to Literary and Cultural Theory*. 3rd ed. Manchester: Manchester University Press, 2009.
Bauerlein, Mark. "Where Are the Literary Scholars/Theorists?" *Chronicle of Higher Education* (April 26, 2010). http://www.chronicle.com/blogs/brainstorm/where-are-the-literary-scholars-theorists/23481.

Benn Michaels, Walter and Stephen Knapp. "Against Theory." *Critical Inquiry* 8.4 (Summer 1982): 723–742.
Bové, Paul A. *In the Wake of Theory*. Hanover, NH: Wesleyan University Press, 1992.
Cole, Andrew. *The Birth of Theory*. Chicago: University of Chicago Press, 2014.
Crews, Frederick. *Postmodern Pooh*. New York: North Point Press, 2001.
Crews, Frederick. *The Pooh Perplex*. Chicago: University of Chicago Press, 2003.
Dews, Peter. *Logics of Disintegration*. London: Verso, 1987.
Ehrenreich, Barbara. *Bright-Sided: How Positive Thinking Is Undermining America*. New York: Metropolitan Books, 2010.
Felski, Rita. *The Limits of Critique*. Chicago: University of Chicago Press, 2015.
Fish, Stanley. "Always Academicize." *The New York Times* (November 5, 2006). https://opinionator.blogs.nytimes.com/2006/11/05/always-academicize-my-response-to-the-responses/.
Jameson, Fredric. *Archaeologies of the Future*. London: Verso, 2005.
Jameson, Fredric. "Introduction." *The Ideologies of Theory*. London: Verso, 2008.
Lentricchia, Frank. *After the New Criticism*. Chicago: University of Chicago Press, 1980.
Mitchell, W. J. T., ed. *Against Theory: Literary Studies and the New Pragmatism*. Chicago: University of Chicago Press, 1985.
Mitchell, W. J. T., ed. "Introduction: Pragmatic Theory." *Against Theory: Literary Studies and the New Pragmatism*. Chicago: University of Chicago Press, 1985.
Morton, Michael. *Herder and the Poetics of Thought: Unity and Diversity in On Diligence and Several Learned Languages*. University Park: The Pennsylvania University Press, 1989.
North, Joseph. *Literary Criticism: A Concise Political History*. Cambridge: Harvard University Press, 2017.
Parry, Marc. "What's Wrong with Literary Studies?" *Chronicle of Higher Education* (November 27, 2016). http://www.chronicle.com/article/Whats-Wrong-With-Literary/238480.
Ricoeur, Paul. *Freud and Philosophy: An Essay on Interpretation*. Trans. Denis Savage. New Haven: Yale University Press, 1970.
Said, Edward W. *The World, the Text, and the Critic*. Cambridge: Harvard University Press, 1982.
Tally, Robert T., Jr. *Fredric Jameson: The Project of Dialectical Criticism*. London: Pluto, 2014.
Williams, Jeffrey. "Prodigal Critics." *The Chronicle of Higher Education: The Chronicle Review* (December 6, 2009): B14–B15.

How Not to Be Governed Like That: Theory Steams On

Robin Truth Goodman

Dare to know!

—Immanuel Kant

"What is critique?" asks Foucault, and, "How does meaning occur?"[1] In explaining his views on Kant and the Enlightenment, Foucault, in this essay on critique where he asks such questions, privileges the nineteenth century as the historical point where the problem of the critical enterprise is given a "concrete hold."[2] In the rest of his essay, as is well known, Foucault explains that the nineteenth century developed processes of rationalization for governing, but that this governing rationalization cannot be dissociated from the question of the limits of such rationalization: "how not to be governed *like that*."[3] The "core of critique," says Foucault, is the relationship between power, truth, and the subject: "critique is the movement by which the subject gives himself the right to question truth on its effects of power ... critique will be the art of voluntary insubordination."[4] Although Foucault clearly does not share Kant's admiration of Enlightenment as the moment when institutions of knowledge demanded obedience, he reads in Kant's "public use of reason," the discovery of autonomy in speaking back to knowledge.

In today's political climate, Foucault's insistence that critique should raise the question of "how not to be governed *like that*"—the question of the subject—is urgent, maybe more urgent than ever. Yet, increasingly prominent trends in critical theory are turning away from—if not turning against—such inquiry. A minority of critical theorists is gaining growing credibility and volume by suddenly discovering the elixir of an immediate relation to texts or to objects, types of reading affected by "mood" rather than concepts and questions, or a dismissal of epistemological, phenomenological, or semiotic frameworks in favor of acknowledging the "object-in-itself" beyond human finitude and subjectivity. All this is arising at a time of increasing political cynicism, apathy, and indifference and a popular rejection of scientific knowledge, when criticism is most needed to stave off political manipulation that could lead to the destruction of the planet.

Arguing that questions of the subject do not give due consideration to objects outside of the subject's finitude and its standpoints, critics are increasingly bracketing the question of the subject as an encumbrance. "While we spent years trying to detect the real prejudices hidden behind the appearance of objective statements, do we now have to reveal the real objective and incontrovertible facts hidden behind the *illusion* of prejudices?"[5] derisively complains, for example, Bruno Latour, suggesting that theory's skepticism is to blame for the current dismissal of science and fact. Latour, however, never specifically defines the critique he is, in fact, critiquing, but infers that critique teaches suspicion and disbelief and demands that the critic unbury "what is really going on..., hidden in the dark"[6] or that the critic be "the one who debunks" or "the one who lifts the rugs from under the feet of the naïve believers."[7] In other words, critique, for Latour, sees itself as tearing away the illusory layers of an individual's consciousness in order to bring forth the shining truth from beneath the veil—or ideology analysis. Casting aside the past fifty years of critical debate and complexity in a diverse range of perspectives—from psychoanalysis, formalism, and structural linguistics through poststructuralism, feminism, and postcolonialism, for example—Latour resurrects an archaic and naïve strawman as his target and blames scholarly critique for the overreaches of science deniers.

Foucault explicitly says that critique is not predominantly in the business of "attempting to find out what is true or false,"[8] legitimate or illegitimate—in other words, of revealing truth concealed under the narratives spun to distort it by the ruling class. Rather, Foucault explains critique as a procedure that locates elements or groups of elements that constitute coercive mechanisms of knowing, and he identifies the types of knowledge and discourse that connect to those mechanisms. Though certainly not the only formulation of critique current in the humanities and social sciences, Foucault's idea of critique does not isolate objects and then recognize subjective content only as overlays that alienate, conceal, or get in the way of "real" meaning that stands essentially apart from the subject. In Foucault's view, the clinic, the prison, the school, and the mental health system are subjective modes that connect bodies of general, accepted knowledge in objectified, institutional forms while posing breaking points in power's techniques. The relationship between power and knowledge in the social and political field is limited, then, by its historical situatedness and context, its thinking subject.[9] Foucaultian critical analysis is therefore about revising our sense of the subject as it operates and struggles historically in fields of knowledge and power rather than demonizing it as concealing the "real" that supposedly shines forth in objects.

For Foucault, as a time when accepted ecclesiastical teachings were losing their claim to authenticity, the nineteenth century was an anchoring point for "the critical attitude." In the nineteenth century, he notes, the idea of natural law and rights was put forward as a limit to the law's interventions, giving birth to critique as the question of the limits to government and nongovernmental authority.[10] Though Foucault would not call "critique" antagonistic, his critical subject is still poised to attend to power's transience and points of breakage. The following two sections of this chapter analyze a nineteenth-century text where a social object or institution is becoming visible through a newly forming relationship of knowledge and the law, where knowledge of the law is posing limits to the law, and so appearing as a critical subject. This analysis leads, in the last section, to a return to Foucault in light of recent criticisms of critique.

Diamond Knowledge

The connection between power and knowledge that Foucault is concerned with is coterminant with the rise of financialization in the late nineteenth century. I focus on Anthony Trollope's 1873 novel *The Eustace Diamonds*, which, I argue, treats as narrative a transition in the concept of property the necklace represents: a type of property which depends on a distance—or even an antagonism—between the object and its representation. According to Mary Poovey, financialization produced social anxiety when objects could no longer be considered the holders of "intrinsick value," and conventions of imaginary writing were ushered in not only to teach the public to accept these new forms of conferring power by producing knowledge but also to create value out of representations disconnected to substantial objects. The question of how meaning is conferred is struggled over and is unsettled, creating uncertainty—or resistance—in meaning's applications. Reflecting in the legacy of this division between words and things, Poovey writes,

That so many of us still imagine observations can be systematic accounts of the world speaks to the success of the long campaign to sever the connection between description and interpretation.... At the same time ... that so many of us believe description ... never was—and never can be—freed from the theoretical assumptions that seem implicit in all systematic knowledge projects implies the campaign to free description ... from interpretation has not been a complete success.[11]

The unreconcilability between knowledge of an object and the object itself brings into play the subject of critique.

The Eustace Diamonds is Lady Lizzie Eustace's story, with Lizzie's character modeled on Becky Sharp of Thackeray's 1848 novel *Vanity Fair* (though Trollope's hatred of satire is well known). Lizzie is critique: her antics make visible the conferral of institutional meaning, name, and value that the Eustace lawyers want to assume is unmediated and unquestionable in the object. When her father the Admiral dies and leaves her in debt, caused in part by her obsession with wearing fake jewelry, Lizzie resolves her financial burdens by marrying Sir Florian Eustace, who dies a year later, bequeathing a fortune to her and his heir. Part of Eustace's possessions had been a diamond necklace that he may have given to Lizzie as a gift but did not mention in his will. The Eustace estate lawyers try to take it back into the family estate through legal demands. For this, they need to create new narratives for it that would determine if it could be said to be a family heirloom, a chattel, a gift, or a piece of paraphernalia; whether she could legally sell the diamonds; and whether her son's rights to property limit her own. None of these options is totally clear, despite the lawyers' best attempts to make the Eustaces's right to possession absolute as they extract precedent to define the diamonds as part of the Eustace line. The novel obsesses over the status of the diamonds that remains categorically indeterminable throughout the novel and is never resolved.

As readers, we are supposed to hate everything about Lizzie: her tenacity about having the diamonds as much as her taste for what Trollope sees as the false floweriness of her lyric poetry language and moods that she appropriates from Byron, Shelley, and Tennyson. Mostly, though, we are meant to fault her for her lies and her lack of concern for conventions. Her claim to her fortune is, for the most part, a pretense against which she overspends, and, displaying the diamonds, she overstates her wealth as a lure, toward marriage, of a series of prominent men. "She would tell any number of lies to carry a point," Trollope begins his description. "It was said of her that she cheated at cards. In backbiting no venomous old woman between Bond Street and Park Lane could beat her,"[12] and Trollope's venom against what he sees as Lizzie's moral failings continues relentlessly. Though, as Alan Roth writes in the *Stanford Law Review*, "professors will never concoct a fact pattern so compelling"[13] as *The Eustace Diamonds*, much of what obscures the factual attribution of the diamonds as property is Lizzie's lying: for example, the diamonds are more likely to be "chattels" if given to her in Scotland with the rest of the properties in the Eustace castle, so she says that they were, and the writing in the jeweler's ledger is smudged so the potential lie cannot be proven right or wrong.[14] She even steals her own diamonds, the first time, and lies to the police about the circumstances of the second theft as well.

The diamonds are, then, Lizzie's field of play. They are nodes where social discourse and imaginative language materialize even as they embody literary conventions, posing imagination to offset the power of objects to anchor social relations as solidly "real." Lizzie's character and literary taste are contrasted with her nemesis and childhood friend, the "solid" Lucy Morris—referred to as "good as gold"[15] or a "firm rock"[16]—who, likewise orphaned, is ugly and poor though virtuous, and whose sincere and worthy engagement to Frank Greystock, a Conservative member of Parliament, Lizzie, through her lies, nearly ruins. Unlike Lizzy, we *can* trust what Lucy says.[17] A lawyer, Greystock himself had risen to political prominence by "saving" the gold standard against encroachments that the City of London was trying to inflict through legal action; he defends the Bank of England by reconstructing its bullion-cellars.[18] Much of the novel takes place in the suspension of Frank's promise to Lucy Morris, a promise that inserts a delay or anticipation about whether or not his word is real, as he eventually does return to her but only a good seven hundred pages later. My contention here is Lizzie's claims to the diamonds trouble the authority, morals, good word, and social understanding to which she—as well as the social class to which she aspires—pretends. As an imposter, she implies they all are imposters.

The question of how the stone relates or does not relate to categories of knowledge and history is thus the quest and the central question of the novel. Some of the characters seek to ground the necklace's value in the solidity of the family name, but ineffectually. "Would the Law do a service, do you think," asks the legal expert Dove rhetorically,

> if it lent its authority to the special preservation in special hands of trinkets only to be used in vanity and ornament? Is that a kind of property over which an owner should have a power of disposition more lasting, more autocratic, than is given him even in regard to land? The land, at any rate, can be traced. It is a thing fixed and known. A string of pearls is not only alterable, but constantly altered, and cannot easily be traced.[19]

Yet, the lawyers never fully ascertain that the diamonds *are not* that kind of property. Like land, the diamonds seem to be weighty, as when the tall footman lifts the iron box made to keep the necklace in, he buckles "as though it were a thing so heavy that he could hardly stagger along with it,"[20] although Lizzie thinks she can carry them on her own, and we soon learn, when the box is stolen and forced open, that the box is empty. While traveling, Lizzie carries the box holding the diamonds sometimes on her lap, sometimes under her feet, where it is, to her, an obstruction to her comfort, or hyper visible and drawing attention, although the box is meant to make the diamonds invisible and unattainable. The necklace adopts so many guises that characters question if it is the same one throughout that was bought and passed down by the grandfather Eustace, or if it is "no more than paste."[21] The diamonds make visible the arbitrariness of value inside the institutional representation of its power.

While the coercive power of the class society is expected to stabilize the diamonds' inherent meaning and value, the antagonistic, irreconcilable claims of the law specialists, the class society, commercial traders, interested others, and Lizzie herself pose three general limits on the conferral of meaning on the diamonds: (1) aesthetics, and qualities associated with aesthetics (most prominently romantic-lyrical or popular literature, lying, and femininity), appear as necessary but shallow deceits that threaten the moral balance, the seeming permanence of social hierarchies, and faith in the stability of meaning in things; (2) debt allowed that those who did not inherit names and power could act as though they did, mimicking the conduct of the landholding and political classes and so making uncertain and discontinuous what had been known to be the concrete reality of power; and (3) the diamonds tied the British credit system, through debt, to colonial domination, thus linking the "fakery" of the nonpropertied classes to the "fakery" of colonial claims to sovereignty.

Heirloom Power

Like Lizzie's diamonds—which are neither heirloom nor paraphernalia nor movable commodity but may be any of these and we will never know—the colony in *The Eustace Diamonds* is an object that falls between knowledge spheres as they coalesce into mechanisms, techniques, and institutions of power. Like the diamonds, the colony follows a similar pathway as Kant's reflective judgment in the third critique, where the beautiful object does not fit prior categories of cognitive or practical representation and understanding and so demands a recirculation of the authority of those categories.[22] Implicated with imagination, judgment irritates the understanding and stokes the understanding's insufficiencies. For Kant as for Foucault, the subject of critique can first be discerned in this gap; that is, the subject of critique appears in the historical recognition of knowledge reflecting on its categories.

Finance's fictitiousness and resultant cognitive uncertainty in *The Eustace Diamonds* occasion at least partly from the diamonds' connection to imperial speculation. Evoking imaginary lands beyond the territorial boundaries of England, the diamonds—with their ornamental, exotic, mystical, and aesthetic qualities that Trollope hates—are excessive to their objective form as determined in the language of English law.[23] The excess of meaning in the diamonds parallels the Parliament's irresolvable disagreements about what to do about a colony resisting the known mechanisms of control, its being governed *like that*. The 1857 Indian Mutiny (called the Sepoy Rebellion in India) exposed what Jenny Sharpe has called a "crisis in British authority"[24]—the lie behind the legitimacy of Britain's hold on empire. Though Sharpe is concerned with the rise of false reports about sexual assaults of native men on white women in India, anxieties about colonial control for economic exploitation might likewise be said to expose "a British failure to command authority,"[25] where the certainties of supremacy and domination might be disclosed as but an empty shell. In fact, in *The Moonstone*, Wilkie Collins's 1868 sensationalist detective novel—often considered "the first" detective novel—on which Trollope bases the plot of *The Eustace Diamonds* (despite Trollope's well-known distaste for sensationalist literature), the diamonds are stolen from an Indian temple in Mysore at the tail-end of the Indian Mutiny, and their British inheritors cannot keep hold of them: no matter what security British banks offer to the diamonds, the Indians steal them back, seemingly with the help of ritualistic magic. The excess of meaning conferred on the diamonds by their relation to finance's forms of representation—their ability to be everywhere and nowhere at once—borrows from the excess of meaning that in *The Moonstone* emanates from their secretive provenance in exoticized, mystical practices of Hinduism.

Set in the midst of a Parliamentary debate about how to govern India, the story of Lizzie and the diamonds frames another story about the fate of Indian self-rule. The difficulty of conferring meaning on the diamonds is partly a result of the diamonds' connection to the difficulty of securing a governing apparatus that would assure control in the colony. The mystical or unearthly character of meaning in the diamonds suggests an "Oriental" origin on which is projected a magical or spiritual power that cannot be reliably attributed, held, known, named, categorized, or instrumentalized. The diamonds thus also upset the metropolis' hold on colonizing knowledge, or the knowledge of how to govern *like that*. Though what Goodlad calls the "heirloom establishment"[26] of parliamentary politics—where offices and favors are passed down for generations ritualistically, consolidating class rule—does not dominate *The Eustace Diamonds* as it does the other Palliser novels,[27] parliamentary debate ensues about the fate of an Indian prince, the Sawab, in the wake of the Indian Mutiny. A rendition of a historical incident in Mysore, the Sawab wants his adopted son to inherit the throne after his death while the liberals in power want, instead, to arrest him. That is, liberals in Parliament promote colonization as part of a "free trade" policy in India, or annexation, whereas Conservatives rally for "direct rule,"[28] where the Sawab and his descendants, adopted or not, would be local stand-ins to enforce British domination through practices of local ritual. As with the diamonds, the question of the Sawab's claims is a question of legal representation, whether his principality is like a British "heirloom," an object that can be handed down through generations, or a false claim like Lizzie's, with his adopted son a usurper of power, an imposter.[29]

The parliamentary question circles around whether British law should accommodate Indian claims or whether, like Lizzie, the Sawab is an intentional counterfeit, a fraud. Lizzie's betrothed, the somewhat incompetent and weak liberal Lord Fawn, expresses the liberal line when writing to Lizzie, begging her to release him from his ill-considered engagement: he had, he laments, encouraged her "to place the diamonds in neutral hands" just as, he thinks to himself, he "was often called upon to be neutral in reference to the condition of outlying Indian principalities."[30] Lord Fawn recognizes the similar legal error in the Sawab's sovereign claims for his princedom and Lizzie's for the diamonds, declaring, "As far as I can see, lawyers always are wrong. About those nine lacs of rupees for the Sawab, Finlay was all wrong. Camperdown [the Eustace lawyer] owns that he was wrong. If, after all, the diamonds were hers, I'm sure I don't know what I am to do."[31] Lizzie's imposture grants her possession of the diamonds (allowing her to socialize amidst the propertied classes) that is simultaneously legitimate and illegitimate. The Indian prince's claim to a right of sovereign power over British heirloom possessions and governance is similarly based on the claim that he is "like" the British by imitating British "heirloom" elite power and advancing their power interests. The question of Lizzie's right to the diamonds is, as Goodlad suggests, attached to the question of imperial right in the colonies and opens the question of how Britain should rule. Because Parliament cannot resolve how best to govern, another question hovers just below the surface: whether British knowledge is adequate to the task of colonial governance, whether Britain should rule *at all like that*.

Lizzie's infiltration into high society's dinner parties, hunting parties, friendships, betrothals, and the like does not succeed in toppling class power. She is not let into the class to which she aspires nor completely rebuffed, but rather, by dressing the part, she brings out and ridicules the security of that class in the knowledge that maintains their hold on power. Lizzie's lies bring to light the inconsistencies in the forms of knowledge that consolidate the power of professional and land-owning classes—Parliament, the Church, the family, and the bank. In Foucaultian terms, Lizzie is the singularity, the event—she "shows the conditions of acceptability of a system and follow[s] the breaking points which indicate its emergence" and thus reveals in history "the arbitrary nature in terms of knowledge, its violence in terms of power, in short, its energy."[32] Critique is knowledge reflecting back on itself from within its own processes of rationalization. This is what Foucault calls "the critical attitude": "an act of defiance, … a challenge, … a way of limiting these arts of governing and sizing them up, transforming them, of finding a way to escape from them or, in any case, to displace them, with a basic distrust."[33] Yet to be written is a critical reading of *The Eustace Diamonds* that would *commend* Lizzie—though she fails in the end—as a hero, for using the symbols of privilege against themselves and thereby confusing the rituals that uphold wealth and ruling-class authority, upending their social and political control.

Antitheory

The turn in cultural and literary scholarship toward antitheory relies on a purposively misguided mis-assessing of critique's assessments of Immanuel Kant's contemporary legacy. Latour, for example, explicitly blames theory's skepticism about statements of fact on theory's being "too faithful to the unfortunate solution inherited from the philosophy of Immanuel Kant."[34] Now, he says, as critics, we need to return to what Kant gave up on: the thing-in-itself, the part of reality that is devoid of subjectivity. Likewise, Rita Felski faults Kant for critique's assuming "the unknowability of the real world."[35] Those engaged in critique are therefore, for Felski, haughty and always in a bad mood, expressed in their "*againstness*"[36] to accepted meanings that inhere in things and texts. For Felski, this bad mood induced by assuming, as she claims theory does, the unknowability of the real world carries an arrogance that all critics are guilty of when they claim superior insight, where the supercilious, paranoid, and nevertheless narrow-minded critic attributes simplicity and naivete to alternative modes of thought and ways of reading including description. Such critics should leave texts and their readers alone, she inveighs. What is more, because critique is mired in "'ideological' styles of criticism,"[37] truth is conveyed "beneath, behind, or to the side of these words"[38] to those considering themselves smart enough to see it, Felski insists, echoing Latour's regressive distortions of what critique is and does inside a condemnation of the styled attitude of the critic.

Meanwhile, Stefano Harney and Fred Moten blame Kant for critique's neglect of the history of feeling because "[t]o feel others is unmediated, immediately social, amongst us, our thing."[39] Most explicitly, Quentin Meillassoux impugns Kant for setting philosophy on a dangerous path where, lamentably (for him), "the sensible only exists as a subject's relation to the world"[40] and relegating any different viewpoint as *"pre-critical,"*[41] and therefore "naïve,"[42] simplistic, irrelevant, absurd, or "regressive"[43]: orthodox Kantianism, he notes, means that "postcritical" philosophers who see themselves as moving beyond dogmatism "will maintain that it is naïve to think we are able to think *something* … while abstracting from the fact that it is invariably we who are thinking that something."[44] Meillassoux is most interested in claiming the importance of the Kantian thing-in-itself as a mathematical exteriority, or an object outside of its mediate relationships with subjectivity, in order to think of time in planetary or ecological, rather than human, scale.[45]

These antitheorists interpret Kant as saying that the only possible relation of the subject to the object is an essential one where the subject entraps the object, conferring a meaning on the object from which the object cannot escape. They therefore call for describing the possibility of the object's existence outside of its relations with any particular human being. Yet, most critique is more engaged with Hegelian interpretations of Kant, where the object-in-itself is the place where History with a big H reveals itself temporally, in human time, as Subject. In other words, Hegel reads the Kantian subject not as an individual human subject or the subject of finite experience but rather as a non-humanized or idealized spirit of knowledge-forms, or Consciousness, within which humans at a particular moment interact. Critique is not therefore giving up on fact—as Latour alleges— as much as saying that knowledge exists in History and that History is bigger than human scale, so that facts exist insomuch as they have limits. For critique, the thing-in-itself is not an unmediated fact that a guilty subject is ill-treating— as Felski and Meillassoux both accuse critique of—as much as an encounter with a fact registering more than its particular manifestation at a moment in history with a small h, or, that is, more than the individual's engagement with the thing in time. In the time of the Subject, critique is not the state of being in a bad mood because of the hardship and onerousness of having to ask questions but rather the possibilities offered in knowledge's reflections on itself in order to free itself from being confined to history in the moment, its finiteness. In other words, what antitheory is giving up in its purposeful misreading of critique's use of Kantian reason is critique's imperative—like Lizzie's with the diamonds—to engage fact while striving to free it from the domination of knowledge and its restricting temporalities, for the benefit of power. Antitheory wants to leave power alone and just describe it.

The antitheorists' turn to feeling and sensibility—which they say is lost to critique—seems to be their way of insisting on the separation of political and social things from individual experience and perception, in conformity with the reading of Kant they dislike but insist upon. This conclusion relies on a reading of Kantian experience as an isolated subject encountering the isolated object disinterestedly. The individual here represents the sensible body to itself as an immediacy. Yet, critique (including but not only Foucault's version of it) has already laid bare this reading of Kant for walling off sheer emotion and the senses away from taking account of the community of feeling—politics—that the object projects in sensibility. As Kant specifies, "the person making the judgment feels himself completely free with regard to the satisfaction that he devotes to the object, he cannot discover as grounds of the satisfaction any private conditions, pertaining to his subject alone, and must therefore regard it as grounded in those that he can presuppose in everyone else."[46] To experience the object demands a knowing, bigger than the individual, that limits the individual's certainty of itself. He goes on: "there must be attached to the judgment of taste, with the consciousness of an abstraction in it from all interest, a claim to validity for everyone without the universality that pertains to objects, i.e., it must be combined with a claim to subjective universality."[47] This universalizing subject may take the form of a prison, a clinic, or an asylum, with all the knowledge that circulates through those institutions, a knowledge that poses the individual judgment as both their effect and the limit of their reason. The subject of critique is the subject who does not restrict itself to knowing within the limits of its finite existence, earthly interest, and familiar institutional categories—that is, what it feels it knows through direct experience—but displaces those limits in acts of voluntary insubordination.

In today's political climate, we cannot afford to turn away from critique. Felski believes that the humanities needs to accommodate itself to the "what is" even if the "what is" is destructive to the humanities: "Faced with an accelerating skepticism about the uses of the humanities in a market-driven age, literary studies find themselves in the throes of a legitimation crisis, casting about for ways to justify their existence."[48] Despite what Felski says, close reading, pure description, and unmediated experience of texts are not going to fend off a "legitimation crisis" in literary studies in the face of market culture—in fact, literary studies is not really even facing a legitimation crisis at all but a defunding of educational institutions and a demonizing of educators, caused by market culture, that is part of an attack on critique involving Felski herself. When it casts the subject as an isolated body of sensibility, the subject's relation to the world is what demands critique. Just as Lizzie Eustace could not afford to accept conferrals of meaning on objects by social elites and financial enforcers, defenders, exploiters, administrators, and professionals, we must engage with facts to limit today's social and political rationalizations—the coercion of knowledge—in the face of which we should be skeptical, and we must keep asking how not to be governed *like that*. To say so feels simplistic and obvious. And yet, here we go again.

Notes

1   Michel Foucault, "What Is Critique?" *The Politics of Truth*, ed. Sylvère Lotringer, trans. Lysa Hochroth and Catherine Porter (Los Angeles: Semiotext(e), 2007), 51.
2   Ibid., 50.
3   Ibid., 44.
4   Ibid., 47.
5   Bruno Latour, "Has Critique Run Out of Steam?" *Critical Inquiry* (Winter 2004), 227.
6   Ibid., 229.
7   Ibid., 246.
8   Foucault, "What Is Critique?," 59.
9   "Foucault makes clear that what he seeks in the characterization of Enlightenment is precisely what remains unthought within its own terms" (Butler, "Critique," 789).
10 Ibid., 46.
11 Mary Poovey, *A History of the Modern Fact: Problems of Knowledge in the Sciences of Wealth and Society* (Chicago and London: The University of Chicago Press, 1998), xxv.
12 Anthony Trollope, *The Eustace Diamonds*, Revised Edition (New York: Penguin Classics, 2004), 42.

13 Alan Roth, "He Thought He Was Right (But Wasn't): Property Law in Anthony Trollope's 'The Eustace Diamonds,'" *Stanford Law Review* 44.4 (April 1992), 879.
14 As Walter Kendrick expresses it, Lizzie "is Trollope's attempt to represent realistically the opposite of realism" (Walter M. Kendrick, "The Eustace Diamonds: The Truth of Trollope's Fiction," *ELH* 46.1 [1979], 137).
15 Trollope, *The Eustace Diamonds*, 305, 309, 314 (e.g.).
16 Ibid., 151.
17 As Kendrick concludes, "If Lucy Morris ruled the world, there would be no novels in it" (Kendrick, "The Eustace Diamonds," 156).
18 Trollope, *The Eustace Diamonds*, 67.
19 Ibid., 295.
20 Ibid., 435.
21 Ibid., 495.
22 "If, however, only the particular is given, for which the universal is to be found, then the power of judgment is merely reflecting" (Immanuel Kant, *Critique of the Power of Judgment*, ed. Paul Guyer, trans. Paul Guyer and Eric Matthews [Cambridge, UK and New York: Cambridge University Press, 2000], 67). Another term of Kant's that might be useful here is "imagination": "The powers of cognition that are set into play by this representation are hereby in a free play, since no determinate concept restricts them to a particular rule of cognition" (Ibid., 102). The difference is that "reflecting judgment" is linked to an experience of nature as nature herself gives order, whereas the "imagination" is linked to the representations inside intuition.
23 Until 1867, when diamonds were discovered in South Africa and other colonies, all diamonds, including most prominently Queen Victoria's own, came from India and involved exploitative extraction, but the discovery of more mines meant that the precious jewels might find themselves in hands other than royal ones.
24 Jenny Sharpe, *Allegories of Empire: The Figure of Woman in the Colonial Text* (Minneapolis, MN and London: University of Minnesota Press, 1993), 4.
25 Ibid., 87.
26 Lauren M. E. Goodlad. *The Victorian Geopolitical Aesthetic: Realism, Sovereignty, and Transnational Experience* (Oxford, UK: Oxford University Press, 2015), 100.
27 The six Palliser novels compose Trollope's second series after his famous series, the Chronicles of Barsetshire (1855–1867). They span from *Can You Forgive Her?* in 1864 to *The Duke's Children* in 1879. Whereas the Barsetshire novels deal with politics among the clergy in villages, the Palliser novels focus on parliamentary politics, mostly in London but also in the country homes of the elite. *The Eustace Diamonds* is the third in the Palliser series.
28 Parliament would decide "as to whether the Sawab of Mygawb should have twenty millions of rupees paid to him and be placed upon the throne, or whether he should be kept in prison all his life" (Trollope, *The Eustace Diamonds*, 63).

29 According to Goodlad, Trollope was "at best ambivalent" (*Aesthetic*, 87) about British dominion in India even as he supported British territorial expansion through settlement in places like Canada, Australia, Ireland, and the West Indies, where he thought the indigenous populations would die out.
30 Trollope, *The Eustace Diamonds*, 647.
31 Ibid., 547–548.
32 Foucault, "What Is Critique?," 63.
33 Ibid., 45.
34 Latour, "Has Critique Run Out of Steam?," 231–232.
35 Rita Felski, *The Limits of Critique* (Chicago and London: The University of Chicago Press, 2015), 36.
36 Ibid., 17.
37 Ibid., 29.
38 Ibid., 31. She repeats this mechanically: "What sustains their [critics'] assurance that a text is withholding something of vital importance, that their task is to ferret out what lies concealed in its recesses and margins" (5).
39 Stefano Harney and Fred Moten, *The Undercommons: Fugitive Planning & Black Study* (Brooklyn, NY: Automedia, 2013), 98.
40 Quentin Meillassoux, *After Finitude: An Essay on the Necessity of Contingency*, trans. Ray Brassier (New York and London: Continuum, 2010), 3.
41 Ibid., 3.
42 Ibid.
43 Ibid.
44 Ibid., 4.
45 I thank my colleagues Aaron Jaffe, Raymond Stricklin, and Christopher Michaels for our lively discussions of these texts in 2018.
46 Kant, *Critique*, 96–97.
47 Ibid., 97.
48 Felski, *The Limits of Critique*, 14. Also: "Literary studies is currently facing a legitimation crisis, thanks to a sadly depleted language of value that leaves us struggling to find reasons why students should care about Beowulf or Baudelaire" (5).

Works Cited

Butler, Judith. "Critique, Dissent, Disciplinarity." *Critical Inquiry* 35.4 (Summer 2009): 773–795.

Felski, Rita. *The Limits of Critique*. Chicago and London: The University of Chicago Press, 2015.

Foucault, Michel. "What Is Critique?" *The Politics of Truth*. Ed. Sylvère Lotringer. Trans. Lysa Hochroth and Catherine Porter. Los Angeles: Semiotext(e), 2007.

Goodlad, Lauren M. E. *The Victorian Geopolitical Aesthetic: Realism, Sovereignty, and Transnational Experience*. Oxford, UK: Oxford University Press, 2015.

Harney, Stefano and Fred Moten. *The Undercommons: Fugitive Planning & Black Study*. Brooklyn, NY: Automedia, 2013.

Kant, Immanuel. *Critique of the Power of Judgment*. Ed. Paul Guyer. Trans. Paul Guyer and Eric Matthews. Cambridge, UK and New York: Cambridge University Press, 2000.

Kendrick, Walter. M. "The Eustace Diamonds: The Truth of Trollope's Fiction." *ELH* 46.1 (Spring 1979): 136–157.

Latour, Bruno. "Why Has Critique Run Out of Steam? From Matters of Fact to Matters of Concern." *Critical Inquiry* 30 (Winter 2004): 225–248.

Meillassoux, Quentin. *After Finitude: An Essay on the Necessity of Contingency*. Trans. Ray Brassier. New York and London: Continuum, 2010.

Poovey, Mary. *A History of the Modern Fact: Problems of Knowledge in the Sciences of Wealth and Society*. Chicago and London: The University of Chicago Press, 1998.

Roth, Alan. "He Thought He Was Right (But Wasn't): Property Law in Anthony Trollope's 'The Eustace Diamonds.'" *Stanford Law Review* 44.4 (April 1992): 879–897.

Sharpe, Jenny. *Allegories of Empire: The Figure of Woman in the Colonial Text*. Minneapolis, MN and London: University of Minnesota Press, 1993.

Trollope, Anthony. *The Eustace Diamonds*. Revised Edition. New York: Penguin Classics, 2004.

8

Antitheory in Postcolonial Perspective

Nicole Simek

It has become commonplace to note that postcolonial studies, like literary criticism more generally, has been traversing a crisis of conscience and methodology over the past decades, as scholars have questioned the purpose and efficacy of literary critique and pondered the future of the academy itself in precarious times. In the following pages, I would like to think through the relationship between debates internal to postcolonial studies and those playing out within the various antitheory strands of thought that have emerged in literary criticism under the banners of surface reading, distant reading, or description. These antihermeneutic trends all take issue with suspicion as a critical method and mood or affect and seek to overcome what they view as the hubristic excesses of the theory era: an overly confident belief in literary criticism's—and the literary critic's—contribution to emancipatory politics, a narrow and limiting antagonistic approach to its objects of analysis, and the contradictory reproduction of elitist hierarchies among critics ostensibly dedicated to democratization as an ideal. Postcolonial studies scholars have been raising similar questions about the adequacy of postcolonial models of critique for addressing new configurations of power in a globalized era—or, indeed, for rectifying older forms of colonial exploitation that proceeded apace despite the field's critical interventions. Yet given the field's investment in critique and a hermeneutics of suspicion, it is not surprising that postcolonial critics would evidence strong skepticism about the values of neutrality, interpretive-free or interpretive-light description, or the benevolence of algorithms and machine-assisted research invoked by thinkers like Franco Moretti or Stephen Best and Sharon Marcus.

Given the differences between, on the one hand, a postcritical position emphasizing the pursuit of "minimal critical agency" and "undistorted, complete descriptions," as Best and Marcus put it in their 2009 introduction to a special issue of *Representations* devoted to "The Way We Read Now,"[1] and a postcolonial position emphasizing, on the contrary, the ideological function of claims to neutrality and objectivity, it is striking that many of the stated aims or motivations of the antitheory turn seem to converge with those of the hermeneutic traditions they repudiate. In privileging neutral description over prescriptive critique, surface readers, for example, argue that we need to correct for theory's formulaic and instrumental use of texts in the service of a predefined political program. In so doing, they aim to cultivate a respect and openness to the text that is not so far removed from critical theory's desire to root out instrumental rationality, or postcolonial studies' goal of elucidating and reforming relations of domination and exploitation. My interest here is in exploring the appeal or pull of these converging and diverging lines of argument, the stakes that are held to be at play, and the kinds of investments that shape our various understandings of worth—our understandings of what questions are worth asking and why. This is as important for postcolonial critics who wish to extend or refresh the power of critique, as it is to descriptive readers who see suspicion as an obstacle or a drain on creative resources.

Beyond Crisis: Challenging Disappointment

A sense of present urgency marks much of the writing proposing a turn against or away from theory. While some of this concern can be attributed to a "fashion-conscious" drive toward the next new thing, as Bruce Robbins notes,[2] much stems as well from a sense of failure and fatigue as literary scholars take stock of the decline of stable employment opportunities in the profession, hostility toward public education in general and the university in particular on the political right, resurgent fascist movements across the globe, and the catastrophic warming of the planet—abetted, critics like Bruno Latour have argued, by the theory era's investment in an epistemological skepticism too easily coopted by climate change deniers and purveyors of alternative facts. "Entire Ph.D. programs are still running," Latour famously wrote in 2004, "to make sure that good American kids are learning the hard way that facts are made up, that there is no such thing as natural, unmediated, unbiased access to truth, ... and so on, while dangerous extremists are using the very same argument of social construction to destroy hard-won evidence that could save our lives."[3] Similarly commenting on the lessons of the George W. Bush presidency, Best and Marcus note that the "demystifying protocols" of a hermeneutics of suspicion seem "superfluous in an era when images of torture at Abu Ghraib and elsewhere were immediately circulated on the internet," when "the real-time coverage of Hurricane Katrina showed in ways that required little explication the state's abandonment of its African American citizens; and many people instantly recognized as lies political statements such as 'mission accomplished.'"[4] In his contribution to Elizabeth S. Anker and Rita Felski's collection, *Critique and Postcritique*, Eric Hayot likewise observes of the crisis facing higher education in the United States:

> One no longer needs the Marx of *The German Ideology* or even Althusser theorizing the ideological state apparatus to understand that conservatives in the United States want to destroy not only the humanities but indeed the entire apparatus of scientific research, and that this desire stems not only from a political resentment (of, e.g., research on climate change) but from an understanding that such a project would allow for the creation of a more vulnerable and hence more pliable class of worker-citizens.[5]

Yet while drawn to the idea of moving beyond critique, Hayot underlines the importance of historicizing this current antitheory moment—and of questioning the governing paradigm of crisis that informs it—before attempting to move toward new, post-theory modes of analysis. Movements that style themselves as messianic breakthroughs overcoming a theory become repetitive, predictable, or toothless in the contemporary moment rely on an often implicit, assumed periodization that necessarily impacts our understanding of what counts as contemporary and how that present is related to the past and future. Noting the weight given to the Bush regime as evidence of the need to move beyond critique in both Latour's and in Best and Marcus's pieces, Hayot wonders about the underlying logics involved in taking this particular example as support for a shift in critical approaches. "What theory of historical presentness," he asks, "allows the extended anecdotal example of an eight-year presidency in the United States to justify arguments about philosophical method?... Imagine what things would look like," he suggests, "if 'contemporary' meant fifty or even one hundred years."[6]

Antitheory movements, Hayot argues, risk repeating the same modes of historicizing—the same "logic of succession and decline," the same "frantic representation of elegy and crisis"—marking the way scholars in the 1970s and 1980s conceptualized the series of competing theoretical schools and thinkers following closely on one another's heels.[7] If we are to avoid foreclosing futures by reproducing preconceived interpretive frameworks, if we are to avoid "adopting too readily historical models (and models of affective relation to history) that determine in advance our understanding," Hayot continues, we must give an account not just of the overlapping personal, disciplinary, institutional, and global political structures and movements that have led to the decision to move beyond theory but also of the theory of history underpinning our historicization itself, "a theory of history that ... gestures also toward the possibility of a new future, that contains, therefore, a concept of futurity itself, of the kind of future that can exist, and a theory of how one gets there."[8]

Hayot's intervention resonates with that of David Scott, who also foregrounds historicization as a problem of both relating to the past and imagining the future in his push for postcolonial studies to renew its critical edge. In his 2004 book, *Conscripts of Modernity*, Scott proposes the concept of problem-space as a means for orienting postcolonial criticism in ways that help maintain the field's vitality that help generate "new and unexpected horizons of possibility," as he puts it.[9] A problem-space is first "a discursive context, a context of language," but more than that, it is a horizon of investment and struggle, "an ensemble of questions and answers around which a horizon of identifiable stakes (conceptual as well as ideological-political stakes) hangs."[10] If we recall, Scott argues, that a problem-space is "a context of argument and, therefore, one of *intervention*," we can begin to shift our interpretation of the past—the objects we choose to analyze and, especially, the questions we ask about them, in ways that help us intervene in the present.[11] Criticism's capacity to effect change hinges first, Scott contends, on the questions we ask, not just the answers we develop. We need to be concerned not just about truth but, strategically, about which truths—which questions and answers—most urgently need exploration and argument. "Problem-spaces alter historically, because problems are not timeless and do not have everlasting shapes," writes Scott. "In new historical conditions old questions may lose their salience, their bite." Thus, postcolonial criticism, as he puts it, "ought always to seek to clarify whether and to what extent the questions it is trying to answer continue to be questions worth having answers to."[12] What, as he puts it later, are our readings of the past and present "meant to do" or "enable" within the discursive contexts of our problem-spaces?[13]

What is at stake in the problem-space Scott seeks to intervene in is the future of the new nations created out of the mid-twentieth-century anticolonial movements, nations that, in his view, have hit a dead end, that have exhausted their creative energy and political imagination, that are plagued by corruption and authoritarianism, and that are deploying "old languages of moral-political vision and hope" out-of-step with current conditions.[14] In rereading C. L. R. James's seminal study of the Haitian Revolution, *The Black Jacobins*, Scott seeks to refashion postcolonial scholars' understanding of modernity and the ways in which they read revolutionary anticolonialism within the story of modernity they tell. Postcolonial scholars, influenced by an older anticolonialist perspective shaped by a pre independence horizon of struggle for liberation and therefore concerned with demonstrating the capacity of the oppressed for actively resisting European power, have criticized James's study for paying too much attention to European values over the agency of the resisters and the African cultural heritage on which such agency rested. Yet to focus on the question of slave resistance today, within a different, postcolonial horizon or problem-space, Scott argues, is to obscure the more strategically important question: How European power changed the very conditions for action themselves? "What is at stake here," he writes, "is not whether the colonized accommodated or resisted, but how colonial power transformed the ground on which accommodation or resistance was possible in the first place, how colonial power reshaped or reorganized the conceptual and institutional conditions of possibility for social action and its understanding."[15] Shifting our focus to these questions allows us to reread the story of anticolonial revolution (James's and others') with different expectations in mind, which alters not only what we see there (a sufficient or insufficient attention to the Africanist basis for slave agency versus a sufficient or insufficient analysis of the conditions of modernity shaping West Indian subjectivity and action) but also our affective response to it, and more precisely, "the nature of the dissatisfactions we come away from it with."[16]

What comes to the foreground in Scott's argument is a concern for reconsidering the hope critics place in clean breaks, in the revolutionary act that sweeps away the old to make room for a new order, and also the paralysis or despair that arises when older questions and answers no longer speak to our reality. Significantly, as Scott repeats at several points, revising our questions does not necessarily require viewing the previous answers as wrong or operating a break with prior critics; rather, what Scott proposes here is a shift in focus and sense of purpose, a different attention to continuities between past and present—an attention that then shapes the paths we are able to conceive as leading to different futures.

Hayot, too, provocatively questions the nature of critical dissatisfaction evidenced in the turn away from theory in the new millennium:

> To declare ... that the old ways are tired, and new ones are needed, is a gesture of the most profound historical provincialism, and a failure of the historical imagination. The truly radical thing, the truly insane gesture, would be to imagine ourselves a relation to the disappointing past that would be essentially

continuous. At which point the terms of the disappointment would surely also have to be reimagined and rewritten.[17]

Significantly, what Hayot argues here is not that we must refuse disappointment, which would be tantamount to refusing to learn from it. Rather, it is our relation to disappointment that we must examine. As Hayot states clearly, his disappointment and boredom with theory, and critique, have led him to question his life's work and the entire endeavor of teaching, of passing on to students "an empty, broken practice" that leads only to "the miseries of disappointed hope."[18] Yet, he continues, in a striking passage:

> I want—I want, in a gesture that for me is pretheoretical, and whose desire has not yet been fully understood—to be suspicious of that disappointment, to be wary of its conservatism and its self-indulgence, to remember the Gramscian lesson of the optimism of the will. And to be suspicious, more intellectually, of the too-rapid abandonment of ideas that, in my reading, my writing, my teaching, still have the power to create hope, to alter relations to the world, to be suspicious also of the ways in which we do not challenge ourselves enough to rethink the basic historical presumptions that we allow to govern us, many of which can be subsumed under the general rubric of the then and the now.[19]

Disappointment challenges: we must both challenge the basis of our disappointment and also accept the challenge of living and thinking in disappointment, of stumbling on the blocks it throws in our path, potentially altering our trajectories and our energies.[20] We must also, Hayot argues, situate that disappointment in relation to multiple histories moving at different paces and structured by differing periodicities and shapes (parabolic rises and falls, but also cyclical repetitions or irregular, nonlinear paths)—the developments of our individual lives and careers as we move from youth to midlife to end-of-life; the histories of the academic institutions and disciplines in which we work; the movements of global economics and politics—in order to avoid both misattributing and neglecting relations of causality between world historical events, institutional changes, disciplinary fashions, and psycho biographical dynamics.

The Politics of Description

In directing our attention to the affects of theorizing and to the entanglement of theory and post- or antitheoretical projects, Hayot's and Scott's work echoes some of the points Eve Kosofsky Sedgwick made in her influential essay on paranoid reading and reparative reading, an essay that has served as a source of inspiration for postcritical readers. What Sedgwick highlights in her essay are the ways that privileged modes of knowing can fail performatively, can fail to produce progressive effects regardless of the truths they uncover. Speaking of AIDS activism, and the critical energies one might devote to tracing out the structural inequalities and systemic forms of discrimination that led to the epidemic's spread, Sedgwick muses that "whether or not to undertake this compelling tracing-and-exposure project represents a strategic and local decision, not necessarily a categorical imperative."[21] Paranoia—the "terrible alertness" to danger and self-defensive anticipation of danger, of bad news— both reveals and overlooks truths.[22] Paranoia, Sedgwick argues, "knows some things well and other things poorly"; the mode of "vigilant scanning" deployed by feminists and queers enables us to engage some practices of violence better than others.[23] Namely, exposing hidden violence is most efficacious, she observes, in a "cultural context ... in which violence would be deprecated and hence hidden in the first place."[24] One problem we face today is that some forms of violence are "hypervisible," and the struggle against them is a struggle not, then, to make them visible and graspable, but "to displace and redirect ... its aperature of visibility."[25] Commenting on examples of torture and mass rape intended to terrorize and serve as warnings, Sedgwick asks, "What does a hermeneutics of suspicion and exposure have to say to social formations in which visibility itself constitutes much of the violence?"[26] But moreover, the exercise of violence—both judicial and extrajudicial—is not always deprecated and does not always scandalize. In such a framework, a framework in which violence is desired, is viewed with satisfaction, exposure of a violent practice itself may fail to surprise, disturb, or motivate, may fail to register. The question facing critics is not whether or not paranoid reading can reveal truths, but rather whether these truths are the ones most urgent to know in a given place and time, in a given problem-space.

As Sedgwick repeatedly stresses, reparative practices—practices of relating and building up—"infuse" paranoid projects of critique; pleasure and depression, following Melanie Klein, are interdependent, and "paranoid exigencies" as Sedgwick writes, "... are often necessary for nonparanoid knowing and utterance."[27] The task at hand is to inhabit and negotiate both of these positions, to draw from the resources of both. This task is in part an epistemological one, but also very much a political one concerned with the purchase criticism has or not on the life of the polis, on the way we live—or die—together.

Yet what critics mean by politics, and how they see the relationship between literary criticism, epistemology, and politics remains a major source of contention in debates over the modes of reading that have emerged in opposition to, or in the wake of, theory.[28] It is in the name of better, more effective politics that scholars like Latour advocate a renewed focus on ontology (an interest in the non-human world of objects) to correct for the cooptation by extremists of the epistemological concerns of the theory era (a preoccupation with mediation), or that Elizabeth S. Anker, writing from the perspective of a scholar in law and literature studies, argues for a critical agenda that recognizes both the disabling but also the enabling functions of different legal regimes in their service of justice, and that "develop[s] metrics gauged to meticulously and rigorously discriminate between just and unjust social realities."[29] Still other articulations of the goals of postcritique highlight instead goals of neutrality, objectivity, or non-bias that can sound very much like a withdrawal from politics altogether. One goal of surface readers, as Best and Marcus describe it, is to find "ways of studying culture that would neither attack nor defend it," to adopt a position of descriptive "neutrality" towards objects of study, where one would refrain from evaluation and "refuse to celebrate or condemn them."[30] As they put it in a later piece coauthored with Heather Love, scholars working in this vein seek to bracket judgment, to honor and "bear witness" to the object of study, and "to experiment with what it might mean to describe, explain, and analyze rather than to theorize or critique."[31] If depth hermeneutics seeks to account for hidden structures, for that which goes unaccounted for, obscured by ideology and habit, surface reading aims to account better for that which "eludes observation" because it parades in plain sight, to account for that which depth hermeneutics fails to notice in its pursuit of what lies below the obvious or evident.[32] Such an accounting is designed to overcome "selectivity" and improve accuracy, to get critics closer to facts, to truth.[33] Surface readers take issue with what they view as an overly deterministic political agenda that dictates interpretation in advance, and, using language that echoes much postcolonial thought, Best and Marcus call for an attentiveness to texts and particulars that does not assume that ideology will take a particular form within them: "We think," they assert, "that a true openness to all the potentials made available by texts is also prerequisite to an attentiveness that does not reduce them to instrumental means to an end and is the best way to say anything accurate and true about them."[34] Such a claim indicts a kind of false openness to texts, a failure of openness that, in this instance, is really only an openness to that which in a text can verify, or be made to verify, prefabricated claims about the obfuscations of ideology, the force of hidden structures, or the authenticity of suppressed histories. No matter the motivation, to read in effect with an eye *only* for hidden meanings amounts to a failure to account for texts, to be accountable to their difference and their surprises.

The vocabulary of objectivity and neutrality that Best and Marcus deploy can be puzzling or even infuriating to postcolonial critics who have strenuously worked to show how description is not value-neutral, but functions normatively and violently—in the power-knowledge relations linking colonial ethnography and colonial governance, for example. As postcolonial scholar Christopher L. Miller has put it, "Few undertakings have proven more prone to ethical pitfalls than the description of other peoples."[35] Neutrality so strongly evokes positivist conceptions of science as a disinterested march towards objective truth, that the stated goals of its proponents—commitment to a kind of freedom and ethical respect for particular—seem disingenuous. At the same time, surface readers look askance at the postcolonial field's similarly motivated commitment to self-reflexive distancing, hearing in calls for such distancing a regressive mind-body, cognitive-affective dualism, a form of dualism that bolsters the individual knowing subject at the expense of relationality. The debate here ends up circling around mutual accusations of mastery. While antisuspicion critics denounce the assumption of a privileged, masterful viewpoint implied by the activities of demystification and denaturalization, postcolonial studies has privileged modernist aesthetic techniques foregrounding self-reflexivity as the means by which critical thought and agency become available to increasingly broader audiences. As Rey Chow notes, self-reflexive techniques aim to make thinking—and attendant forms of political agency—visible and available to all: "the point of the [Brechtian] alienation effect is to politicize reflexivity by making it *vulgar*: thought is no longer deep and refined, but crude; it sticks out where you least expect it to; it takes on unsubtle, obtrusive shapes."[36] Within such a horizon, which associates the disturbance of aesthetic absorption not with mastery but with a check on mastery, a check on entrenched powers and habits of thought, extolling the virtues of neutrality and literal-mindedness appears not as a means of disrupting the current status quo, but rather as a return to the old, as a disavowal of the inherent partiality of every act of representation.

Best and Marcus anticipate such a reaction in their 2009 piece, noting that "surface reading, which strives to describe texts accurately, might easily be dismissed as politically quietist, too willing to accept things as they are."[37] To this, they counter that surface reading and description are often, first, very much invested in freedom (though this freedom is conceived variously by different proponents as a freedom to anti-instrumental aesthetic or intellectual enjoyment, as a freedom to study a wider range of objects, or as a freedom from a pre-given political agenda), and second, compatible with critique. At the same time, within surface reading they also observe emerging trends in tension with these investments, including a "political realism about the revolutionary capacities of texts and critics, and doubts about whether we could ever attain the heightened perspicacity that would allow us to see fully beyond ideology" as well as "a skepticism about the very project of freedom, or about any kind of transcendent value we might use to justify intellectual work."[38] On this view, politics has too often been equated in critique with revolutionary politics (and, allegedly, with a naive belief in the critic's capacity to stand outside ideology) and defined as the goal of literary criticism (or "intellectual work" more broadly), which then in turn determines the direction of the analysis regardless of the example at hand.

The skepticism of skepticism described in this short passage evokes a host of consequential lines of inquiry for any debate over the future and goals of literary studies. These include the nature of ideology and how to traverse it; the nature and efficacy of revolutionary versus progressive or incremental politics and the priority we should accord to one or the other; the relationship between philosophical realism (observable in the New Materialist and descriptive ontological turns in the humanities) and political realism (a term with multiple and varied vernacular and theoretical understandings); the transcendental versus immanent bases on which disciplinary or institutional values are founded (impacting teaching, research, and labor practices more generally); and the broad, long-standing question of the precise ways in which knowledge-power nexuses—dynamic, mobile nexuses—take shape in a given moment, shifting the valences and effects of what we deem political, apolitical, or nonpartisan stances.

From a postcolonial perspective, then, a basic yet crucial question for literary criticism remains, in what relationship to politics does the pursuit of knowledge stand? But if this question is to give any traction to debates over our collective critical endeavors, it must be taken seriously as an unsettled question, as an inquiry into the precise dynamics of our moment (including the temporal boundaries of that moment), not simply as an occasion to recall that the study of literature inevitably unfolds within relations that are inescapably political and economic. This latter point certainly bears repeating (especially in the face of arguments claiming that the field is inconsequential and unworthy of student time, effort, or funding), yet it is not sufficient. In the context at hand, in what precise circumstances, we should ask, under what horizons, does a postcritical approach to literary texts constitute a resistant practice of freedom (one in which, as Best and Marcus put it, summarizing Marjorie Levinson, aesthetic absorption "frees us from the apathy and instrumentality of capitalism by allowing us to bathe in the artwork's disinterested purposelessness"[39]), a democratizing expansion of the aesthetic attachments critics consider worthy of upholding rather than denigrating (a concern of Rita Felski's *The Limits of Critique*[40]), or, conversely, a renunciation—be it politically realist or quietist—of the notion that literature and literary criticism have any direct or indirect purchase on moral values or political pursuits such as freedom and democracy?

Facts and Friction

Returning to the unsettling question of how scholars should respond to the cooptation of skepticism for environmentally destructive, authoritarian, and racist ends, I would like to end by fleshing out some ways in which we might define our contemporary problem-space, with the goal of discerning how we might work dialectically with the resources of critical and reparative, prescriptive and descriptive modes of interpretation, how we might locate and walk, as Terry Eagleton puts it, the "narrow line between cynicism and credulity."[41] To do so, I would like first to reconsider an anecdote with which Christopher L. Miller launches his 1985 book, *Blank Darkness: Africanist Discourses in French*, an insightful work of critique that builds on Edward Said's *Orientalism* to study the processes of desire and distortion at work in European accounts of Africa.[42]

Miller's study begins with a question about a paradox:

> In the middle of the nineteenth century a book about Africa was published in France. It purported to contain "information" and was written in a style of scientistic precision. The title was *Renseignements sur l'Afrique centrale et sur une race de Niam-Niam ou "hommes à queue" qui s'y trouverait, d'après les nègres du Soudan* [*Information on Central Africa, and on a nation of Niam-Niams or 'men with tails' who are said to live there, according to the Negroes of the Sudan*]. Many centuries after Herodotus had reported that Africa was filled with "dog-eared men, and the headless that have eyes in their chests," when a discourse of purified realism called science had supposedly distinguished itself from fable, how was this possible?[43]

The ensuing, animated academic debate over the existence of Africans with tails—involving French scholars at the Société de Géographie de Paris, the Académie des Sciences, and the Société Orientale—is just one example Miller cites of the ways mistaken assumptions—assumptions about the monstrosity of Africans—shape our perception of evidence, leading in this case to perceiving leather clothing shaped like tails as anatomical tails. Colonial history abounds with other examples of scientific conclusions based on what today would seem like obviously false data. For example, Miller writes, "Empirical evidence, readily available and highly valued in eighteenth-century England, somehow conformed to Edward Long's claim that 'Europeans and Negroes did not belong to the same species,' and therefore that 'mulattoes were unfertile hybrids.'"[44] Such errors cannot simply be attributed to the role of fantasy and distortion in retransmissions and second-hand retellings; as Miller points out, Edward Long "was a resident of Jamaica, living in the midst of a slave population," and would thus have had ample occasion to observe evidence to the contrary.[45] Similarly, Enlightenment contemporaries like the Abbé Demanet could claim, in a dissertation on physics, that black babies are born white and that black people turn white when they die, claims that defy what should have been easily known at the time.[46]

How does a society like that of France's nineteenth-century scientific community come to hold contradictory beliefs? Under what circumstances do people who value procedures like testing assumptions, weighing evidence, comparing testimonies, and correcting hypotheses when new evidence disproves them come to accept fable as fact? Looking back at the Niam-Niam example helps bring into relief some interpretive dilemmas that we face today as a community. In tracing the history of long-standing and pervasive ideas about Africa that persisted in Europe despite the accumulation of data, despite increased cultural contact and multiple opportunities to disprove earlier fables, we can extrapolate some lines of inquiry pertinent to contemporary circumstances: we can look, for example, at how knowledge was disseminated, how academic and political institutions contributed to reproducing old ideas. Yet what stands out most urgently in this example, however, is not that it highlights (once again) that knowledge is always produced in a social context and dependent on the values, priorities, and preconceptions at play in that context. Rather, the Niam-Niam debate shows that if skepticism and realism can produce similar factual errors, the antidote to the one is not always the other. Put differently, reestablishing trust in realism may not be the only or primary issue at stake in the problems of climate change denial, ascendant fascisms, and hypervisible state or nonstate acts of violence and repression. Indeed, as the infamous term "alternative facts" suggests, the problem is not so much an absolute form of skepticism—the belief that knowledge of truth is impossible—but rather a trust in "facts" (and those who claim to know them) that lend support to the fantasies structuring the psychic and social realities of the believers—particularly in the absence of a common understanding or literacy in the specialized procedures by which evidence is gathered and tested, and conclusions supported, revised, and refined. While skepticism leads us, sometimes to our peril, to reopen otherwise settled debates, belief also shuts down skepticism, stubbornly resisting salutary debate, segregating and insulating communities from interpretive friction and argument. Just as skepticism must resist congealing into a simplified caricature of itself, today's new realisms cannot afford to do without skepticism, without engaging with the very production of observations, arguments, and evidence— the dialogical constitution of shared understandings that we come to call truth.

The role of friction in this continual renegotiation—and the problem of self-segregation and insulation from debate—is difficult to overstate in our current moment. The interrelation of paranoid and reparative practices, of readings that perform the dismantling or smashing work of taking apart, of analyzing, on the one hand, and those that put together, relate, and join, on the other, does *not* mean that a happy and static methodological synthesis awaits us just over the horizon. There is no sure-fire, "mid-level" reading practice between the close and the distant, between the deep and the shallow, the realist and the critical, that could escape this dynamism, that we could rest on. Still less, I believe, have we arrived at a moment in which criticism can annihilate itself, standing aside to allow texts, objects, or data to speak for themselves, as if meaning could simply manifest, unmediated. Quite the contrary, interrelationality is also incommensurabilty, and the persistence of difference, of the difference between making and unmaking, highlights the dynamism and unpredictability of interpretation, the intricacies of shifting problem-spaces. In what sorts of practices and modes of knowing efficacy lies should remain an unsettled question, continually asked and asked again.

Notes

1 Stephen Best and Sharon Marcus, "Surface Reading: An Introduction," *Representations* 108 (2009): 17, 18.
2 Bruce Robbins, "Fashion Conscious Phenomenon," *American Book Review* 38.5 (2017): 5.
3 Bruno Latour, "Why Has Critique Run Out of Steam? From Matters of Fact to Matters of Concern," *Critical Inquiry* 30.2 (2004): 227.
4 Best and Marcus, "Surface Reading," 2.

5   Eric Hayot, "Then and Now," in *Critique and Postcritique*, ed. Elizabeth S. Anker and Rita Felski (Durham: Duke University Press, 2017), 291.
6   Ibid., 291.
7   Ibid., 288, 289.
8   Ibid., 293.
9   David Scott, *Conscripts of Modernity* (Durham: Duke University Press, 2004), 1.
10 Ibid., 4.
11 Ibid.
12 Ibid.
13 Ibid., 108.
14 Ibid., 2.
15 Ibid., 119.
16 Ibid., 130.
17 Hayot, "Then and Now," 289.
18 Ibid., 293.
19 Ibid., 294.
20 In a similar vein, Simon Critchley states that "philosophy begins in disappointment," with the realization, that is, of the impossibility of absolute knowledge, our lack of direct access to the world of things, and our own finitude (Simon Critchley, *Infinitely Demanding: Ethics of Commitment, Politics of Resistance* [London: Verso, 2007], 1).
21 Eve Kosofsky Sedgwick, "Paranoid Reading and Reparative Reading, or, You're So Paranoid, You Probably Think This Essay Is about You," in *Touching Feeling* (Durham: Duke University Press, 2003), 124.
22 Ibid., 128.
23 Ibid., 130, 132.
24 Ibid., 140.
25 Ibid.
26 Ibid.
27 Ibid., 129.
28 For a critical assessment of these modes of reading within a feminist context, see also Nicole Simek, "Reading," in *The Bloomsbury Handbook of Twenty-First Century Feminist Theory*, ed. Robin Goodman (New York: Bloomsbury, 2019).
29 Elizabeth S. Anker, "Postcritique and Social Justice," *American Book Review* 38.5 (2017): 10.
30 Best and Marcus, "Surface Reading," 17, 18.
31 Sharon Marcus, Heather Love and Stephen Best, "Building a Better Description," *Representations* 135.1 (2016): 3.
32 Best and Marcus, "Surface Reading," 18.
33 Ibid., 17.

34   Ibid., 16.
35   Christopher L. Miller, *Theories of Africans: Francophone Literature and Anthropology in Africa* (Chicago: University of Chicago Press, 1990), 34.
36   Rey Chow, *Entanglements, or Transmedial Thinking about Capture* (Durham: Duke University Press, 2012), 24.
37   Best and Marcus, "Surface Reading," 16.
38   Ibid.
39   Ibid., 14.
40   Rita Felski, *The Limits of Critique* (Chicago: University of Chicago Press, 2015).
41   Terry Eagleton, "Not Just Anybody," review of *The Limits of Critique* by Rita Felski, *London Review of Books* 39.1 (2017).
42   Christopher L. Miller, *Blank Darkness: Africanist Discourses in French* (Chicago: University of Chicago Press, 1985).
43   Miller, *Blank Darkness*, 3.
44   Ibid., 21.
45   Ibid.
46   Ibid.

Works Cited

Anker, Elizabeth S. "Postcritique and Social Justice." *American Book Review* 38. 5 (2017): 9–10.

Best, Stephen and Sharon Marcus. "Surface Reading: An Introduction." *Representations* 108 (2009): 1–21.

Chow, Rey. *Entanglements, or Transmedial Thinking about Capture*. Durham: Duke University Press, 2012.

Critchley, Simon. *Infinitely Demanding: Ethics of Commitment, Politics of Resistance*. London: Verso, 2007.

Eagleton, Terry. "Not Just Anybody." Review of *The Limits of Critique* by Rita Felski. *London Review of Books* 39.1 (2017).

Felski, Rita. *The Limits of Critique*. Chicago: University of Chicago Press, 2015.

Hayot, Eric. "Then and Now." In *Critique and Postcritique*. Ed. Elizabeth S. Anker and Rita Felski. Durham: Duke University Press, 2017. 279–295.

Latour, Bruno. "Why Has Critique Run Out of Steam? From Matters of Fact to Matters of Concern." *Critical Inquiry* 30.2 (2004): 225–248.

Marcus, Sharon, Heather Love, and Stephen Best. "Building a Better Description." *Representations* 135.1 (2016): 1–21.

Miller, Christopher L. *Blank Darkness: Africanist Discourses in French*. Chicago: University of Chicago Press, 1985.

Miller, Christopher L. *Theories of Africans: Francophone Literature and Anthropology in Africa*. Chicago: University of Chicago Press, 1990.

Robbins, Bruce. "Fashion Conscious Phenomenon." *American Book Review* 38.5 (2017): 5–6.

Scott, David. *Conscripts of Modernity: The Tragedy of Colonial Enlightenment*. Durham: Duke University Press, 2004.

Sedgwick, Eve Kosofsky. "Paranoid Reading and Reparative Reading, or, You're So Paranoid, You Probably Think This Essay Is about You." In *Touching Feeling*. Durham: Duke University Press, 2003.

Simek, Nicole. "Reading." In *The Bloomsbury Handbook of Twenty-First Century Feminist Theory*. Ed. Robin Goodman. New York: Bloomsbury, 2019.

Eaten Alive, or, Why the Death of Theory Is Not Antitheory

Christian Haines

Theory kills. This is the shorthand version of Lisa Ruddick's argument in "When Nothing Is Cool," an essay that attributes to critical theory the power to throw students into a state of "confusion, inhibition and loss"—a general existential "malaise" not unlike the passive vertigo of Meursault in Albert Camus's *L'Étranger*. Ruddick argues that "the anti-individualist ideology of left postmodernism" undermines the integrity of the inner self and, in doing so, contributes to the atrophy of moral faculties. To be clear, Ruddick isn't making the argument of an Allan Bloom or a Lynn Cheney; she doesn't lament the loss of a stable Western tradition, nor does she bemoan the rise of identity politics. Instead, she stakes her claims on the level of affect. Her aim is to rescue a version of the humanities that would shelter passionate attachments to objects of study (especially literature) and that would allow the individual subject to grow, to revitalize herself, through the activity of criticism. In contrast, the theoretical humanities obey a "drive to flatten anything (except politics) that might nourish a human being with its aliveness."[1] Too busy attempting to achieve a posture of "academic cool," theory-driven (anti-)humanists sacrifice the liveliness of students to the altar of professional advancement.

There is much one could criticize in Ruddick's essay. It constructs a series of reductive oppositions between the individual and collective, the concrete and abstract, the warm and the cold. Such categorical distinctions do little justice to artistic or cultural practices, especially those invested in estranging us from our habits of perception, nor do they serve as an adequate basis for understanding social life, including the group dynamics of the classroom. Ruddick also models the ideal version of the connection between scholar and text on the basis of heteronormative romance, elaborating an implicit analogy between study and long-term monogamy. Not only does this analogy risk complicity with structural violence against queer life, it also suggests a conservative mode of study, one whose tenderness toward its object implies maintenance of the status quo. Passion, in this context, is passion for self-sameness, for repetition that consolidates identity, rather than disrupting it. All that being said, I want to call attention to a certain truth in Ruddick's words. Ruddick is right to associate theory with death. There is a mortification proper to theory, a death-work that is related to mourning and elegy. Ruddick uses a figure of speech that is telling in this regard. "[S]omething in this intellectual environment," she writes of passionate English majors, "is *eating them alive*" (emphasis added).[2] The image of a student's flesh being torn apart by a theorist's fangs is perhaps too literal a reading of "eating them alive," but it does call attention to a peculiarity in Ruddick's argument, namely, that theory is a place in which life and death mix together. Theory lives in and on the zone of indistinction between life and death. It situates itself in the moment when life passes over into death but also, conversely, in the space in which death creeps into life. Theory rarely kills, but it does "sacrifice," and the ritualistic dimension of the latter term makes a difference. Theory is a ritual of self-destruction, or identity overload, but it is also a ritual of rebirth and revitalization. Theory mortifies, but, in death's midst, it enables new life to appear.

Ruddick identifies theory with death not only in the sense that it deadens students but also in the sense that theory itself is dead, or, more precisely, undead—a creature shuffling on after its own demise. Theory, after all, was declared dead years ago. The obituaries of theory are numerous, ranging from Walter Benn Michaels and Steven Knapp's well-known screed regarding the logical fallacies of contemporary critical theory to Terry Eagleton's Marxist call to substitute tragic morality for postmodern relativism to the *New York Times*' mean-spirited and obtuse obituary for Jacques Derrida.[3] John Mowitt has described these constantly renewed burial rites as "offering theory," a phrase that plays on several senses of "offering," including "to off" (to murder; to dispose of), "to give or gift" (to act out of generosity, to surrender over, but also to transmit and, in doing so, to put the other into one's debt) and, finally, "to sacrifice" (to ritualistically end the life of; to reproduce the *polis* by executing specific forms of life).[4] Theory is not in decay—its decline is neither steady nor irreversible—rather it lives its own death, renews itself by way of its expiration. Mowitt crystallizes the living death of theory in the figure of "Limbo":

> If theory must be repeatedly killed anew, it is because it stubbornly survives its death. In fact, given the cycle of reviling and reviving theory—for every, "Against Theory" or *In Theory* there is an equal or greater *Theory as Resistance* or *The*

Future of Theory—I think we are obliged to draw the conclusion that theory has assumed the restless, even perpetually agitated, status of the living dead. Theory is not simply in Limbo, it *is* Limbo in the sense that it has come to designate the zone of indistinction, the *limbus*, between life and its others.[5]

Mowitt's analysis addresses the institutional position of theory, as well as the demand or obligation that it places on teachers: the "legacy" of theory—the rubric under which Mowitt writes—is such that the representatives of theory (for instance, the professor tasked with teaching an English Department's "Introduction to Literary Theory") becomes a bearer of death, a figure of the place in which life becomes indistinguishable from its others. It is this professor who asks her students to face the mutability of existence, the historicity of first principles, the ideological nature of even the most common-sense principles; it's this professor, in other words, who replaces assumptions regarding the given—assumptions that not infrequently sustain certain passions—with interrogation of the categories of thought. This sort of reflection does involve at least a symbolic, if not a literal, death, because it redefines what we mean by life; it asks not so much that one discard personal identity as allow that identity might be a contingent matter, less foundational substance than fiction with ambivalent effects. From this perspective, Ruddick's complaint against theory is a reaction formation in respect to the death that is immanent to theory; Ruddick attempts to separate out life and death, passion and speculation, literature and philosophy, by repressing the vitality (and, I would add, the pleasure) of theory's death.

Mowitt makes a critical distinction between thinking that grapples with the properly theoretical intimacy between life and death and thinking that transforms theory into bare life. The former comportment acknowledges that the generosity of theory—the gift of thought that it offers, its surplus in respect to the knowing and the known—is not without cost; theory demands its pound of flesh, which is to say that it conscripts the subject of thought—student and teacher alike—into a sacrificial economy: one surrenders oneself to speculation, to the virtual domain of thought, and, in doing so, abandons the security of certainty in knowledge. I confess to extending Mowitt's own thinking beyond the parameters it declares for itself by suggesting that the economy of sacrifice that Mowitt sketches involves the productive dismembering of student life: students cannot learn theory without sacrificing themselves—their security in their sense of self, their confidence in their assumptions—to theory's insights. In contrast, the other comportment—call it antitheory—does not so much sacrifice theory as foreclose it; it transports theory to a zone of abandonment in which theory can be killed without ceremony. (Mowitt draws on Giorgio Agamben's theorization of bare life as the disavowed ground of sovereignty.⁶) This manner of administering the life and death of thought secures the student against theory not so much by concealing certain texts, thinkers, or concepts but rather by eliminating the theoretical impulse as such. The health of the student body depends, in this instance, on a preemptive strike against the alterity of theory. "Antitheory" thus names not the death of theory but the foreclosure of it. It is one thing to suggest, for example, that deconstruction has run its course insofar as its meditations on textuality have failed to adequately account for racialized alterity.⁷ It is quite another to suggest that the passion for literature depends on securing the classroom and, by implication, the academy from theory in the first place. The annihilation of theory is thus distinct from its death, for while the latter contributes to theory by ritually ending it so that it might begin again, the former leaves no space for theory. It seals thinking off from theory in the name of security.

In this chapter's remainder, I consider the scene of theory as a drama of life and death, gift and sacrifice, subjectivization and desubjectivization. The following section contends that the recent valorization of critical "modesty," announced by the turn to surface reading, description, and postcriticism, constitutes a mode of antitheory insofar as, in privileging the vitality of the given over the paucity of the virtual, it preempts speculation and allows lines of theoretical inquiry to go into attrition. These polemics against critique involve a fantasy of self-presence—specifically, a fantasy of the object's presence to itself without mediation—that is more about security (institutional security but also self-security) than fidelity to the text or to the matters of life. I propose another way of considering the relations among vitality, death, textuality, interpretation, and speculation by conceptualizing the life of the theorist as a thinking through death, as a thinking of life by way of death. It is only by reckoning with the death at the heart of theory that thought exceeds the order of things or introduces the possibility of another world. In the final instance, I argue that one is only a teacher of theory to the extent that one is a student of theory, and to be a student of theory is to sacrifice one's sense of security but it is also to discover the pleasure of being eaten alive.

Antitheory for Life

Rita Felski's *The Limits of Critique* outlines "the idiom of critique" in order to make the case for its replacement by an affirmative criticism. Critique, according to Felski, is conflictual, haughty, dismissive, skeptical, and detached—in short, it is characterized by an unremitting negativity. This negativity is a matter not only of how it characterizes its objects—as naïve, unwittingly complicit, or false—but also of the way in which it positions the intellectual as "exceptional, embattled, oppositional, and radical."[8] Felski articulates the difference between critique and affirmative reading as a difference between transcendence and immanence. Even so-called immanent critique involves a critic who "carves out a distance from the words and worlds of others, espousing a stance irreducible to the tyranny of the given."[9] In contrast to critical criticism, Felski proposes a "postcritical reading," a mode of interpretation that is not "uncritical" but accepts our entanglements with the given and insists on the positive aspects of reader-text encounters:

> Foreswearing suspicion, we are confronted not only with the text but with our implication and entanglement with that text. Aggressivity gives way to receptivity, detachment mingles with an acknowledged attachment, a text's pastness does not trump its evident presentness, and aesthetic pleasures and sociopolitical resonance are intertwined rather than opposed. The aim is no longer to diminish or subtract from the reality of the texts we study but to amplify their reality, as energetic coactors and vital partners in an equal encounter.[10]

I cannot exhaustively account for Felski's provocation, but allow me to make a few observations: First, Felski maps an opposition between immanence (postcritical) and transcendence (critical) onto an opposition between positivity and negativity—immanence entails an experience of the given as a kind of wealth, a surplus of the sensuous, while transcendence entails a kind of existential poverty. Second, this ontological claim depends on presenting a twofold negativity as if it were singular: Felski's argument treats epistemological negativity, or skepticism, as synonymous with, or at least inextricable from, affective negativity (haughtiness, arrogance, etc.). Finally, the previous two points imply a continuity between the subject formation of the critic and the activity of criticism; that is, they imply that the critic acts out of a specific way of being in the world. Consequently, the critical critic is poor in the world not only in regard to her critical activities but, more generally, in regard to life itself; she misses out on rich experiences because of her commitment to critique. Doing away with critique is therefore as much a matter of public welfare as it is a question of best practices in the humanities.

Felski's argument shares much in common with Ruddick's, even if Felski is more nuanced in her account of the contemporary landscape of criticism and theory. For both scholars, critique—understood as more or less synonymous with critical theory, if not theory *tout court*—takes away from life or, more precisely, it asks its practitioners to subtract from the vitality of the given in the name of intellectual superiority. Ruddick and Felski participate in a trend in literary criticism that Jeffrey Williams has usefully designated "the new modesty." The new modesty involves "embracing empirical description, shedding a suspicious stance, and looking for methods from other places [i.e. adopting methods from the social sciences, computation, and other supposedly more 'objective' forms of inquiry]."[11] Williams includes in this tendency not only Felski's postcriticism but also Stephen Best and Sharon Marcus's manifesto for surface reading, Franco Moretti's distant reading, and Heather Love's descriptivism.[12] Discrepant in their approaches and objects of inquiry, these critics nonetheless share a desire to recover the innocence of objectivity, to save the given from its corruption by willful interpretation. Best and Marcus are of particular note in this regard not only because their articulation of surface reading has garnered a great deal of attention but also because of the way in which they associate surface reading with a "political realism about the revolutionary capacities of both texts and critics" and with "a paradoxical space of minimal critical agency."[13] Surface reading, they argue, searches after "the neutrality of description"—it "strive[s] to produce undistorted, complete descriptions of them ['things']"—and this neutrality implies an exchange of speculation for self-presence, of alterity for ipseity.[14] Modesty, in this context, means surrendering to the given, the implication being that concrete existence is much richer than the clouds of speculation.

This surrender to sheer facticity is antitheory, or at least a species of it. The valorization of the given leaves little space for the speculative element of theory. As Carolyn Lesjak has argued, "The impulse to be affirmative, to talk about what texts do rather than what they don't do, occludes the negation upon which such affirmation is based ... but unlike a dialectical reading, offers no way of actually registering or thinking the occlusion that structures the surfaces being privileged."[15] It is not so much that surface reading and other postcritical reading methods are not savvy enough to realize that their objects are getting one over on them. More importantly, these methods empty their objects of qualitative or modal complexity, replacing the constitutive non identity of texts with a fantasy of pure self-presence. They operate on the premise that the potentiality of a text, its virtual dimension, is exhausted in its actuality. There is a tautological bent to such thinking, as the postcritical critic dispels the objections of the critical critic by pointing to her object and saying, "It is what it is. Merely see." Ellen Rooney points out that this maneuver amounts to an attempt to exculpate the act of reading, to shed the complicity that passes between interpretation and text:

> There is no position more potent, no interpretive stance more powerful, than one that claims merely to "indicate what the text says about itself" [Rooney quotes from Best and Marcus], in effect, not to be interpreting at all. The claim this critical stance makes to modesty is itself the strategy by which the imagined reader accrues to herself all the authority of what the text is said to reveal in its own voice for its own purposes alone.[16]

Rooney is less interested in any supposed hypocrisy on the part of surface readers than in the impossibility that they paper over, namely, the impossibility of pure description. Interpretation requires not only a gap between one text and another—between what the critic writes and what the critic reads—but also a zone of indistinction between the text and its interpretation: criticism only occurs by entering into the text, by reading/writing one's way into the text, and, in doing so, it marks the text's nonidentity with itself, the potentiality that haunts the words on the page, the slippage between the literal and the figurative that makes every text into an allegory of itself.[17] With this in mind, it becomes evident that far from being arrogant or detached in their reading practices, critical critics—Rooney's example is Louis Althusser—acknowledge the "guilt" of reading, the undeniable violence that enters into any encounter with object or text, precisely because such encounters are never unmediated, never free of the history that precedes them. We make our own readings but not in conditions of our own choosing. In contrast, the pursuit of pure description, the search after a method that would let texts speak for themselves, assumes an innocence on the part of the critic, which is to say that it commits itself to a disavowal of the agency involved in criticism, "a fantasy of stepping outside the subject altogether."[18]

The postcritical turn is an odd bird, because it calls attention to the life of the critic only so as to vanish the critic to a scholarly afterlife—a fantastic realm in which texts read themselves. Reading is simultaneously the practice through which postcriticism calls attention to the figure of the critic—her attitude, affect, comportment, and agency—and the means by which it elides the critic in favor of the fantasy of a wholly autonomous object, a well-wrought urn, as it were. Lesjak suggests that "the substitution of reading for theory both harkens back to a more innocent time of ordinary, commonsensical reading ('just reading' [the phrase belongs to Sharon Marcus]) and, as we have seen, easily allows for a complacent accommodation to the given."[19] Moreover, as Jeffrey Williams worries, this new modesty also gives up on "the utopian impulse of criticism," or the role of criticism in cultivating the possibility of another world by attending to the traces of difference and potentiality in this one. The paradox, here, is that this strand of antitheory declares itself *for life*; that is, it operates on the assumption that it's rescuing life and literature from the violence of theory and critique. Postcriticism turns out to be for certain kinds of life—those that respect and care for the integrity of aesthetic and cultural objects—and not so much for others. Here is Felski, again, this time in collaboration with Elizabeth S. Anker: "In spite of their differences, these [postcritical] critics are all committed to treating texts with respect, care, and attention, emphasizing the visible rather than the concealed in a spirit of dialogue and constructiveness rather than dissection and diagnosis."[20] Anker and Felski want to save the positivity of difference, or the sensuousness of the particular, from those who would prefer to read against the grain, read allegorically, read speculatively, or read critically. They want to secure opportunities to build and collaborate from the corrosive influence of critical critics. However, they can do so only insofar as they draw a line of critical antagonism on one side of which lies the future of criticism (the classroom as a space of public health, as a group therapy session in which students and teachers spare themselves from an unjust world through recourse to aesthetics) and on the other side lies the broken dreams of critique (the outdated, cranky, too hopeful visions of liberation through critical agency). As Bruce Robbins argues, for all that the postcritical turn laments the aggression of critique, it can only sustain itself as a coherent project through its own acts of aggression, albeit ones conducted in the name of all that is beautiful in life and text.[21]

Postcriticism promises to bring the passion back to criticism, to shelter students from the knowingness of their professors. This is a paradox, because if life involves movement, if the life of objects is not inert substance, then reading for life cannot really be a matter of pure givenness. Life is not self-presence but rather the co-implication of the actual and the virtual, or, to paraphrase Gilbert Simondon, what distinguishes life is that its potentiality is not exhausted in a given form of life, that its stability is only ever provisional, that, in short, it changes again and again.[22] Postcriticism saves the life of reading from theory's death only insofar as it zombifies thought, eliminating reflexivity and negativity in favor of tautology—the object is what it is, reading should be just reading. Put differently, a life without death, a living without negativity, is an unthinking life, or no life at all. In contrast, a criticism for life would have to participate in the incompletion of the text, in the partiality of a form that doesn't exhaust its potential for thought. It would have to acknowledge not only its own guilt—the complicities that mediate its encounters—but also the potentials that open up in the encounter with the text, including the potential death of the reader. This death, I explain below, is not the reader's effacement but her sacrifice to the possibilities of theory. It is the experience of being eaten alive.

Criticism and Theory for Life

Few texts speak so eloquently to the liveliness of theory as the eulogies composed by Jacques Derrida and collected in *The Work of Mourning*. In each one, Derrida lingers with the life and thought of the deceased, struggling to formulate the singularity of her voice. I use the term "eulogy" in a broad manner, one which comprehends retrospectives published in journals, as well as the texts that Derrida read at funerals. Despite their differences, these texts share a place of thought, a place in which life and death mingle, less opposites than companions. This intimacy between life and death relates metonymically to the intimacy between philosophy and grief, or, more broadly, between speculation and feeling. Remembering Barthes, for instance, Derrida doesn't separate his thought from his life, nor his death from his living, but instead demonstrates that so much of Barthes's life was devoted to thinking through death, to thinking of death in order to make sense of life: "The death of Barthes' mother on October 22, 1977 was a devastating blow from which Barthes, according to his own account, never fully recovered."[23] Derrida goes on to suggest that the concept of the *punctum*, as articulated in *Camera Lucida* (1980), is not merely a significant conceptual distinction (the opposite of the *studium*) but also a form of mourning, a way in which Barthes speaks of and to his mother.

> The word *punctum*, moreover, translates, in *Camera Lucida*, one meaning of the word "detail": a point of singularity that punctures the surface of the reproduction—and even the production—of analogies, likenesses, and codes. It pierces, strikes me, wounds me, bruises me, and, first of all, seems to concern only me. Its very definition is that it addresses itself to me. The absolute singularity of the other addresses itself to me, the Referent that, in its very image, I can no longer suspend, even though its "presence" forever escapes me, having already receded into the past.... But it is always the singularity of the other insofar as it comes to me without being directed towards me, without being present to me; and the other can even be "me," me having been or having had to be, me already dead in the future anterior and past anterior of my photograph.[24]

The surface of the photograph is a ruse not because there is depth or meaning that lurks behind it but because it arrives broken by a detail, a detail without which it cannot surface for the reader. What makes a photograph, or, more generally, a text, singular is not an accumulation of positive traits (as postcriticism would have it) but a *punctum*, a singular wound that unsettles the identity not only of the text but also of the life that encounters the text. The idea that travels, here, between Barthes and Derrida, that they share as they commune not beyond life and death but in the place where the two touch, is that thinking involves the experience of one's own death: "and the other can even be 'me,' me having been or having had to be, me already dead in the future anterior and past anterior." This death comes through "the singularity of the other," which is to say that one experiences one's own death when one's personal integrity gives way to heterogeneity, to an encounter with difference that does not permit one to remain the same. One thinks only insofar as one allows one's self—one's self-sameness—to die and, in doing so, invites difference into a life. To read after theory, to practice criticism in the wake of theory, is therefore an exercise in self-criticism, an exercise in abandoning the security of what one already knows for the sake of what surprises.

To sacrifice oneself to theory is neither an aberration nor a moment of theoretical excess, but a necessity, so long as one is committed to theoretical thought, to thought that asks what the situation of thought is. I am aware, of course, that the genealogy of "Theory" in the Anglo-American context is particular and peculiar, all too often limited by a narrow set of proper names, most of them belonging to dead white men, many of them French. Changing the term to "Critical Theory" expands the scope to include Germans, as a well as a range of thinkers who would once have been identified with the "Third World." This genealogical narrowness was, of course, always a fiction; bell hooks, Gayatri Spivak, Edward Said, Eve Sedgwick, Lisa Lowe, Jack Halberstam, and countless others are always already unsettling the boundaries of "Theory." These thinkers do not so much call theory into question as mobilize and invent the plurality of thought that goes by the name of "theory." The recent deaths of theory—for instance, in the so-called new materialisms or in speculative realism and object-oriented ontology[25]—is salutary insofar as, far from being examples of antitheory, they represent the dissemination of theory, the decline of an arboreal model of "Theory" in favor of the rhizomatic proliferation of theories. This proliferation should not, however, disguise that this death qua surplus of life was always already at the heart of "Theory." To theorize has always been to participate in conversations, or conversions, between life and death, speculation and passion, positivity and negativity.

A criticism for life would make good on the death at the heart of theory by asking after the possibilities for life that such death opens up. This preparation for death is how I understand the utopian impulse of theory or criticism. Theory enables one to think the real possibility of another world by teaching the historical, material, social, and political contingency of the self; speculation, in the sense of the imagination of radical difference, requires not only that the object of thought change but also the subject. Antitheory, at least in its most recent incarnation as the postcritical turn, is fundamentally antiutopian. When Ruddick, Felski, or Best and Marcus ask scholars to return to "just reading," to get literal or to surrender suspicion to affirmation, they are also asking scholars to leave well enough alone, to submit to the world as it is. The reward for this submission comes in the form of ideological and disciplinary legitimation for the pleasures of "just reading"; that is, by surrendering theory or critique, one wins the right to enjoy culture, art, or literature without asking after the situation of thought. Whether or not this form of legitimacy protects one from the whims of administrators or legislators is quite another question. In contrast, theory and critique admit that there is no innocence in enjoyment, that the world in which we exist permits no site of noncomplicity, no space outside racism, capitalism, heteropatriarchy, misogyny, settler colonialism, transphobia, and empire. At the same time—and this is a crucial distinction that antitheory slides over without comment—this admission of complicity doesn't cancel enjoyment but produces another space of pleasure, a space within and against the situation in which we find ourselves, a space for another kind of desire. According to Fredric Jameson, this learning to desire otherwise defines the utopian impulse, which it turns out has less to do with a specific social content than with "a kind of desiring to desire, a learning to desire, the invention of the desire called Utopia in the first place, along with new rules for fantasizing or daydreaming of such a thing."[26] Jameson is concerned in particular with the way in which utopia entails a thinking of collectivity beyond the individualism that functions as the ideological supplement of capitalism, but his point, I would suggest, holds more generally for theoretical practice: theory is pedagogical in the sense that it not only requires that we learn to read differently but also requires that we learn to desire differently, or to live in another manner. This is, of course, what many find troubling in theory. The fear of theory is a fear of change; it is fear of the other but also fear of becoming other. The postcritical turn, with its fetishization of the literal object, is nothing less than a preemptive strike against theory, a security measure against the difference—the death—that theory makes.

I want to conclude this chapter by outlining some different manners of experiencing the death at the heart of theory. These different ways of living and dying through theory imply processes of radical conversion or practices of becoming other than oneself in the name of justice, desire, truth, and pain. The first comes from Michel Foucault's account of the Cynics in the final lectures he delivered at the Collège de France. It would be unadvisable to extract from

Foucault's work a normative principle in regard to thought, not least because he so often dedicated his thinking to unsettling norms. Instead, I simply want to suggest that Cynicism was so interesting to Foucault because it wagered the value of thought on a life lived in proximity with death. For Cynics, the first principle of thought is "[t]he principle of altering the *nomisma* [the currency]," of "changing the custom, breaking with it, breaking up the rules, habits, conventions, and laws."[27] Thinking begins by breaking the habitual course of things. For the Cynics, it is not so much the content of this or that thought that is the measure of thinking as the life in which that thought is embedded. Foucault remarks that many commentators describe the life of the Cynic as a "dog's life" (*bios kunikos*). The qualities that earn the Cynic this description include shamelessness ("a life which does in public, in front of everyone, what only dogs and animals dare to do"); indifference (it is "content with what it has, and has no needs other than those it can satisfy immediately"); and combativeness (it is "a life which barks, a diacritical [*diakritikos*] life, that is to say, a life which can fight, which barks at enemies, which knows how to distinguish the good from the bad, the true from the false, and masters from enemies").[28] The Cynic embodies negativity not only in the sense of opposing the status quo but also in abasing himself before others. By incarnating worthlessness, the Cynic introduces a void into the world, a point of indistinction between positivity and negativity through which alterity takes its distance from the given. This is what Foucault terms the "active poverty" of Cynicism, which is "not the kind of poverty that would be satisfied with giving up all concern with wealth, acquisitive conduct, and economy" but which must "also be 'an operation one carries out on oneself in order to obtain positive results of courage, resistance, and endurance."[29] Courage, here, is twofold, for it not only means sacrificing "the traditional forms of existence" in favor of the true life, an "other life."[30] It also means militant opposition to the world itself:

> Thus you see that the Cynic is someone who, taking up the traditional themes of the true life in ancient philosophy, transposes them and turns them round into the demand and assertion of the need for an *other life*. And then, through the image and figure of the king of poverty, he transposes anew the idea of an *other* life into the theme of life whose otherness must lead to the change of the world. An *other* life for an *other* world.[31]

This logic of transposition, according to which self-negation begets another life and this other life, in turn, constitutes the condition of possibility of another world, is what one might call the courage of theory. In the classroom, this courage refuses to let thought conclude with the given; it grants the endurance to dwell in questions without easy answers and to experience one's own death as the letting go of passionate attachments to the status quo. That being said, this courage neither describes the sum of theoretical practice nor exhausts the potentiality of theory. If it did, theory would risk being little more than the mirror image of antitheory, an affirmation of the subject that merely inverts postcriticism's affirmation of the object. The recent work of Catherine Malabou on plasticity complicates the courage of theory by introducing a consideration of trauma. In *Ontology of the Accident*, Malabou theorizes metamorphosis in terms of moments of destruction: "We must all of us recognize that we might, one day, become someone else, an absolute other, someone who will never be reconciled with themselves again, someone who will be this form of us without redemption or atonement, without last wishes, this damned form, outside of time."[32] Malabou shares Foucault's interest in thinking the passage from one form of life to another, but she reminds us that this passage isn't always of our own volition, that sometimes it happens to us, the effect of illness, a car accident, or a breakup. This is a moment when the subject becomes object, when the materiality of existence exceeds volition. It is worth noting that Malabou articulates this ontology as a zone of indistinction between life and death or, more specifically, as a living death through which one body transforms into another: "Between life and death we become other to ourselves."[33] If for Foucault metamorphosis implies freedom, for Malabou it implies the ambiguity of existence, the significance of chance and contingency in the order of things. Malabou thus offers a way of thinking that does away with the desire for redemption, that replaces the search for saving grace with an acknowledgment of being's plasticity, or, as she puts it, "[T]he history of being itself consists perhaps of nothing but a series of accidents which, in every era without hope of return, dangerously disfigure the meaning of essence."[34]

Malabou suggests that theory needs to think vulnerability as much as courage.[35] To be a student of theory is to participate not only in the passion for freedom but also in shared suffering, in grief over the accidents of being. "Accident," however, does not adequately account for what it means to be stripped of being, for what it means to be subject to systemic exploitation, oppression, enslavement, and/or genocide on the basis of race, ethnicity, gender, sexuality, class, nationality (or lack thereof). There are, of course, numerous genres of critical theory dedicated to considering the question of what it means to be deprived of the material conditions for living or living well: critical race theory, disability studies, critical ethnic studies, trans studies, queer theory, gender studies, American Studies, Native American and Indigenous Studies, Black Studies—one could go on. It is by way of the last that I wish to conclude this chapter, in particular, by repeating the question, asked over a century ago by W. E. B. Du Bois: "How does it feel to be a problem?"[36] As is well known, Du Bois responds with the concept of double consciousness, which introduces the phenomenology of blackness as a matter of "twoness"—a state of being both for oneself and for a white other. Blackness comes into play as a constitutive fracture in racialized existence. To feel oneself a problem, to apprehend one's own existence as mediated by racism, is to live out the split between essence and existence, to find oneself caught between the two, constantly grasping the right to claim the former, while being abandoned to the latter.

This state of existence without essence, or of life without the right to live, is at the core of Black Studies, or at least a significant strand of it. Frantz Fanon diagnoses the racializing apparatus of colonialism as producing "a zone of nonbeing, an extraordinarily sterile and arid region, an incline stripped of every essential from which a genuine new departure can emerge."[37] Orlando Patterson argues that slavery generates social death, that it introduces a limbo between biological death and social recognition.[38] Hortense Spillers thinks through the ungendering of black life, through processes of racialization involving the theft of the body and the mutilation of the flesh.[39] There are, of course, any number of additional thinkers that one could cite—Sylvia Wynter, Saidiya Hartman, Cedric Robinson, Aimé Césaire, and Denise Ferreira da Silva, for example—but what they share is a sense that blackness plays itself out between being and nothingness, essence and existence, surplus and void. In the last decade or so, scholars have spoken of an ontological turn in African American or Black Studies, but, as this all-too-brief survey suggests, ontological matters have always been at the heart of this field. This "turn" is perhaps less a shift in the activities of the field than the belated recognition that to think blackness, to reckon with historical processes of racialization, is to think *theoretically*. Indeed, insofar as the constitution of theory—the specific genealogy of "Theory" but also its global historical conditions—has always depended on situations of racialized inequality, it would be better to say that theory has always been thinking of blackness. I take this to be the fundamental lesson of Nahum Chandler's *X—The Problem of the Negro as a Problem for Thought*, a book which makes a compelling case for reading Du Bois as a critical theorist. Du Bois, Chandler explains, does not presuppose blackness as an object of thought but rather transforms it into a question, a question whose response "demands that we rethink the premises of all concepts of historicity and sociality by which such entities are demarcated."[40] Blackness is not a given; it escapes, undoes, and improvises on conceptual frameworks; it is deconstruction *avant la lettre*, mapping the architectonics of Western thought only insofar as it also undermines them.

Du Bois and Chandler, as well as the other scholars cited above, suggest a different way of thinking about the death at the heart of theory, one that has as much to do with systemic violence as freedom. However, this distinction is not a stable opposition. One of Chandler's central contentions is that the rift of double consciousness is not only the effect of a history of violence but also a gift:

> Du Bois marks the structure of possibility of subjectivation that arises with this sense, which he calls 'double-consciousness' at the level of the subject and 'second-sight' at the level of the socius in general, with both a positive and negative sign. It manifests not only as a kind of loss, a disarticulation of ostensible purpose, but also a kind of 'gift,' a distantiation of ostensible horizon as a limit.[41]

The "actual experience" of this "sense" is negative, determined by historical conditions, an effect and a relay of violence, but this actuality is itself traversed by a surplus of potentiality.[42] This surplus "desediments" blackness; it opens up the historical production of blackness as a space not only of critique but also of invention.[43] It's what Chandler calls "a certain exorbitance," and this exorbitance is what allows avant-garde practices like M. NourbeSe Philip's *Zong!* or social actions like the protests in Ferguson to not only recall the injustices of slavery but also experiment with new ways of living in the world.[44]

It's important not to conflate "the problem of the Negro" with a generic logic of theory; blackness describes a zone of indistinction between life and death, positivity and negativity, being and nothingness, that is singular in its history, operations, and implications. At the same time, this singular problem has something to teach critical theory as a whole. First, it shows that theory's delineation of thinking, its self-reflexive reckoning with the situation of thought, is at one and the same time determination, or setting of limits, and the putting into play of indeterminacy—improvisation in the sense of the doubling of the seen by the unseen, or the given by the virtual. Theory never contents itself with the facticity of existence, because being itself is never merely given. Finally, theory is not a luxury but a necessity. For some, in fact, it's a matter of survival. #BlackLivesMatter theorizes not simply to account for the historical conditions from which it has emerged but also to mark the difference between the everyday experience of black folks and the possibility of justice (i.e., between the given and the to come). Or, to cite another case of grave import, theory enables the direct actions of a group such as ACT UP to register not only as antinormative—a break with heteronormative and homophobic institutions and practices—but also as contributions to networks of mutual support that allow life and death to signify otherwise. Finally, there is no struggling against the inequalities produced by capitalism without that mode of symptomatic reading which theorizes literal economic exchanges as figures of a social totality. One could cite many other cases that make demands on theory for the sake of life, but my point, here, is simply to suggest that, far from being detached, haughty, or arrogant, the theoretical practices associated with critique constitute ways of engaging with the world otherwise. To call for postcriticism as a remedy to violence in the classroom is therefore to ignore the way in which the death of theory is also life, a means of passing from one state of being to another, a moment in which being folds back onto itself, revealing the violence of "just reading," as well as the hope of what is to come. Theory is grief, suffering, and trauma; theory is pleasure, freedom, and utopia. Theory is the passage between these extremes in an experience of living one's own death, of becoming another. Theory means that one cannot truly live without being eaten alive.

Coda

Part of what fuels the antitheoretical tendency of the postcritical turn is concern regarding the health of the humanities. Declining enrollments in and funding for the humanities certainly raises questions about what students want from their education and what the public expects from its scholars. Without having easy answers to these questions, I have to agree with Christopher Breu when he argues that the postcritical turn is an attempt to resolve socioeconomic problems, or material contradictions, through affective and symbolic means.[45] Postcriticism wants to repair the shabby state of the humanities by renewing a passion for humanistic values, and it marks the specificity of its project by way of its contrast to the practice of critique, which it argues is, at best, bad at drawing students into the classroom and, at worst, directly responsible for undermining the outreach efforts of the humanities. Postcriticism seems to suggest that the humanities is suffering from a public relations failure—an inability to adequately communicate what makes the humanities so significant. Anker and Felski again:

> At a time when higher education is under siege, it seems urgent to articulate more compelling accounts of why the humanities matter and to clarify to larger audiences why anyone should care about literature, art, or philosophy. Accustomed to the rhetoric of dismantling and demystification, critique lacks a vocabulary and set of established rationales for mounting such defenses.[46]

Leaving to the side the question of whether or not critique/critical theory lacks the means to respond to this situation, Anker and Felski mistake the material crisis facing higher education with a crisis of values, as if the problem were moods and dispositions, rather than, say, neoliberalism and the privatization of education. It's not that language, aesthetics, and affect aren't material—they are—but rather that they exhaust neither the material conditions that produce "the crisis in the humanities" nor the avenues for responding to them. If I put "the crisis in the humanities" in scare quotes, it's because the phrase doesn't really manage to encompass the depth and breadth of the general crisis of higher education, which has more to do with funding structures for students and institutions than with the particular values of the humanities.[47] Critical theory won't solve this crisis, but the postcritical turn's preemptive strike against critical theory strips students and faculty of the equipment we need for addressing the conditions we face. For my part, I would rather be eaten alive than confuse neoliberalism with a public relations failure.

Notes

1   Lisa Ruddick, "When Nothing Is Cool," *The Point Magazine*, 2015. https://thepointmag.com/2015/criticism/when-nothing-is-cool.
2   Ibid.
3   See, respectively, Steve Knapp and Walter Benn Michaels, "Against Theory," *Critical Inquiry* 8.4 (Summer 1982): 723–742; Terry Eagleton, *After Theory* (New York: Basic Books, 2003); and Jonathan Kandell, "Jacques Derrida, Abstruse Theorist, Dies at 74," *New York Times* (October 10, 2004).
4   John Mowitt, "Offering Theory," *Canadian Review of Comparative Literature* (September–December 2006): 269–282.
5   Ibid., 272.
6   See Giorgio Agamben, *Homo Sacer: Sovereign Power and Bare Life*, trans. Daniel Heller-Roazen (Stanford: Stanford, University Press, 1998).
7   See, for instance, Rey Chow, *The Age of the World Target: Self-Referentiality in War, Theory, and Comparative Work* (Durham: Duke University Press, 2006).
8   Rita Felski, *The Limits of Critique* (Chicago: University of Chicago Press, 2015), 50.
9   Ibid., 127.
10 Ibid., 184–185.
11 Jeffrey Williams, "The New Modesty in Literary Criticism," *The Chronicle of Higher Education* (January 5, 2015).

12　See, respectively, Stephen Best and Sharon Marcus, "Surface Reading: An Introduction," *Representations* 108.1 (Fall 2009): 1–21; Franco Moretti, *Distant Reading* (New York: Verso, 2013); Heather Love, "Close but Not Deep: Literary Ethics and the Descriptive Turn," *New Literary History* 41.2 (Spring 2010): 371–391.

13　Best and Marcus, "Surface Reading," 15–16, 17.

14　Ibid., 18. It is worth noting that there has been a follow-up to the issue of *Representations* that introduced surface reading, with an Introduction written by Sharon Marcus, Heather Love, Stephen Best, "Building a Better Description," *Representations* 135.1 (Summer 2016), Special Issue: "Description across Disciplines": 1–21. The introduction is less polemical and more nuanced than the previous issue's introduction, but its conflation of description as a practice with description as a project implicitly repeats the earlier essay's foreclosure of theory (3). The essay's defense of description—a practice that the authors acknowledge is constitutive of most critical practices—is, in actuality, a proposal to make description the terminal point of criticism. That is, their call to suspend skepticism regarding description amounts to another instance of insisting tautologically on the literal or the given (15).

15　Carolyn Lesjak, "Reading Dialectically," *Criticism* 55.2 (Spring 2013), 247.

16　Ellen Rooney, "Live Free or Describe: The Reading Effect and the Persistence of Form," *differences* 21.3 (2010), 125.

17　I am thinking here of Paul De Man's insights in *Allegories of Reading: Figural Language in Rousseau, Nietzsche, Rilke, and Proust* (New Haven: Yale University Press, 1979).

18　Lesjak, "Reading Dialectically," 247.

19　Ibid., 249.

20　Elizabeth S. Anker and Rita Felski, "Introduction," in *Critique and Postcritique* (Durham: Duke University Press, 2017), 16.

21　In a review of Anker and Felski's edited collection, *Critique and Postcritique*, Bruce Robbins writes: "Can we paint a composite portrait of the Postcritiquer? … One distinctive element is indeed a passive-aggressive tone that does not seem to notice that it is engaged in obliterating 'whole fields' and dissing all the people working in them, most of whom have been doing exactly what she thinks they should be doing. Give me honest aggression any time. (And yes, I do mean like my own.) Another element is extreme self-satisfaction with their beliefs, attachments, and feelings (which can't be disputed) and with the comfortable perch in the world where divine providence has seen fit to place them. *They* certainly don't need to trouble themselves with social injustice. Life is beautiful. Texts are beautiful." Robbins, "Fashion Conscious Phenomenon," *American Review of Books* 38.5 (July/August 2017), 6.

22 Simondon defines life as a "permanent activity of individuation," or a process of "becoming" that renews itself in the living being's encounters with worldly problems. Gilbert Simondon, *L'individuation psychique et collective* (Paris: Aubier, 1989 [1964]), 16–18. Translations mine.
23 Jacques Derrida, *The Work of Mourning*, ed. Pascale-Anne Brault and Michael Naas (Chicago: University of Chicago Press, 2003), 33.
24 Ibid., 39.
25 Although I don't have the space to discuss the matter at length, I would suggest that the turn to the object, to the facticity of existence, and to materiality by theories that fall under the rubric of object-oriented ontology, speculative realism, and the new materialisms are not so much forms of antitheory as deaths of theory. In particular, the shifts from epistemology to ontology, from language to materiality, and from the subject to object institute a break with "Theory" as it has circulated within the humanities and some of the social sciences since the 1970s, or the introduction of new kinds of theoretical practices through the burial of old kinds. This death is also a renewal of theory, as these shifts do not so much evacuate the former terms as introduce new conceptual problems in respect to them.
26 Fredric Jameson, *The Seeds of Time* (New York: Columbia University Press, 1996), 90.
27 Michel Foucault, *The Courage of Truth: The Government of Self and Others II. Lectures at the Collège de France, 1983–1984*, ed. Frédéric Gros, trans. Graham Burchell (New York: Picador, 2012), 243.
28 Ibid., 243.
29 Ibid., 258.
30 Ibid., 245.
31 Ibid., 287.
32 Catherine Malabou, *The Ontology of the Accident: An Essay on Destructive Plasticity*, trans. Carolyn Shead (Hoboken: Wiley, 2012), 2–3.
33 Ibid., 34.
34 Ibid., 91.
35 She is not unique in this insistence, of course. See, for instance, Judith Butler, *Precarious Life: The Powers of Mourning and Violence* (New York: Verso, 2004) and *Frames of War: When Is Life Grievable?* (New York: Verso, 2009).
36 W. E. B. Du Bois, *The Souls of Black Folk*, in *Writings*, ed. Nathan Huggins (New York: Library of America, 1986), 363.
37 Frantz Fanon, *Black Skin, White Masks*, trans. Richard Pilcox (New York: Grove Press, 2008 [1952]), xii.
38 See Orlando Patterson, *Slavery and Social Death: A Comparative Study* (Cambridge: Harvard University Press, 1982).

39 See Hortense Spillers, "Mama's Baby, Papa's Maybe: An American Grammar Book," *Diacritics* 17.2 (Summer 1987): 64–81.
40 Nahum Chandler, *X—The Problem of the Negro as a Problem for Thought* (New York: Fordham University Press, 2013), 59.
41 Ibid., 36.
42 Ibid.
43 Chandler is very close to Fred Moten in this respect, an affinity that does not go unremarked by the latter. For both thinkers, thinking blackness does not mean articulating a positive ontology to replace the "zone of nonexistence" to which blacks have been confined. Instead, they bring into play a para-ontology, a way of inhabiting the in-between of being and nothingness that is as inventive as it is painful. See Fred Moten, *In the Break: The Aesthetics of the Black Radical Tradition* (Minneapolis: University of Minnesota Press, 2003) and "Blackness and Nothingness (Mysticism in the Flesh)," *South Atlantic Quarterly* 112.4 (Fall 2013): 737–780.
44 Chandler, *X,* 37.
45 Christopher Breu, "The Humanities as Contradiction: Against the New Enclosures," Special Issue, "Saving the Humanities from the Neoliberal University," ed. Ronald Strickland, *Humanities* 7 (July 2018): 1–16.
46 Anker and Felski, "Introduction," 19.
47 For more nuanced takes on the crisis of the university in the United States, see, for example, Christopher Newfield, *The Great Mistake: How We Wrecked Public Universities and How We Can Fix Them* (Baltimore: Johns Hopkins University Press, 2016); and Melinda Cooper, *Family Values: Between Neoliberalism and the New Social Conservativism* (Cambridge: Zone Books, 2017), Ch. VI: "*In Loco Parentis*: Human Capital, Student Debt, and the Logic of Family Investment."

Works Cited

Agamben, Giorgio. *Homo Sacer: Sovereign Power and Bare Life*. Trans. Daniel Heller-Roazen. Stanford: Stanford, University Press, 1998.

Anker, Elizabeth S. and Rita Felski. "Introduction." In *Critique and Postcritique*. Durham: Duke University Press, 2017.

Best, Stephen and Sharon Marcus. "Surface Reading: An Introduction." *Representations* 108.1 (Fall 2009): 1–21.

Breu, Christopher. "The Humanities as Contradiction: Against the New Enclosures." Special Issue, "Saving the Humanities from the Neoliberal University." Ed. Ronald Strickland. *Humanities* 7 (July 2018): 1–16.

Butler, Judith. *Precarious Life: The Powers of Mourning and Violence*. New York: Verso, 2004.

Butler, Judith. *Frames of War: When Is Life Grievable?* New York: Verso, 2009.

Chandler, Nahum. *X—The Problem of the Negro as a Problem for Thought.* New York: Fordham University Press, 2013.

Chow, Rey. *The Age of the World Target: Self-Referentiality in War, Theory, and Comparative Work.* Durham: Duke University Press, 2006.

Cooper, Melinda. *Family Values: Between Neoliberalism and the New Social Conservativism.* Cambridge: Zone Books, 2017.

De Man, Paul. *Allegories of Reading: Figural Language in Rousseau, Nietzsche, Rilke, and Proust.* New Haven: Yale University Press, 1979.

Derrida, Jacques. *The Work of Mourning.* Ed. Pascale-Anne Brault and Michael Naas. Chicago: University of Chicago Press, 2003.

Du Bois, W. E. B. *The Souls of Black Folk.* In *Writings.* Ed. Nathan Huggins. New York: Library of America, 1986.

Eagleton, Terry. *After Theory.* New York: Basic Books, 2003.

Fanon, Frantz. *Black Skin, White Masks.* Trans. Richard Pilcox. New York: Grove Press, 2008.

Felski, Rita. *The Limits of Critique.* Chicago: University of Chicago Press, 2015.

Foucault, Michel. *The Courage of Truth: The Government of Self and Others II. Lectures at the Collège de France, 1983-1984.* Ed. Frédéric Gros. Trans. Graham Burchell. New York: Picador, 2012.

Jameson, Fredric. *The Seeds of Time.* New York: Columbia University Press, 1996.

Kandell, Jonathan. "Jacques Derrida, Abstruse Theorist, Dies at 74." *New York Times* (October 10, 2004).

Knapp, Steve and Walter Benn Michaels. "Against Theory." *Critical Inquiry* 8.4 (Summer 1982): 723-742.

Lesjak, Carolyn. "Reading Dialectically." *Criticism* 55.2 (Spring 2013): 233-277.

Love, Heather. "Close but Not Deep: Literary Ethics and the Descriptive Turn." *New Literary History* 41.2 (Spring 2010): 371-391.

Malabou, Catherine. *The Ontology of the Accident: An Essay on Destructive Plasticity.* Trans. Carolyn Shead. Hoboken: Wiley, 2012.

Moretti, Franco. *Distant Reading.* New York: Verso, 2013.

Moten, Fred. *In the Break: The Aesthetics of the Black Radical Tradition.* Minneapolis: University of Minnesota Press, 2003.

Moten, Fred. "Blackness and Nothingness (Mysticism in the Flesh)." *South Atlantic Quarterly* 112.4 (Fall 2013): 737-780.

Mowitt, John. "Offering Theory." *Canadian Review of Comparative Literature* (September-December 2006): 269-282.

Newfield, Christopher. *The Great Mistake: How We Wrecked Public Universities and How We Can Fix Them.* Baltimore: Johns Hopkins University Press, 2016.

Patterson, Orlando. *Slavery and Social Death: A Comparative Study.* Cambridge: Harvard University Press, 1982.

Robbins, Bruce. "Fashion Conscious Phenomenon." *American Book Review* 38.5 (July/August 2017): 5–6.

Rooney, Ellen. "Live Free or Describe: The Reading Effect and the Persistence of Form." *differences* 21.3 (2010): 112–139.

Ruddick, Lisa. "When Nothing Is Cool." *The Point Magazine* (2015). https://thepointmag.com/2015/criticism/when-nothing-is-cool.

Simondon, Gilbert. *L'individuation psychique et collective*. Paris: Aubier, 1989.

Spillers, Hortense. "Mama's Baby, Papa's Maybe: An American Grammar Book." *Diacritics* 17.2 (Summer 1987): 64–81.

Williams, Jeffrey. "The New Modesty in Literary Criticism." *The Chronicle of Higher Education* (January 5, 2015).

10

Theory as Meat Grinder

Harold Aram Veeser

I've been interviewing prominent critics for a book about this to my mind greatest generation of North American theorists. I've been struck by their metaphors for theory: theory is fluoride in the water, or an illuminating flash of lightning, or a meat grinder. In the course of talking to them, I came to believe that theory can improve your life. What follows here is a brief account of how I came around to this visceral phenomenological take on theory. Some of these critics hope for more from theory than an "A" on a paper or a dissertation idea. A few of them even claim that theory can improve our human attachments. I was very puzzled. What could they mean? This chapter is a stab at figuring that out.

My undergraduate adviser and favorite English professor was a theorist. This I dimly understood from his amazingly theoretical undergraduate lectures on British Victorian and Modernist literature. He, Edward Said, approved when I connected the novel *New Grub Street* and the philosophy of Pessimism. I was excited by the project and his reaction, and when the next year I had five papers to write, in five different classes, I remembered Said's praise for the Marxist theories of Georg Lukács. I used my drug money to buy the newly released hardcover of Lukács's *History and Class Consciousness*, I read the book overnight, and I used his theories as a meat grinder. I worked everything through Lukács's theory, all my exams and term papers, from Modern Drama to Aesthetics to *The Day of the Triffids*. I made the dean's list.[1] The meat grinder's power was evident. I had a conversion experience.

Other theorists whom I interviewed experienced the uncanny power of theory. Richard Macksey convened the first real theory conference in North America. He remembers meat grinding moments: "New Criticism would say, as soon as you figure out what rhetorical machine the author is using, you've got the mainspring of the watch."[2] He explained that "you can seem to master a subject that appeals to you. That is what I suspect drew some people to literary theory, because we don't have to work so hard."[3] But for him meat grinding was too easy; it violated Macksey's sense of fair play. W. J. T. Mitchell, shaper of our discipline, started as a math major whose first English paper took a theoretical turn: "So my first really important essay in English literature was on the idea of reason and nothingness in [Blake's] *Urizen*. The idea of nothingness I took from Sartre's *Being and Nothingness* because I was taking a philosophy course in French philosophy."[4] I felt like Mitchell's cousin, since I too in my first paper for Said had used a Continental philosopher (Schopenhauer) to interpret a British literary classic (*New Grub Street*). This sort of meat grinder couldn't be so bad if the distinguished Mitchell had done it, too. But the specter of the meat grinder troubled Wai Chee Dimock, current editor of *PMLA*. When she was a grad student, she and her peers were all writing dissertations day and night in the new Yale word-processor lab. Seeing each other there all the time, "we were joking that it was actually the Yale computer program that was actually producing all these scripts in different ways."[5] A powerful machine that autonomously writes your work is a version of the meat grinder. Dimock offered another version, too. For her, theory came to be personified in Walter Benn Michaels and Michael Fried, and in that form, theory also took over the writing of her first book on Melville. "Their Berkeley NEH seminar had a profound and kind of shocking effect, it just completely overturned my take on Melville. I got rid of my original dissertation and wrote a totally different book."[6] For Dimock, at least in this anecdote, Fried and Michaels had turned into a poststructural Rosemary's baby, colonizing her body and speaking through her.

Theory's fatal attractions, according to these theorists, include the following: it is portable, can be applied to anything, and churns out predictable interpretations; it is also too easy to use and can short-circuit scholarly invention and originality. Michael Bérubé told me not to worry that "the next big thing in Theory" would be, as Sophia McClennen bitingly put it, "just so 'eighties a project":

> So, yeah, I don't really think in terms of next big thing, because the 'eighties part of it you mentioned, the shoulder-padded part of it, the puffy hair, leg-warmer part of it, a moment where it did feel like we ate and chewed up Baudrillard last year, and then the year before that it was Bakhtin. Now, [ghoulish leering voice] who's next? So I think, it's not like that, it's not like This Year's Model. It's more like, Rita Felski was saying this she was giving a lecture at the Cornell School of Criticism and Theory two years ago, the Anti-Critique lecture. And she was really being pushed on this, I mean, "this is the School for Criticism and Theory. We're not giving up on critique, thank you."[7]

Rita Felski is another shaper of the field, having revolutionized *New Literary History* and launched a tumultuous reform movement in literary theory:

> But I will say, compared to a lot of narratives about the decline of theory, I'm actually very excited about where things are going now. I think the whole shift away from the rhetoric of unmaking and undermining and disrupting towards how do we theorize our passion about things, how do we theorize our attachments?[8]

I understand what she is saying about unmaking and undermining. She means that literary criticism has settled into habits of detecting and exposing hidden evils in literary texts. Calling such work a hermeneutics of suspicion or symptomatic reading, critics have spent forty years unmasking, reading for absences, and exposing complicities and evils shrouded in classic texts and popular culture. That resonated with me: I too felt this had become tiresome. But the second part of her statement, the part about theorizing our passions and attachments: What could that mean? I had no idea. In desperation I looked into Bruno Latour, the theorist whom Felski named as her most profound influence. Latour was mostly too abstract and addicted to sociological jargon, but I did find this comment:

> Apart from religion, no other domain has been more bulldozed to death by critical sociology than the sociology of art. Every sculpture, painting, *haute cuisine* dish, techno rave, and novel has been explained to nothingness by the social factors "hidden behind" them. Nowhere has social explanation played more the role of a negative King Midas transforming gold, silver, and diamonds into dust. And yet, as one sees in religion, if you are listening to what people are saying, they will explain at length how and why they are deeply *attached, moved, affected* by the works of art which "make them" feel things.[9]

Latour's distaste for critical sociology, the sociology of art, and social explanation is clearly the same as Felski's distaste for hermeneutics of suspicion, symptomatic reading, unmasking, and undermining. But I still don't quite get what he is saying about attachment to art. Perhaps the answers are to be found in the new theories of affect proposed by many recent scholars.[10] Sentimentality has been theorized heavily, as have "ugly feelings" and attachment to the earth.[11] I admit to cringing whenever someone explains why he or she is "deeply attached, moved, affected" by works that "make them" feel things. Felski and Latour may possibly be saying that, when theories have evolved to where they can analyze these inchoate feelings, then we may all have to cringe less.

Given Felski's attack on theory as critique, was theory out of steam and destined to become extinct? I asked an influential book editor who helped to shape the theory generation, Bill Germano editorial director of Routledge:

I'm not sure that (a) there was an it and (b) that it's over. I think it's more like a big container of some concentrate that fell into the ocean. Now it's... it's like fluoride. Maybe that's the actual analysis. It's like fluoride. We have fewer cavities because of it.[12]

Germano also said that theory swings in and out of fashion. But he added, "I don't really like the pendulum theory because part of it would be to imply that we are ready to go back to drawing the blinds and just reading Tennyson."[13]

Many critics felt theory had come to stay. Marjorie Garber said, "A lot of theory is going to turn out to be 'wrong.' The *phlogiston*. It doesn't exist, but the idea of phlogiston made people think about alchemy and chemistry differently. That way of using theory, as a bridge ... is never going to be over."[14] Literary theory has certainly splattered itself all over Leitch's theory map: Leitch's word for this, *disaggregated*, seems an understatement. But Ken Warren said, "there are probably more continuities than not," and he didn't dismiss my "eighties" question about what will be the next big thing. "In a way there are big things," Warren said, "but they manifest in a more diffuse kind of way."[15]

Jane Gallop agreed that theory survives: "it's become actually foundational. Which is a weird place for it to be since it's kind of an anti-foundationalism." Theory stood outside the bounds of normalcy, like the Sex Pistols. But now every English department offers grad and undergrad theory classes. And while it used to be "seen as this Thing, now it's the intellectual background of the work that people do."[16] Gerald Graff agreed: "theory has seeped into the culture enough to make people begin to realize that, yeah, essentialized categories like race, black and white, homosexual, gay/straight, that there's a problem with essentializing those categories."[17] Even Fish agreed: "Theory has been absorbed into the general vocabulary of American literary studies. And so notions that once were hotly contested, or in some quarters the cause of suspicion, are now routinely appearing."[18]

But there are problems when something born to rebel becomes the status quo. Walter Benn Michaels finds many uses of theory redundant, with beginning scholars "producing as a kind of gospel things de Man said thirty years ago, as if, as if there'd never been any discussion or argument about, not what the politics of it was, or what the morality was, whether it actually made any fucking sense."[19] As the author of a notorious article, "Against Theory," Michaels used to urge scholars to abandon theory. Today, he admits that theory still matters: "There are certain issues with futures."[20]

Vincent Leitch, our most influential commentator on theory as The Norton Anthology of Theory and Criticism's general editor, glossed the current flowering of theory: "In a world in which there are 6,800 mutual funds, 20,000 wines reviewed annually in *Wine Spectator*, and innumerable sneakers to choose from, proliferation and fragmentation should come as no surprise."[21] But he stops short of explaining current theory as just more commodification: "In relation to theory, concepts of commodities, fashion, and shelf life compose a degraded picture."[22] Leitch would prefer to call it a theory renaissance, with ninety-four subdisciplines circling around twelve major topics, all of them with their own major figures, sympathetic journals, book series, and MLA discussion groups.

My own preferred metaphor is neither commodification nor renaissance but rather a version of the nomad war machine. This metaphor was coined long ago by Gilles Deleuze and Felix Guattari.[23] Deleuze and Guattari would have welcomed what they surely would have called the rhizomatic spread of nearly 100 literary theories. Theory thus dispersed has a guerrilla-like organization. Guerrilla theory has curtailed the clout of gurus and celebrities; diluted the influence of established journals, departments, and presses; and launched new networks and minor centers of power. The Dow Jones-style big brands such as feminism and deconstruction have been replaced by peasant-insurgent-like journals, presses, and scholarly collectives. A journal such as *symplokē* is a fine example of this. Like the assemblages of weapons used by the nomad war machine, the newer theory seldom uses whole-hog any of the methods of canonical feminism or deconstruction. Current theorists seem instead to knock together impromptu, partial borrowings from established theories. The resulting machinic assemblages are ad hoc contraptions more fitting for the new objects of English Department study.

Jeffrey Nealon, another historian of theory, has said that, in the past

> you could churn literary objects through New Historicism or psychoanalysis or whatever—and churn them through is probably not the right phrase because it makes it seem like it's a grinder again—but you could work them through the theory and the theory could tell you something you hadn't seen before in Shakespeare or in Milton or whatever. Now, the objects are no longer primarily literary objects.[24]

English Department objects now go well beyond *Hamlet*, *Pride and Prejudice*, and *The Dream of the Rood*. They include debt studies, food studies, geocriticism, comparative transpacific, subcultures, gaming studies, new media, social media, critical pedagogy, digital humanities, discourse analysis, life writing, oratures, sentimentality, trauma, pulp fiction, feminist theory, and disability literature—plus seventy-five more. Theories designed to interpret the classics are over the hill. Nealon got it right: the meat grinder wears out, goes obsolete. "Circa 1985 if you could point out the hidden subversiveness beneath commodified practices you were doing interesting work. But you can't pick it up and move it 40 years further, because now there is nothing but subcultures."[25]

Felski's whole against-critique project seems to have sprung from her misgivings about moral meat-grinding: "Puritanism led to denouncing counter-positions and hyper-policing."[26] As an Australian trained in England, she is well positioned to detect North American traces of Puritan culture, especially the grim moralism and yearnings for purity. It grew on her that North Americans had twisted French theory into tense postures of judgment and self-examination. The suspicious vigilance of identity theories has been not just defensive but also insistently redundant; it was decades ago that Eve Sedgwick first denounced "paranoid reading." Fish agrees that paranoid reading, or reading for symptoms, has run its course. "I felt it had run its course the first time it appeared. ... The hermeneutics of suspicion, there it is. That's the big debate I have with Judith [Butler]. Judith is still holding out for critique. Critique of critique of critique of critique."[27]

Sedgwick's long-ago call for "reparative reading" to replace paranoid reading went unheeded, and it remains to be seen whether or not Felski's call will even be heard. Theorizing our attachments and passions certainly sounds preferable to self-righteous unmaskings and denunciations. Felski's recommended turn to larger actor-networks reminds me of Gerald Graff's urgings to stage conflicts with theoretical adversaries. But her program has a decidedly positive spin. "Rather than looking behind a text for hidden causes and motives, literary scholars should place themselves in front of it and reflect on what it suggests and makes possible."[28]

Similarly, Janet Lyon says of a projected Felski-esque theory,

> not that it's some external thing or meat-grinder. It's something that lights up important elements in things, that whole concatenation of anthropocene, and deep time, and post-humanism, and all that stuff. And this is just another way of suggesting how theory works. It's something that lights up important elements in things.[29]

Still, it is hard to know what specific program is being recommended. What sort of literary criticism or theory would "shining a light" entail? Lyon emphasizes lighting up elements hitherto unseen. But this capacity to find the new has always been part of theory's portfolio. Fish observes of one of his own creations: "nobody else has ever done anything like that, actually—anatomize what anti-professionalism is."[30] But he doesn't take credit for it; he gives the credit to

Theory: "Anti-professionalism is a logical outgrowth of the anti-foundationalist insight."[31] He is equally modest about his game-changing Milton book, *Surprised by Sin* (1967). Theory wrote it, not he himself, he confessed. Had he not published it that year, someone else would have. Theory takes on a life of its own, an eerie capacity to produce new thought, like a Frankenstein's monster with a life of its own. Bérubé's case goes right along with this: he wrote his essay "Life as We Know It" thinking it was cultural studies, but he found out—after the fact—that it was the first great work of disability studies. It was another Rosemary's baby, gestating in him without his knowledge or even necessarily his desire.

I have not answered all the pressing questions that I posed. Theory as commodity, as fashion cycle, as meat grinder, as fluoride, as one-on-one basketball, as puritanical inquisition, as shining light, as Frankenstein's monster, as Rosemary's Baby: the metaphors proliferate no less than the theories themselves. My focus on metaphors is a creaky old-fashioned style of literary analysis, and my interest in critics' thoughts and "the next big thing" has the "eighties" flavor of puffy hair and legwarmers. But that is the best I can do. The crystal ball remains cloudy. Once meat grinders have been replaced by networks, machinic assemblages, and theories of attachment, it is not at all clear what sort of work English professors will do.

These interviews with critics impressed me nonetheless with how fully the critical machinery had taken up residence inside the human psyche. While interviewing Homi Bhabha, I heard his story about his mother who for ninety years always requested books she was unable to understand. She read the adolescent Homi poetry by Ezra Pound but she couldn't explain it. What could this odd story mean? Bhabha drew from it the lesson that, when you meet something terribly difficult, you should not turn away from it and exclaim, "Oh, how pretentious." Rather you should give it a chance, stick with it, and hope that something will eventually emerge. This moral of Bhabha's story might be thought of as antifoundationalism in action: like Bhabha's mother, we have no external prop or theory that can guarantee a good result.

The question of theory came down to this: How can theory improve your life?[32] As a principle of behavior, his mother's embracing of difficulty might not change the way you shop, board a plane, make your coffee, brush your teeth, or set up a router. But it just might help you to hang in there until you get to the root of your brother's habit of telling embarrassing stories about you in front of your new romantic interest, the significance of your partner's flirtations with other men, or your department chair's last-minute decision to change your teaching schedule. Theoretical interventions such as hybridity, disavowal, third space, and proximity, as well as Bhabha's attention to the grain of the voice as a theoretical category, also if less obviously than the tolerance of difficulty, all can improve our lives. Theory has become part of the background, the common sense, and the premise of daily life. The machinery of theory has entered the human psyche and made us, in a happy way, posthuman.

On this phenomenological level, theory will survive because it can make lives better.[33]

Notes

1. Georg Lukács, *History and Class Consciousness: Studies in Marxist Dialectics*, trans. Rodney Livingstone (Cambridge: MIT Press; The Merlin Press, 1971).
2. Richard Macksey, interview with H. Aram Veeser, Baltimore, MD, August 7, 2015.
3. Ibid.
4. W. J. T. Mitchell, interview with H. Aram Veeser, Austin, TX, January 8, 2016.
5. Wai Chee Dimock, interview with H. Aram Veeser, Vancouver, Canada, January 10, 2015.
6. Ibid.
7. Michael Bérubé, interview with H. Aram Veeser, State College, PA, July 25, 2015.
8. Rita Felski, interview with H. Aram Veeser, Vancouver, Canada, January 9, 2015.
9. Bruno Latour, *Reassembling the Social: An Introduction to Actor-Network Theory* (Oxford and New York: Oxford University Press, 2005), 236.
10. For example, Stephen Best and Sharon Marcus, "Surface Reading: An Introduction," Special issue, *The Way We Read Now*, ed. Stephen Best and Sharon Marcus, *Representations* 108 (2009): 1–21.
11. For example, Rey Chow, *Sentimental Fabulations: Contemporary Chinese Films: Attachment in the Age of Global Visibility* (New York: Columbia University Press, 2007), and Lauren Berlant, *The Female Complaint: The Unfinished Business of Sentimentality in American Culture* (Durham and London: Duke University Press, 2008).
12. William P. Germano, interview with H. Aram Veeser, New York, July 9, 2015.
13. Ibid.
14. Marjorie Garber, interview with H. Aram Veeser, Cambridge, MA, March 4, 2015.
15. Kenneth Warren, interview with H. Aram Veeser, Chicago, IL, July 29, 2015.
16. Jane Gallop, interview with H. Aram Veeser, Vancouver, Canada, January 9, 2015.
17. Gerald Graff, interview with H. Aram Veeser, Chicago, IL, July 25, 2015.
18. Stanley Fish, interview with H. Aram Veeser, New York, January 27, 2015.
19. Walter Benn Michaels, interview with H. Aram Veeser, Vancouver, Canada, January 11, 2015.

20 Ibid.
21 Vincent B. Leitch, interview with H. Aram Veeser, transcript provided by Leitch, March 16, 2015.
22 Ibid.
23 Gilles Deleuze and Félix Guattari, *A Thousand Plateaus: Capitalism and Schizophrenia*, trans. Brian Massumi (Minneapolis and London: University of Minnesota Press, 1987), 351–423.
24 Jeffrey Nealon, interview with H. Aram Veeser, State College, PA, July 25, 2015.
25 Ibid.
26 Felski, interview with H. Aram Veeser.
27 Fish, interview with H. Aram Veeser.
28 Rita Felski, *The Limits of Critique* (Chicago and London: The University of Chicago Press, 2015), book jacket back cover.
29 Janet Lyon, interview with H. Aram Veeser, State College, PA, July 25, 2015.
30 Fish, interview with H. Aram Veeser.
31 Ibid.
32 Homi Bhabha, interview with H. Aram Veeser, Cambridge, MA, September 17, 2015.
33 I am grateful to Christina Garidis for her help with this chapter. I am grateful to the panelists who took part in the MLA session at which this chapter was first presented.

Works Cited

Berlant, Lauren. *The Female Complaint: The Unfinished Business of Sentimentality in American Culture*. Durham and London: Duke University Press, 2008.
Bérubé, Michael. Interview with H. Aram Veeser. State College, PA. July 25, 2015.
Best, Stephen and Sharon Marcus. "Surface Reading: An Introduction." Special issue, *The Way We Read Now*. Ed. Stephen Best and Sharon Marcus. *Representations* 108 (2009): 1–21.
Bhabha, Homi. Interview with H. Aram Veeser. Cambridge, MA. September 17, 2015.
Chow, Rey. *Sentimental Fabulations: Contemporary Chinese Films: Attachment in the Age of Global Visibility*. New York: Columbia University Press, 2007.
Deleuze, Gilles and Félix Guattari. *A Thousand Plateaus: Capitalism and Schizophrenia*. Trans. Brian Massumi. Minneapolis and London: University of Minnesota Press, 1987.
Dimock, Wai Chee. Interview with H. Aram Veeser. Vancouver, Canada. January 10, 2015.
Felski, Rita. Interview with H. Aram Veeser. Vancouver, Canada. January 9, 2015.
Fish, Stanley. Interview with H. Aram Veeser. New York. January 27, 2015.

Gallop, Jane. Interview with H. Aram Veeser. Vancouver, Canada. January 9, 2015.
Garber, Marjorie. Interview with H. Aram Veeser. Cambridge, MA. March 4, 2015.
Germano, William P. Interview with H. Aram Veeser. New York. July 9, 2015.
Graff, Gerald. Interview with H. Aram Veeser. Chicago, IL. July 25, 2015.
Leitch, Vincent B. Interview with H. Aram Veeser. Transcript provided by Leitch. March 16, 2015.
Lukács, Georg. *History and Class Consciousness: Studies in Marxist Dialectics*. Trans. Rodney Livingstone. Cambridge: MIT Press; The Merlin Press, 1971.
Lyon, Janet. Interview with H. Aram Veeser. State College, PA. July 25, 2015.
Macksey, Richard. Interview with H. Aram Veeser. Baltimore, MD. August 7, 2015.
Michaels, Walter Benn. Interview with H. Aram Veeser. Vancouver, Canada. January 11, 2015.
Mitchell, W. J. T. Interview with H. Aram Veeser. Austin, TX. January 8, 2016.
Nealon, Jeffrey. Interview with H. Aram Veeser. State College, PA. July 25, 2015.
Warren, Kenneth. Interview with H. Aram Veeser. Chicago, IL. July 29, 2015.

Part Three

Philosophy, Theory, and Antitheory

11

Theory Does Not Exist

Paul Allen Miller

I want to argue that theory, as such, does not exist. I realize the perversity of this claim being made by a scholar who has written more than his fair share of books and articles in which the names of Derrida, Foucault, and Lacan, Kristeva, Irigaray, and Kofman loom large. Moreover, I fully appreciate the grave historical irony of this claim after Brexit and the Trump election in a cultural and political context in which the very project of enlightenment modernity seems increasingly imperiled, in which racism, sexism, and homophobia are on the rise, and in which the value of scientific reason (or reason *tout court*) is increasingly questioned. The fact that the science deniers themselves thrive in a media culture that is almost totally dependent on technology never seems to give them pause.

I speak, moreover, as someone who sits in the Provost's office of a major research university and is witnessing the flight of our students from subjects of real inquiry in both basic science and the humanities and who hears the demands of their parents for immediate returns on their investments and of governing boards that insist that the university be run "as a business," that outcomes be measurable and preferably spendable. I think we must also pause in this time of crisis and ask very seriously, "What are we doing as scholars of critical theory?" Are we fiddling while Rome burns? The climate is rapidly degrading, racial nationalism is on the rise throughout the West, neofascists and their close kin are holding rallies and gaining electoral traction, children of immigrants have been put in cages, and the left opposition is too often bogged down in infighting and finger-pointing. It feels all too close to Europe in the 1930s. And here we are doing what academic students of theory do: dissecting the finer points of Derrida, consigning Latour to the ash heap of history, celebrating geocriticism, or investigating the depths of poetry and the Lacanian Real. Have we really nothing better to do? Perhaps not. *Indeed*, perhaps not: for I would argue that sometimes when we most seem to be doing nothing, we are in fact doing something crucial, something that must be done, precisely because it is no thing, because it is not an object with clearly defined borders that can be produced, consumed, commodified, and assessed, because it offers the opportunity to rethink the ontic world as it has been given.

Increasingly I think the correct metaphor is not to picture ourselves as an elite collection of mandarins—which we must admit is how we appear to an all too large a group in the public—occupants of the ivory tower who grow our fingernails long and argue about irrelevancies, while feeding at the trough of public education or on the largesse of the wealthy families who pay steep private school tuitions. Rather than thinking of Nero playing his lyre amidst the decadence of empire, when I consider my colleagues in the humanities who work long hours for mediocre pay and increasingly little job security to teach often-apathetic undergraduates, to prepare graduate students for an all but nonexistent job market and to produce scholarship on topics they love deeply but do not expect even their nearest and dearest to understand, I reflect back instead on the Irish monks of the fifth and sixth centuries, who out on their windswept island copied ancient manuscripts by hand, manuscripts that the surrounding population and the barbarian hordes overrunning Europe could not read or understand and that they would have more readily burned for warmth than spent hours carefully, meticulously annotating and copying. It was those monks who in many ways preserved the conversation we name Western civilization, who through founding schools and monasteries across northern England produced figures such as Alcuin of York, who would go on to establish the cathedral school system under Charlemagne. That system in turn produced the Carolingian renaissance and later grew into the beginnings of the great universities of Europe and, in a sense, eventually brought us all to be contributors to this collection.

Civilization is a delicate web that depends on long conversations extending over great expanses of time, and we should not fool ourselves about how easily its thread is snapped. The Dark Ages actually happened, as did Nazism, Pol Pot, and ISIS. Basic questions about meaning, truth, justice, and ethics; about the importance of reading, thinking, writing, and reflecting; about the nature of the beautiful, the abject, and the sublime can only be posed in terms of the history of their previous usages, predications, and definitions. The capacity to interrogate our present condition, to imagine alternatives to it, and to persuade others to join us in trying to realize those alternatives—as well as the conceptual quality and texture of those alternatives—is precisely dependent on the continuity and context of this conversation. The inability for the next generations to continue it or to understand the complex nature of its genealogy and the subtle determinations that differentiate it from calculations of pure utility or economic rationality is a real possibility. War, ecological disaster, educational mediocrity, the unwillingness to recognize or support that which cannot be subjected to a brutal immediate use all threaten to snap the threads that weave the text of this conversation.

If Irish monks seem too distant a metaphor for the role humanist scholarship plays in the preservation of civilization, think instead of a Jewish French philosopher of Algerian origin buying a postcard in the gift shop of the Bodleian library in Oxford. Derrida's famous postcard is itself taken from the frontispiece to a thirteenth-century work of fortune-telling by Matthew of Paris. The carefully hand-drawn image depicts two figures: one is seated at a desk producing a manuscript, in much the same manner as those very Irish monks would have done and as the actual monk who produced this work did; the other is standing behind the first and giving directions, perhaps even dictating what is being written. They are labeled respectively Socrates and Plato.

There are many ironies here, most of which Derrida himself unpacks in the course of *La carte postale* (1980), which begins as an epistolary novel, continues with Derrida's reading of Lacan's seminar on Poe's "Purloined Letter," and ends with an interview on the relation between Derrida's work and psychoanalysis. The frontispiece to Matthew of Paris's work eventually becomes the cover of Derrida's own. Among the many ironies is the reversal of roles that seems to take place in the postcard's depiction of Plato and Socrates. By tradition, and indeed in accordance with what can be presumed to be historical fact, Socrates did not write. He is the first philosopher in the West, the one from whom all subsequent ancient schools claimed their descent—the Platonic, Stoic, Cynic, Cyrenaic, Peripatetic, and Epicurean—yet he left no writings, and we know him only from the writings of his followers. Most famously, we know Socrates from the writings of Plato. The Socrates of Plato's *Apology, Symposium, Phaedrus*, and the *Republic* is etched in most of our minds and melds with Socrates himself for the vast majority of us. Yet he was hardly the only one. A very different Socrates emerges if you read Xenophon's *Apology, Symposium, Memorabilia*, or *Oikonomika*. Theodectes, whose work is now lost, produced yet another,[1] and we would be very negligent if we were not to include the Socrates of Aristophanes's *Clouds*, whom Kierkegaard considered closest to the historical Socrates.[2] The point here is not to determine which of these is the real Socrates, but rather to see that what a conventional intellectual history would view as a straight line from Socrates to Plato to Plato's readers, ultimately including Derrida and us, is anything but straight. The Socrates that we know both really existed and no doubt had a profound influence on Plato as well as many others. He also so aggravated his uncomprehending fellow citizens that they had him executed, precisely for asking them uncomfortable questions. What is justice? What is the good? What is the beautiful? How should we organize the state so as to bring those forms into being? Yet, this same Socrates is also very much Plato's creation. Indeed, Socrates in a real sense took Plato's dictation. It was he who received Plato's inscription to precisely the extent that Plato was the young disciple able to receive his. The linear depiction of intellectual history, of philosophical debate, of the conversation that constitutes the thin but binding web of civilization is an illusion. That history is a dialogue whose recursive temporality flows in both directions and whose content is never simply there to be received but must be actively constructed and responded to at each point of transmission or transference, at each postal relay.

And this is very much Derrida's point. His stance is ironic and mischievously humorous, but nonetheless deadly serious when he argues in *La carte postale* that we should not underestimate the influence of Freud's *Beyond the Pleasure Principle* on Plato's *Philebus*.[3] The claim is at least a paradox. Traditional intellectual history assumes a univocal, irreversible system of transmission. Socrates teaches Plato. Plato teaches Aristotle. Jesus teaches the disciples. The disciples and the church fathers found the church. And the Western *logos* is established and handed down to us: a divine mixture of Hellenic wisdom and Hebraic faith, in which Sigmund Freud, Matthew Arnold, and Charles Maurras all play their parts. Platonism's function has been to anchor that system of knowledge. Derrida's interrogation of Plato in relation to Freud, however, serves to show not simply the debt of Freud to Plato but the way in which debt per se is the condition of possibility for any investment, the way in which each step forward must recreate its own past in a movement of double conditioning that is, yes, "always already" decentered. Thus, any given relay in the system of transmission of meaning must be radically historicized not only in terms of its debt to the past but also in terms of the way that past itself becomes an object of transmission and hence potentially of appropriation and misappropriation as a condition of entering that system, of becoming a project, of becoming the future. The *Philebus*, as we know it, as we read it today, would not exist without Freud, Derrida argues, to precisely the same degree that Socrates would not exist without Plato, and there is no *Philebus* and no Socrates for us other than the ones we know.[4]

Nonetheless, it is all too easy to forget the contingencies upon which that postcard from the past depends if it is to reach its destination, and indeed as Derrida argues within the same work against Lacan,[5] the letter does not in fact always arrive at its destination, or at least we must always keep open the possibility of its destruction or its loss. The entire structure of Derrida's meditation depends not only on the recursive temporality of his dialogue with Freud, Plato, and Socrates, and the vicissitudes that allowed the works of Plato to survive when so much from antiquity did not, including all the dialogues of Aristotle. It also depends on the production and preservation Matthew of Paris's book of prognostications; on the monks who drew Plato and Socrates in their own image; on the commitment to build and preserve the Bodleian library in 1602; on the invention, continuation, and disruption of the epistolary novel, beginning with Ovid's *Heroides*; and on the commodification and reproduction of culture represented by the postcard itself. At any point, the links in this chain, some salutary, others less so, could have been easily broken and what we take now for civilization could have been lost. There is nothing necessary about any of this surviving or continuing to survive, even though as we gather in our seminar rooms, give our lectures, and write our papers, we all too often take for granted that it will.

What then does any of this have to do with theory or with antitheory for that matter? Everything and nothing. I am asking us to think seriously about what do we mean when we say we teach *theory*, we use *theory*, we apply *theory*, or we have moved beyond/after *theory*? Is theory a thing? Does it have an ontology? Is it something that was invented in Paris on or around 1968 or in American English and Comparative Literature Departments in the 1970s and 1980s? Or, like the poor, has it always been with us? Is it not in many ways the very conversation I have just described as the fabric of civilization itself? Is it not what makes possible, though not as simply a series of operations or reproducible skills, not as *technē*, but as a fundamental questioning of the constitution of our object world that also, in a real sense, brings that world into being as an object of thought, experience, and radical change? And do we not in just as many ways do it a disservice by turning that conversation into a thing that one can either use or reject, adopt or dismiss?

Moreover, if it is a thing, if one can be either for or against theory, does it have different varieties or flavors? Can we move through our intellectual cafeteria line and take a helping of psychoanalysis, a bit of deconstruction, a side of Marxism, and a lovely little dollop of the new materialism for dessert? Is this not what our primers and introduction to theory courses too often lead our students and those who would condemn us to believe, that these "methodologies" are separate entities that both somehow all fall under the magical term "theory" and yet are separable, and you can choose between them as your desire, your hunger, or your nutritional need sees fit? But is this not exactly what Derrida, in many ways the prime exemplar of theory and the "theoretical turn," in a work like *La carte postale* demonstrates not to be true, showing instead that Plato, Socrates, Freud, medieval monastic culture, theory, philosophy and postmodern capitalism are so interimplicated that the very notion that they could be separated from one another and dealt with as semiautonomous entities is precisely as absurd as trying to read Plato today without thinking of Freud.

In 1976, Michel Foucault delivered his annual course at the Collège de France, entitled that year, *Il faut défendre la société*. In it, he argues that history as a discourse has had two primary functions in Western society after antiquity. The first, from the Middle Ages through the eighteenth century, was to legitimate the powers of the sovereign by tracing their origin to Rome. This strategy can be seen in sources as disparate as Geoffrey of Monmouth's twelfth-century *History of the Kings of Britain* and Ronsard's *Françiade*, as well as in Petrarch's famous statement, "what is there in history that is not the praise of Rome."[6] The second function, however, is to conceptualize the history of nations as the chronicle of a war between opposed races. These were not initially understood to be biological races, and these discourses certainly did not correspond to a racist worldview or to a scientific racism, such as became prominent first in the nineteenth century and would later go on to underwrite Nazi ideology, Jim Crowe, manifest destiny, and European imperialism. Nonetheless, in many ways, these early, often obscure, historical works, Foucault argues, provide the rhetorical and intellectual foundations that make those later social and epistemic formations possible. They also provide a set of analytical and storytelling tools that underlie a variety of later models of historical development that see the primary motor of history as being an irreconcilable conflict between mutually exclusive, opposed populations, ranging from social Darwinism to the Stalinist purges.

This second type of history, which knows no analogue in either the ancient or the Medieval world, was initially proposed as a counterhistory. It opposed to the royal narrative of continuity and linear descendance from antiquity to the present a counterstory of conquest, oppression, resistance, and wars of liberation. It was initially produced by writers seldom read today, such as Hotman, Boulainvilliers, and Thiers, as well as others long forgotten. These were often the writers of reaction, defending the rights of the nobility against an increasingly centralized monarchy, which had founded its legitimacy on arguments of continuity and lineal transmission. But at the same time, these reactionary counterhistorians were also forging the discourse of revolution. They present modernity as a break from antiquity, an illegitimate usurpation. Their discourse is founded on unearthing the secret history of the conquest of the nation, whether in the form of the Norman Conquest in England or of the invasion of the Franks and the Merovingian conquest of the indigenous Gallo-Romans. These writers comb the archives to build their narratives, stories that would be decisive, as Foucault shows, both for Walter Scott and Marx himself.[7]

For many, Foucault's name is virtually as synonymous with theory as Derrida's. Together with Lacan, these three made up the ruling troika of what used to be known as "French theory." They were antihumanist Nietzscheans bent on upending the centrality of the subject, the self-evidence of liberalism, and the quiet verities of postwar American literary formalism. If the barbarians were at the gates, they spoke French, and if this was theory, then we should definitely be against it, as the likes of William Bennett (1992), Allan Bloom (1987), E. D. Hirsch (1987), or even René Wellek (1983) assured us.[8] Theory, as thus portrayed, was indeed a thing, and it was bad: a vile abstraction that threatened to swamp all we valued beneath a welter of incomprehensible jargon and half-digested philosophy.

Yet what kind of "thing" was Foucault actually up to here and what would it mean to be for it or, for that matter, against it. If we ask him, the metaphor he offers is oddly enough not so dissimilar from that of the Irish monks I offered at beginning of this chapter. He presents himself less as the Nietzschean superman and much more as the Nietzschean philologist. If he is a theorist, his theory is not one that can be either abstracted or generally applied; nor is it contemplative in the Aristotelian sense of *theoria*, but rather it is very much the product of the archive and the barely audible, often arcane, conversations contained therein:

> After all, the fact that the work I have presented you had this simultaneously fragmentary, repetitive, and discontinuous manner of presenting itself, would correspond closely to something that one could call a "feverish laziness," which characteristically affects the lovers of libraries, of documents, of references, of dusty writings, of texts that have never been read, of books which, as soon as they are printed, are closed up and sleep then on the shelves from which they are taken only several centuries later. All of this would go well with the busy idleness of those who profess a knowledge to no end, a sort of extravagant knowledge, the wealth of the parvenu whose exterior signs, as you well know, are found spread across the bottoms of their pages. That would be suitable for all those who identify with one of those most ancient but also most characteristic secret

societies of the West, one of those strangely indestructible secret societies... which were formed early in Christianity, during the time no doubt of the first convents, on the border of the invasions, the fires, and the forests. I mean the great, tender and passionate free masonry of useless erudition.[9]

Of course, Foucault here does not so much mean that this knowledge is completely useless, anymore than the manuscripts copied, annotated, and illuminated by those Irish monks were useless, even though no single one of those monks ever imagined the uses to which those manuscripts and their collective efforts would be put. Rather these are knowledges that are not completely subjected to or exhausted by immediate use, knowledges that have been swept aside or subjected by new, hegemonic configurations of power, knowledges that once unearthed reveal both the capillaries of knowledge and power that have nourished the dominant synthesis of the present and thereby offer new possibilities of thought, new forms of knowledge and truth.

They do not so much offer a "global theory" as the possibility of a local critique. Foucault's next remarks here are prescient. They recall very much the impasse faced by the humanities in the modern American university, where we are constantly asked to justify our existence in terms of outcomes assessment, value added, and the income levels of our graduates. What contribution does a commentary on Origen's homily on the Song of Songs, a new reading of Montaigne's "Des cannibales," or a study of postcolonial film make to the reduction of student debt, postgraduate income levels, and to powering the infernal machine of endlessly increasing commodity production and consumption? Foucault's response is neither to fall back on claims of timeless values, which are only too obviously time bound, nor to submit to a narrowly conceived utilitarianism, but to call for and foster an insurrection of "subjected knowledges":

> [A] local critique is accomplished, it seems to me, through what we might call the "returns of knowledge." By "returns of knowledge," I mean the following: if it is true that in recent years we have often encountered at least on a superficial level a recurring motif: "not more books but life!" "not more knowledge, but reality," "not books, but cash," etc., it seems to me that under, across, and within this recurring motif, what we have seen produced is what might be called the insurrection of "subjected knowledges."[10]

Now Foucault in these passages was as much addressing the anti-intellectualism of the Cultural Revolution as of the neoliberal state.[11] There is a sense in which the demand for immediate political utility is the obverse of the insistence on the assessment and commodification of all knowledge. But the subjected knowledges to which he is referring, the dusty tomes to which his attention was turned, revealed a world of hidden conversations and debates, which not only had been subjected to later hegemonic narratives but also can be shown to have created the intellectual substructure of many of the best-known discursive formations of the next two centuries. In the coming years, his attention would turn to the language of the confessional, of Stoic philosophy, and of ancient justifications for the courage to stand before your prince, your people, or your soul and tell the truth. These discourses, of course, spoke to a variety of contemporary concerns from the genealogy of psychoanalysis to the creation of a counterhistory of philosophy as a set of practices and forms of self-relation, rather than a body of doctrine, but in no case do they offer a global theory. They inform what Foucault termed the ontology of the present, that is, the being of our present moment, the way in which reality is defined and exists for us, not in the form of a transcendental deduction, but as a thousand barely audible voices and institutions that inform, contradict, and determine one another and exist in a recursive relationship between present and past that in turn constitutes the future as a determined set of possibilities.[12]

What then do we mean by theory? For Zahi Zalloua, theory is defined by its opposition to philosophy. If philosophy seeks a world of pure thought, then theory is messy, impure, interdisciplinary. If philosophy seeks certainty, theory strives to be skeptical, to put itself forever in question, to be forever critical. If philosophy aims for the truth, the incontrovertible, the certain, theory is fictive, constructed, contingent. Hegel's *Logic*, Russell and Whitehead's *Principia Mathematica*, and Wittgenstein's *Tractatus* are philosophy by this definition, or at least that is what they very much aim to be. Kierkegaard, Nietzsche, and Derrida are theory, messy, literary, and skeptical. Zalloua in his closely argued and powerful book, *Theory's Autoimmunity* (2018), offers a ringing defense of theory as the critical self-analysis of reason from the standpoint of its own inscription.

Autoimmunity refers to the way in which the protective system of the body turns against itself as in such autoimmune disorders as lupus, rheumatoid arthritis, or ulcerative colitis. It is what happens when the body identifies the same as other, when the self starts to defend itself from itself, from the other that always exists within the self. Theory then names a move whereby reason, and more precisely reason's inscription into the material, its practice by a self, its critical recognition of its own historical contingency, turns on itself and undermines philosophy's claims to pure reason, to unadulterated certainty, to the absolute truth, at least insofar as those claims are actually made. Theory on this view is what turns reason from a protective coating into a gaping wound that allows the external to penetrate within us, to become recognized as the already internalized. It is what makes us vulnerable to the event: "Without autoimmunity nothing would happen; there would be no presence, no event of any kind. The event punctures the psychic shield afforded by our habits, which constitute our lifeless or quasi-mechanistic horizon."[13] Without the piercing of the envelope of self-protective identity, there is no encounter with the event or the other, but instead, as in *Beyond the Pleasure Principle*, or the *Philebus* for that matter, a return to a homeostatic sameness that is impossible to differentiate from either death or immortality.

And this, in turn, is precisely the argument in Plato's *Symposium*. Human beings can never possess wisdom but only the love of wisdom, *philosophia*, because to possess wisdom fully would mean to reach perfection, and the perfect is that from which nothing is missing. Those from whom nothing is missing do not experience love or desire because you cannot desire that which you fully possess. Therefore, only the gods possess wisdom and insofar as they must be completely bereft of desire, they must also be completely unmoved and unmoving, and therefore in the perfection of their immortality, they are indistinguishable from the dead.[14] They are literally beyond the pleasure principle. But we humans—in our wounding imperfection,[15] in our openness to the other we do not possess, in our desire, in our traumatic autoimmunity and its shuddering *jouissance*— must settle for mere philosophy, which names not certainty, not the possession of knowledge, but its simultaneous pursuit and lack. And so at the very origins of philosophy, when Plato dictates to Socrates, to Socrates who is the source of Plato's wisdom, we find theory, as defined by Zalloua, not opposed to philosophy, but as the very conditions of its existence qua philosophy.

The search for wisdom, however, comes to us in a variety of practices, none of which can be separated from their various forms of embodiment and inscription. It may be instructive at this point to turn our attention briefly to monks in a very different tradition from those in Ireland. Specifically, I would ask you to consider the Buddhist monks and hermits of China and Japan, the searchers for truth and enlightenment, who would leave their lives behind, sometimes lives of great privilege, go out and sit facing a wall for years at a time, practicing what in the vocabulary of the later Foucault would be termed "technologies of the self" or "the arts of existence."[16] As he would contend in his final lectures at the Collège de France, which focused on the ancient philosophy of the West rather than the East, these "technologies" and "arts" were best understood as "spiritual practices," practices of self-formation and reflection that prepared the subject to receive the truth and to perform acts of truth, or *alèthurgies* to use the term he coined in 1980 when beginning his examination of early Christian practices of confession and profession.[17] As Plato emphasizes in his seventh letter, such practices, while deeply learned, did not simply involve the receiving and repeating of predigested information (or misinformation) but involved *tribē*: a labor, a continuous friction, that leads to the "spark" or "flame" of enlightenment.[18] This is true philosophy according to Plato, and in this philosophical tradition, to which Foucault clearly affiliates himself, but in which he would also include Nietzsche, the Kant of *What Is Enlightenment*, the Stoics, and the Cynics, the truth is never fully separable from the act that produces it, even as that act, to be an act of truth, an *alèthurgie*, must point beyond itself.[19] The monks of Iona who produced the *Book of Kells* and other masterpieces of early Celtic art did not simply transmit the information that makes up our civilization, as if the conversation could be reduced to its separable referents, but they maintained, elaborated, and transmitted its practice, a form of writing and inscription that can never be reduced merely to the immediate utility of its products.

Bodhi Darma came from the West. He sat for nine years facing a wall on Mount Song, bringing Buddhism and the practice of the Chan to China. To make sure he did not fall asleep but continued his meditation with full awareness, he slit his eyelids, seeking the moment of enlightenment. In an early Chan text, the *Song of the Jewel Mirror Awareness*, we read:

> Filling a silver bowl with snow
> Hiding a heron in the moonlight
> When you array them they are not the same;
> When you mix them, you know where they are.
> The meaning is not in the words,
> Yet it responds to the inquiring impulse.[20]

These other monks, these *rishis*, are the Buddhist seekers of enlightenment who know they have reached it precisely at the moment when the search itself becomes what is sought. The event, the moment when Being beyond the opposites,[21] beyond the binary nature of opposed truths reveals itself, is also the moment of its simultaneous disappearance.[22] The fetishization of truth, the fantasy that you can possess it and be the god of Plato's *Symposium*, is also the moment when truth disappears, when enlightenment becomes both death and immortality, but also delusion.[23] The search for the truth, for the *event* in the moment of its disclosure, is no less authentic for the fact that in the grasping of the event, it vanishes in a moment of self-occultation. The event itself is no thing, and the attempt to reduce it to a thing, a reproducible entity, is to deny its status precisely as the event, a something beyond the endless reproduction of the given. An early Chan text tells the following anecdote:

> Once as Yaoshan [a Chan monk of the Tang dynasty] was sitting, Shitou [his master] saw him and asked "what are you doing here?" Yaoshan said, "I'm not doing anything." Shitou said, "Then you are just sitting idly." Yaoshan said, "if I were sitting idly, that would be doing something." Shitou said, "You said you are not doing; what aren't you doing?" Yaoshan said "Even the saints don't know."[24]

The moment of aporia in these practices, as in the early Socratic dialogues, becomes the search for truth itself. Such koans, as in Socratic practice, force the practitioner to think beyond the categories of the given. That search is not opposed to study. It is indeed founded on study, a study that always moves toward the truth, toward that which breaks through the fetishization of different formations of power, discourse, and knowledge, but not in the name of a cynical claim that there are no facts, that knowledge does not exist, but in the endless pursuit of a truth whose fundamental realization, as the event, as the triumph of the autoimmune response, is both the destruction of the sovereign self, as Zalloua recognizes so well, *and* its absolute realization. As the thirteenth-century Zen master Dogen writes:

> To study the Buddha way is to study the self. To study the self is to forget the self. To forget the self is to be actualized by myriad things. When actualized by myriad things, your body and mind as well as the bodies and minds of others drop away. No trace of realization remains, and this no trace continues endlessly.[25]

Let us take just a moment to examine what is happening in this extremely dense passage. Dogen tells us that the study of Buddhism is on a fundamental level after a form of self-realization or spiritual practice in the Foucauldian sense. But rather than producing a shallow New Age focus on the self, as a bounded, centered entity, as a thing, the search for enlightenment instead leads to a deconstruction of the narcissistic self, to the recognition that the self has no existence apart from the myriad things out of which and in relation to which it is constituted. This recognition in turn both undermines the mind-body distinction and the radical separation of self from other on which that distinction depends. That undermining, in turn, means that the realization of the self is its disappearance, its reduction to a trace that both continues endlessly and has no definable ontic existence.

What the Chan and Zen traditions bring to this discussion, even if only briefly, is to reframe the problematization of what is theory and what is philosophy in a larger, less ethnocentric context. What Foucault would argue has become lost in the teaching of much academic philosophy but is central to the philosophical tradition—and I think it is important to realize that neither he nor Derrida ever self-identified as theorists but always as philosophers—is the valorization of practices of truth, *askeses*, that undo the opposition of theory and philosophy, that foreground not truth as endlessly reproducible information, not as what any ass can google and then present as *his* truth, but as an intersubjective practice that always includes its own processes of reflection, verification, and materialization as integral to the act of veridiction.[26]

And this in turn really is the point. Philosophy *is* this practice, this conversation, across the centuries, across genres, ultimately across entire civilizations, that reflects, produces, and criticizes acts of truth. It exists as processes of reflection, verification, and materialization, whether that is in the rarefied forms of philosophies of science and formal logic or in Socrates on the streets of Athens challenging his fellow Athenians to say what it is they know, to define justice, and to care for themselves. Philosophy is constituted in all its manifold forms by this dialogue with its own archive and by the debates on what constitutes that archive. Theory, insofar as it seeks to challenge the hegemony of a certain vision of philosophical purity, is always dependent on its reinsertion in the dialogue with philosophy. In Socrates's great speech in the *Phaedrus*, we are not presented with a series of deductions, we are not offered a method of adjudicating the truth or falsity of a given set of propositions, nor are we offered a set of truths that can be formalized separately from their textual formulation. In the vision of the parade of souls approaching the gods and catching ever so slight a glimpse of the forms of beauty and the good, of the souls who guide their chariots pulled by the horse of spirit and the horse of sexual desire,[27] we have a complex myth of love that is self-consciously poetic and derivative, even as it seeks to oppose itself to the rhetorical manipulations of Lysias's cynical speech and Socrates's first speech. Myth in Plato is not a mere accidental ornament or illustration but a necessary supplement to the *logos* and dialectic, as can be illustrated in a wide variety of dialogues from the *Republic*, to the *Symposium*, the *Gorgias*, and the *Timaeus*.[28] The archive of received semblances in Plato—myths, speeches hidden under one's cloak, writing itself—in the final analysis can never be completely dissociated from the truth philosophy claims to speak and to adjudicate. Thus, even the myths deployed by Socrates in his great speech are derived from the poetic tradition, the lore of Pythagoreanism, the mysteries, and Egyptian myth.[29] As Berger argues, the great speech pretends "to be a spontaneous ecstatic outburst when it is actually a citational pastiche."[30] It undermines philosophy's attempt to immunize itself against the other. It is in short theory: present at the birth of philosophy even in its vision of the ideal. Theory is the precondition, supplement, and transcendence of philosophy. Theory is antitheory, and as theory qua theory, as a *thing*, it does not exist.

In the ancient world, the other of philosophy is not named theory but rhetoric, and this opposition is precisely what is put into play in the *Phaedrus*, which begins as an examination of the power of Lysias's cynical demonstration speech, advocating that a young man should only yield to one who is not in love with him, since all lovers are mad. The dialogue famously ends with a philosophical examination of how speeches should be made and an argument for the philosophical *logographer* or speechwriter. The *Phaedrus* in fact is the first example of a philosophical examination of rhetoric and, as such, is the great predecessor to Aristotle's *Rhetoric* and such important later works as Cicero's *De Oratore*. In the middle of the *Phaedrus*, we find Socrates's great speech, one of the most brilliant virtuoso displays of rhetoric in the entire ancient tradition. It turns Lysias's argument on its head, contending that the beloved should *only* yield to the suitor who is in love, precisely because he is mad, like the poet and ultimately the philosopher. Thus the central exemplar of philosophy's superiority to rhetoric, both as philosophy and as rhetoric, is a poetic speech in which the philosopher argues for his own constitutive madness.

Philosophy can never be pure. It is always derivative from rhetoric and poetry, from various practices of embodiment. In the end, this conclusion is not the product of a deconstructive reading or an elaborate theoretical argument but is directly stated within the dialogue. Philosophy is a response to a preexisting set of conversations, acts of imagination, acts of truth, and acts of persuasion. When Socrates begins his critique of Lysias's speech, Phaedrus is incredulous. He asks, "Where have you heard a better speech than this?" Socrates replies:

> Now I really can't say. But it's clear I've heard them, whether they be lovely Sappho or wise Anacreon or some prose writers? What sort of proof do I offer in support? I have a strange fullness in my breast, divine Phaedrus, and I perceive that I am able to say different things, which would not be worse, on this same topic. I know well that I have not at all thought about these matters, being conscious of my own ignorance. Indeed, I think, the only possibility left is that I have been filled through my ears from the streams of others, like a pitcher. But on account of a certain stupidity, I have forgotten this very thing, how and from whom I heard them.[31]

This passage has gone all but unnoticed in the scholarship. It claims simultaneously that Socrates is ignorant and filled with information, with the citations of others. He is, of course, being ironic, but not simply sarcastic. Every phrase in this passage overflows with meaning rather than simply points to its opposite. It also points to a fundamental aporia. If there is no original word, then, at what point do we distinguish internal from external, philosophy as the authentic pursuit of truth from rhetoric or theory as the secondary manipulation of language? The first answer is we don't. The moment such a distinction is made, the moment the play of difference is arrested, then language, words themselves become dead letters. The play of transmission is arrested; the letter ceases to arrive at its destination. The second answer, though, is to acknowledge the infinite irony of this temporal play. *Primary* and *secondary, inside* and *outside* are not fixed terms with fixed meanings, but neither are they meaningless. Rather only when Socrates ceases to ask questions, when he simply accepts being the wisest of men, does he cease to be in a complex, recursive, and mutually constitutive relationship with Plato, Freud, and us, to be our inspiration and creation. Filled with the knowledge of others, like a pitcher, and completely ignorant, inspired and utterly derivative of the poets and writers of prose: philosophy is constituted both as itself and its other, as both theory and antitheory.

We make then a fundamental mistake in arguing for or against theory, as if theory were a thing that can be simply refused or accepted, anymore than can philosophy or rhetoric, at least within a world in which people still seek to discuss, persuade, or imagine. Rather, what I would contend we must do in our seminar rooms, our lecture halls, our journal articles and books is relentlessly to expose the myriad ways in which the very possibility of the existence of our civilization is dependent on this work, on the continuity of this work, even when it might appear to those outside that we are doing nothing. The very possibility of a self that cares for itself in relation to others, that distinguishes in a coherent and sustained fashion between truth and falsity, that is able to conceptualize and defend a moral universe beyond immediate utility, beyond the crushing brutality of pure exchange value, and that is not consumed by fear and hatred, by the death drive, is dependent upon the practices of truth, imagination, and persuasion that we preserve, refine, and continue in this conversation. The ontology of the present, as a present, is made up of the discourses that contribute to that conversation and of the practices that constitute them. By making those practices visible, we both transmit them and open them up to interrogation, criticism, and change. We make articulate resistance possible. By unearthing the dusty subjected knowledges and the barely audible voices that created them, we both enliven them and make new discursive options available. We make it possible to think, and thus to act, differently.[32] In doing so, we reveal the constitutive debt that the future not only owes the past but the past owes the future, that Socrates always in a sense took dictation from a Plato that only Freud made possible. In doing so, we reveal the postal system, the material substructure that allows the letter to arrive at its destination: a gossamer-like structure that is all too fragile in the strands that bind it together.

Yaoshan while meditating said in response to his master's query,

> "I'm not doing anything." Shitou said, "Then you are just sitting idly." Yaoshan said, "if I were sitting idly, that would be doing something." Shitou said, "You said you are not doing; what aren't you doing?" Yaoshan said "Even the saints don't know."[33]

The fact that even the saints don't know is precisely what makes this practice, our practice, at least *in potentia*, a radically transformative act: for when we sit in our studies, discuss in our seminar rooms, and lecture in our auditoriums, we may appear to be doing nothing, and indeed what we are doing is *no thing*. Yet I would contend that the conversation in which we are participating—the conversation that we name variously theory, philosophy, rhetoric, and literature, the search for truth—is itself both fundamental to the constitution of the world of things as things, as a set of defined ontic categories, and to the possibility of revolution in ways yet to be imagined.[34]

Notes

1 Gabriel Danzig, "Apologizing for Socrates: Plato and Xenophon on Socrates' Behavior in Court," *Transactions of the American Philological Association* 133 (2003).
2 Søren Kierkegaard, *The Concept of Irony with Continual Reference to Socrates*, ed. and trans. Howard V. Hong and Edna H. Hong (Princeton: Princeton University Press, 1989), 128–156.
3 Jacques Derrida, *La carte postale: De Socrate à Freud et au-delà* (Paris: Flammarion, 1980), 120; Paul Allen Miller, *Postmodern Spiritual Practices: The Construction of the Subject and the Reception of Plato in Lacan, Derrida, and Foucault* (Columbus: Ohio State University Press, 2007), 139–141.
4 Derrida, *La carte postale*, 36, 60–70, 180–207; Miller, *Postmodern Spiritual Practices*, 151–166.
5 Derrida, *La carte postale*, 439–524.

6   Michel Foucault, *"Il faut défendre la société": Cours au Collège de France. 1976*, ed. Mauro Bertani and Alessandro Fontana (Paris: Gallimard and Seuil, 1997), 65.
7   Foucault, *"Il faut défendre la société,"* 69, 87.
8   Jacques Derrida, *Memoires for Paul de Man*, The Wellek Library Lectures at the University of California Irvine, trans. Eduardo Cadava, Jonathan Culler, Cecile Lindsay, and Avital Ronnell (New York: Columbia University Press, 1986), 12, 41–43n5; Jacques Derrida, *Mémoires pour Paul de Man* (Paris: Galilée, 1988), 34–35n2; Paul Allen Miller, "Ghosts in the Politics of Friendship," *Dead Theory: Derrida, Death, and the Afterlife of Theory*, ed. Jeffrey R. Di Leo (New York: Bloomsbury, 2016a).
9   Foucault *"Il faut défendre la société,"* 6.
10 Ibid., 8.
11 David Macey, *The Lives of Michel Foucault* (New York: Pantheon, 1993), 217–219; Benoît Peeters, *Derrida* (Paris: Flammarion, 2010), 269–296; Paul Allen Miller, *Diotima at Barricades: French Feminists Read Plato* (Oxford: Oxford University Press, 2016), chapter 2.
12 Michel Foucault, *Le gouvernement de soi et des autres: Cours au Collège de France, 1982-1983*, ed. Frédéric Gros (Paris: Gallimard and Seuil, 2008), 4–5, 22, 273, 285–286.
13 Zahi Zalloua, *Theory's Autoimmunity* (Evanston: Northwestern University Press, 2018), Introduction.
14 200a–203a.
15 CF Aristophanes's myth of the androgyne.
16 Michel Foucault, *L'Usage des plaisirs: Histoire de la Sexualité*. Vol. 2 (Paris: Gallimard, 1984), 35; Michel Foucault, "L'écriture de soi," in *Dits et écrits: 1954–1988*. Vol. 4, ed. Daniel Defert et François Ewalt (Paris: Gallimard, 1994), 415; Michel Foucault, "A propos de la généalogie de l'éthique: un aperçu du travail en cours," in *Dits et écrits: 1954–1988*. Vol. 4, ed. Daniel Defert et François Ewalt (Paris: Gallimard, 1994), 617; Michel Foucault, *L'herméneutique du sujet: Cours au Collège de France, 1981–82*, ed. Frédéric Gros (Paris: Gallimard, Seuil, 2001), 241–242; Angèle Kremer-Marietti, *Michel Foucault: Archéologie et Généalogie*, 2nd ed. Rev. (Paris: Livre de poche, 1985), 251, 277; Alexander Nehamas, *The Art of Living: Socratic Reflections from Plato to Foucault* (Berkeley: University of California Press, 1998), 168–169; Frédéric Gros, "Situation du cours," in Michel Foucault, *L'herméneutique du sujet: Cours au Collège de France. 1981–82*, ed. Frédéric Gros (Paris: Gallimard, Seuil, 2001), 524–525.
17 Pierre Hadot, *Qu'est-ce que la philosophie antique* (Paris: Gallimard, 1995), 21–22; Foucault, *L'herméneutique du sujet*, 16–17; compare A. J. Festugière, *Contemplation et vie contemplative selon Platon*, 2nd ed (Paris: Vrin, 1950), 21–22; Michel Foucault, *Du gouvernement des vivants: Cours au Collège de France, 1979-80*, ed. Michel Senellart (Paris: EHESS, Gallimard, 2012), 8, 48, 79–81, 111–112, 151–157.

18 Plato, "Seventh Letter," 340a–344e; Foucault, *Le gouvernement de soi et des autres*, 51–56, 192–234.
19 Foucault *L'herméneutique du sujet*; Foucault, *Le gouvernement de soi et des autres*, 8–9, 29–36, 64, 322; Michel Foucault, *Le courage de la vérité: Cours au Collège de France, 1984*, ed. Frédéric Gros (Paris: Gallimard, EHESS, and Seuil, 2009).
20 Thomas Cleary, ed. and trans., *Timeless Spring: A Soto Zen Anthology* (Tokyo and New York: Weatherhill, 1980), 39.
21 Benjamin Radcliff and Amy Radcliff, *Understanding Zen* (Boston: Charles E. Tuttle and Company, 1993), 13–33.
22 Cf. (Mumonkan Case 19). "Nanquan said, 'The Way is not in the province of knowledge, yet not in the province of unknowing. Knowledge is false consciousness, unknowing is indifference. If you really arrive at the inimitable Way, it is like space, empty and open; how can you insist on affirmation and denial?' At these words, Zhaozhou was suddenly enlightened" (Thomas Cleary, ed. and trans., *No Barrier: Unlocking the Zen Koan* [New York: Bantam, 1992], 94). Thanks to Charles Platter for the reference.
23 Shunryu Suzuki, *Zen Mind, Beginner's Mind: Informal Talks on Zen Meditation and Practice*, ed. Trudy Dixon (New York and Tokyo: Weatherhill, 1970), 21–22.
24 Cleary, *Timeless Spring*, 35.
25 Kazuaki Tanahashi, ed., "Actualizing the Fundamental Point," in trans. Robert Aitken and Kazuaki Tanahashi, *Moon in a Dewdrop: Writings of Zen Master Dōgen* (New York: North Point Press, 1985), 70.
26 Foucault, *Le gouvernement de soi et des autres*, 318.
27 Plato, *Phaedrus*, 246e–248c.
28 Léon Robin, "Notice," in *Platon: Phèdre* (Paris: Société d'Edition "Les Belles Lettres," 1966), xcvi; Catherine H. Zuckert, *Postmodern Platos: Nietzsche, Heidegger, Gadamer, Strauss, Derrida* (Chicago: University of Chicago Press, 1996), 218.
29 Robin, "Notice," lxxix–lxxxvii, 44n1, 50n3; 158–160; W. H. Thompson, *The Phaedrus of Plato with English Notes and Dissertations* (New York: Arno Press, 1973), xxvi–xxvii, 43–74; Michael L. Morgan, "Plato and Greek Religion," *The Cambridge Companion to Plato*, ed. Richard Kraut (Cambridge: Cambridge University Press, 1992), 231–239; Ernst Heitsch, *Phaidros* (Göttingen: Vandenhoeck & Ruprecht, 1993), 95, 98–107.
30 Harry Berger Jr., "*Phaedrus* and the Politics of Inscriptions," *Plato and Postmodernism*, ed. Steven Shankman (Glenside, PA: Aldine Press, 1994), 102.
31 Ibid., 235c1–d3.
32 Foucault, *L'Usage des plaisirs*, 14–15.
33 Cleary, *Timeless Spring*, 35.
34 Many thanks to Anna Kornbluh and Irving Goh, whose articulate questions both at the initial presentation and in subsequent conversation helped to sharpen my

focus and make this a better chapter. Thanks also to Steven Shankman for his constructive feedback and encouragement and to my audience at the English Department at Ewha Woman's University in Seoul who heard a later version of this chapter and whose lively response I greatly appreciated.

Works Cited

Bennett, William J. *The De-Valuing of America: The Fight for Our Culture and Our Children*. New York: Touchstone, 1992.

Berger, Harry, Jr. "*Phaedrus* and the Politics of Inscriptions." *Plato and Postmodernism*. Ed. Steven Shankman. Glenside, PA: Aldine Press, 1994. 76–114.

Bloom, Allan. *The Closing of the American Mind*. New York: Simon and Schuster, 1987.

Cleary, Thomas, ed. and trans. *Timeless Spring: A Soto Zen Anthology*. Tokyo and New York: Weatherhill, 1980.

Cleary, Thomas, ed. and trans. *No Barrier: Unlocking the Zen Koan*. New York: Bantam, 1992.

Danzig, Gabriel. "Apologizing for Socrates: Plato and Xenophon on Socrates's Behavior in Court." *Transactions of the American Philological Association* 133 (2003): 281–321.

Derrida, Jacques. *La carte postale: De Socrate à Freud et au-delà*. Paris: Flammarion, 1980.

Derrida, Jacques. *Memoires for Paul de Man*. The Wellek Library Lectures at the University of California Irvine. Trans. Eduardo Cadava, Jonathan Culler, Cecile Lindsay, and Avital Ronnell. New York: Columbia University Press, 1986.

Derrida, Jacques. *Mémoires pour Paul de Man*. Paris: Galilée, 1988.

Festugière, A. J. *Contemplation et vie contemplative selon Platon*. 2nd ed. Paris: Vrin, 1950.

Foucault, Michel. *L'Usage des plaisirs. Histoire de la Sexualité*. Vol 2. Paris: Gallimard, 1984.

Foucault, Michel. "L'écriture de soi." In *Dits et écrits: 1954–1988*. Vol. 4. Ed. Daniel Defert et François Ewalt. Paris: Gallimard, 1994. 415–430.

Foucault, Michel. "A propos de la généalogie de l'éthique: un aperçu du travail en cours." In *Dits et écrits: 1954–1988*. Vol. 4. Ed. Daniel Defert et François Ewalt. Paris: Gallimard, 1994. 609–631.

Foucault, Michel. "*Il faut défendre la société*": *Cours au Collège de France. 1976*. Ed. Mauro Bertani and Alessandro Fontana. Paris: Gallimard and Seuil, 1997.

Foucault, Michel. *L'herméneutique du sujet: Cours au Collège de France. 1981–82*. Ed. Frédéric Gros. Paris: Gallimard, Seuil, 2001.

Foucault, Michel. *Le gouvernement de soi et des autres: Cours au Collège de France. 1982–1983*. Ed. Frédéric Gros. Paris: Gallimard and Seuil, 2008.

Foucault, Michel. *Le courage de la vérité: Cours au Collège de France. 1984*. Ed. Frédéric Gros. Paris: Gallimard, EHESS, and Seuil, 2009.

Foucault, Michel. *Du gouvernement des vivants: Cours au Collège de France. 1979–80*. Ed. Michel Senellart. Paris: EHESS, Gallimard, 2012.

Gros, Frédéric. "Situation du cours." In Michel Foucault, *L'herméneutique du sujet: Cours au Collège de France. 1981–82*. Ed. Frédéric Gros. Paris: Gallimard, Seuil, 2001. 487–526.

Hadot, Pierre. *Qu'est-ce que la philosophie antique*. Paris: Gallimard, 1995.

Heitsch, Ernst. *Phaidros*. Göttingen: Vandenhoeck & Ruprecht, 1993.

Hirsch, E. D. *Cultural Literacy: What Every American Needs to Know*. New York: Houghton Mifflin, 1987.

Kierkegaard, Søren. *The Concept of Irony with Continual Reference to Socrates*. Ed. and trans. Howard V. Hong and Edna H. Hong. Princeton: Princeton University Press, 1989.

Kremer-Marietti, Angèle. *Michel Foucault: Archéologie et Généalogie*. 2nd ed. Rev. Paris: Livre de poche, 1985.

Macey, David. *The Lives of Michel Foucault*. New York: Pantheon, 1993.

Miller, Paul Allen. *Postmodern Spiritual Practices: The Construction of the Subject and the Reception of Plato in Lacan, Derrida, and Foucault*. Columbus: Ohio State University Press, 2007.

Miller, Paul Allen. "Ghosts in the Politics of Friendship." In *Dead Theory: Derrida, Death, and the Afterlife of Theory*. Ed. Jeffrey R. Di Leo. New York: Bloomsbury, 2016. 111–132.

Miller, Paul Allen. *Diotima at Barricades: French Feminists Read Plato*. Oxford: Oxford University Press, 2016.

Morgan, Michael L. "Plato and Greek Religion." *The Cambridge Companion to Plato*. Ed. Richard Kraut. Cambridge: Cambridge University Press, 1992. 227–247.

Nehamas, Alexander. *The Art of Living: Socratic Reflections from Plato to Foucault*. Berkeley: University of California Press, 1998.

Peeters, Benoît. *Derrida*. Paris: Flammarion, 2010.

Radcliff, Benjamin and Amy Radcliff. *Understanding Zen*. Boston: Charles E. Tuttle and Company, 1993.

Robin, Léon. "Notice." *Platon: Phèdre*. Paris: Société d'Edition "Les Belles Lettres," 1966. vii–ccv.

Suzuki, Shunryu. *Zen Mind, Beginner's Mind: Informal Talks on Zen Meditation and Practice*. Ed. Trudy Dixon. New York and Tokyo: Weatherhill, 1970.

Tanahashi, Kazuaki, ed. "Actualizing the Fundamental Point." Trans. Robert Aitken and Kazuaki Tanahashi. *Moon in a Dewdrop: Writings of Zen Master Dōgen*. New York: North Point Press, 1985. 69–73.

Thompson, W. H. *The Phaedrus of Plato with English Notes and Dissertations*. New York: Arno Press, 1973.

Wellek, René. "Destroying Literary Studies." *New Criterion* 2 (1983): 1–8.
Zalloua, Zahi. *Theory's Autoimmunity*. Evanston: Northwestern University Press, 2018.
Zuckert, Catherine H. *Postmodern Platos: Nietzsche, Heidegger, Gadamer, Strauss, Derrida*. Chicago: University of Chicago Press, 1996.

12

(Anti)Theory's Resistances

Tom Eyers

Prologue

I come to the question of theory—what it is, the pathos of its repeatedly announced deaths, its vulnerable afterlives, those various postcritical movements that would now, belatedly, oppose it: I come to these bearing multiple dislocations, disciplinary, and otherwise. I went to university initially to read English literature, and a fortuitous encounter with Jacques Derrida's *Writing and Difference* at age eighteen set me on the path to a determinately literary theory. English at Cambridge, however, appeared from the off hostile to theory in its very marrow (the atmosphere at my college—the proudly conservative Trinity—no doubt contributed to my perception of this), and so I migrated to sociology, and eventually to social anthropology, while maintaining my literary interests and studying as much European philosophy as I could. Meanwhile, the philosophy department at Cambridge, preoccupied as it was with the parochial concerns of the analytic school, would not have been welcoming. I alighted on the anthropology department in large part because of Marilyn Strathern, a formidable feminist theorist who, in her short time as acting chair of the department, encouraged transdisciplinary risk taking.[1] By the time I wrote my Ph.D. dissertation, I was based in a philosophy research center in London that specialized in a politically radical variant of that curiously secondhand, usefully homeless practice known as Anglophone "Continental" philosophy. And yet, writing on Jacques Lacan, a psychoanalyst of course, I never quite identified with philosophy, "Continental" or otherwise, even as my dissertation and first book bore the marks of an intensive graduate training in the Kantian and post-Kantian traditions.[2]

Now tenured in one of the rare philosophy departments in the United States that focuses on the "Continental" variant, I still feel like something of an internal exile in philosophical circles, especially as my literary interests have returned with a vengeance. (I am aware, needless to say, of how lucky I am to have a job and tenure at all, in this nigh-apocalyptic job market for Ph.D. graduates). I have, in the last few years, published works of straight literary theory and essays that center above all on close reading of literary language, poetry especially, and yet I am not straightforwardly a literary scholar, either; I don't quite fit with any one historical period or specialty. Being neither quite a philosopher nor quite a literary critic, I am, I suppose, a *theorist*. And yet, as is well known, theory, or French theory, or structuralism, or poststructuralism, found a home in the United States principally in literature departments, and so even as I identify, more or less, with it, whatever that "it" is, I am employed in the name of a discipline, philosophy, that, even in its marginalized Continental wing, remains largely peripheral to cutting-edge critical-theoretical, certainly literary-theoretical, discussion, and publication. When I give talks, they are almost always at literary conferences or in departments of literature, even as these institutional spaces have become less and less welcoming to theoretical speculation on the trans- if not a-historical character of literary language. Needless to say, the vertiginous dislocations that began in my undergraduate years have persisted, intensified even.

I test your patience with this autobiographical preamble to make clear that, whatever my views on "antitheory," to be aired soon enough, theory itself is, for me, a site of anxious unbelonging, by no means a settled thing. It would be easy to romanticize or generalize such insecurity as a necessary condition for theory "proper," but one should always remember that full-bore or "high" theory was permitted access to the central precincts of the academy for a very short time and that it was this brief institutional security that allowed it to flourish—and even then, there were strings attached. In 2018, my guess is that the would-be future Fredric Jamesons, or Lauren Berlants, or Stuart Halls, or Eve Sedgewicks, or Judith Butlers, or Gayatri Spivaks are too busy teaching five or more courses a semester as adjuncts to rustle up the energy to *épater les professeurs*. The predictable reversion after the 1990s to idealist-historicist periodization in literary course manuals and job advertisements has had a similarly chilling effect on literary theory, producing generations of cuttingly intelligent literary scholars who nonetheless write pathologically conventional cultural histories, sometimes garnished as an afterthought with French proper names and often lacking sustained attention to the knots and stubborn stains of literary language.[3]

There is one further twist to this story, which is that the moment of theory, in the US academy at least, coincided with an acceleration of the neoliberalization of the university.[4] Two competing temporalities are at work here: the first, now well documented, concerns the belated impact of sociopolitical upheavals on the content of university curricula, at least in the capitalist core. "Theory" represents the belated reflection in those universities, institutions situated at the heart of world capitalism and yet partially insulated from it for purposes of social reproduction, of the now fatally anthologized 1960s, that still only partially understood roiling of bourgeois and Left certainties alike. The second temporality, ultimately far more decisive for our time, is the accelerated incursion from the early 1980s on of neoliberal economics onto university campuses. That these two temporalities coincided, with the resulting irony that the humanities at their most apparently radical benefited from a momentary surge of money and a resulting star system that was by definition neoliberal to the core,[5] makes of theory a decidedly ambiguous phenomena, politically speaking and otherwise—ambiguity being one of theory's presiding fetishes, of course.[6] The too easy conclusion to be avoided, not least because it is ignorant of the relative and inevitable discordance of these historical trends, indeed of the multiple and staggered historical temporalities that Althusser showed us compose the capitalist *socius* per se,[7] is that "theory" and "neoliberalism" therefore necessarily go hand in glove. That one historical process meets the other is no proof of causation, one way or the other, although much contemporary literary-historical scholarship would be nothing if not for just such a conflation. And if all of this is so with respect to theory, it must also be true for "antitheory," too; while there is no doubt some truth to the newly minted canard that the digital humanities, say, align suspiciously well with neoliberal imperatives of impact and quantification in the contemporary academy, to merely notice the appearance of congruence, to performatively repeat the correlation in place of an investigation of its no-doubt contradictory ripples and detours, is to confuse too easy polemic with analysis.

But what is "theory," this threatening thing the opponents of which have, after all, motivated this very volume? Suffice to say that, despite their retrospective collation under the theory header, deconstruction, on the one hand, say, and post-Saidian cultural studies, on the other, had almost nothing to do with one another. The one insisted on the epistemological perturbations, the antihumanist disruptions, the textual interrelations, that surreptitiously adhere to and disrupt any appeal to "context," to reference, to pseudo-naturalized historical periodizations, without of course *discarding* those things. The other tended to consider the dwelling on such quandaries as by definition politically quietist, preferring instead to multiply the sources from which a more or less Bourdieuan sociology of literature might arise and reinstalling in the process a more or less liberal historical humanism, if a globalized one, as the horizon and limit of literary and cultural scholarship. It is to the considerable discredit of the antitheorists that they have often taken little heed of these distinctions, although the defenders of theory are frequently just as guilty, passing quickly over the divisions in their own camp, the better to skewer the ostensibly unified enemy. My point is that to argue "for" theory and "against" antitheory is no simple matter and may well, indeed, be a quixotic enterprise; there are trends in scholarship ranged before the banner of theory that I would have little interest in defending, and I suspect that "antitheory," whatever it may be, is as internally disordered as the intellectual forces it would choose to oppose.

All general categories, when peered at long enough, crumble into particularities, it is true, although my sense is that "theory" and "antitheory" take on whatever meaning they have now in an intellectual field that lacks almost any common denominator. This disintegration of any sense of unified endeavor in the humanities, a product in part of relentless assaults on the always-relative autonomy and critical function of the university (to say nothing of the speciousness of previous claims to a unified, universal humanistic project), means that both "theory" and "antitheory" possess an almost tragic valence now, mimicking as they do postures of commitment, community, and continuity that can only now appear melancholically anachronistic. One must, in this connection, register the affect of pathos, sliding often into an uncomfortable comedy, that saturates much discussion of theory in our time, for and against—this muted absurdity produced by the performative address of something that is, for all intents and purposes, no longer historically available as an institutionally encouraged critical mode. And yet as I alert the reader to the potential laughter and/or tragedy involved, I will blunder comedically and/or tragically ahead myself and arrive in the latter half of this chapter on the idea of *auto-resistance* as a tool to define and disturb the various rhetorical poses of theory and antitheory both. Before staking such a claim, and before "antitheory" can emerge here as a legible phenomenon, it is necessary to treat an alliance that rarely now speaks its name—that of theory and philosophy.

Theory/Philosophy, Once Again

Theory, as a retrospectively constructed and romanticized "outsider" discourse, one temporarily, institutionally grounded at the very moment of its upmost claim to outsiderness, was, among other things, displaced philosophy.[8] This is to say that theory emerged, in all of its heterogeneity, as both an alternative to the world-building ambitions of canonical philosophy and a surreptitious reintroduction of philosophy in an appropriately chastened, and apparently historically self-aware, state, with the stick bent at least in part away from the universal and toward the particular. Antitheory, then, is inexplicable without some understanding of its relation to philosophy, philosophy being the shadow that ghosts the former's often passive aggressive addresses to literary and cultural theory *tout court*.

Ghosts multiply and haunt other ghosts in this context. Philosophy's metaphysical ambitions, when they do still emerge, can now only appear ersatz. The old philosophical categories have been definitively overrun by history itself and by the irreversible breaking of the dam that introduced questions of politics, class, and race into a previously and formatively idealist space. Philosophy in such an exalted state appears now as something of an undead discourse, although it putters along quite happily in its increasingly well worn and inconsequential grooves. Philosophy haunts theory, in turn, even as theory is, perhaps, also self-haunted, constitutively afraid of its own shadow. Theory, this is to say, has often wished to stay silent on its dependence on the hulking canonical-philosophical monolith to its right, even as an initial, open rejection of philosophy has so often conditioned the emergence of much self-definitionally "radical" theoretical discourse. In the present, theory is reminded at every turn of its status as the garnish on a largely historicist-empiricist intellectual menu. Recent theoretical discourse—the revived idealisms of the ironically named "new materialism" being a case in point—has vanishingly little to do with the urgent projects of Marxist and psychoanalytic political-theoretical synthesis, of immanent conjunctural analysis, of the materialist renovation of historiography, of leaping innovations in epistemology, that characterized the first wellsprings of what became "theory" in 1960s France.[9] (And it is worth remembering, for all the too easy talk of theory as an Atlanticist dumbing down of Philosophy Proper, that Louis Althusser's influential book series, an attempt to promote a new, philosophically sophisticated Marxism, bore the title Théorie—*not* Philosophie, and for good reason.)[10]

These interlaced conundrums—redolent as they are of theory's always-contested but now nigh-anachronistic status, anachronism to be construed here not in a purely negative sense but as potentially both critical and constructive, if by no means radical per se—have produced in their wake various sublimations, distortions, and denials, in both theory's proponents and antagonists. Overly comfortable defenders of theory—all of them with different definitions of the latter—have largely missed their chance to diagnose the present conditions that have blocked any mass emergence of new, truly disruptive theorizing in the academy. Instead, they have often mimicked the descriptive empiricism that theory once vociferously opposed, producing backward-looking maps and networks of putative theoretical growth and influence.

In the pages of books such as Vincent Leitch's recent *Literary Theory in the 21st Century: Theory Renaissance*, a once iconoclastic discourse does battle with its remaining specters, resists various of its own claims to self-definition, shaves off its stubborn edges, settles into empty proclamations of survival (even renaissance!), and ultimately concedes to a nostalgic belatedness that at least threatens banality. According to Leitch, "In a nutshell, the way I see it, theory provides many resources: cultural capital, fertile canons and traditions, critique, useful tools, a professional lingua franca ... This has motivated innumerable franchising operations, part of Theory Incorporated."[11] The problem here is not the interpolation of corporate lingo; Leitch is clearly being playful. The limitation is rather that such a definition of theory could well apply to myriad other intellectual formations. None of the things that Leitch lists, coming toward the end of his book and designed to inspire confidence in the robustness of theory's future, are particular to theory at all, whether "high," "cultural," or otherwise. One should always be attentive to what is being evaded when such lists begin to proliferate, especially when each item is more or less interchangeable with the last, and when the items intended to exemplify and particularize a general category—in this case "theory"—are clearly enough general categories in their own right, in no clear way dependent on the priorly posited universal type.

It is hard not to characterize this as that storied Hegelian night in which all cows are black. If the aforementioned "new materialism" is a species of antitheory, its subspecies "object-oriented ontology" also resolves obsessively and constantly to lists, in this instance of various medium-sized objects, the better to dazzle the reader into accepting the more than questionable claim that a proliferation of descriptive analogies and stunted metonymies is enough to swerve past 100 years or more of the critique of metaphysics.[12] Leitch has a critical sense far surpassing such nostalgic attempts to resuscitate the ahistorical empire building of pre-Kantian philosophy. Nonetheless, I worry that his enumerative drive—his admirably capacious but also undiscriminating urge to descriptively map the manner in which "theory" is used—mutes the manner in which theory, at its best, disrupts just such ideas of application and use of "before" and "after," of concept and object.

My principle theme for the remainder, at any rate, will be that of auto-resistance in theory and antitheory, a topic that has, in fact, already begun to coalesce. (The impossibility of making theory a consistent set, addressed above, is itself an instance of the auto-resistance that I will elaborate below, and the empirical list, now common to both defenses of theory and its enemies, is an example of an attempted formalization that issues only in a nonanalytical, open-ended dispersal—see my immediate references above to object-oriented ontology and to Leitch.) My claim, in brief, is that antitheory, understood as a heterogeneous constellation of interventions and critical moods that advance a more or less self-cancelling critique of critique, emerges in part out of defensive moments of resistance to the very auto-resistance or constitutive self-dislocation *in theory itself*. Such auto-resistance is acknowledged and even championed by theory and disavowed almost universally by those who position themselves self-consciously against it. I will begin to define what I mean by auto-resistance by turning to Paul de Man's "The Resistance to Theory," the now-unfashionable de Man also serving as a reminder that contemporary antitheory often seems content to reinvent the wheel. I will turn then briefly to Freud, clearly an indispensable reference on the theme of resistance, before offering a concise reading of what I take to be an exemplary instance of twenty-first-century antitheory and its constitutive blindnesses to formative self-difference or auto-resistance. Antitheory, I will argue, is more than happy to recognize difference per se (it, too, adores lists), but *self*-difference, the material-linguistic, peskily internal gap that both makes critique a possibility and prevents its collation into an empirically satisfying whole entirely eludes its shiny apertures.

Auto-Resistance in De Man and Freud

Initially written in the early 1980s on the request of the MLA, Paul de Man's "The Resistance to Theory" was rejected—was resisted, perhaps—as unsuitable for its projected purpose as a conspectus of literary theory, both in the present and future. As de Man explains, "I found it difficult to live up … to the minimal requirements of this program [set by the MLA] and could only try to explain … why the main theoretical interest of literary theory consists in the impossibility of its definition."[13] Those familiar with de Man will recognize that curious mixture of irony and melancholy that courses through his writings. Familiar too will be the gathering together of an apparently consequential endeavor—in this case, a summary by one of its most important exponents of literary theory—

and its stopping up short in, not merely *incompletion*, but a kind of sublime *impossibility*. Such a negative sublimity's sense of perverse enjoyment in defeat threatens, as in so much of de Man's work, to borrow under cover of darkness some of the very same effusive metaphysical energy that defines the "aesthetic ideology" that it would otherwise wish to oppose. Our ongoing definition of theoretical auto-resistance, and its doubling resistance in turn by antitheory, will require a desublimation of this rather stagey, dramatical negativity.

What kind of inception does the apparent impossibility of literary theory, or at least its thwarted summation, announce? We get a clue when de Man attempts to distinguish literary theory proper from its others, not least literary history. "Literary theory can be said to come into being when the approach to literary texts is no longer based on non-linguistic, that is to say historical and aesthetic, considerations"; "Literary history ... is still the history of an understanding of which the possibility is taken for granted."[14] If literary history, with its sequential ordering of blocks of time, must assume a priori the cognizability of the objects that it subsequently arranges, theory instead adopts what could hastily be construed as a semi-Kantian posture, investigating the conditions of possibility (and, in the Derridean twist, impossibility), to say nothing of the evasions and exclusions, that permit the very congealing of literary texts into more or less coherent objects for any subsequent act of cognition. De Man, at any rate, considers the analytical procedures proper to literary history to show little of the overt resistances and torsions that attend literary theory, that make it a site of acute epistemological tension.

But while it seems clear why literary theory, on this analysis, is a rather more contentious endeavor than literary history, at least as it has been understood to be, we are still in the dark as to why any *summation* of literary theory, its progressive encompassing in a provisional but comprehensive accounting, is an *impossibility*, instead of something that is simply difficult to achieve. The answer lies in the particular model of *resistance* that de Man's essay eventually sketches. I say "eventually" because de Man is quick to first acknowledge the external forces that, at the time of the essay's composition, were ranged against theory, this of course being the moment of the culture wars. But such forces, while often possessed of considerable institutional power, had no general bearing on the epistemological possibility or impossibility of theorizing theory, of producing a meta-account of its own deductive procedures. The most consequent threat to such a project was rather internal and thus constitutes a mode of resistance that is immanent to, even generative of, rather than external to, theorization per se. As de Man writes, "Resistance may be a built-in constituent of its discourse," and "[t]he resistance to theory is a resistance to the use of language about language. It is therefore a resistance to language itself or to the possibility that language contains factors or functions that cannot be reduced to intuition."[15]

Jacques Lacan was onto the same insight with his aperçu that "no metalanguage can be spoken."[16] All discourses that must adopt language as both object and vessel, literary theory and psychoanalysis being exemplary of this, are, it would seem, formatively subject to such tangles. But perhaps there is a further twist to this story, insofar as theory—psychoanalysis being paradigmatic of the latter—is constitutively *aware* of its internal reflexivity, of its complicitous debt to that which it should otherwise prefer to coolly understand. Such foreknowledge seems inherent to theory's necessarily, generatively thwarted attempts at self-summation, this being the gist of the "impossibility" sketched by de Man. And yet ironically, it is, I would wager, this self-awareness of auto-resistance, this almost tragic knowledge of the necessity of theory's internal resistance to itself, that marks theory out as distinct from nontheoretical discourses, and perhaps especially to those who would explicitly oppose theory or critique. At the very moment at which an apparent impossibility is reached—theory's constitutive inability to self-summarize—one may convert an impediment into an opportunity: for it is this that allows us to summarize theory after all, all "theory" bearing the mark of this bind, all non- and antitheory conspicuously lacking it. Those readers who would worry that such a definition excludes all but the most language-centric of theoretical formations, with deconstruction and psychoanalysis at center stage, should have no fear. While I lack the space here to fully argue the point, queer theory, critical race studies, postcolonial theory, with their varying emphases on mourning, on the erasures of the archive, on the convergence of material and semantic violence, can be read as so many reproductions, amplifications, or disruptions, of theory's formative moments of auto-resistance.

Sigmund Freud gives us a useful model of the necessity of theoretical self-summation and its intriguing impossibilities. The very notion of resistance, of course, which in psychoanalysis is always also a kind of auto-resistance, would have no meaning without Freud's intervention. In an odd text with the title "Freud's Psycho-Analytic Procedure," published in 1904 in a book by Loewenfeld on obsessional neurosis, Freud writes of himself in the third person. The effect is uncanny, perhaps no more so than when the topic of resistance arises: "The factor of resistance has become one of the corner-stones of his theory. The ideas which are normally pushed aside on every sort of excuse ... are regarded by him of derivatives of the repressed psychical phenomena (thoughts and impulses), distorted owing to the resistance against their reproduction." And: "The greater the resistance, the greater is the distortion. The value of these unintentional thoughts for the purposes of therapeutic technique lies in this relation of theirs to the repressed psychical material."[17]

It is not uncommon in Freud to find moments of theorization that seem determined to erase their very traces. One thinks of those definitional moments of hesitation, of compulsive self-revising, that mark the writings, early and late, somehow both reporting on and embodying the stutters and self-revisions of his analysands' speech. Here, however, something else seems at work. In a form that, from a certain angle, appears almost as a parody of his famous self-analyses—those forbiddingly byzantine, this encyclopedia-like summary almost laughably reduced—Freud self-summarizes. Perhaps in an attempt to head off at the pass the semantic knots that come from writing about a certain kind of writing—the speech of the analysand writing itself into contradictions the better to reveal the contradictions that underpin it, the writing of that writing doing much the same with all the more distortion—the use of third person here might justifiably be expected to provide some reassurance or distance.

To the contrary, however, the curious self-erasure of Freud's "I," combined as it is with a precipitously early attempt of self-accounting whose very rhetorical surety begins unsettlingly to signal its opposite, gives positive shape to a quandary that lies at the center of psychoanalysis and theory both: to write about that which self-resists is to only redouble and strengthen that resistance, producing symptomatic effects that, in this case, literalize the inevitable, tragic self-distance or necessary failure of self-accounting that imposes upon the very need to theoretically take stock. Freud disappears, this is to say, at the moment at which a summary of his achievements requires him to be fully in view. I am, of course, aware that such self-written anonymous dictionary or encyclopedia entries were a notable feature of nineteenth-century intellectual life. But there's no escaping the glaring overlap of medium and content here, this being a fusion especially meaningful in light of Freud's theoretical but also personal concern for self-distancing, for his simultaneous insistence that psychoanalysis is, indeed must be, an objective science, and his testifying to something like the opposite conclusion in the form of the confessional self-analyses that, as much as anything else, birthed psychoanalysis as a medium of auto-resistance.

I underline the conflicted pathos here in part to remind the reader of a remark I made toward the beginning of this chapter, where I pointed to the tragic/comic mood of the very idea of a "defense" (defenses being, of course, types of resistance) of theory in the era after its institutional eclipse, and in part to revise that sentiment. In light of this more fundamental mechanism of tragic auto-resistance, the former affect of tragedy, of a kind of sad belatedness that threatens to make the very noun "theory" seem embarrassing, was perhaps always there, always a possibility, always lurking as a threat but also a goad. My guess is that any genuinely new theoretical work in this putatively post-theoretical era must not shrink from confronting this in-built absurdity, but must rather exacerbate it, kneedling its bruises in the hope that new forms may emerge from the precipitous distance it reveals between theoretical work and our current historical common sense.

Antitheory, Finally

All of this strikes me as rather far from how the antitheorists tend to characterize their opposing numbers. The charges are now well known: theorists are overly invested in suspicion, have little to say about the pleasures of reading and writing (Barthes, anyone?), and are too willing to prostrate to the postures of mastery. Paradoxically loud are the calls for a new humbleness in criticism. And yet might it not be the case—this being an instance of something like psychoanalytic cliché—that such overt gestures toward modesty may well conceal the opposite? Freud, in any case, and de Man after him seem rather more interested in casting suspicion on themselves than on others, indeed on the very likelihood of finally succeeding in their respective projects. In this final section, I analyze an exemplary instance of contemporary antitheory, in order to demonstrate that while a recognized and affirmed auto-resistance is by definition absent in antitheory, other, more comedically overt forms of symptomatic emergence are very much in evidence.

My exhibit will be Sharon Marcus and Stephen Best's influential introduction to their special edition of the journal *Representations* on "Surface Reading." Published almost a decade ago in 2009, the edition was one of the first salvos in the most recent wave of writing critical of theory, although dating antitheory is no easy matter; robust polemics against apparent theoretical excesses are as old as theory itself, theory's self-resistance generating in the same moment an externalization of its spectral self-battles. What is it that Best and Marcus take themselves to be opposing, or at least hoping to displace? Theory, for them, with Marxism and psychoanalysis identified as the ringleaders, is characterized above all by suspicion, and by a spatial metaphorics that would have us dive deep into texts' murky depths. Theory takes meaning to be "hidden, repressed, deep, and in need of detection and disclosure by an interpreter."[18] That which has most value in a text, so this gloss on theory goes, is that which is not most immediately apprehensible. Interpretation may only gain a political edge within such an ideology if latent forces are finally exposed to unforgiving sunlight.

Who could object to such a characterization? Well, not to put too fine a point on it, anyone who has ever seriously read the most important progenitors of what came to be known as "theory." Indeed, one of the defining quirks of the avant-garde French philosophy that in large measure gave birth to theory is its troubling of any straightforward spatial metaphorics in criticism. Think of Lacan's definitional repudiation of psychoanalysis as a depth psychology, his insistence on the topological involutions that define the permeable borders of subject and object, of consciousness and the unconscious. Consider Althusser's rejection of any vulgar Marxism of base and superstructure, in favor of complexly striated, overdetermined conjunctures with relatively autonomous levels and instances. Conjure Derrida's disturbance of the binary opposition in the name of the becoming-space of time and the becoming-time of space, all of this on behalf of a *différance* that would loop back to partially condition, partially disable, its own possibilities. Paul de Man's writings on the auto-impositional violence of literary language have little to do with any naïve concern with the revelation of a text's buried secrets; he would have considered any such critical procedure as laughably gauche, as inattentive, at best, to the materiality of the signifier. This is not to say that these theoretical interventions were faultless, or that we need only continue on, disciple like, in their shadows. But it is to say that any argument made for a new type of reading—in this instance, "surface reading"—would do well to announce itself with instances of good, rigorous, accountable, reading, rather than with lamentable caricature.

Whatever their understanding, or lack thereof, of the practices that they seek to replace, what kind of criticism should, ideally, emerge from Best and Marcus's surface revolution? The answers are surprisingly familiar. Such criticism would inspect textual surfaces for the ways in which "texts can reveal their own truths because texts mediate themselves; what we think theory brings to texts (form, structure, meaning) is already present in them."[19] In such a criticism, "depth is not to be found outside the text or beneath its surface …; rather, depth is continuous with surface and is thus an effect of immanence."[20] The elementary gesture in the latter toward a complication of surface/depth spatialities reads as a simplified primer to what was ubiquitous in theory's heyday, "immanence" of course being a theoretical keyword par excellence. And the notion of texts revealing their own truths—a beginner's description of ontological immanence—echoes faintly with Derrida's insistence that deconstruction is always-already at work in a text, although one surely needn't be a hardcore Derridean to hold the hardly controversial belief that the properties of a text preexist our reading of them.

Notice, at any rate, how a definitional textual property, that of self-reference, is neutralized here in advance. It's a feature, what I've called auto-resistance, that, in theory proper, with its recognition that the uncanniness of textual self-address is in no way reducible to mere "interpretation" or suspicious uncovering, leads to a vertiginous but productive expansion of the possibilities for criticism. It's one that tends toward the idea that the historical materiality of the text might both exceed and enable its sense, for instance; or how historical time itself might be treated as a material force irresponsive to, but formative for, calls for hermeneutic closure. Or, how the natural world, for all its seeming indifference to literary coding, displays equivalent properties of resistance and withdrawal that disjunctively repeat themselves, in very different linguistic-material contexts, in our fraught, self-negating artistic cultures. All of this seems off-limits to the easy straw-manning of the antitheorists, who would recommend caution, smallness, a corseting of speculation, at the very historical moment when thinking beyond our baleful present is, I would suggest, an existential necessity.

The conclusion should not simply be that reading suffers when attempts to reinvent the wheel replace careful, mediated analysis of literary complexity, although this seems true enough. It is rather that, in a strange way, antitheory, at least as it has manifested here in Best and Marcus, begins to resemble its own simplified vision of what theory is or was. Without the redoubling awareness of auto-resistance that, I have argued, characterizes theory "proper," antitheory seems driven to cast undue suspicion on its ostensible opponents, while corseting itself in its own ghostly imagining of that with which it does phantom battle. And so perhaps there *is* a certain epistemological torsion at the center of antitheory after all, one different in kind from theory's auto-resistance but comparable to it in its very uncanniness. Upon inventing a fictional other, "theory," with the intention of leaving behind exhausted past possibilities, it is finally only past possibilities, and rather simplified versions thereof, that result. Caricature begets caricature, one might say. In reducing theory's auto-resistance to something as empirically manageable as self-reference or suspicion, antitheory remains caught in a disabling feedback loop generated by its fear of uncertainty. Theory at its best puts such uncertainty to creative, constructive use, the better to conceive of the historical present as less weightily inevitable, less stuck, than it so often seems to be.

Notes

1. Strathern's masterpiece remains *The Gender of the Gift*. See Marilyn Strathern, *The Gender of the Gift: Problems with Women and Problems with Society in Melanesia* (Berkeley, CA: University of California Press, 1990).
2. A revised version of my dissertation was published as Tom Eyers, *Lacan and the Concept of the "Real"* (New York: Palgrave, 2012).
3. This is precipitous generalization, of course, but I think it captures in its hyperbole a growing reality in the academy, and risky generalizations, after all, are one of the useful outrages that theory made possible.
4. Vincent Leitch, of whom I will be mildly critical presently, has written with real insight on the overdetermined relationship between the corporate takeover of the university and theory. See Vincent Leitch, *Literary Criticism in the 21st Century: Theory Renaissance* (London: Bloomsbury, 2014), 149–150.
5. For a fascinating debate on the origins, meanings, and consequences of the theory star-system, see first David R. Shumway, "The Star System in Literary Studies," *PMLA* 112.1 (January 1997): 85–100, and the response by Bruce Robbins, "Celeb-Reliance: Intellectuals, Celebrity, and Upward Mobility," *Postmodern Culture* 9.2 (January 1999). http://pmc.iath.virginia.edu/text-only/issue.199/9.2robbins.txt.
6. For a well-judged account of the production of "French theory" in the US academy, see François Cusset, *French Theory: How Foucault, Derrida, Deleuze, & Co. Transformed the Intellectual Life of the United States* (Minneapolis: University of Minnesota Press, 2008).
7. See especially the expanded version of *Reading Capital*. Louis Althusser et al., *Reading Capital: The Complete Edition*, trans. Ben Brewster and David Fernbach (New York: Verso, 2016).
8. Peter Osborne's account of the dialectical complexities of the theory-philosophy relation is the most persuasive that I have come across. See Peter Osborne, "Philosophy after Theory: Transdisciplinarity and the New," in *Theory after "Theory,"* ed. Jane Elliott and Derek Attridge (New York: Routledge, 2011), 19–34.
9. The French journal *Cahiers pour l'Analyse*, published by students of Althusser between 1965 and 1969, including a young Jean-Claude Milner and Alain Badiou, provided the high watermark of this experimental moment, one comparable to the upsurge of literary modernisms at the turn of the twentieth century. See the two volume collection *Concept and Form*, ed. Peter Hallward and Knox Peden (London: Verso, 2012). My second book placed *Cahiers pour l'Analyse* center stage in its broader exploration of the intersection of psychoanalysis, epistemology, Marxism, and literary theory in 1960s France. See Tom Eyers, *Post-Rationalism: Psychoanalysis, Epistemology, and Marxism in Post-War France* (London: Bloomsbury, 2013).

10 Althusser changed his mind repeatedly on the philosophy/theory relation, but two representative texts are Louis Althusser, "On the Materialist Dialectic," in *For Marx*, trans. Ben Brewster (London: Verso, 2008), 161–219; and Louis Althusser, "Lenin and Philosophy," in *Lenin and Philosophy and Other Essays* (New York: Monthly Review Press, 2001), 11–45.

11 Leitch, *Literary Criticism*, 152.

12 For an especially trenchant critique of this tendency in Bruno Latour and more recent "object oriented ontology," see Ray Brassier, "Concepts and Objects," in *The Speculative Turn: Continental Materialism and Realism*, ed. Levi Bryant, Nick Srnicek, and Graham Harman (Melbourne: Re Press, 2011), 47–66.

13 Paul de Man, "The Resistance to Theory," in *The Resistance to Theory* (Minneapolis: University of Minnesota Press, 1986), 3.

14 Ibid., 7.

15 Ibid., 13.

16 Jacques Lacan, "Subversion of the Subject and the Dialectic of Desire," in *Écrits*, trans. Bruce Fink (New York: W.W. Norton, 2007), 813.

17 Sigmund Freud, *The Standard Edition of the Complete Psychological Works of Sigmund Freud VII: A Case of Hysteria, Three Essays on Sexuality, and Other Words*, trans. James Strachey (New York: Vintage, 2001), 253–254.

18 Steven Best and Sharon Marcus, "Surface Reading: An Introduction," *Representations* 108.1 (Fall 2009): 1.

19 Ibid., 11.

20 Ibid.

Works Cited

Althusser, Louis. "Lenin and Philosophy." In *Lenin and Philosophy and Other Essays*. New York: Monthly Review Press, 2001. 11–45.

Althusser, Louis. "On the Materialist Dialectic." In *For Marx*. Trans. Ben Brewster. London: Verso, 2008. 161–219.

Althusser, Louis et al. *Reading Capital: The Complete Edition*. Trans. Ben Brewster and David Fernbach. New York: Verso, 2016.

Best, Steven and Sharon Marcus. "Surface Reading: An Introduction." *Representations* 108.1 (Fall 2009): 1–21.

Brassier, Ray. "Concepts and Objects." In *The Speculative Turn: Continental Materialism and Realism*. Ed. Levi Bryant, Nick Srnicek, and Graham Harman. Melbourne: Re Press, 2011. 47–66.

Cusset, François. *French Theory: How Foucault, Derrida, Deleuze, & Co. Transformed the Intellectual Life of the United States*. Minneapolis: University of Minnesota Press, 2008.

de Man, Paul. "The Resistance to Theory." In *The Resistance to Theory*. Minneapolis: University of Minnesota Press, 1986.

Eyers, Tom. *Lacan and the Concept of the "Real."* New York: Palgrave, 2012.

Eyers, Tom. *Post-Rationalism: Psychoanalysis, Epistemology, and Marxism in Post-War France*. London: Bloomsbury, 2013.

Freud, Sigmund. *The Standard Edition of the Complete Psychological Works of Sigmund Freud VII: A Case of Hysteria, Three Essays on Sexuality, and Other Words*. Trans. James Strachey. New York: Vintage, 2001.

Hallward, Peter and Knox Peden, ed. *Concept and Form*. London: Verso, 2012.

Lacan, Jacques. "Subversion of the Subject and the Dialectic of Desire." In *Écrits*. Trans. Bruce Fink. New York: W.W. Norton, 2007.

Leitch, Vincent. *Literary Criticism in the 21st Century: Theory Renaissance*. London: Bloomsbury, 2014.

Osborne, Peter. "Philosophy after Theory: Transdisciplinarity and the New." In *Theory after "Theory."* Ed. Jane Elliott and Derek Attridge. New York: Routledge, 2011. 19–34.

Robbins, Bruce. "Celeb-Reliance: Intellectuals, Celebrity, and Upward Mobility." *Postmodern Culture* 9.2 (January 1999). http://pmc.iath.virginia.edu/text-only/issue.199/9.2robbins.txt.

Shumway, David R. "The Star System in Literary Studies." *PMLA* 112.1 (January 1997): 85–100.

Strathern, Marilyn. *The Gender of the Gift: Problems with Women and Problems with Society in Melanesia*. Berkeley, CA: University of California Press, 1990.

13

Forget Latour

Zahi Zalloua

A touchstone for many antitheorists, or post-theorists, is the French anthropologist and sociologist of science Bruno Latour. Latour's often-quoted 2004 article, "Why Has Critique Run out of Steam?" could have been titled, "Why Has Theory Run out of Steam?" In his polemical article, Latour makes a series of accusations about theory's overreach, unproductive habits, and waning relevance. I stress that these are accusations, displaying a dearth of cited evidence, and thus lacking a serious engagement with any theorists. Latour decries the arrogance of theorists, and critique's excessive paranoia. For Latour, the path of critical theory—the path taken by the Frankfurt School, psychoanalysis, and deconstruction, among others—is dangerous and unsustainable, doing more harm than good. Latour himself assumes partial responsibility, making a *mea culpa* for the current state of affairs: "The mistake we made, the mistake I made, was to believe that there was no efficient way to criticize matters of fact except by moving away from them and directing one's attention toward the conditions that made them possible."[1]

Waving the banner of social constructivism is no longer the sign of the courageous fight against the hegemony of the given and common sense. The spirit of critique, so goes the argument, is more prevalent in the circles of climate change deniers or deployed for an aggressive geopolitical agenda. Theory, in this respect, has unwittingly armed the other side, the side of militarism and antiscience. Its damage is also felt closer to home, at the university, where "the Zeus of Critique rules absolutely, to be sure, but over a desert."[2] The imperatives to disenchant, to denaturalize, to defetishize: all have led to a weakening of the humanities. Latour pleads for an alternative model, urging critics to move away from their debunking ethos—theory's *"critical barbarity,"*[3] as he calls it—to one of caring and protection, from a feeling of superiority to one of collaboration and generosity. In short, Latour's new critic needs to "add" to reality rather than "subtract" from it, generate more ideas rather than destroy existing ones.[4]

In what follows, I want to push back against Latour's understanding of theory and scrutinize—or, better yet, critique—the antitheoretical turn, the postcritical turn, he has helped spur in the humanities.[5] The imperative to "forget Latour" is meant as a call to reinvest in theory's critique, an invitation to exit our current inhospitable climate to theory.[6] I will first situate Latour's argument within the larger antitheory camp, looking at the movement of speculative realism and its subset or variant, object-oriented ontology, two approaches to reality at odds with theory's perceived idealism and overinvestment in language. Then, I address Latour's growing influence in literary studies, asking: What does Latour offer literary critics? What does it mean to read antitheoretically, postcritically? How do we deal—can we deal—with the question of ideology after Latour? In answering these questions, I turn to Ari Folman's 2008 *Waltz with Bashir*, an Israeli animated docufilm that deals with the trauma of the 1982 Sabra and Shatila massacre. Analyzing this film, I argue, shows the limits of a Latourian approach to literary studies, more specifically, and reaffirms the need to expose, to theorize, more generally.

Latour's antitheory project aligns closely with that of speculative realists. Latour and the speculative realists repeatedly call for a cognitive reinvestment in the study of reality, for "renewing empiricism,"[7] as Latour puts it, or, in the words of the editors of *The Speculative Turn*, for "speculating once more about the nature of reality independently of thought and of humanity."[8] The speculative turn can be seen as a strictly philosophical response to the idealism of the linguistic turn, to the strand of continental philosophy that gave us theory—at the moment that philosophy, in the eyes of theory's detractors, took a decisively wrong *linguistic* turn.

Against the antirealism pervading contemporary thought, the speculative turn urges a return to the object, a renewed attachment to the external world. Quentin Meillassoux is often credited for initiating this philosophical rebellion against the linguistic turn. In his 2006 *After Finitude*, Meillassoux conducts a severe critique of post-Kantian philosophies. From Marxism and phenomenology to psychoanalysis and deconstruction, continental thought has suffered the limitations of what Meillassoux calls "correlationism." Correlationism maintains that "we only ever have access to the correlation between thinking and being, and never to either term considered apart from the other."[9] Since we do not have a rational access to things-in-themselves, all we have after Kant, all we are allowed to discuss philosophically, are the transcendental conditions for knowledge.[10] Any claim of knowledge is immediately followed by a qualification:

by "for us," that is, *for us finite beings*.¹¹ As a result, Meillassoux argues, we have forsaken ontology, have settled for a toothless epistemology, and have foreclosed any genuine access to the external world.

On Meillassoux's reading, theory would be the latest face of correlationism. Theory has remained preoccupied with these Kantian concerns, removing us further and further away from ontology, enlarging the gap between *verba* and *res*, words and things. As a corrective to theory's obsessions with subjectivity and representation, speculative realists endorse a "flat ontology" and promote a posthumanist ethos. Posthumanism, unlike antihumanism, is not primarily concerned with demystifying the origins of meanings; it is more interested in diffusing and multiplying their origins rather than recentering them in some impersonal structures. The speculative turn pushes back against a paralyzing fixation with interpretation. Proponents of these shifts object not so much to the interpretation of objects—which remains, at some level, a necessity—but rather to the excessive weight given in analysis to the conditions that govern interpretation. Theory's self-reflexivity has come at a great cost: reality itself. Theory stands accused of leading us astray with its excessive preoccupation with mediation; it made us settle for too little, turning our gaze inward, away from what Meillassoux calls "the great outdoors [*le grand dehors*]."¹²

In the same vein, Latour calls for a return to the "world": "Down with Kant! Down with the Critique! Let us go back to the world still unknown and despised."¹³ While theory is "on the side of knowing" (focused on the subject of knowledge—at the cost of neglecting the world and its nonhuman objects), Latour's brand of antitheory is "on the side of the known," the objects of knowledge, the given, the readily accessible.¹⁴ Latour has little patience with the plight of theorists and their critical or deconstructive hermeneutics. He wants to leave behind the revolutionary energy of May 1968 that produced a whole generation of French intellectuals. As Latour puts it, "we don't wish to have too much to do with the twentieth century."¹⁵ While theorists typically foreground reflexivity and the opacity of signifiers, Latour wants to talk about things in the world, freed, as it were, from the self-defeating preoccupations of theory.

As an alternative approach to hermeneutics as usual, to human-centered inquiry, Latour champions actor-network theory, which underscores the posthumanist insight that

> *any thing* that does modify a state of affairs by making a difference is an actor—or, if it has no figuration yet, an actant. Thus, the questions to ask about any agent are simply the following: Does it make a difference in the course of some other agent's action or not?¹⁶

Latour's actor, as Rita Felski puts it, "is not freighted with assumptions about intention, consciousness, or autonomy but designates any and all phenomena whose existence makes a difference."[17] To be sure, Latour's emphasis on relationality puts him at odds with a number of object-oriented ontologists who are more interested in reviving a concern for objects as substances, objects that withdraw and resist relations. Still, they do endorse the ways Latour's actor-network theory foster a "democratization" of interpretation, enacting a categorical rejection of human exceptionalism.

Limiting agency and interpretation to humans is indeed unduly restrictive. Antitheory is a posthumanism. In a flat ontology, agency and interpretation are effectively redistributed and reconceptualized as otherwise than anthropocentric. Latour boldly asserts: "Hermeneutics is not a privilege of humans but, so to speak, a property of the world itself."[18] This contrasts staunchly with theory's hermeneutics, its labor of suspicion and critique. "What's the difference between deconstruction and constructivism?" Latour asks wryly.[19] The difference, he answers, is clear: constructivism displays a respect for objects (and the people who believe in them), whereas deconstruction does not.[20] And fortunately, Latour tells us, objects do not comply with theory's interpretive predilections; they refuse to be "ground to dust by the powerful teeth of automated reflex-action deconstructors."[21]

Likewise, for object-oriented ontologists such as Graham Harman and Timothy Morton, objects must be freed from the persistent humanist subject/object prism. Harman stresses that objects are "entities ... quite apart from any relations with or effects upon other entities in the world"[22]; and Morton says, "we've become so used to hearing 'object' in relation to 'subject' that it takes some time to acclimatize to a view in which there are only objects, one of which is ourselves."[23] Human beings thus delude themselves in elevating themselves to the exceptional and exclusive status of *subjects*. All objects are on equal footing; all there is are objects interacting with other objects.

If the speculative turn is where Latour's impact on philosophy is perhaps most visible, the descriptive turn reflects Latour's undeniable mark on literary studies. It is to Latour that Felksi, for example, repeatedly turns in her 2015 *The Limits of Critique*. Latour offers Felski and others a way out of theory's orbit of suspicion, pointing to an alternative ways of imagining literary studies.[24] Felski's version of the descriptive turn, her investment "in a care or concern for phenomena, a preference for description over explanation, a willingness to attend rather than to analyze"[25] is made to stand against theory's overtly suspicious attitude, its alleged uncare of the text.

So if, for the proponents of the speculative turn, theory is too obsessed with itself, with subjectivity, and the question of representation, for those of the descriptive turn, theory is too suspicious, ruining the experience of literature. The same critics often align Eve Sedgwick's critical remarks on paranoid modes of reading with Latour's indictment of critique. Both Sedgwick and Latour find the paradigm of suspicion too mechanical, deprived of its earlier inventive energy. Like Latour, Sedgwick presents herself as a reformed theorist in her memorable 1997 essay, "Paranoid Reading and Reparative Reading, or, You're So Paranoid, You Probably Think This Essay Is about You." Latour and Sedgwick attribute theory's flaws to a fear of being duped or becoming compromised by the unexpected. Simply stated, theorists are by training traumatophobic. Theorists are paranoid; they want to minimize interpretive vulnerability; they are allergic to anything laden with surprise:

> The first imperative of paranoia is "*There must be no bad surprises,*" and indeed, the aversion to surprise seems to be what cements the intimacy between paranoia and knowledge per se ... because there must be no bad surprises, and because to learn the possibility of a bad surprise would itself constitute a bad surprise, paranoia requires that bad news be already known.[26]

On Sedgwick's reading, theory compels you to turn your gaze forward and backward; "at once anticipatory and retroactive,"[27] paranoid thinking works to master the past (what has happened; what lessons can we draw from this or that example) and foreclose any deviation from a projected future. A rhetoric of exemplarity soothes, as much as possible, a paranoid mind. It gives the paranoid hermeneut tools to tame temporality's alterity, to convert the "new" into something always already known.

For Latour and Sedgwick, theory's will to mastery is at the root of its demise, or at least of its diminishing value. If theory were to undergo a conversion, it would have to shed its hermeneutics of suspicion, its investment in ideology critique. Literary studies after theory, under the "democratic" regime of antitheory, would be decisively more descriptive, less judgmental, and, most importantly, more inclusive in what it cares about. *Waltz with Bashir*, with its expansive treatment of trauma, seems ideally situated for a Latourian reading. I will first sketch out such a reading, highlighting elements of the film most receptive to a Latourian approach, contrasting it with a critique-oriented reading, and then return to the stubborn questions of ideology and suspicion (although I will propose to swap suspicion for skepticism).

Waltz with Bashir opens with a pack of rabid dogs, racing at night through Tel Aviv streets, finally gathering beneath a man's apartment window. We then quickly discover that this scene is the actual dream of the man in the window, who is recounting the dream to his friend Ari Folman. He explains to Folman that he has been having this recurrent nightmare, whose origins he speculates lie in his experience of the 1982 Lebanese invasion, where, as a soldier, he was ordered to kill dogs so as to prevent them from barking at soldiers entering Lebanese villages. Distraught by his dreams, he asks Folman if he is experiencing any lingering traces of the war. Folman claims no memories of his military service in Lebanon. This absence of memory comes to puzzle Folman, triggering his meditation on his involvement in Lebanon, which circles back to the Sabra and Shatila massacre. Folman eventually arrives at the realization that he was an actual witness to the tragic event, and, moreover, that he, alongside other Israeli forces, assisted the Lebanese Christian Phalangist militia, either by launching flares or by helping to contain the Palestinian refugees while the Phalangists were running their operation. The film ends with an interruption of the animation, which is replaced with actual video footage of the aftermath of the massacre showing dead bodies and the lamentations of a Palestinian mother.

While *Waltz with Bashir* has been highly acclaimed, it has received a critical reception among literary critics, at least from critics still invested in critique. For example, Raz Yosef is rightfully suspicious of the turn to the actual footage, claiming that it does nothing to counter the film's depoliticized and depoliticizing narcissistic bent:

> The horrifying archival images of slaughtered Palestinian men, women and children at the end of the film are ... detached from their historical and political context and provide a kind of catharsis for the protagonist: now he remembers and is released from the trauma that had been haunting him; now he is cured and redeemed from the wounds of the past and can apparently carry on with his life.[28]

The displacement of the Palestinians is further felt by Yosef in an exchange between Folman and his psychologist friend, Uri Sivan, who interprets Folman's trauma in relation to his parents' trauma of Auschwitz, perversely suggesting that the trauma of Sabra and Shatila is not really about the Palestinians themselves, that the "true" causes of his disturbance lie spatially and temporally elsewhere. Here the ostensive victims, the Palestinians, are displaced by Folman's split identifications with both victims (the Jews of Auschwitz) and victimizers (Sivan describes Folman's behavior at the Sabra and Shatila camps as Nazi-like).

But for Latour such a type of reading is in the business of negating and demystifying. It tells its readers: Don't be fooled by the film's ideology, its veneer of complexity. A Latourian response would claim that Yosef's reading reflects a transcendent perspective on the world, one that is premade, ready to be applied "critically" to any cultural product that does not tell the story of the Palestinians. A Latourian reading would set itself apart from Yosef and other demystifiers of the film. It would acknowledge the attachment of that a spectator may have for the cultural artifact and ask a reparative question: How does the film add to our understanding of trauma, of the horrors of war? It would reorient the spectator to the film's posthumanist distribution of trauma, to the ways it multiplies the connections to trauma. It might stress that this is not the exclusive story of Ari Folman: a journey into his phantasmatic and solipsistic working through of trauma. We can imagine a Latourian reading carefully describing the ways dogs, Israeli soldiers, Phalangists, Palestinians refugees, and even the materiality of the film (its animation and documentary footage), all emerge as actors in the film, some as strong actors (the Phalangists and Israeli soldiers) and some as weak actors (the dogs and the Palestinians). The film, with its mixture of human and nonhuman actors, performs a flat ontology. A critic's task is simple: he or she needs to translate, trace out, and pay attention to the ways actors in the film do not exist in themselves, in isolation, but in their relationality, that is, in their networks of association.

Yes, but lingering questions of ideology persist. The distinction between victim and victimizer is not the same type of division as subject and object. While the latter is precisely what an actor-network theory wants to overcome, it is important to stress that not all binaries are equally problematic. Folman's trauma—that he could become that type of Nazi-person—is not a sufficient condition for victimhood. Aggressors are not immune to trauma, but this fact alone does not make them victims on equal ethical and political footing with the victimized. The film appears to be guilty of this dubious conflation; a flat ontology-inspired interpretation risks compounding that problem.[29]

But what about Latour's objection that critique has become too mechanical: "Are we not like those mechanical toys that endlessly make the same gesture when everything else has changed around them?"[30] In the context of the Israeli–Palestinian conflict, we may ask what exactly has changed? From the Sabra and Shatila massacre in 1982 to the last devastating Gaza War in 2014, there is a strong continuity in the Israeli disregard for Palestinian lives. Perhaps the change lies in the attitude of *some* Israelis. This is after all a film made by an Israeli in Israel against Israel's hawkish ways. We might point to Folman's interview statement that he made an antiwar film, a film obliquely critical of Ariel Sharon's leadership during the Lebanese invasion. Here Latour might caution leftist critics not to let their paranoia cloud the "positive" message of the film. Antitheory would urge a reparative perspective, evaluating the film for what it does (its impact on other actors) rather than what it is (ideologically tainted from the start), for what it opens up rather than what it excludes. Simply stated, the slogan of Latourian antitheory is: Opt for hermeneutic generosity rather than critical hermeneutics.

The persuasiveness of Latour's argument relies on the validity of that choice: hermeneutic generosity or critical hermeneutics? To which I'm tempted to answer, "Yes, Please!"[31] Slavoj Žižek has made productive use of this type of response non response when confronted with a fake choice. Generosity and critique are not intrinsically at odds with one another. It also depends on the kind of hermeneutics that one deploys, that is operative in our discussion of theory and antitheory. We all know the key distinction that Paul Ricoeur makes between a hermeneutics of faith and a hermeneutics of suspicion. But it is also important to remember that Ricoeur evokes two additional types of hermeneutics. There is an aborted hermeneutics—a hermeneutics of skepticism (nihilistic in its orientation), and a projected hermeneutics—a hermeneutics of postcritical faith.

Whereas Ricoeur insisted on the difference between skepticism and suspicion, hoping for a dialectics of faith that transverses suspicion, resulting in a hermeneutics of postcritical faith, antitheory has tended to efface the distinction between suspicion and skepticism. An anti-antitheory might be well served to return to Ricoeur's aborted hermeneutics. And I would further add that it is not paranoia but hysteria that fuels such a hermeneutics of skepticism. The theorist as hysteric is never satisfied with the Master's answers, constantly questioning their interpellation as a would-be knower and desiring subject: What do I know? What do I want? What the critic-hysteric says about an object is always tentative, subject to expansion and revision.

But is the hysteric too enthralled by their own negativity, too captivated by their non identity? Not necessarily. Skepticism can also be reparative; its negativity is also what incites its practitioner to want more, to know more. A deconstructive skepticism is not any less faithful to its object than Latour's object-oriented ontology.

By way of conclusion, I want to return to the last scene of the film in a way that is "reparatively critical." I read the scene, at least in part, as a rebuff of Sivan's allegorical interpretation of Folman's trauma. We must not forget that the psychologist is only a character in the film and does not necessarily represent the film as a whole. We shouldn't just assume that he is the mouthpiece of the director, as some critics have done. In any case, the Saying of the Palestinian woman (here I'm using Saying in its Levinasian sense, as the expression of a desire to communicate; its phatic function) reminds the audience that the scene of violence is (should be) about the Palestinians. Her Saying jolts the spectator out of his or her comfortable consumption of a Lebanese War aestheticized through the subjective gaze of its protagonist. It throws the viewer back to the morally bewildering place of Sabra and Shatila.

But is this return of the real, or raw, account of the massacre too late and thus incomplete? The spectator is confronted with the Saying of the woman, but her Saying is left without a response. Folman declines to engage with her story, her collective story. He does not directly express any sense of personal responsibility for Palestinian suffering—he does not ask for their impossible forgiveness (you can only forgive the unforgivable, as Derrida has taught us)—or collective responsibility for the Lebanese invasion, not to mention the Nakba, which brought the refugee camps into existence in the first place.

As these difficult questions go unexplored, Folman leaves his spectators with a generalized sense of responsibility, but this universalization of responsibility risks reifying the Palestinians' Saying by presenting it as undigested (it is left untranslated for Folman's Israeli and Western audiences) and by depoliticizing Israel's involvement: if everyone is responsible, no particular one is responsible. To be sure, telling the other's story, speaking for them, is a thorny interpretive adventure. Folman chooses to engage with what he knows—which is first and foremost his own experiences as an Israeli solider. In an interview, Folman describes entertaining the possibility of "making a *Rashomon* of 1982, showing the conflict from the differing viewpoints of all those involved. But it was not for him. 'Who am I to tell their stories?' he says of the Palestinians. 'They have to tell their own stories.'"[32] But one wonders if this expression of humility serves rather a self-protective function, foreclosing contact with the other rather than making room for their voice. It is after all never a simple choice between speaking for others or only speaking for oneself/one's people. In any case, when it came to the Palestinians, Folman refused to engage their trauma, opting for hermeneutic fasting or withdrawal, perhaps out of a desire to respect the opacity of the other, but at the expense of prolonging a dialogue with the survivors and the memory of the victims.

Against Latour, theory here does not adopt the position of the all-powerful Zeus judging and condemning others (the director, the film, the naïve spectator, etc.) for their fetishes and mystifications. Theory, in its deconstructive guise, is more hysteric than paranoid, more skeptical than suspicious. Its attentiveness to ideology does not follow the logic outlined by Latour and others. To insist that ideology matters, to expose Waltz with Bashir as ideological, is to say, first, that a certain framing and making of Palestinian suffering is fraught, that there is something problematic about making the Israeli subject complex, self-reflexive, while maintaining the Palestinian other as an object of pathos, ossified, as it were, in her suffering, and also to insist that more is going on (in reality, in the film)—whence the labor of hermeneutics, the impetus to reread and remake, to translate otherwise, to see different connections, and so on. In this light, Latour's crucial distinction between constructivism and deconstruction is ultimately a dubious one. To the Latourian question, "Constructivism or deconstruction?" we must answer again, "Yes, Please!"[33]

Notes

1. Bruno Latour, "Why Has Critique Run Out of Steam? From Matters of Fact to Matters of Concern," *Critical Inquiry* 30 (2004): 231.
2. Ibid., 239.
3. Ibid., 240.
4. Ibid., 232.
5. See Zahi Zalloua, *Theory's Autoimmunity: Skepticism, Philosophy, and Literature* (Evanston: Northwestern University Press, 2018).
6. The title also calls to mind Jean Baudrillard's book *Forget Foucault*, which questionably faults Foucault's model of discourse for its purported complicity with power, for being "a mirror of the powers it describes" (Jean Baudrillard, *Forget Foucault*, trans. Nicole Dufrense [Cambridge: Semiotext(e), 2007], 30). In our case, however, what we are after is not a critique of critique, but a critique of anti-critique, of an anti-critique masquerading as a richer account of reality.
7. Latour, "Why Has Critique Run Out of Steam?," 231.
8. Levi Bryant, Nick Srnicek, and Graham Harman, "Towards a Speculative Philosophy," in *The Speculative Turn: Continental Materialism and Realism*, ed. Levi Bryant, Nick Srnicek, and Graham Harman (Melbourne: re.press, 2011), 3.
9. Quentin Meillassoux, *After Finitude: An Essay on the Necessity of Contingency*, trans. Ray Brassier (New York: Continuum, 2008), 5. Meillassoux elaborates further on his concept: "Correlationism rests on an argument as simple as it is powerful, and which can be formulated in the following way: No X without givenness of X, and no theory about X without a positing of X. If you speak about something, you speak about something that is given to you, and posited by you. Consequently, the sentence: 'X is,' means: 'X is the correlate of thinking' in a Cartesian sense. That is: X is the correlate of an affection, or a perception, or a conception, or of any subjective

act. To be is to be a correlate, a term of a correlation. And in particular, when you claim to think any X, you must posit this X, which cannot then be separated from this special act of positing, of conception. That is why it is impossible to conceive an absolute X, i.e., an X which would be essentially separate from a subject. We can't know what the reality of the object in itself is because we can't distinguish between properties which are supposed to belong to the object and properties belonging to the subjective access to the object" (Meillassoux, "Speculative Realism: Presentation by Quentin Meillassoux," *Collapse* 3 [2007]: 409).

10 Meillassoux distinguishes between two forms of correlationism: a weak version and a strong one. Weak correlationism rules out knowledge of the noumenal real, of the in-itself, yet without dismissing its thinkability. Strong correlationism excludes the possibility of even its thinkability: "According to Kant, we know *a priori* that the thing-in-itself is non-contradictory and that it actually exists. By way of contrast, the strong model of correlationism maintains not only that it is illegitimate to claim that we can know the in-itself, but also that it is illegitimate to claim that we can at least think it" (Meillassoux, *After Finitude*, 35).

11 Meillassoux decries a certain fetishization of the prefix "co-" from Kant to Derrida: "The 'co-' (of co-givenness, of co-relation, of the co-originary, of co-presence, etc.) is the grammatical particle that dominates modern philosophy, its veritable 'chemical formula.' Thus, one could say that up until Kant, one of the principal problems of philosophy was to think substance, while ever since Kant, it has consisted in trying to think the correlation" (Meillassoux, *After Finitude*, 5–6).

12 Meillassoux, *After Finitude*, 7.

13 Bruno Latour, "The Politics of Explanation," in *Knowledge and Reflexivity*, ed. Steve Woolgar (London: Sage, 1988), 173.

14 Ibid., 173.

15 Bruno Latour, "An Attempt at a 'Compositionist Manifesto,'" *New Literary History* 41 (2010): 471–490, 476.

16 Bruno Latour, *Reassembling the Social: An Introduction to Actor-Network-Theory* (Oxford: Oxford University Press, 2005), 71. The posthumanism of Latour and others is not incompatible with theory's critical practices. Slavoj Žižek, for example, does not object to a focus on nonhuman factors in a critique of ideology. On the contrary, he credits Jane Bennett's wider account of how actants relate to one another at a polluted trash site: "how not only humans but also the rotting trash, worms, insects, abandoned machines, chemical poisons, and so on each play their (never purely passive) role. There is an authentic theoretical and ethico-political insight in such an approach" (Žižek, *Disparities* [New York: Bloomsbury, 2016], 60). Developing an ecological eye, Žižek argues, will serve critique much better than a human-centered perspective, which has not been able to mobilize adequate resistance to capitalism's ruling ideology. See Jane Bennett, *Vibrant Matter: A Political Ecology of Things* (Durham: Duke University Press, 2010), 4–6.

17 Rita Felski, "Latour and Literary Studies," *PMLA* 130 (2015): 738.
18 Latour, *Reassembling the Social*, 245.
19 Latour, "Why Has Critique Run Out of Steam?," 232.
20 "We can see why there is no question, if we want to restore meaning to constructivism, of giving ourselves over to the temptations of the critical spirit [deconstruction and the likes]" (Latour, *An Inquiry into Modes of Existence*, trans. Catherine Porter [Cambridge: Harvard University Press, 2013], 156). See also Bruno Latour, "The Promises of Constructivism," in *Chasing Technoscience: Matrix for Materiality*, ed. Don Ihde and Evan Selinger (Bloomington: Indiana University Press, 2003), 41.
21 Latour, "Why Has Critique Run Out of Steam?," 243.
22 Graham Harman, "The Well-Wrought Broken Hammer: Object-Oriented Literary Criticism," *New Literary History* 43.2 (2012): 187. A philosophy that does justice to objects cannot be "a philosophy of access to the world" (Harman, *The Quadruple Object* [Winchester: Zero Books, 2011], 136).
23 Timothy Morton, "Here Comes Everything: The Promise of Object-Oriented Ontology," *Qui Parle* 19.2 (2011), 165. Again: "It is Kant who shows ... that things never coincide with their phenomena. All we need to do is extend this revolutionary insight beyond the human-world gap. Unlike Meillassoux, we are not going to try to bust through human finitude, but to place that finitude in a universe of trillions of finitudes, as many as there are things—because a thing just is a fit between what it is and how it appears, for any entity whatsoever, not simply for that special entity called the (human) subject" (Morton, *Hyperobjects: Philosophy and Ecology after the End of the World* [Minneapolis: University of Minnesota Press, 2013], 18).
24 Today's antitheory is not the antitheory of old. It does not desire to return to some pristine, pre-Lapsarian condition; instead, today antitheory—of which Rita Felski is exemplary—wants to move beyond the stalemate of theory, beyond theory's obsession with signifiers and mediation.
25 Rita Felski, *The Limits of Critique* (Chicago: University of Chicago Press, 2015), 107. "Latour draws us away," Felski writes, "from the prototype of the knowing, ironic, detached critic" (Felski, "Latour and Literary Studies," 740).
26 Eve Kosofsky Sedgwick, "Paranoid Reading and Reparative Reading, Or, You're So Paranoid, You Probably Think This Essay Is about You," in *Novel Gazing: Queer Readings in Fiction*, ed. Eve Kosofsky Sedgwick (Durham: Duke University Press, 1997), 9–10.
27 Sedgwick, "Paranoid Reading and Reparative Reading," 24.
28 Raz Yosef, "War Fantasies: Memory, Trauma and Ethics in Ari Folman's *Waltz with Bashir*," *Journal of Modern Jewish Studies* 9.3 (2010): 323–324.
29 Felski wants to reassure other literary critics that Latour still allows them to be politically engaged in their criticism: "Actor-network theory does not exclude

the political—it is deeply interested in conflicts, asymmetries, struggles—but its antipathy to reductionism means that political discourse cannot serve as a metalanguage into which everything can be translated" (Felski, "Latour and Literary Studies," 740). But I question the effectiveness of a politics that willfully evacuates ideology from its interpretive toolbox. Isn't there a place in ANT for a model of ideology critique that is not reductive and totalizing?

30 Latour, "Why Has Critique Run Out of Steam?," 225.
31 "In a well-known Marx Brothers joke, Groucho answers the standard question 'Tea or coffee?' with 'Yes, please!'—a refusal of choice ... [O]ne should answer in the same way the false alternative today's critical theory seems to impose on us: either 'class struggle' (the outdated problematic of class antagonism, commodity production, etc.) or 'postmodernism' (the new world of dispersed multiple identities, of radical contingency, of an irreducible ludic plurality of struggles). Here, at least, we can have our cake and eat it" (Žižek, "Class Struggle or Postmodernism? Yes, Please!" in *Contingency, Hegemony, Universality: Contemporary Dialogues on the Left*, ed. Judith Butler, Ernesto Laclau, and Slavoj Žižek [New York: Verso, 2000], 90).
32 Jonathan Freedland, "Lest We Forget," *The Guardian* (October 25, 2008). http://www.theguardian.com/film/2008/oct/25/waltz-with-bashir-ari-folman.
33 Support from the Louis B. Perry Research Award made this research possible. I also would like to thank Chloe Casey for his help on this project.

Works Cited

Baudrillard, Jean. *Forget Foucault*. Trans. Nicole Dufrense. Cambridge: Semiotext(e), 2007.
Bennett, Jane. *Vibrant Matter: A Political Ecology of Things*. Durham: Duke University Press, 2010.
Bryant, Levi, Nick Srnicek, and Graham Harman. "Towards a Speculative Philosophy." In *The Speculative Turn: Continental Materialism and Realism*. Ed. Levi Bryant, Nick Srnicek, and Graham Harman. Melbourne: re.press, 2011. 1–18.
Felski, Rita. "Latour and Literary Studies." *PMLA* 130 (2015): 737–742.
Felski, Rita. *The Limits of Critique*. Chicago: University of Chicago Press, 2015.
Freedland, Jonathan. "Lest We Forget." *The Guardian* (October 25, 2008). http://www.theguardian.com/film/2008/oct/25/waltz-with-bashir-ari-folman.
Harman, Graham. *The Quadruple Object*. Winchester: Zero Books, 2011.
Harman, Graham. "The Well-Wrought Broken Hammer: Object-Oriented Literary Criticism." *New Literary History* 43.2 (2012): 183–203.
Latour, Bruno. "The Politics of Explanation." In *Knowledge and Reflexivity*. Ed. Steve Woolgar. London: Sage, 1988. 155–177.

Latour, Bruno. "The Promises of Constructivism." In *Chasing Technoscience: Matrix for Materiality*. Ed. Don Ihde and Evan Selinger. Bloomington: Indiana University Press, 2003. 27–46.

Latour, Bruno. "Why Has Critique Run Out of Steam? From Matters of Fact to Matters of Concern." *Critical Inquiry* 30 (2004): 225–248.

Latour, Bruno. *Reassembling the Social: An Introduction to Actor-Network-Theory*. Oxford: Oxford University Press, 2005.

Latour, Bruno. "An Attempt at a 'Compositionist Manifesto.'" *New Literary History* 41 (2010): 471–490.

Latour, Bruno. *An Inquiry into Modes of Existence*. Trans. Catherine Porter. Cambridge: Harvard University Press, 2013.

Meillassoux, Quentin. "Speculative Realism: Presentation by Quentin Meillassoux." *Collapse* 3 (2007): 408–449.

Meillassoux, Quentin. *After Finitude: An Essay on the Necessity of Contingency*. Trans. Ray Brassier. New York: Continuum, 2008.

Morton, Timothy. "Here Comes Everything: The Promise of Object-Oriented Ontology." *Qui Parle* 19.2 (2011): 163–190.

Morton, Timothy. *Hyperobjects: Philosophy and Ecology after the End of the World*. Minneapolis: University of Minnesota Press, 2013.

Sedgwick, Eve Kosofsky. "Paranoid Reading and Reparative Reading, Or, You're So Paranoid, You Probably Think This Essay Is about You." In *Novel Gazing: Queer Readings in Fiction*. Ed. Eve Kosofsky Sedgwick. Durham: Duke University Press, 1997. 1–37.

Yosef, Raz. "War Fantasies: Memory, Trauma and Ethics in Ari Folman's *Waltz with Bashir*." *Journal of Modern Jewish Studies* 9.3 (2010): 311–326.

Zalloua, Zahi. *Theory's Autoimmunity: Skepticism, Philosophy, and Literature*. Evanston: Northwestern University Press, 2018.

Žižek, Slavoj. "Class Struggle or Postmodernism? Yes, Please!" In Contingency, Hegemony, *Universality: Contemporary Dialogues on the Left*. Ed. Judith Butler, Ernesto Laclau, and Slavoj Žižek. New York: Verso, 2000. 90–135.

Žižek, Slavoj. *Disparities*. New York: Bloomsbury, 2016.

After Anti-Foundationalism: Ten Theses on the Limits of Antitheory

Christopher Breu

1. Theory is dead! Long live theory!

At the beginning of the twenty-first century, Terry Eagleton, long-time warrior on behalf of theory, wearied, perhaps, from ceaseless struggle, laid down his arms, departed from the battlefield, and declared theory dead.[1] This declaration came as a shock to many of us who had devoted graduate careers to gaining partial knowledge of the capacious, scattered, speculative, and obsessive discourse we call theory. It felt like one of the generals of the culture wars (forgive the bellicose metaphors, but they seem to work in this case) suddenly departed the field, declaring defeat. Many of us true believers in the cause of theory were dismayed, feeling betrayed by one of our own. Many of us also felt like it takes a certain position of professional privilege to declare the field that your work was associated with to be over.

It also, perhaps, takes a certain kind of honesty. It involves stepping back from one's life work and reflecting on whether it remains vital and current. It involves an assessment of whether there is more work to do in a given approach. Thus, we find the proliferation of essays like "What Was Postcolonialism?" or "Queer and Then."[2] On one level, such moments may betoken professional exhaustion as much as any larger sea change in the profession. It is not surprising that such essays are often written by well-established scholars in a given field looking back over a life's work. If you have a restless intellect, it is hard not to grow a bit tired reading the same arguments all the time, especially when they are versions of arguments you helped establish.

Yet, on another level, such essays often do represent moments of significant sea change in a given field or discipline. Thus, while the death of theory that

Eagleton proclaimed was not so much the death of theory as such, but rather the waning of the power and intellectual rewards yielded by a certain version of theory, it did in fact mark a shift in theoretical discourse. As with the regular declarations of the death of jazz, rock, or classical music, the claims about the death of theory are greatly exaggerated. Yet, there is often something at stake in such moments that produce the inflated claims of demise. For example, classical music may not be dead, but it certainly has mutated in locations and forms from orchestral composition designed for symphony halls to the computer-based composition that can be performed or reproduced in any of a number of sites. So-called neoclassical music or contemporary composition also tend to fuse with other genres such as jazz, improvisation more generally, and experimental electronic music. So classical music isn't dead, but its shape and definition have certainly changed in major ways. This is not our parents' classical music and even the descriptor "classical" may not make a lot of sense at the moment (given its emphasis on a canonical repertoire). Similarly, theory hasn't died; It has shifted forms however (and in contrast to classical music, I find the term "theory" still the best available one to capture the work done by speculative thought in the present). The turn-of-the-century moment in which Eagleton's book appeared did mark a shift away from the forms of antifoundationalism and constructivism that were central to much theoretical discourse in the seventies, eighties, and nineties and toward a partial reclaiming of foundations and foundational questions. Issues of ontology, materialism, and realism are being raised again in ways that cut against the antifoundationalist common sense that was enshrined by theory in the late twentieth century.

2. Antitheory positions are, of course, theoretical.

Antitheory positions have been around as long as theory itself. Indeed, echoing Jacques Derrida's account of writing being necessary to conceptualize speech, or Judith Butler's assertion that, as a concept, homosexuality predates heterosexuality, it wouldn't be a surprise to find out that the antitheory position predates the concept of theory itself.[3] And, if we take the foundations of the field of literary studies as our origin moment (one that, like all origin claims, is performative and excludes more than it includes), the twin midcentury formations of Leavisism and new criticism can be read as forms of antitheory *avant la lettre*. Both approaches worked to separate the aesthetic and thematic account of the literary object from biographical, historical (other than literary historical), and social contexts. So, there was a form of antitheory (excluding anything "extraneous" to promote the apprehension of the text itself) before that thing we call theory appeared on the scene, at least by its proper name. Yet Leavisism and new criticism were in turn responding to what they saw as unproductive approaches to the study of literature from an earlier moment of biographical criticism, psychological criticism, moral criticism, and German-style philology. So, depending on your definition of theory, their antitheory position could be seen as a response to earlier moments of theory. Thus, the origin narrative slides ever backward.

Rather than looking for an origin for theory or antitheory, then, I think it is more productive to define theory and antitheory as different theoretical accounts of the existence of theory as such. While seemingly paradoxical, such a definition affirms Gerald Graff's argument that antitheoretical positions are indeed theoretical.[4] They are theories about the uselessness or destructiveness of theory. To argue that even antitheory is a theory seems to preclude the need for argument about the advantages and limitations of theory, antitheory, and post-theory as positions. If everything is a theory, then why argue for or against theory as such? If it is inevitable, there is no point in debating it. Yet, a profession's or a field's attitude toward theory shapes the quality of the theoretical discourse it produces. If its official position is that theory is at best a distraction and at worst destructive of the fabric of the field's legitimate objects of study, then the theory produced by such an approach will be attenuated at best and incoherent and unsystematic at worst.[5] Whether we see theory as a legitimate dimension of literary studies matters. It matters not only for how we apprehend literature and culture but also for how sophisticated our field is in understanding its own intellectual endeavors and first principles. It also helps us situate our own endeavors and first principles in relationship to those of other fields. Thus, theoretical discourse is necessary for interdisciplinarity.

3. Theory can be posited as both transhistorical and as having a definite history.

In making this claim, I am daring to echo Althusser's infamous and gnomic claims that ideology has no history and yet specific ideologies have histories.[6] I think we have to think of theory in a similar way. It has many histories but it can also be posited as well-nigh transhistorical. While it is often crucial to historicize in order to denaturalize what are often seen as natural formations (this was one of the crucial forms of work done by antifoundationalist theories and forms of historicism in the late twentieth century), it can be equally necessary to emphasize that something represents more than merely a passing historical phenomenon—that there are fundamental (sometimes transhistorical or ontological) questions staged by a given discourse that are not reducible to merely one historical moment or stage. Thus, Althusser emphasizes the transhistorical dimensions of ideology precisely to indicate that the problem of ideology will not disappear with the disappearance of class society.

Similarly, we may posit theory as a discourse that in the United States emerged in the seventies with the reception of French structuralism and poststructuralism and British cultural studies in the humanities and social sciences. This is the version of theory that Eagleton declared dead, and it has indeed morphed into something else in the present. Moreover, while the French influence remains strong as does the American reception, it has transformed into a more genuinely global discourse (although one too often conducted in English). So this understanding is one version of theory. It may be changing in the present enough to be given the name "post-theory," if the latter can be taken to be a different version of speculative discourse (one that forms less in opposition to the foundational discourses of continental philosophy and contemporary science, but more on this below) rather than a rejection of theory as such. Yet, I prefer to stick to the term "theory," if only because of the ambiguity of the prefix "post-" itself. Post discourses can indicate a relationship to what came before, but it also often indicates the death or problematic nature of the earlier formation (take postmodernism, poststructuralism, and postcolonialism as three examples of such). For this reason, I want to maintain the term "theory" even in this local history of the concept and even though I am critical of aspects of the version of theory, with its emphasis on constructivism and antifoundationalism, that was enshrined in the late twentieth century.

However, this local manifestation of theory can be taken as one version of a larger will to speculative rationality that we term "theory." Such a conception would encompass continental philosophy (and Anglo-American philosophy for that matter) rather than setting itself in contradistinction to it. This latter version of theory doesn't disappear so much as take different historical forms. While we might see the disappearance of such forms of theory from the curriculum, one of the dangers of the current neoliberal restructuring of the academy in relationship to testable knowledge and prepackaged content, it takes a much greater dystopian vision to imagine the destruction of speculative rationality as such. It is, finally, the idea of theory as speculative rationality I will defend here, one that can take many different forms but one that is at its most powerful when it is nurtured as an interdisciplinary discourse that works to undo the reification of knowledge in different disciplines. It also works to ask crucial questions about the working assumptions of the disciplines and institutions in which we work. Finally, and most forcefully, it also posits the possibility of the world being otherwise. To argue for the end to such a theoretical practice is not only difficult but fundamentally hostile to the very core of intellectual inquiry.

4. The new new criticism is not the way forward.

One of the more unexpected developments of the new century is the calls within the field of literature to attend to and appreciate the text itself more fully. This assertion, often framed as an antidote to the preponderance of critique and the reduction of literary texts to mere examples in theoretical discourse, has gone by a number of names, each of which offers a distinct approach, but ones that share a new emphasis on deriving meaning (and pleasure) from the literary text itself. These include such diverse movements as postcritique, the new aestheticism, and object-oriented literary criticism. Each of these movements is different and each has a relationship to theory. Isobel Armstrong has defined new aestheticism as a return to the category of the aesthetic as the lynchpin of literary study.[7] The new aestheticism is valuable to the degree that it complicated and challenged the dismissal of the aesthetic in too much cultural studies and cultural Marxism, yet it also rejected much of the crucial critical work done by those same bodies of theory that situated understandings of the aesthetic in the context of both ideology and history.

Rita Felski's articulation of postcritique draws both upon Eve Sedgwick's articulation of a reparative reading practice and Bruno Latour's argument that critique has "run out of steam."[8] Yet Latour's and Sedgwick's projects were about a different emphasis within theory, one aimed toward repair and building rather than tearing down. These are still theoretical positions, indeed crucial ones, as any Marxist account of utopian thinking would also assert. While Felski also recognizes that she is articulating a theoretical position, the position itself is about subordinating critique to reaffirm the "incandescent, extraordinary, sublime and utterly special" dimensions of the work itself.[9] Her position affirms the new-critical notion of the autonomy of the text, although, in this case, recognizing that it also intersects with (but is not determined by) the social and affirming the effect of the text on the reader (so there is a hint of reader-response criticism in it as well). This concern with readerly reception is particularly marked in the "Introduction" to *Critique and Postcritique*, jointly edited by Felski and Elizabeth S. Anker, where they fault critique for encouraging an "antagonistic and combative attitude toward the public world."[10] Yet, while I certainly want to affirm the need to build as well as dismantle (which was always a dimension of Marxist critique—Fredric Jameson always emphasized the utopian as well as ideological registers of critique), I think the image of the public here is a rather genteel (and thus class-inflected) one. Eleanor Courtemanche has demonstrated that the online public, rather than being cowed by critique, has made it the dominant mode of social media.[11] These forms of online critique borrow the language of, if not always the dialectical dimensions and concern for context of, 1990s cultural studies. So in the present, we do not need to cede to a new (or refurbished old) autonomy of the work of art; if anything, we need better and more nuanced ways to theorize the relationship between text and context as well as writings in various media and the various publics with which they intersect. Recent work in media studies, with its theorization of not only the interactive dimensions of a given text but the infrastructure of its encoding and delivery and the complex and mediated dimensions of both its production and reception, suggests a much richer vein for theorizing textual production in the present.[12] Moreover, the best of this work theorizes the aesthetic, but with an emphasis on the qualitative and sensuous experience of the aesthetic rather than articulating hierarchies of value or insisting on the autonomy of texts.

One might hope for an attention to such a context in Graham Harman's account of object-oriented literary criticism, but one finds instead the same emphasis on the autonomy of the literary object that characterizes the new aestheticism and postcritique.[13] Harman, of course, is merely applying his object-oriented ontology, which represents an important, if contested, development in philosophy, to the logic of the literary text. One of the more controversial (and I might add problematic) aspects of Harman's philosophy is the emphasis on the object's autonomy. While I understand his desire to emphasize the aspects of a given object or material formation that exceed human perception and forms of human action (which is an important materialist emphasis to my mind, although Harman does not define himself as a materialist), it does not follow that objects have an autonomous core that is "withdrawn" from *all* interactions with any other object. Partial autonomy and partial excess (or withdrawal) are important and explain why entities are in fact entities—that they don't just simply dissolve into larger or smaller systems or units (what Harman describes as overmining and undermining) but to emphasize complete withdrawal and autonomy is to reify objects in a way that denies their macrological and micrological situatedness in systems both larger and smaller. It fundamentally denies both the economic and the ecological organization of objects (or entities, or forms of materiality, however you want to theorize this). Thus what we wind up with in Harman's account of the literary object is an argument against acculturation as such: "The call for 'the death of the author' needs to be complemented by a new call for the 'death of the culture.'"[14] What this argument winds up doing is affirm disciplinarity (which Harman starts out with as a given) and refuses the crucial contextual work that is done by any materialism worthy of the name, whether it is political economic, ecological, or postphenomenological. It is, in sum, a new reification and a new version of the new criticism. This is not what we need the face of contemporary theory to be.

5. We need to redefine theory so that it is adequate to the world in which it performs its work.

In the introduction to the *Valences of the Dialectic*, Fredric Jameson makes a distinction between philosophy and theory, one that it is crucial to recognize, even as I want to argue for the need of the two categories to be understood as necessarily entangled.[15] Of course, if we take the capacious definition I provided above, that theory can be equated with speculative thought as such, then philosophy and its history can be folded into the category of theory, and the opposition between them vanishes. Rather than taking this route, which too quickly resolves a dialectical opposition that needs to be appreciated in its negativity, I want to stay with this opposition for a moment in the present discussion. Jameson means something distinct by theory, which he historicizes as a discourse that emerged in the later half of the twentieth century and offers "a space outside the institutions and outside the rehearsal of such compulsory rationalization, and its claims of theory (if not its achieved realities) which allow us to grasp the limits of philosophy as such, very much including dialectical philosophy."[16] He goes on to argue, "I believe that theory is to be grasped as the perpetual and impossible attempt to dereify the language of thought, and to preempt all the systems and ideologies which inevitably result from the establishment of this or that fixed terminology."[17] This opposition situates theory as a kind of solvent, unclogging philosophy's pipes, if you will, and making thought flow again. And, of course, flow was one of the fetishized terms in the heyday of anti-essentialism. In the Deleuzian and French feminist language of the era, everything was flows.

Yet, what happens when flow itself has become just one more calcified term? What happens when the crucial denaturalizing process that we associated with anti-essentialism at its best becomes merely another institutional discourse? Jameson, ever the dialectician, articulates just such an understanding of theory's status in the present:

> One may very well welcome the current slogans of anti-foundationalism and anti-essentialism—and reread Marx himself as well as Hegel in light of the demands they make on us—without ignoring the obvious namely that these preeminently theoretical slogans and programs have already themselves become thematized and reified—in other words, have themselves begun to turn into foundationalisms and philosophical systems in their own right.[18]

So how do we in turn dereify the paradoxical reification of the language of dereification? How do we denaturalize theories that post denaturalization as their *modus operandi*? Do we continue to just radicalize the work of denaturalization, interrogating each statement or claim for ever-more precise traces of essentialism or foundationalism? Can anti-essentialism itself be turned into a permanent revolution?

On one level, the answer is yes. We need the powerful work of reflexivity that is central to the work undertaken by anti-essentialism at its best. All truth claims should be able to be reflexively interrogated. This is the necessary work of theory as permanent revolution (to rework a term from Trotsky). Yet, on another level, this endless will toward interrogating foundations becomes its own foundation, but one that is incapable of producing something more than self-reflexive critique. In this way, anti-essentialism becomes very much like those parties that claim to embody the work of permanent revolution and then calcify political power into a permanent, unchanging structure. So the answer is also no. Theory must move beyond its anti-essentialist phase and posit structures and foundations in order to do the work of producing a better world. It must posit a praxis and a vision for the future as well as continue the work of critique. Felski and Latour are right in this regard. We can't be comfortable with critique alone. We can't just tear down, interrogate, disrupt, and dismantle.

We also need to build; we need to theorize about what kind of future we want. We need to confront the most pressing problems of our times, including the devastation produced by climate change and ever-growing global inequality. We can't do this by merely critiquing. We also need to theorize foundations, institutions, practices, and edifices from which to do this work. If one of the dangers of the present, as I've been arguing, is that a permanent, reified formation is institutionalized in the name of anti-institutionalization, then one of the ways of avoiding this risk is by actively constructing theories, practices, and institutions that build self-critique into their very functioning while also daring to posit positive visions and ontological claims about what exists and what kinds of better existence could be possible. Theory needs to turn away from the reflexive mirror and turn again to the world, both the world of human shaping and the world that exceeds and exists in tension with the human. Fortunately, much scholarship in the present is beginning to do this work from the turn to ontology, ecology, and political economy, to much of the work that is taking place under the rubrics of speculative realism and new materialism. This brings us to our next thesis.

6. Contemporary theory needs to be poised between foundationalism and antifoundationalism.

We need foundations. We need concepts and sites from which to theorize a better world. We also need institutions in the humanities and social sciences that can work to bring the practice of theory into dialogue with the social and political world. We need to protect and build what we have created during the theory revolution. Theory in the present is like a state in the postrevolutionary moment. After the fervor of the revolution, how can a state, and an economy, and an ecology be built that will instantiate and maintain the core tenets of the revolution? If all that revolutionary struggle is not to be in vain, structures, institutions, and practices need to be put into place to maintain its political and ethical force. Theory itself must be ontologized on a certain level (hence my Althusserian description of it above as having no history).

Part of this new definition of theory, then, would be a partial turn back to philosophy, which would also be a moving past the hard-and-fast opposition between theory and philosophy that Jameson both posits and complicates. Theory in the present is again asking the fundamental questions of ontology. It has begun to move beyond the epistemological limitations and distortions of the linguistic and cultural turns. If language and culture were the metaphor through which we understood everything, then everything became shaped by these metaphors. Moreover, the paradigm became a thoroughly constructivist one. Everything was linguistically or culturally constructed, and that which resisted, set limits on, or differed from such constructions was not theorized. While various forms of mediation were theorized, even these were conceptualized primarily in terms of the logics of language (discourse for Foucault, or the endless play of deconstruction in language for Derrida). Different structures and different temporalities and forms of mediation were collapsed into language as the generalized metaphor for what exists. Even the Marxism of the time, while exceedingly rich, emphasized the cultural and the superstructural, taking their leads from the work of Jameson and Althusser.

As Levi Bryant, who is a much more capacious and interdisciplinary thinker in the object-oriented mode than Harman, has argued, within such a framework both nature and materiality (what he calls objects) are bracketed, the exception being the materiality of the medium of representation itself.[19] Thus, while the subject and representation were complexly theorized within the linguistic turn, the object, materiality, and what Jason Moore has termed the "world-ecology" all were undertheorized if theorized at all.[20] Theodor Adorno warned about the danger of the attenuation of attention to the object at the beginning of the period that we later came to name as postmodernity (or the period of the cultural and linguistic turns); this warning was indeed prescient.[21]

Fortunately, much of the work that has appeared under the rubrics of new materialism, speculative realism, and posthumanism has returned an emphasis on all that was left out of the linguistic turn. Much like art in the same moment, we have gone from the self-referentiality of Jeffrey Koons or even the powerfully politicized work of the Guerilla Girls (with its autocritique of art as a gendered practice and commodity) to the mixed media paintings of Ana Teresa Barboza or the instillation work of John Okomfra, which differently mark the intersections of the material body with trauma and constructions of femininity in patriarchal cultures, on the one hand, and articulates the psychosocial workings of racism in relationship to ecological and political economic violence, on the other. Art, like theory, has exited the ironic or even politicized hall-of-mirrors of commodification and self-reference and turned outward toward the systems, structures, and materialities in which human life is situated. Theory should follow suit.

7. Theory adequate to our Anthropocene present needs to theorize both human and nonhuman agency, and it needs a robust but critical realism for doing so.

At first, the argument for a partial return of theory to philosophy might seem counterintuitive. Wasn't it modern philosophy that has argued, after Kant, that we need to bracket things-in-themselves? We can discuss the representation of things or what things are or mean for us, but there is no way of positing the reality of things other than for us. This was the first antirealist move that modern philosophy made that laid the groundwork for powerful critiques of essence, nature, and foundation. In many ways, the powerful anti-essentialist and antifoundationalist work done by the cultural and linguistic turns flow, with a few twists and turns, directly out of a specific reading of Kant. This point has been made by Quentin Meillassoux, who in his critique of correlationism, argues that Kant's prohibition on considering things in themselves means that we can only "have access to the correlation between thinking and being, and never to either term consider apart from each other."[22] Meillassoux goes on to argue that we can, and need to, posit the existence of things separate from human apprehension of them. He stages this argument in terms of time, positing what he terms "ancestral" events, like the birth and formation of the universe, that are known as real by science (although science itself can change its notion of the real) even as there were clearly no humans anywhere to apprehend them. While the temporal dimensions of the critique of correlationism are important to posit, we might also want to think about the critique in terms of spatiality (or spatiotemporality) and relationality. In a world in which various ecosystemic by-products are shaping the habitability of the planet as such, in which algorithms engage in financial transactions with other algorithms at speeds imperceptible to humans, in which code and a vast digital infrastructure constructs and constrains communication, entertainment, and the infrastructural functioning of everyday life in the present, it seems crucial to think about how various nonhuman entities and materialities interact with each other, shape each other, and how, in turn, such interactions shape our interactions with them.

While such forms of materiality, infrastructure, and world-ecology are certainly humanly produced, this doesn't mean that they are fully human controlled or that they don't take on a force and agency of their own. The critique of posthumanism as effacing human responsibility and agency in the face of primarily humanly produced violence like climate change misses the mark. Jodi Dean is right to argue that we need to be careful not to abdicate our human agency when it is most needed and that our attention to material objects and actors should not come at the cost of forestalling human action.[23] Making this argument, though, is one thing. Refusing to recognize the force and power of the nonhuman structures, systems, and materialities that we have had a powerful hand in building and shaping is another. It is profoundly idealist to subscribe to the idea that the only form of agency to exist is human. It may hinder our ability to adequately predict and intervene in the damage done by climate change and other largely humanly produced, but not fully controlled, forms of violence. Such a position is finally to confuse agency and mastery. Dean's argument seems to long for a moment of pre-ecological thinking in which the human relationship to the world around us can be one of sheer instrumentality. I think we can adequately theorize human agency while also attending to the force, complexity, resilience, and insistence of nonhuman actors and formations. Any materialism that will help to save us from climate change and transform our relationship to the larger world will need to give the material (or the object, in Adorno's terms) its due.

We need a critical realism, one that retains the self-reflexive dimensions of theory during the linguistic turn, but one also that understands the necessity of positing real actors and entities in the world that don't depend completely on human construction. Such a realism would not minimize human agency. As Jason Moore has demonstrated, we have had a profound, transformative effect on the world-ecology, and most of this impact has been driven by capitalism, so much so that he renames the "Anthropocene" the "Capitaloscene." Capitalism represents the single greatest threat to the survival of all sorts of species, the human being the most notable. Yet, recognizing human agency does not mean enshrining human mastery. We need to understand how our actions intersect with and affect other forces. In order to do this on a theoretical level, we need to venture new ontologies (while continuing to interrogate them on the level of epistemology). This is why the recent ontological turn has felt so necessary. At the same time, this turn should not be an invitation toward apolitical mysticism. Too much speculative realism has put the emphasis on the speculative rather than the realism. We need a robust, politicized, understanding of realism, one that engages the most pressing political issues of our present. It needs to be able to think in terms of both ecologies and the political economy, which brings me to my next thesis.

8. Theory needs to be able to think the political economic and the political ecological as well as the ethical and the political together.

Much recent theory presents us with a stark set of binary choices. Moreover, these choices are often narrated in terms of a simple account of the "old" and the "new" or the moment before and after a "turn." This language can be helpful as a way of tracking transformations in the field. They can give us a sense of the "structure of feeling" (to use Raymond Williams' decidedly old, but excellent, theoretical language) of where theory or the field is in the present.[24] Yet, they also perform a subtle work of persuasion. They implicitly favor the new while marking the old as obsolete. So, when rhetorically effective, they tend to compel you to choose the new over the old. What is presented as a choice is, on a rhetorical level, no choice at all.

While I have sometimes used this language as a shorthand in this chapter, I have also argued that we need to move beyond this binary thinking. We need to retain what was best about earlier moments of theory while also embracing what is best in the new. The implicit injunction to embrace the new and eschew the old is particularly problematic in two recent "turns": the ethical turn and the ecological turn. Both of these "turns" are crucial developments (especially the ecological), but neither should be considered a thorough-going replacement for their binary others: the political and the political economic. Indeed a robust and attentive theory for the present needs to theorize the relationship between and among both terms of these binary pairs. One might argue that these oppositions might be deconstructed, echoing the call in much of the best recent ecocriticism to deconstruct the opposition between nature and culture. Yet while the logic of deconstruction isn't supposed to work this way, what often happens in such cases is the opposition often becomes replaced by one of the terms as a stand-in for both. Thus, recent ecocritical deconstructions of the nature culture divide, culture is folded into nature, and the latter term does the work of both. While certain crucial insights are achieved this way—it refuses the backgrounding or bracketing of nature and the thoroughly constructivist conception of culture that accompanies such an approach—it also refuses to recognize the specific province of culture as a part of a larger nature. It runs the danger of renaturalizing everything such that the powerful critiques of nature that were part of anti-essentialism become lost. The straightforward inversion of terms is rarely a solution. Even Marx's materialism was not a crude rejection of idealism but a complex dialectical account of the intertwining of the material and the ideal. In what follows, then, I want to emphasize the dialectical tension between categories, as well as their necessary entangling.

We need to take this approach to recent work that emphasizes ethics and the ecological. Ethics cannot merely replace politics, without the danger of a depoliticization of the fields of the political economic and political ecological. Ethics orient us toward collective practices that enable a better, more sustainable, and just present and future. The ethical is not fundamentally antagonistic. It is, at its best, collective and attentive to inter-entity relations rather than personal. But we also need politics, particularly in the context of neoliberal pressures, to transform collective political struggle into personal moral hygiene. Ethics without the conflict of politics can very quickly descend into individualized moral prescriptions. We need both the antagonism at the heart of politics and the collective practice that is ethics at its best. Politics always comes into being, as Jacques Rancière has argued, when the current contingent organization of the polis is challenged by "the part of those who have no part."[25] We need the agonistic dimensions of politics to ensure that all entities and actors can challenge the composition of the field. We also need ethics to generate the fundamental good toward which political struggle and its aftermath are oriented. To return to an earlier metaphor, we need a real permanent revolution and such a revolution never suspends the possibility of the political, such a revolution is also oriented around a constant ethical renewal.

A similar position needs to be argued about political economy and political ecology, or between an account of the capitalist world system and what Jason Moore describes as the world ecology. Of course any political economy is part of a larger ecology. Moreover, there are often different ecosystems that intersect with a given political economy. But what political economy emphasizes, at least in the Marxian and world systems traditions, is a fundamental antagonism: that is, between capital and labor (whether paid or unpaid, and however racialized, gendered, and sexualized). Ecosystems are often multipolar and factor in multiple axes of intersection and difference. If one of the dangers of political economy is to reduce everything to one single antagonism or causal explanation, one of the dangers of ecological thinking is that, in its emphasis on relationality and multipolar causality, it can tend toward a kind of functionalism, in which each part is necessary in its place for contributing to the whole. So we need to think the antagonism of political economy alongside the complexity and multipolar dimensions of ecology. The best definitions of each concept thus echo each other. Take this definition of political economy from Anwar Shaikh:

> [A]lthough the book attempts to demonstrate that the capitalist economic system generates powerful ordered patterns that transcend the historical and regional particularities, the forces that shape these patterns are neither steely rails nor mere constellations of circumstance. They are rather moving limits whose gradients define what is easy and what is difficult at any moment of time. In this way they channel the temporal paths of key economic variables. Indeed, these shaping forces are themselves the results of certain immanent imperatives, such as "gain-seeking behaviors" that define the social form in all of its historical

expressions. It is not a matter of contrasting ahistorical laws to historically contingent outcomes. Agency and law coexist within a multidimensional structure of influences. But this structure itself is deeply hierarchical, with some forces (such as the profit motive) being far more powerful than others. The stage on which history plays out is itself moving, driven by deeper currents ... [T]he resulting systemic order is generated in-and-through disorder ... Order-in-and-through-disorder is of a piece, an insensitive force that tramples both expectations and preferences.[26]

This definition is striking in a number of related ways. It provides a precise definition of what Marx means by materialism. Material formations are not "steely rails" nor "ahistorical laws" but rather temporal and spatial forces that shape "what is easy and what is difficult at any time." Moreover, capitalism and its political economic functioning is not merely a horizontal relationality as is favored by ecologically minded critics like Manuel De Landa but needs to be understood in its necessary hierarchy.[27] Such a hierarchy, produced by the force of the profit motive, creates antagonisms around class, labor, accumulation, and exploitation even as it also has to be understood as functioning within and helping to produce a political ecology (i.e., a politically inflected account of its functioning within multiple ecological registers). Some of the crucial dimensions of Shaikh's vision here is its emphasis on systemic contingency as well as structuration, spatiotemporal transformation as well as organization.

In thinking ecologically, we also need to think about the contingent and the structured as well as the spatiotemporal. Ecological thinking also asks us to think about vastly different scales and the intersections and intertwinings as well as disjunctions among these scales. Jeffrey Jerome Cohen frames these scalar disjunctions in terms of the following question: "What of the catastrophic, the disruptive, urban ecologies, the eruptive, heterogeneous microclimates, inhumanly vast or tiny scales of being and time, the mixed spaces where the separation of nature and culture are impossible to maintain?"[28] While this question runs the danger, as Ray Brassier points out, that so much work influenced by Bruno Latour demonstrates of merely providing a heterogeneous list as if it were a developed argument, it emphasizes several crucial things about ecosystemic thinking. At its best, such thinking is in no way functionalist.[29] It is instead about the disruptions as much as the continuities associated with different ecological relationships and actors. It also indicates that the scale of ecological thinking is necessarily multiple and potentially discontinuous. How do we think at the level of the microbe and the planet at once? Yet ecological thinking insists that we do think at these different scales. We may want to affirm, for reasons of praxis and conceptual clarity, Moore's account of a world-ecology as a singular account of a large-scale ecology that echoes world-systems theorists accounts of capitalism as a single world system, yet we also need to recognize that such work is inevitably about examining ecological phenomena at a certain scale and within a given framework.

Within a world-ecology framework, the echoes between political economy and political ecology are particularly notable. Yet, if political economy tends toward the singular and the antagonistic, then ecology, in all its complexity, tends toward the multiple and the entangled. Take, for example, this account of new ecological thinking in history and the humanities from Timothy J. LeCain:

> Yet today convincing new evidence is telling us that humans are both far more embedded in material things than we had previously realized and that these things with which we are entangled are far more dynamic and creative than we had once understood. If these propositions are true, as I will argue, then we humanists need to create a less anthropocentric history of our species, one in which what we had once understood as solely "our" intelligence, creativity, culture, power, technologies, and cities are emerging in significant part from a broader world of intelligent and creative animals, plants, metals, and other material things that have made us. In this book I want to explore some of the many ways in which humans are the products of an infinitely generative partnership with the things that surround us—a partnership that can be both wonderful creative and horrifically destructive.[30]

While we may want to take issue here with the idea of intelligent metals and LeCain's language may tip a bit too much toward humans being passive sites of constitution or creation, at its best, this passage echoes the Shaikh passage in arguing for an understanding of complex material systems that shape possibilities and probabilities of human and systemic or social action. Humans are not passive here but partners with the material world. Yet, with its language of embeddedness, it is also less about conflict than cooperation and co-constitution. We need to recognize these material sites of co-constitution, but we also need to think about them as potential sites of antagonism and value creation.

A revitalized materialism would think the insights of political economy and political ecology together. Maintaining the tensions between the singular and the plural, the vertical and the horizontal, the micro and the macro, constraint and agency, the structured and the disruptive, and space and time is the work of a vibrant contemporary speculative materialism. It is also the work of an ecologically informed Marxism and a Marxist-inflected ecological critique. Both are necessary if we are going to intervene in climate change and the ecological and economic devastation produced by capitalism.

9. Theory needs to maintain its ambitions but let go of fantasies of mastery.

Criticisms of theory often see it as overstepping its boundaries. It is not properly disciplined or disciplinary. It chases after dreams of totality. It tries to offer an account of everything existing (and quite a few things that don't). In short, it is problematically broad and ambitious. It is like that first-year philosophy student who wants to answer all the big questions of the universe all at once. Yet, as I have just argued, the ambitions of theory's scale are necessary if we are going to address the most pressing ecological and economic issues of the moment. Theory needs its ambition. It needs to attempt to engage the planetary scale on which both global capitalism and climate change function. It also needs to be able to think about the micrological and its relationship to such macrological structures. As the research of the Petrocultures Research Cluster has demonstrated, not only do we need to think about the impact of fossil-fuel products on climate change but we also need to think about their ecological impact on a cellular level in relationship to bodies.[31] So theory needs its ambition. It needs its will to speculation and interdisciplinarity.

What it needs to let go of, though, is its fantasies of mastery. As Julietta Singh has demonstrated, mastery has problematic legacies in relationship to colonialism, racial violence, and our relationship with other animals.[32] It also has a problematic legacy in relationship to knowledge production. Too much of academic life is organized around fantasies of mastery. Such fantasies wind up rendering knowledge both monumental and dead. Such dead knowledge becomes, for Lacan, the discourse of the university.[33] His whole psychoanalytic discourse was designed to forestall such knowledge. The only true knowledge is disruptive knowledge, the "kind of thought that tries to come to grips with the real," as Bruce Fink describes it.[34] It is the discourse of the analyst that works to produce such knowledge, a discourse of which the analyst herself is not in control. Instead, such a discourse hews as closely as possible to uncomfortable truths and refuses comfortable categorization. Knowledge is at its most powerful when it is unmastered, when it intervenes in a given situation by introducing what is occluded by it. Such forms of knowledge are not only disruptive but alive. They catalyze agency, forestall the everyday workings of the university, and produce a different symbolic and material situation.

As I argued earlier, refusing mastery is not refusing responsibility. We can recognize the power and force of nonhuman actors of all sorts (including the economy) without rejecting the power of human agency, world construction, and responsibility to ourselves and those other than ourselves. To say we construct worlds does not mean that we are the only ones constructing such a world. It also does not mean that once constructed, worlds do not take on a life of their own. To emphasize the agency of the subject does not mean we need to forego what Adorno describes as the object's preponderance.[35] Not only are subjects more complicated than we often recognize, hence the invocation of Lacan above, but so are objects. They are shaped by our agency but are not fully reducible to it. The need to attend to both the world and our agency in relationship to it brings us to our final thesis.

10. Theory in the present needs to balance hope and realism, possibility and the difficulty of genuine transformation.

While I have a number of issues with much of what has been published under the name of speculative realism, the name itself I think may be the best descriptor there is for what theory is at its best. Theory needs to be both speculative and realist. It needs speculation to forestall being reduced to forms of empiricism or being in thrall to the reification of what is. As part of its return to foundational forms of knowledge, theory has come to value science and various forms of empirical knowledge again. This development is all to the good. What theory needs to avoid, however, is subordinating its will to speculation to the claims of science. We need to value the power of scientific experimentation and insight, while also maintaining a commitment to what Adorno and Horkheimer describe as "critical rationality," or the necessity to think of any critical insight in relationship to the whole of what exists.[36] This insistence on totality is one of the things that makes theory distinctive and distinctively speculative.

We also need to attend to the realist half of what theory as speculative realism involves. Theory needs to insist on the problems and challenges of this world. While the material turn has been an important development for all the reasons I have already outlined, too much work that goes on in it emphasizes the speculative while foregoing realism. We need political, economic, and ecological realisms in the present. We need to confront the challenge that climate change represents for the planet as a whole. Such is what a robust and nonreified realism would enable us to do.

However, and this is perhaps the negation of the negation, we also need hope. We need our realism to be limned with hope, with the possibility of futures that can be genuinely different from the present. If out of the Pandora's Box that is contemporary theory hope comes to us at last, it will be just what we need.

Notes

1. See Terry Eagleton, *After Theory* (New York: Basic Books, 2003), esp. 23–40.
2. Mishra Vijay and Bob Hodge, "What Was Postcolonialism," *New Literary History* 36.3 (Summer 2005): 375–402. Michael Warner, "Queer and Then?: The End of Queer Theory?," *The Chronicle of Higher Education*, January 1, 2012. https://www.chronicle.com/article/QueerThen-/130161.
3. See: Jacques Derrida, *Of Grammatology, 40th Anniversary Edition*, trans. Gayatri Chakravorty Spivak (Baltimore: Johns Hopkins University Press, 2016); Judith Butler, *Gender Trouble: Feminism and the Subversion of Identity*, New Edition (New York: Routledge, 2006).
4. Gerald Graff, *Beyond the Culture Wars: How Teaching the Conflicts Can Revitalize American Education* (New York: W.W. Norton, 1992), 64–85.
5. For just such a disparaging attitude toward theory, see *Theory's Empire: An Anthology of Dissent*, Daphne Patai and Will H. Corral, eds. (New York: Columbia University Press, 2005); for a good critique of this volume, see Vincent B. Leitch, *Literary Criticism in the 21st Century: Theory Renaissance* (New York; London: Bloomsbury, 2014), 11–32.
6. Louis Althusser, *On the Reproduction of Capitalism*, trans. G. M. Goshgarian (London: Verso, 2014), 174–176.
7. Isobel Armstrong, *The Radical Aesthetic* (New York: Wiley-Blackwell, 2000).
8. Rita Felski, *The Limits of Critique* (Chicago: University of Chicago Press, 2015); Eve Kosofsky Sedgwick, *Touching Feeling: Affect, Pedagogy, Performativity* (Durham: Duke University Press, 2003), 123–152; Bruno Latour, "Why Has Critique Run Out of Steam? From Matters of Fact to Matters of Concern," *Critical Inquiry* 30 (Winter 2004): 225–248.
9. Elizabeth Anker and Rita Felski, "Introduction," in *Critique and Postcritique*, Elizabeth Anker and Rita Felski, eds. (Durham: Duke UP, 2017), 11.
10. Ibid., 19.

11 Eleanor Courtemanche, "The Peculiar Success of Cultural Studies 2.0," *Arcade: Literature, the Humanities, and the World.* https://arcade.stanford.edu/blogs/peculiar-success-cultural-studies-20.
12 For an understanding of how rich and complex media studies can be in depicting the relationships among the production, mediation, distribution, and reception of texts, see the essays in *Critical Terms for Media Studies*, W. J. T. Mitchell and Mark B. N. Hansen, eds. (Chicago: University of Chicago Press, 2010).
13 Graham Harman, "The Well-Wrought Broken Hammer: Object-Oriented Literary Criticism," *New Literary History* 43.2 (Spring 2012): 183–212.
14 Ibid., 201.
15 Fredric Jameson, *Valences of the Dialectic* (London: Verso, 2010).
16 Ibid., 9.
17 Ibid., 9.
18 Ibid., 10.
19 Levi Paul Bryant, *The Democracy of Objects* (Ann Arbor: Open Humanities Press, 2011), 14–15.
20 Jason W. Moore, *Capitalism in the Web of Life: Ecology and the Accumulation of Capital* (London: Verso, 2015), 3.
21 See Theodor W. Adorno, *Negative Dialectics*, trans. E. B. Ashton (London: Continuum, 1972).
22 Quentin Meillassoux, *After Finitude: An Essay on the Necessity of Contingency*, trans. Ray Brassier (London: Continuum, 2008), 5.
23 Jodi Dean, "The Anamorphic Politics of Climate Change," *e-flux* 69 (January 2016). https://www.e-flux.com/journal/69/60586/the-anamorphic-politics-of-climate-change/.
24 Raymond Williams, *Marxism and Literature* (Oxford: Oxford University Press, 1977), 128.
25 Jacques Rancière, *Disagreement: Politics and Philosophy*, trans. Julie Rose (Minneapolis: Minnesota, 1999), 11.
26 Anwar Shaikh, *Capitalism: Competition, Conflict, Crises* (Oxford: Oxford University Press, 2016), 5.
27 See Manuel De Landa, *A Thousand Years of Nonlinear History* (New York: Zone Books, 1997), 67–70.
28 Jeffrey Jerome Cohen, "Introduction," in *Prismatic Ecology: Ecotheory beyond the Green*, ed. Jeffrey Jerome Cohen (Minneapolis: University of Minnesota Press, 2013), xxii.
29 Ray Brassier, "Concepts and Objects," in *The Speculative Turn*, ed. Levi Bryant, Graham Harman, and Nick Srnicek (Melbourne: Re.press, 2011), 47–66.
30 Timothy J. LeCain, *The Matter of History: How Things Create the Past* (Cambridge: Cambridge University Press, 2017), 8.

31 For more on the Petrocultures Research Cluster, see http://petrocultures.com/.
32 See Julietta Singh, *Unthinking Mastery: Dehumanism and Decolonial Entanglements* (Durham: Duke University Press, 2018).
33 See Jacques Lacan, *The Other Side of Psychoanalysis: The Seminar of Jacques Lacan book XVII*, trans. Russell Grigg (New York: Norton & Norton, 2007), esp. 147–148.
34 Bruce Fink, "The Master Signifier and the Four Discourses," in *Key Concepts of Lacanian Psychoanalysis*, ed. Danny Nobus (New York: Other Press, 1999), 34.
35 Max Horkheimer and Theodor W. Adorno, *Dialectic of Enlightenment: Philosophical Fragments*, trans. Andrew Jephcott (Stanford: Stanford University Press, 2002), 183.
36 Ibid., 1–34.

Works Cited

Adorno, Theodor W. *Negative Dialectics*. Trans. E. B. Ashton. London: Continuum, 1972.

Althusser, Louis. *On the Reproduction of Capitalism*. Trans. G. M. Goshgarian. London: Verso, 2014.

Anker, Elizabeth and Rita Felski. "Introduction." In *Critique and Postcritique*. Eds. Elizabeth Anker and Rita Felski. Durham: Duke UP, 2017. 1–28.

Armstrong, Isobel. *The Radical Aesthetic*. New York: Wiley-Blackwell, 2000.

Brassier, Ray. "Concepts and Objects." In *The Speculative Turn*. Eds. Levi Bryant, Graham Harman, and Nick Srnicek. Melbourne: Re.press, 2011. 47–66.

Bryant, Levi Paul. *The Democracy of Objects*. Ann Arbor: Open Humanities Press, 2011.

Butler, Judith. *Gender Trouble: Feminism and the Subversion of Identity*. New Edition. New York: Routledge, 2006.

Cohen, Jeffrey Jerome. "Introduction." In *Prismatic Ecology: Ecotheory beyond the Green*. Ed. Jeffrey Jerome Cohen. Minneapolis: University of Minnesota Press, 2013. xv–xxxv.

Courtemanche, Eleanor. "The Peculiar Success of Cultural Studies 2.0." *Arcade: Literature, the Humanities, and The World*. https://arcade.stanford.edu/blogs/peculiar-success-cultural-studies-20.

Dean, Jodi. "The Anamorphic Politics of Climate Change." *e-flux* 69 (January 2016). https://www.e-flux.com/journal/69/60586/the-anamorphic-politics-of-climate-change/.

De Landa, Manuel. *A Thousand Years of Nonlinear History*. New York: Zone Books, 1997.

Derrida, Jacques. *Of Grammatology*. 40th Anniversary Edition. Trans. Gayatri Chakravorty Spivak. Baltimore: Johns Hopkins University Press, 2016.

Eagleton, Terry. *After Theory*. New York: Basic Books, 2003.

Felski, Rita. *The Limits of Critique*. Chicago: University of Chicago Press, 2015.

Fink, Bruce. "The Master Signifier and the Four Discourses." In *Key Concepts of Lacanian Psychoanalysis*. Ed. Danny Nobus. New York: Other Press, 1999. 27–47.

Graff, Gerald. *Beyond the Culture Wars: How Teaching the Conflicts Can Revitalize American Education*. New York: W.W. Norton, 1992.

Harman, Graham. "The Well-Wrought Broken Hammer: Object-Oriented Literary Criticism." *New Literary History* 43.2 (Spring 2012): 183–212.

Horkheimer, Max and Theodor W. Adorno. *Dialectic of Enlightenment: Philosophical Fragments*. Trans. Andrew Jephcott. Stanford: Stanford University Press, 2002.

Jameson, Fredric. *Valences of the Dialectic*. London: Verso, 2010.

Lacan, Jacques. *The Other Side of Psychoanalysis: The Seminar of Jacques Lacan book XVII*. Trans. Russell Grigg. New York: W. W. Norton, 2007.

Latour, Bruno. "Why Has Critique Run Out of Steam? From Matters of Fact to Matters of Concern." *Critical Inquiry* 30 (Winter 2004): 225–248.

LeCain, Timothy J. *The Matter of History: How Things Create the Past*. Cambridge: Cambridge University Press, 2017.

Leitch, Vincent B. *Literary Criticism in the 21st Century: Theory Renaissance*. New York: Bloomsbury, 2014.

Meillassoux, Quentin. *After Finitude: An Essay on the Necessity of Contingency*. Trans. Ray Brassier. London: Continuum, 2008.

Mitchell, W. J. T. and Mark B. N. Hansen, eds. *Critical Terms for Media Studies*. Chicago: University of Chicago Press, 2010.

Moore, Jason W. *Capitalism in the Web of Life: Ecology and the Accumulation of Capital*. London: Verso, 2015.

Patai, Daphne and Will H. Corral, eds. *Theory's Empire: An Anthology of Dissent*. New York: Columbia University Press, 2005.

Rancière, Jacques. *Disagreement: Politics and Philosophy*. Trans. Julie Rose. Minneapolis: University of Minnesota Press, 1999.

Sedgwick, Eve Kosofsky. *Touching Feeling: Affect, Pedagogy, Performativity*. Durham: Duke University Press, 2003.

Shaikh, Anwar. *Capitalism: Competition, Conflict, Crises*. Oxford: Oxford University Press, 2016.

Singh, Julietta. *Unthinking Mastery: Dehumanism and Decolonial Entanglements*. Durham: Duke University Press, 2018.

Vijay, Mishra and Bob Hodge. "What Was Postcolonialism." *New Literary History* 36.3 (Summer 2005): 375–402.

Warner, Michael. "Queer and Then?: The End of Queer Theory?" *The Chronicle of Higher Education* (January 1, 2012). https://www.chronicle.com/article/QueerThen-/130161.

Williams, Raymond. *Marxism and Literature*. Oxford: Oxford University Press, 1977.

Index

Note: Locators with letter 'n' refer to notes.

abandonment 6, 67, 68, 80, 85, 151, 154, 167
abjection 63, 67, 68
Abrams, M. H. 51, 122
abstraction 25, 42, 43, 49, 52, 96, 101, 144, 205
abstract machines 63
absurd 64, 68, 71 n.17, 99, 116, 143, 204, 223, 230
Abu Ghraib torture 151
accountability 73, 77
actor-network theory (ANT) 15, 17, 127, 192, 238–9, 242, 247–8 n.29
ACT UP 179
ADHD 81
Adorno, Theodor 85, 86, 129, 259, 261, 267
Advertising 83, 123, 126, 221
Aesthetic Education (Schiller) 51
Aesthetic Education in the Era of Globalization, An (Spivak) 46
aesthetics/aesthetic education 46–52, 55, 57
affect 13, 36, 63, 67, 99, 127, 149, 151, 153, 154, 165, 169, 171, 180, 181, 261
After Finitude (Meillassoux) 237–8
After the New Criticism (Lentricchia) 120, 122
"Against Theory" (Knapp and Benn Michaels) 6, 9, 16, 17, 18, 19, 20, 21 nn.7–8, 35, 62, 120, 122, 123, 166–8, 175, 190, 203, 213, 227, 239, 252
Agamben, Giorgio 70 n.14, 167–8
agency 8, 74, 84, 88, 99, 149–50, 153, 157, 170, 171, 172, 239, 259–61, 264, 265, 267
AIDS activism 155
AIG 56
Alaimo, Stacy 27
Alcuin of York 200
alèthurgies 209

alienation, theory of 8, 49, 75, 83, 85–9, 157
allegory 119, 171
Althusser, Louis 3, 26, 119, 151, 171, 222, 224, 231, 233 n.9, 234 n.10, 252–3, 258, 259
"American Left Criticism" 122
American Studies 120, 177
Améry, Jean 68, 70 n.14
analytic philosophy 4, 5, 20 n.4, 92, 93, 100, 105–6 nn.3–4, 108 n.36
anarchism 42
anguish 63, 67, 68
animal studies 28
Anker, Elizabeth S. 151, 156, 172, 180–1, 182 n.21, 255
Anthropocene 259–61
anthropocentrism 45, 47, 192, 239, 259–61, 265
anthropomorphism 28
anti-anticommunism 128
anti-antitheory 11, 128–9, 243
anti-essentialism 2, 27, 257, 260, 262
anti-foundationalism 2, 18, 20, 85, 193, 250–68
anti-hermeneutics 12, 27, 149
anti-philosophy 9, 15, 19, 94, 101–2
anti-professionalism 192–3
anti-Semitism 75
antitheory
    discontentment/argumentative topics 5–20
    forms/types of 1, 2
    limitations 250–70
    and philosophy 4–5, 15–16, 92–105, 199–217, 220–34
    predates the concept of theory 251–2
    rise and developments of 1–5, 9, 115–32
Antitheory 1.0 25–8
Antitheory 2.0 28–38

anxiety 86, 136
Apology (Plato) 201
Apology (Xenophon) 201
Apter, Emily 25
Arac, Jonathan 129
Archaeologies of the Future (Jameson) 128–9
Aristophanes 201
Aristotle 92, 202
Armstrong, Isobel 254
Arnold, Matthew 202
Arrighi, Giovanni 44
art 46–7, 49, 50, 96, 175, 180, 189, 255, 259
art history 37
artificial intelligence 96
askeses 211
Auerbach, Erich 121
Austen, Jane 128
authoritarianism 32, 52, 75, 84, 152, 159
autism 81, 84
autonomy 42, 49, 127, 134, 171, 188, 204, 223, 231, 239, 254, 255–6
auto-resistance 16–17, 220–34
avant-garde 118, 179, 231

Bacon, Francis 93
Badiou, Alain 25, 233 n.9
Bakhtin, Mikhail 49, 188
Balfour, Ian 71 n.18
Balzac, Honoré de 125
Barad, Karen 27, 34
Barboza, Ana Teresa 259
Barry, Peter 130 n.5
Barthes, Roland 119, 173–4, 230
Bataille, Georges 62, 64, 66–8
Baudelaire, Charles 147 n.48
Baudrillard, Jean 188, 245 n.6
Bauerlein, Mark 130 n.7
Bauman, Zygmunt 75
Bear Stearns 56
beauty, power of 46–50, 52, 54, 57, 211
Beckett, Samuel 60, 63
Being and Nothingness (Sartre) 188
being vs. nothingness 178, 179, 184 n.43
Benjamin, Walter 49, 54, 116, 119
Bennett, Jane 27, 246 n.16
Bennett, William 122, 205
Benn Michaels, Walter 6, 9, 14, 17, 19, 21 n.7, 25, 35, 120, 122, 166, 188, 190
Bergmann, Gustav 106 n.4

Berlant, Lauren 221
Bérubé, Michael 188, 193
Best, Stephen 12, 27, 149–50, 151, 156, 157, 159, 170, 171, 175, 230–2
Beyond the Pleasure Principle (Freud) 202, 208
Bhabha, Homi 193–4
biology 18, 34, 96, 97, 98, 100–1
biopolitics 13, 37
birtherism 84
Bivens-Tatum, Wayne 44
Bjerg, Ole 41
Black Jacobins, The (James, C. L. R.) 152–3
#BlackLivesMatter 179
Blackmur, R. P. 120
blackness 178–80, 184 n.43
Black Notebooks (Heidegger) 64
Black studies 76, 177–8
Blake, William 188
Blanchot, Maurice 62, 63
Blank Darkness: Africanist Discourses in French (Miller, Christopher L.) 159–60
Bloom, Allan 122, 125, 165, 205
Bloom, Harold 122
Bodhi Darma 209
Book of Kells 209
Boulainvilliers, Henri de 204–5
Bourdieu, Pierre 80, 87, 119, 223
Bové, Paul A. 121–2, 123, 125
Bradatan, Costica 69 n.5
Brassier, Ray 264
Breu, Christopher 18–19, 180, 250–70
Brexit 61, 199
Broad, Eli 78
Brooks, Cleanth 119
Brooks, Peter 44
Bryant, Levi 259
Buchanan, Pat 122
Buddhism 208, 209, 210
Burke, Kenneth 120
Bush, George W. 85, 150, 151
business cycle 41
Butler, Judith 3, 26, 27, 116, 192, 221, 251
Buying Time (Streeck) 41
Byron, Lord 137

CAEP (Council for the Accreditation of Educator Preparation) 73
Camera Lucida (Barthes) 173–4

Camus, Albert 71 n.17, 120, 165
cancer 85
capitalism 7, 36, 40–57, 60, 62, 85, 87, 88, 159, 175, 180, 204, 222, 246 n.16, 261, 263, 264, 265, 266
Capitalist Realism (Fisher) 80
catatonia 68
Césaire, Aimé 178
Chan 209–11
Chandler, Nahum 178–9, 184 n.43
Chan Zuckerberg Initiative (CZI) 78, 89 n.6
Charlemagne 200
charters 74, 77, 79–81
Chaucer, Geoffrey 118
Cheney, Lynn 122, 165
Chicago, razing of public housing projects 79, 80
Chow, Rey 157
Chronicle of Higher Education 123, 128
church fathers 202
Cicero 212
civilization 16, 200–3, 209, 211, 213
Cixous, Hélène 62, 93
Clarke, Simon 41
class 1, 27, 41, 42, 53
    mobility 87–8
    ruling 80, 82, 83, 135, 141, 142
    struggle 53, 76, 77, 87, 138, 139, 142, 224, 248 n.31, 253, 255, 264
    working 77, 79, 83
climate change 28, 81, 85, 150, 151, 160, 236, 257, 260, 261, 266, 268
Clinton, Bill 41
Clinton, Hillary 82
Closing of the American Mind, The (Bloom, Allan) 122, 125
Clouds (Aristophanes) 201
CNN 82
cognitive science 96, 97
Cohen, Jeffrey Jerome 264
Colbert, Stephen 85
Colebrook, Claire 69, 71 n.18
Collins, Wilkie 140
commercialism 77
Common Core State Standards 74
communism 41, 43, 128
Comparative Literature 4, 93, 97, 121, 203
CompStat 73
computer science 96, 97, 98

Comte, August 76
Conflict of the Faculties, The (Kant) 103
Conrad, Joseph 33, 125
conscious capitalism 57
Conscripts of Modernity (Scott) 152
conspiracy 75, 84
constructivism *vs.* deconstruction 17–18, 239, 245, 251, 253
Continental philosophy 17, 32, 92–3, 106 n.5, 108 n.36, 121, 122, 188, 220–1, 237, 253
Continental theory 106 n.5, 122
corporate culture 77
corporate media 81, 82
correlationism 51, 55, 80, 222, 237–8, 245–6 nn.9–11, 260
corruption 152, 170
Counts, George 76
courage 176–7
Cours de Linguistique Générale (Saussure) 106 n.4
Courtemanche, Eleanor 255
crime statistics 73
Crisis in the Humanities, The (Plumb) 44
"Crisis in the Humanities Officially Arrives, The" (Fish) 54–5
crisis of the humanities 7, 43–5, 57, 115, 181
"Crisis of the Humanities in the South, The" 44
crisis of truth 8, 74, 75, 83, 88
crisis theory/crisis 7, 40–57, 74, 75
Critchley, Simon 162 n.20
critical citizenship 103, 105
critical ethnic studies 177
Critical Inquiry 6, 122
critical pedagogy 8, 75, 85–8, 89, 191
critical race theory 35, 177
critical rationality 267
critical reading 28, 35, 36, 125, 128, 142, 169, 170
critical realism 259–61
critical sociology 76, 189
critical theory 13, 76, 77, 83, 85, 116–19, 123–9, 134, 150, 165, 166, 169–70, 174, 179, 181, 199, 221, 236, 248 n.31
    genres 177–8
critique
    analyses 115–32

Felski's (postcritical) assertion 9–14, 17, 19, 28, 115–18, 123–8, 131 n.26, 142–5, 151, 159, 168–70, 172, 175, 180–1, 182 n.21, 188, 189, 192, 239, 247–8 n.29, 247 nn.24–5, 254–5, 257
    Foucault's idea 134–6, 140, 142–5
    Kant's legacy 134, 139–40, 142–4, 220, 237
    Latour's view 135, 142–3, 254–5
    metaphors 125–7
    postcolonial 152
    vs. criticism/theory/antitheory 116–23, 152, 165–84
Critique and Postcritique (Anker and Felski) 151, 182 n.21, 255
Critique of Pure Reason (Kant) 46
Culler, Jonathan 45
Cultural Literacy (Hirsch) 122
cultural reproduction 76, 87
Cultural Revolution 206
cultural studies 2, 3, 6, 25, 97, 98, 117, 122, 125, 130 n.3, 193, 222, 253, 254, 255
cultural theory 1, 16, 20 n.4, 121, 224
Cynicism 43, 123, 124, 135, 159, 175–6, 201, 209, 210, 211, 212

Dark Ages 200
Dasein 64
da Silva, Denise Ferreira 178
data analysis 27
dead knowledge 266
dead theory 62, 63, 167
Dean, Jodi 260–1
death, role of 13–14
death of theory 14, 37, 62, 99, 108 n.39, 118, 165–84, 250–1
decision making, Derridean notion 28–9
deconstruction 6, 7, 10, 17–18, 28–35, 61–2, 69 n.3, 70 n.6, 118, 122, 131 n.12, 168, 178, 191, 203, 210, 212, 222, 228, 232, 236, 237, 238, 239, 243, 244, 245, 247 n.20, 259, 262
De Landa, Manuel 264
Deleuze, Gilles 6, 25, 27, 34, 62, 63, 68, 69 n.4, 93, 116, 119, 121, 191, 257
de Man, Paul 16–17, 51–2, 190, 226, 227–8, 230, 231
Demanet, Abbé 160
democracy 32, 49, 52, 54, 74, 75, 84, 89, 103, 105, 132 n.30, 149, 159, 239, 240

democratic socialism 54
democratic values 103, 105
demystification 10, 26, 33, 36, 150, 157, 180, 238, 241, 242
denaturalization 8, 18, 88, 157, 236, 252–3, 257
De Oratore (Cicero) 212
depression 67–8, 155
Derrida, Jacques 4–5, 6, 15, 16, 25–38, 41, 51, 60, 62, 63, 69, 93, 108 n.35, 108 n.39, 116, 118, 119, 166, 173–4, 183, 199, 201–5, 207, 211, 220, 227, 231, 232, 244, 251, 259
"Des cannibales" (Montaigne) 206
description 12–14, 19, 20 n.1, 21 n.8, 127, 137, 143, 145, 149–50, 154–9, 168, 170, 171, 176, 182 n.14, 225, 231–2, 239–40, 251, 258, 267
descriptive reading 28, 150
descriptivism 170
désoeuvrement (unworking/inoperativity) 63
desperation 67, 68, 189
"detour through theory" 25, 83
Devos, Betsy 78–9, 81
Dewey, John 53, 54, 76, 95
Dews, Peter 130 n.8
dialectics 20, 41, 42, 51, 159, 170, 211
différance 29, 70 n.6, 231
Di Leo, Jeffrey R. 1–21, 92–109
Dimock, Wai Chee 188
disability studies 177, 193
discrimination 155, 156, 225
disruptive knowledge 266–7
distant reading 27, 149, 170
division of labor 49
Dogen 210
Dosse, François 64
Dostoevsky, Fyodor 121
double conditioning 202
double consciousness 178–9
Dream of the Rood, The 191
D'Souza, Dinesh 122
Du Bois, W. E. B. 178–9

Eagleton, Terry 31, 120, 159, 166, 250, 251, 253
ecology 18, 143, 201, 256, 258, 259, 260, 261–8
education 8, 73–90
    under Obama administration 74–5

radical empiricist approaches 74, 75–80
teacher education policies 73–4
under Trump administration 75, 80–1
Education Next 79
Ehrenreich, Barbara 129
Eliot, T. S. 44, 120
Emerson, Ralph Waldo 93, 106–7 nn.7–8, 109 n.50
Emile (Rousseau) 53
empire 62, 140, 175, 200, 225
English literature 122, 130 n.7, 188, 220
Enlightenment 134, 145 n.9, 160, 199, 208, 209–10
epistemology 1, 45, 52, 85, 135, 150, 155, 156, 169, 183 n.25, 222, 224, 227, 232, 233 n.9, 238, 258, 261
Escape from Freedom (Fromm) 88
esotericism 2, 107 n.27
Essays in Radical Empiricism (James) 94
essence 2, 26, 84, 177, 260
  vs. existence 178
essentialism 26, 27, 33, 257
Eurocentrism 47
Eustace Diamonds, The (Trollope) 11–12, 136–45
existentialism 92, 120
exploitation 7, 13, 60, 62, 140, 149, 150, 177, 264
Eyers, Tom 16–17, 220–34

fact (evidence, argument, and truth) 8, 75, 78, 81, 83, 84, 85–9, 122, 135, 138, 143–4, 160, 201
  alienation of 85–8
failed revolt 62
failure 60–71
  Aztec myth 64–7, 68
  "epic fail" rhetoric 61, 64
  idea of "we" 61
  of public education 77, 78–9, 82
  and resilience 62–3
  role of 7
  test-based 77
  of theory 61–71
Failure of Corporate School Reform, The (Saltman) 87
"fake news" 11, 81–2, 128
Fanon, Frantz 178
fascism 32, 51, 52, 150, 160, 199

Fashion System, The (Barthes) 119
Faulkner, William 120–1
Felski, Rita 9–14, 17, 19, 28, 115–18, 123–8, 131 n.26, 142–5, 151, 159, 168–70, 172, 175, 180–1, 182 n.21, 188, 189, 192, 239, 247–8 n.29, 247 nn.24–5, 254–5, 257
feminism 2–3, 10, 25, 35, 76, 97, 98, 118, 122, 130 n.3, 131 n.12, 135, 155, 162 n.28, 191, 220, 257
Fichte, J. G. 103
financial crisis, 2007–2008 7, 42, 55–6
financialization 7, 41, 43, 56–7, 136–7
Fink, Bruce 266
Fish, Stanley 21 n.7, 43, 54–5, 122, 128, 130 n.9, 190, 192–3
Fisher, Mark 67–8, 70 n.15, 80
Flynn, Mike 81
Folman, Ari 17, 237, 240–5
Forget Foucault (Baudrillard) 245 n.6
formalism 4, 25, 26, 135, 205
for-profits 74–5, 77, 79, 81
fossil-fuel, impact of 85, 266
Foucault, Michel 10, 15, 16, 32, 42, 45, 62, 93, 108 n.35, 116, 118, 119, 121, 129, 130 n.3, 134, 135–6, 140, 142, 144, 145 n.9, 175–7, 199, 204, 205–11, 245 n.6, 259
Frankfurt School 76, 92, 116, 119, 121, 127, 129, 130 n.3, 130 n.8, 236
Franklin, Benjamin 54
freedom 7, 47, 48, 49, 51, 57, 62, 64, 157–9, 177, 179, 180
Freire, Paulo 76, 88
French Revolution 47
French theory 6, 130 n.8, 192, 205, 221, 233 n.6
Freud, Sigmund 10, 16, 116, 119, 120, 121, 124, 127, 131 n.12, 202–4, 226, 228–30
Friedman, Milton 41
Fromm, Erich 88
Frye, Northrop 120
functional literacy 82

Gallop, Jane 190
Garber, Marjorie 190
Gary Plan 76
Gates, Bill 78

Gates, Henry Louis 3, 122
gender studies 2, 3, 25, 27, 97, 177
gender theory 105 n.3
Germano, William 14–15, 189–90
Ghosts of My Life (Fisher) 67–8
Giroux, Henry 76, 88
Gissing, George 125
Glass-Steagall act, repeal of 41
globalization 52, 83, 149, 223
globalization studies 2, 3, 25, 97
global theory 206–7
Goebbels, Joseph 51
Goh, Irving 7, 60–71
Goodlad, Lauren M. E. 141, 147 n.29
Goodman, Robin Truth 11–12, 134–47
Gorgias (Plato) 211
Graff, Gerald 190, 192, 252
Gramsci, Antonio 43, 52, 76, 116, 121, 154
Great Mistake, The (Newfield) 54, 55
Greenblatt, Stephen 122, 130 n.9
Guattari, Félix 6, 25, 34, 63, 68, 69 n.4, 191
Guerrilla theory 191

Habermas, Jürgen 121
Hacker, P. M. S. 106 n.4
Haines, Christian 13–14, 165–84
Haitian Revolution 152–3
Halberstam, Jack 174
Hall, Stuart 25, 221
Hamlet (Shakespeare) 191
Harman, Graham 239, 255–6, 259
Harney, Stefano 143
Harpham, Geoffrey Galt 44, 45, 53
Hartman, Saidiya 178
Harvey, David 42–4, 57
hate crime 61
Hawthorne, Nathaniel 33
Hayek, Friedrich 41
Hayot, Eric 151–5
Heart of Darkness (Conrad) 33
Hegel 25, 28, 32, 43, 119, 121, 143, 207, 225, 257
hegemony 44, 49, 119, 123, 125, 206, 207, 211, 236
Heidegger, Martin 56, 62, 64, 119
Hekman, Susan 27
Heraclitus 4
Herder, Johann Gottfried 131 n.13
hermeneutics 4, 6, 26, 36, 37, 156, 238, 239, 243, 245

hermeneutics of suspicion 11, 12, 13, 27, 28, 35, 37, 99, 104, 115, 116, 123, 124, 127, 149, 150–1, 155, 189, 192, 240, 243
Heroides (Ovid) 203
heteropatriarchy 175
higher education 11, 15, 74, 93, 101, 109 n.48, 116, 117, 122, 123, 128, 151, 180–1
Hill, Paul T. 79
Hinduism 139
Hirsch, E. D. 122, 205
historical events 3, 26, 47, 154
History and Class Consciousness (Lukács) 187
Hitchcock, Peter 6–7, 8, 40–57
Holocaust 84
homophobia 179, 199
homosexuality 190, 251
Horkheimer, Max 267
Hotman, François 204–5
humanism 7, 13, 32, 33, 43, 44, 45, 46, 53, 54, 56, 57, 87, 115, 119, 165, 180, 192, 201, 205, 222–3, 239, 242, 246 n.16, 259, 260, 265
humanitarianism 44
humanities, crisis in the. *See* crisis theory/crisis
Humanities and Public Life, The (Brooks) 44
Humanities and the Dream of America, The (Harpham) 44
humanization 88
humility 13, 63, 67, 68, 69 n.5, 244
hurricane Katrina 79, 80, 151
hybridity 193

idealism 17, 19, 48, 221, 224, 237, 260, 262
identity formation 27
identity politics 1–2, 42, 103–4, 165
ideology 45, 48, 51, 77, 79, 82, 83, 86–7, 88, 135, 151, 156–7, 158, 165, 204, 227, 231, 237, 240, 241–2, 244–5, 246 n.16, 248 n.29, 252, 253, 254
Illiberal Education (D'Souza) 122
immanence 47, 158, 167, 169, 224, 227, 231–2, 263
Indian Mutiny 1857 140, 141
individualism 165, 175
Individuals (Strawson) 106 n.4

infrastructure 18, 42, 45, 255, 260
intentionality 29, 34, 130 n.9, 141
interpretation theory 36, 238
Irigaray, Luce 62, 199
Irish monks 200, 201, 205, 206
irony 93, 119, 122, 199, 213, 222, 226
ISIS 200
Islam 84

James, C. L. R. 152–3
James, Henry 94, 107 n.13
James, William 8, 92–105, 108 n.36
Jameson, Fredric 18, 60, 116, 124–5, 128–9, 131 n.14, 175, 221, 255, 256, 257, 258–9
Jesus 202
Jetztzeit 49
Jews 84, 241
Jim Crowe 204
jouissance 208
journalism 8, 73, 75, 80–5, 88, 98, 115
JSTOR 44
justice 12, 29, 103, 156, 165, 175, 179, 200, 202, 211, 247 n.22

Kant, Immanuel 32, 46, 48, 51, 103, 119, 121, 134, 139, 140, 142–4, 146 n.22, 209, 220, 225, 227, 237–8, 246 nn.10–11, 247 n.23, 259–60
Karamazov Brothers 55
Kermode, Mark 120
Keynes, John Maynard 41
Kierkegaard, Søren 201, 207
Kimball, Roger 49, 50, 51, 122
kinship systems 3, 26
Kirby, Vicki 34
Klein, Melanie 155
Knapp, Steven 6, 9, 17, 19, 21, 35, 120, 122, 166
knowledge production 78, 266
Kofman, Sarah 199
Konstantinou, Lee 128
Koons, Jeffrey 259
Kristeva, Julia 93, 199

Lacan, Jacques 3, 16, 26, 34, 93, 108 n.35, 116, 118, 119, 121, 199, 201, 203, 205, 220, 228, 231, 266, 267
La carte postale (Derrida) 201, 202, 204
Lambert, Gregg 27

language
  Derrida on 28–38
  and literature 34–8
  Saussure on 26–7
La Part maudite (Bataille) 64–7
Lapavitsas, Costas 41
Latour, Bruno 15, 17, 19, 28, 34, 62, 64, 69 n.3, 127, 135, 142, 143, 150, 151, 156, 189, 199, 236–48, 254, 257, 264
Leavis, F. R. 119, 120, 251, 252
LeCain, Timothy J. 265
Lectures on the Theory of Ethics (Fichte) 103
Lehman Brothers 55
Leitch, Vincent 3, 9, 10, 25, 190–1, 225, 226, 233 n.4
Lentricchia, Frank 120, 122
Leonhardt, David 79
Lesjak, Carolyn 170, 171
L'Étranger (Camus) 165
Levinson, Marjorie 159
Lévi-Strauss, Claude 3, 26, 119, 121
"Life as We Know It" (Bérubé) 193
Limited Inc. (Derrida) 28–9
Limits of Critique, The (Felski) 9–10, 28, 123, 124, 127, 159, 168, 239
Linguistic Turn, The (Rorty) 106 n.4, 107 n.9
linguistic-turn theory 3, 4, 6, 17, 20 n.4, 26, 27, 28, 29, 30, 32, 33, 35, 92, 93, 106 n.4, 237, 259, 260, 261
literary criticism 2, 4, 9, 12, 13, 31, 40, 107 n.27, 115, 116, 117, 118, 120, 122, 123, 124, 128, 129, 131 n.12, 149, 156, 158, 159, 170, 189, 192, 221, 237, 241, 254, 255
literary studies 10, 12, 17, 25, 36, 92, 105 n.3, 116, 118, 119, 120, 123, 125, 131 n.12, 145, 147 n.48, 158, 190, 237, 239, 240, 251, 252, 254
literary theory 14, 20 n.4, 21 n.7, 25, 121, 122, 127, 129, 167, 188, 189, 190, 191, 220, 221, 225, 226–7, 228, 233 n.9
Literary Theory: An Introduction (Eagleton) 31, 120
Literary Theory in the 21st Century (Leitch) 225
Llosa, Mario Vargas 2
Locke, John 75–6
logical atomism 93
logical empiricism 93, 107 n.9
Logic (Hegel) 207

Logics of Disintegration (Dews) 130 n.8
logos 30, 49, 202, 211
Long, Edward 160
Love, Heather 28, 156, 170
Lowe, Lisa 174
Lukács, Georg 116, 119, 121, 187
Lyon, Janet 192
Lyotard, Jean-François 93, 119

MacCabe, Colin 118, 130 n.5
Macksey, Richard 187, 188
Making Money—The Philosophy of Crisis (Berg) 41
Malabou, Catherine 177
managerialism 77
Marcus, Sharon 12, 27, 149–50, 151, 156, 157, 159, 170–1, 175, 182 n.14, 230, 231, 232
Marcuse, Herbert 129
Marx, Karl 41, 42, 49, 76, 116, 119, 120, 121, 124, 127, 128, 151, 205, 257, 262, 264
Marxism 3, 6, 25, 40, 41, 43, 57, 98, 105 n.3, 118, 121, 122, 124, 127, 131 n.12, 166, 187, 203, 224, 230, 231, 233 n.9, 237, 254, 255, 259, 266
Marxist Literary Group 118
Marx's Theory of Crisis (Clarke) 41
masters of suspicion 116, 120, 124, 127
mastery 125, 157, 230, 240, 261, 266–7
Material Feminisms (Alaimo and Hekman) 27
materialism 3, 6, 15, 18, 19, 27, 30, 33–4, 44, 54, 174, 183 n.25, 203, 224, 225, 251, 255, 256, 258, 259, 261, 262, 264, 265
Matthew of Paris 201, 203
Maurras, Charles 202
McChesney, Robert 81
McClennen, Sophia 188
McGowan, John 6, 21 n.8
McWilliams, Rebecca 83
meaning 6, 8, 11, 26–33, 35, 36, 40, 42, 50, 51, 73, 82, 84, 88, 115, 121, 122, 124, 125, 127, 134–7, 139, 140, 142, 143, 145, 157, 161, 173, 177, 200, 202, 209, 213, 223, 228, 229–31, 233 n.5, 238, 247 n.20, 254
Meaning of Truth, The (James) 94
meat-grinding metaphor 14, 187–94

media studies 98, 255, 269 n.12
Meillassoux, Quentin 15, 143, 237–8, 245–6 nn.9–11, 247 n.23, 260
melancholia 68, 70 n.15, 226
Melville, Herman 188
Memorabilia (Xenophon) 201
metamorphosis 177
metaphysics 1, 6, 29, 32, 93, 94, 99, 100, 101, 108 n.36, 224, 225, 227
Michaels, Walter Benn 6, 9, 14, 19, 21 n.7, 25, 35, 120, 122, 166, 190
Mill, J. S. 93
Miller, Christopher L. 157, 159–60
Miller, J. Hillis 35
Miller, Paul Allen 15–16, 199–217
Milton, John 35, 118, 191, 193
minimal critical agency 149–50, 170
Mirowski, Philip 41
misogyny 175
Mitchell, W. J. T. 122, 188
modernity 41, 45, 46, 49, 153, 199, 205, 259
modesty 168, 170, 171, 230
Montaigne, Michel de 206
Moonstone, The (Collins) 140
Moore, G. E. 93
Moore, Jason 259, 261, 263, 265
Moretti, Franco 12, 27, 149, 170
Morson, Gary Saul 54
Morton, Timothy 15, 239
Moten, Fred 143, 184
Mowitt, John 166–7
multiculturalism 1
myth 64–8, 69, 211–12, 215 n.15
Myth and Symbol school of criticism 120
Mythologies (Barthes) 119

Nancy, Jean-Luc 62, 63, 67, 70 n.11
Nation, The 83
Native American and Indigenous Studies 177
naturalism 19
nature 6, 18, 33–4, 46, 47, 83, 84, 153, 260, 262, 264
Nazi/Nazism 84, 200, 204, 241, 242
NCATE (National Council for Accreditation of Teacher Education) 73
Nealon, Jeffrey T. 2, 3, 4, 6–8, 11, 25–38, 191

neoliberalism 11, 15, 19, 41, 42, 57, 75, 77, 78, 79, 80, 83, 87, 99, 101, 103, 104–5, 109 n.48, 116, 181, 206, 222, 253, 263
neopragmatism 4, 122, 127
Netflix 10, 13
neutrality 12, 149, 150, 156, 157, 170
Never Let a Serious Crisis Go to Waste (Mirowski) 41
New Age 210
New Criterion 54
New Criticism 11, 35, 92, 119–20, 122, 187, 251, 252, 254–6
Newfield, Christopher 43, 54, 55, 56, 57
New Grub Street (Gissing) 187, 188
new historicism 3–4, 6, 25, 35, 98, 130 n.9, 152, 191
New Literary History 189
new materialism 3, 6, 15, 18, 27, 30, 33–4, 158, 174, 183 n.25, 203, 224, 225, 258, 259
New York Times 79, 82, 95, 166
Nietzsche, Friedrich 5, 68, 116, 119, 120, 121, 122, 124, 127, 205, 207, 209
nihilism 31, 63, 243
No Child Left Behind 86
nonhuman networks 28, 46, 238, 242, 246 n.16, 259–61, 267
non-knowledge 67
Norton Anthology of Theory and Criticism, The 190–1
nothingness 178, 179, 184 n.43, 188, 189
Nussbaum, Martha 43, 52–4

Obama, Barack 74, 80–1
objectivity 27, 73, 82, 86, 150, 156, 157, 170
object-oriented ontology 3, 15, 27, 174, 183, 225, 226, 237, 239, 243, 254, 255, 259
obsessive compulsive disorder (OCD) 44, 86, 87
Occasional Thoughts on Universities in the German Sense (Schleiermacher) 103
OECD PISA score 77
O'Hara, Daniel T. 21 n.7
Oikonomika (Xenophon) 201
oil industry, health risks 85
Okomfra, John 259

ontology 3, 17, 18, 34, 156, 174, 177, 183 n.25, 184 n.43, 207, 213, 225, 226, 238, 239, 242, 243, 251, 255, 258
Ontology of the Accident (Malabou) 177
Orban, Viktor 32
Orientalism (Said) 159
Origen 206
Other, the 119
Ovid 203

Paradise Lost (Milton) 35
paranoia 155, 236, 240, 243
paranoid reading 155, 192
"Paranoid Reading and Reparative Reading, or, You're So Paranoid, You Probably Think This Essay Is about You" (Sedgwick) 240
Parmenides 4
Passeron, Jean 87
Patterson, Orlando 178
Peace of Westphalia 52
Peirce, Charles S. 93, 100
Pełczyński, Zbigniew 32
performativity 27, 29, 32, 119, 155, 222, 223, 251
Perry, Ralph Barton 94, 100, 107 nn.12–13
Pessimism 68, 187
Phaedrus (Plato) 201, 211, 212
Pharmakon 29, 41, 45, 52
phenomenology 29, 92, 120, 135, 178, 187, 194, 237, 256
philanthrocapitalism 78, 89 n.6
Philip, M. NourbeSe 179
philology 4, 120, 205, 252
philosophy
 displaced 16
 and poetry 15
 and theory/antitheory (classical arguments) 199–217, 220–34
 and theory/antitheory (James's work) 8–9, 15–16, 92–105
 and theory resistances 220–34
phlogiston 190
plasticity 177
Plato 15, 16, 122, 201–4, 208, 209, 211, 213, 214
Plumb, John Harold 44
pluralism 93, 98, 99, 104, 108 n.36

PMLA 31, 188
poetry 15, 137, 193, 199, 212, 221
police brutality 61
political economy 42, 46, 49, 64, 256, 258, 259, 261–8
Political Unconscious, The (Jameson) 124–5
Pol Pot 200
Poovey, Mary 136–7
positivism 8, 41, 73, 74, 75–80, 84, 85, 86–8, 157
postcolonialism/postcolonial studies 3, 12, 25, 35, 97, 135, 149–61, 206, 228, 250, 253
   Hayot's work 151–2, 153–4
   Scott's work 152–4
postcritical reading 28, 36
postcriticism 168, 170, 171, 172, 173, 177, 180
postcritique 11, 13, 17, 20, 99, 101, 156, 254, 255. *See also under* critique
posthumanism 28, 238, 239, 242, 246 n.16, 259, 260
poststructuralism 1, 2, 3, 4, 6, 11, 18, 26, 27, 31–2, 76, 92, 93, 97, 105–6 nn.3–4, 116, 117, 127, 130 n.8, 135, 188, 221, 253
posttheory 18, 97, 151, 230
post-truth 32, 85
Pound, Ezra 193
power-knowledge relations 136–42, 157, 266–7
power plays 26, 27
practicalism 87
pragmatism 4, 21 n.7, 76, 85, 93, 94, 95, 100, 108 n.36, 117, 122, 127, 128, 129
Pride and Prejudice (Shakespeare) 191
Principia Mathematica (Russell and Whitehead) 207
Principles of Psychology (James) 95
privatization 41, 55, 74, 77, 78–80, 87, 181
psychoanalysis 105 n.3, 135, 191, 201, 203, 207, 220, 228, 229, 230, 231, 233 n.9, 236, 237
public sector (de)funding 77
punctum 173–4
Puritanism 33, 192, 193
"Purloined Letter" (Poe) 201
Pythagoras 4

QAnon 84
queer theory 2–3, 25, 97, 125, 155, 166, 177, 228, 250

race/racism 1, 159, 175, 178, 199, 204, 259
race and gender studies 2, 3, 25, 97
Rancière, Jacques 263
Readings, Bill 54, 125, 128, 152, 161, 171
Reagan, Ronald 41
Reaganism 121
realism 15, 17, 18, 19, 20, 27, 32, 35, 36, 56, 101, 158, 159, 160, 161, 170, 174, 183 n.25, 237, 238, 251, 258, 259–61, 267–8
"real news" 81
Reardon, Sean 79
reason
   critical 36, 207–8
   Derridean 29
   inclination and 49, 50, 52
   Kantian 134, 144
   as masculine 52
   and nature 46–7
   and nothingness 188
   and philosophy 207–8
   Saussurean 26
   and science 1, 199
remnant 29, 30, 118
reparative reading 28, 36, 155, 159, 161, 192, 242, 243, 254
Representations 150, 230
reproduction 48, 53–4, 55, 57, 87, 149, 173, 203, 210, 222, 228, 229
Republic (Plato) 15, 201, 211
resistance 16–17, 45, 53, 104, 105, 119, 120, 128, 136, 153, 158–9, 166–7, 176, 204, 213, 220–32, 246 n.16
ressentiment 68, 70 n.14
revenge 70 n.14, 83
revisionism 21 n.7
rhetoric 11, 14, 15, 16, 20, 37, 52, 61, 63, 73, 101, 115, 122, 124, 125, 138, 180, 187, 189, 204, 211, 212, 213, 214, 223, 229, 240, 262
Rhetoric (Aristotle) 212
Ricardo, David 41
Richards, I. A. 120
Ricoeur, Paul 115–16, 123–4, 243
Robbins, Bruce 150, 172, 182 n.21
Robespierre, Maximilien 53

Robinson, Cedric 178
Romanticism 47
Rooney, Ellen 170–1
Rorty, Richard 4, 106 n.4, 107 n.9
Roth, Alan 138
Rousseau, Jean-Jacques 46, 52, 53, 76
Rove, Karl 85
Ruddick, Lisa 165–6, 167, 169–70
Ruge, Arnold 128
Russell, Bertrand 93, 207

sacrifice 13–14, 56, 66–7, 70 n.11, 165, 166, 167–8, 172, 174
sadness 67–8
Safire, William 122
Said, Edward 122, 159, 174, 187, 188, 222
Saltman, Kenneth J. 8, 11, 73–90
Sanders, Bernie 54
Sartre, Jean-Paul 120, 128, 188
Saussure, Ferdinand de 3, 4, 6, 26–7, 33, 106 n.4, 118, 119
scapegoating 81, 84
Schelling, F. W. J. 103
Schiller, Friedrich 46–53, 55
Schleiermacher, Friedrich 103
Schopenhauer, Arthur 188
scientific knowledge 135
scientific management 76
Scott, David 152–5
Scott, Walter 205
Scripted Bodies (Saltman) 78
Sedgwick, Eve 25, 28, 155, 174, 192, 240, 254
Seinsvergessenheit 56
self-reflexivity 157, 179, 238, 245, 261
semiotics 119, 135
September 11 attacks 84
Seventeen Contradictions (Harvey) 42–3
sex and gender 1, 3, 26, 177, 263
sexism 75, 199
sexual abuse 140
sexuality 1, 190, 211, 251
sexuality studies 1
Shaikh, Anwar 263, 264, 265
Shakespeare, William 118, 191
shame 63, 67, 68, 101, 176
Sharia Law 81
Sharon, Ariel 242
Sharpe, Jenny 140
Shelley, Percy Bysshe 137
shibboleth 29

signifier/signified 3, 6, 26–7, 31, 42, 119, 231, 238, 247 n.24
Simek, Nicole 12–13, 149–61
Simmel, George 85
Simondon, Gilbert 172, 183 n.22
Singh, Julietta 266
Sivan, Uri 241, 243
skepticism 32, 115, 124, 135, 142, 145, 149, 150, 158, 159, 160–1, 169, 182 n.14, 240, 243
Smarick, Andy 79
Smith, Adam 41
social constructionism 1, 27, 33, 34, 150, 236
social construction of knowledge 1
social Darwinism 204
socialism 43, 54
social justice 12, 103
social reproduction 76, 87, 222
Socrates 4–5, 67, 201–4, 208, 210–14
Some Problems of Philosophy (James) 94, 95, 100, 101
Song of the Jewel Mirror Awareness 209
Southern Humanities Conference 44
speculative realism 15, 17, 18–19, 20, 27, 55, 56, 101, 174, 183 n.25, 237, 238, 258, 259, 261, 267
Speculative Turn, The (Bryant et al.) 237
Spillers, Hortense 178
Spivak, Gayatri 46, 51, 52, 116, 174, 221
Stalinism/Stalinist purges 80, 204
Standardized testing 74, 76–80, 82–3, 85–8
standards movement 77
Stanford Law Review (Roth) 138
state, idea of 7, 10, 45, 46–52, 54–6, 132 n.30, 151
Stein, Gertrude 37
Stoicism 201, 207, 209
storytelling 28, 204
Strathern, Marilyn 220
Strawson, Peter 106 n.4
Streeck, Wolfgang 41
structuralism 1, 2–4, 7, 11, 26, 27, 61–2, 64, 92, 93, 97, 105–6 nn.3–4, 119, 221, 253
structural linguistics 135
style studies 120
stylistics 4
subject
    Foucaultian 134–6, 140, 177, 206–7
    Kantian 134–5, 140, 142–4
    Lacanian 228, 231, 267

Latour's 238–40, 242
Nietzschean 205
supplement 16, 29, 175, 211, 212
surface reading 3, 12, 13, 27, 35, 149, 150, 156–8, 168, 170–1, 182 n.14, 230, 231
surplus *vs.* void 178
Surprised by Sin (Fish) 193
suspicion 17, 99, 124, 135, 149, 150, 169, 175, 190, 230, 232, 239, 240, 243
suspicious reading 10
symbolism 119
symplokē 191
Symposium (Plato) 201, 208, 209, 211
Symposium (Xenophon) 201

Tagore, Rabindranath 52, 53
Tally, Robert T., Jr. 10–11, 12, 17, 115–32
tautology 170, 172, 182 n.14
Taylor, Frederick 76
teleology 43, 63
Tennyson, Alfred Lord 15, 137, 190
Tenured Radicals (Kimball) 122
terrorism 60, 84, 155
Thackeray, William 137
Thales of Miletus 37
Thatcherism 122
Theodectes 201
"Theories of Reading" (Felski) 10
theory. *See also specific topics*
    ambitions 266–7
    defined 207
    genres 191
    historical/transhistorical dimensions 252–4
    limitations 250–68
    as meat-grinding/uncanny 187–95
    resistance to 220–34
    vs. rhetoric 212
    rise of 92–3, 96–102, 119–21
theory after theory 63
theory aside 62
Theory's Autoimmunity (Zalloua) 207
theory's empire 62
Thesis on Feuerbach (Marx) 49
Thiers, Adolphe 204–5
Third World 174
Thoreau, David 93, 106 n.8
Timaeus (Plato) 211
TINA thesis 87

tobacco industry, health risks 85
"To Reclaim a Legacy" (Bennett, William) 122
trace 29, 30, 43, 52, 55, 116, 242
Tractatus Logico-Philosophicus (Wittgenstein) 106 n.4, 207
transcendence 6, 16, 158, 169, 207, 212, 237, 242
transphobia 175
trans studies 177
trauma 17, 177, 180, 191, 208, 237, 240, 241, 242, 243, 244, 259
"Traveling Theory" 122
Trawny, Peter 64
Trollope, Anthony 11, 136, 137–8, 140, 146 n.27, 147 n.29
truism 26
Trump, Donald 32, 36, 75, 78, 80–5, 83, 199
truth, search for 199–214

unconditional hospitality 7, 62
unconscious 3, 26, 231
undocumented immigrants 81
universal harmony 49
University in Ruins, The (Readings) 54
University of Wisconsin system 128
Unmaking the Public University (Newfield) 54
untruth 81, 83, 84–5
Urizen (Blake) 188
Utopia 117, 129, 171, 174–5, 180, 254, 255

Valences of the Dialectic (Jameson) 256–7
Veeser, Harold Aram 14, 187–95
venture philanthropy 18, 78
vouchers 74, 77, 79, 81, 89 n.1
vulnerability 103, 126, 151, 177, 208, 220, 240

Walker, Scott 128
Wall Street 83
Waltz with Bashir (Folman) 17, 237, 240–5
Warren, Ken 190
Wasteland (Eliot) 44
Wellek, René 205
What Is Enlightenment (Kant) 209
"What's Wrong with Literary Studies?" (Felski) 123
"When Nothing Is Cool" (Ruddick) 165

Whewell, William 93
White, Hayden 3, 26
white supremacy 61, 75
"Why Has Critique Run Out of Steam?"
 (Latour) 17, 69 n.3, 236
Will, George 122
Williams, Jeffrey 130 n.9, 170, 171
Williams, Raymond 262
Wilson, Edmund 120
Wimsatt, William K. 119
Wine Spectator 191
wisdom, search for 208–10
Wittgenstein, Ludwig 106 n.4, 107 n.8, 207
Wolfe, Cary 28
Work of Mourning, The (Derrida) 173
writing, Derridean notion 29–30, 60, 220, 251

Writing and Difference (Derrida) 220
Wynter, Sylvia 178

Xenophanes 92
xenophobia 75
Xenophon 201
X—The Problem of the Negro as a Problem for Thought (Chandler) 178

Yale Critics 118–19
Yaoshan 210, 214
Yosef, Raz 241, 242

Zalloua, Zahi 17, 207, 208, 210, 236–48
Zen 210–11
Žižek, Slavoj 243, 246 n.16
Zong! (Philip) 179
Zunshine, Lisa 28